AF519470

Evolution of Constitutional Government and Assam Legislatures

Evolution of Constitutional Government and Assam Legislatures

Makhanlal Kar

Akansha Publishing House
New Delhi - 110059 (India)

Akansha Publishig House
R 37-B, Vani Vihar, Uttam Nagar
New Delhi-110059
E-mail: ektabooks@yahoo.com

Showroom :
4649/21B, Ansari Road
Darya Ganj
New Delhi-110002
Ph. 23263193 / 9811582579

Evolution of Constitutional Government and Assam Legislatures

First Edition : 2005
ISBN 81-87606-88-6

(The responsibility for the facts stated, conclusions reached etc. is entirely that of the Author. The publisher is not responsible for them, whatsoever.)

Printed in India

Published by **M. P. Misra** for *Akansha Publishing House*, New Delhi-110059,Typeset at ***Deep Printers*** New Delhi 110002 and Printed at *Mehra Offset Printers* Delhi-110002.

CONTENTS

Acknowledgement		vii
Maps		ix
Introduction		xiii
Chapter 1	Assam in a Nutshell	1
Chapter 2	Evolution of Constitutional Government in India	27
Chapter 3	Local Bodies and Elective Principles in Assam	131
Chapter 4	Evolution of Legislatures and Electoral Politics	163
Appendix		261
Bibliography		363
Index		379

ACKNOWLEDGEMENT

I am grateful to the Indian Council of Social Science Research, North Eastern Regional Centre, Shillong, for financing this project.

Professors Dr. B. Datta Ray, Dr. K. K. Bhattacharjee, Dr. S. D. Nandi, Shukla Nandi, Abhijit Choudhury and Vinayak Dutta, all reputed scholars of Shillong, always helped me. Sharmistha (Bulbuli), her husband Anuj, their colleagues at Third Eye, a well known computer education centre of Guwahati and Debajyoti (Tubai) of Shillong rendered active cooperation and assistance in the preparation of the manuscript. The final form for publication was shaped by Prof.. B. B. Dam of Guwahati Commerce College and Ruby Art Press, Tarun Nagar, Guwahati. I am indebted to all of them.

Tulika, Jharna, Dola, Babli, Mamoni, Bikash, Aparajit and Baban gave me constant support.

Dispur home is my sanctum sanctorum.

Guwahati
14 July 2004

—Makhanlal Kar

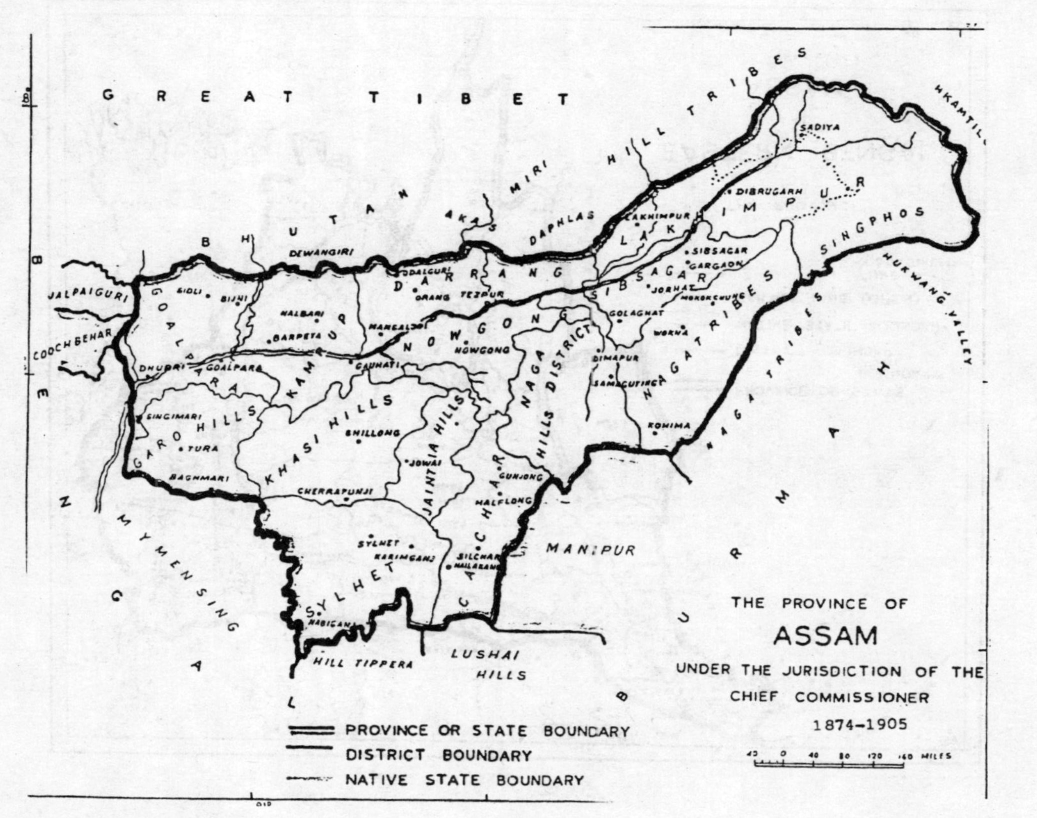
GREAT TIBET
BHUTAN
AKAS
MIRI
HILL TRIBES
DAPHLAS
HKAMTIL
SADIYA
DIBRUGARH
LAKHIMPUR
SINGPHOS
HUKWANG VALLEY
SIBSAGAR
GARGAON
JORHAT
MOKOKCHUNG
GOLAGHAT
WOKHA
NAGA TRIBES
DIMAPUR
SAMAGUTING
KOHIMA
NAGA HILLS DISTRICT
DARRANG
DEWANGIRI
UDALGURI
ORANG
TEZPUR
NOWGONG
KAMRUP
MANGALDOI
NALBARI
BARPETA
GAUHATI
GOALPARA
SIDLI
BIJNI
DHUBRI
JALPAIGURI
COOCHBEHAR
GARO HILLS
SINGIMARI
TURA
BAGHMARI
KHASI HILLS
SHILLONG
CHERRAPUNJI
JAINTIA HILLS
JOWAI
GUNJONG
HALFLONG
CACHAR
SILCHAR
SYLHET
KARIMGANJ
HABIGANJ
MANIPUR
HILL TIPPERA
LUSHAI HILLS
MYMENSING
BENGAL
BURMAH
THE PROVINCE OF
ASSAM
UNDER THE JURISDICTION OF THE
CHIEF COMMISSIONER
1874-1905
40 0 40 80 120 160 MILES
PROVINCE OR STATE BOUNDARY
DISTRICT BOUNDARY
NATIVE STATE BOUNDARY

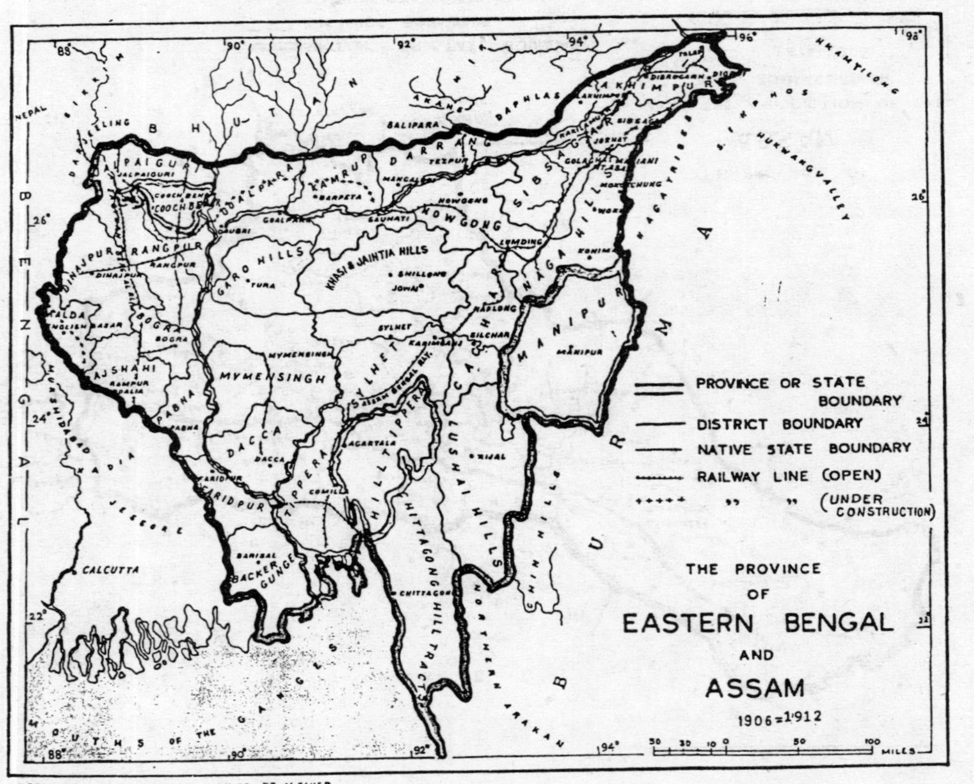

THE PROVINCE
OF
EASTERN BENGAL
AND
ASSAM
1906-1912
PROVINCE OR STATE BOUNDARY
DISTRICT BOUNDARY
NATIVE STATE BOUNDARY
RAILWAY LINE (OPEN)
" " (UNDER CONSTRUCTION)
50 30 10 0 50 100 MILES
BHUTAN
BENGAL
BURMA
NEPAL
SIKKIM
DARJEELING
JALPAIGURI
COOCH BEHAR
RANGPUR
DINAJPUR
MALDA
ENGLISH BAZAR
BOGRA
RAJSHAHI
RAMPUR BOALIA
PABNA
GOALPARA
DHUBRI
KAMRUP
BARPETA
GAUHATI
DARRANG
TEZPUR
MANGALDAI
BALIPARA
AKAS
DAPHLAS
LAKHIMPUR
DIBRUGARH
SADIYA
SIBSAGAR
JORHAT
GOLAGHAT
NOWGONG
LUMDING
NAGA HILLS
KOHIMA
MOKOKCHUNG
GARO HILLS
TURA
KHASI & JAINTIA HILLS
SHILLONG
JOWAI
HAFLONG
CACHAR
SILCHAR
SYLHET
KARIMGANJ
MANIPUR
MYMENSINGH
DACCA
FARIDPUR
TIPPERA
COMILLA
HILL TIPPERA
AGARTALA
BACKERGUNGE
BARISAL
CHITTAGONG HILL TRACTS
CHITTAGONG
LUSHAI HILLS
AIJAL
CHIN HILLS
NORTHERN ARAKAN
NAGA TRIBES
SINGPHOS
HUKWANG VALLEY
HKAMTILONG
MURSHIDABAD
NADIA
JESSORE
CALCUTTA
MOUTHS OF THE GANGES
88°
90°
92°
94°
96°
98°
26°
24°
22°
PREPARED UNDER THE SUPERVISION OF

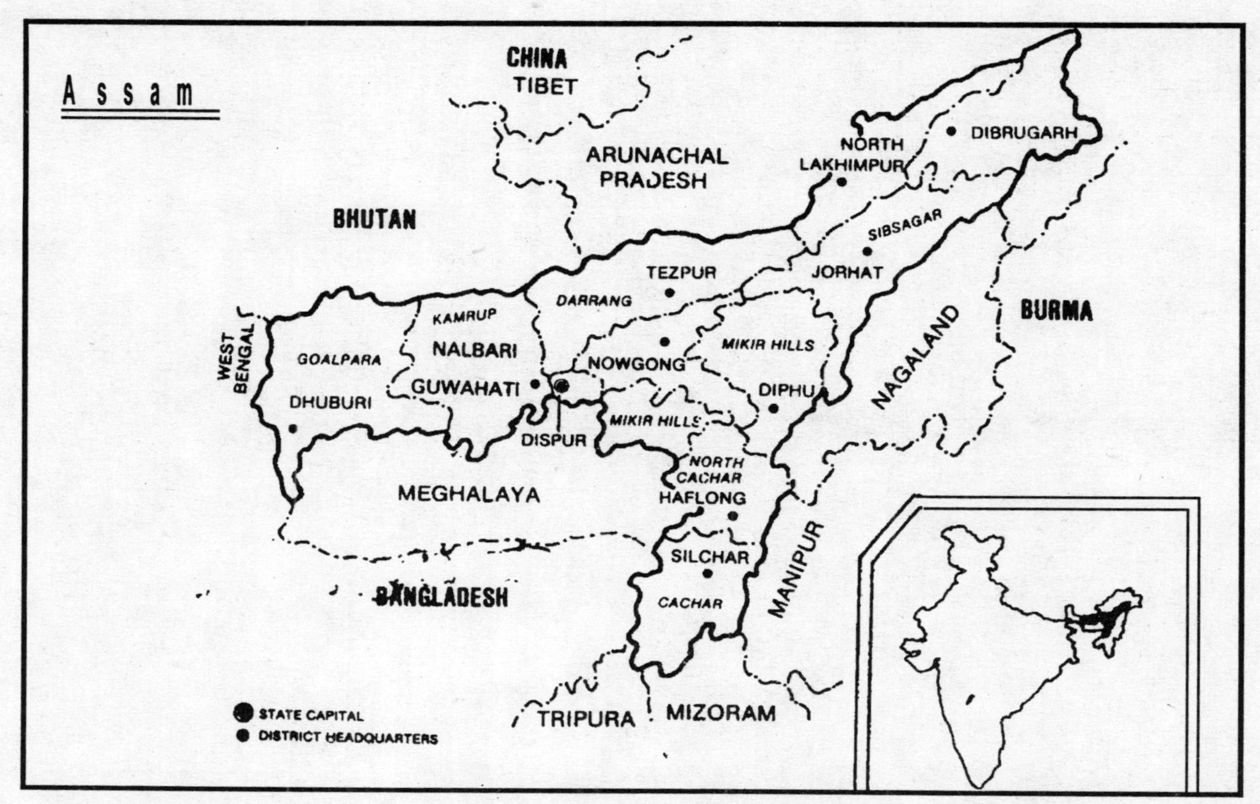
Assam
CHINA
TIBET
ARUNACHAL PRADESH
BHUTAN
NORTH LAKHIMPUR
DIBRUGARH
SIBSAGAR
JORHAT
TEZPUR
DARRANG
KAMRUP
NALBARI
GOALPARA
WEST BENGAL
DHUBURI
GUWAHATI
DISPUR
NOWGONG
MIKIR HILLS
DIPHU
MIKIR HILLS
NORTH CACHAR
HAFLONG
SILCHAR
CACHAR
MEGHALAYA
BANGLADESH
NAGALAND
BURMA
MANIPUR
TRIPURA
MIZORAM
STATE CAPITAL
DISTRICT HEADQUARTERS

INTRODUCTION

A considerable part of India's struggle for political emancipation related to the demand for constitutional and administrative reforms. This was so because the upper echelons of the society who represented it initially had faith in peaceful methods such as prayers and petitions. But the obstinate unwillingness of the British authorities to part with power in any form and their unilateral policies, often oppressive, disappointed the younger generations of the early twentieth century. That led to considerably well-organized and repeatedly violent outburst of the people's political awakening against alien rule. Thus two simultaneous streams of Indian national spirit emerged. While the two major political parties, the Indian National Congress, supported by the Jamait-Ul-Ulema-E-Hind and the All India Muslim League followed non-violent methods for the redressal of national grievances, the revolutionaries were determined to get rid of foreign rule by force.

It is neither easy nor correct to say that non-violent constitutional struggle alone brought us freedom though its eminent role is universally lauded and recognized. That cannot of course mean the negation of the devotion, bravery, patriotism and sacrifice of the people who did not see eye to eye with the principle of non-violence and therefore carried on with armed revolution. Even the last phase of our struggle for freedom was characterised by a combination of peaceful negotiation between the British Government on the one hand and the declaration of war against the imperial power on the other. It was led by no less a person than a former top Congressman turned revolutionary, Netaji Subhas Chandra Bose, the Supreme Commander of the Indian National Army or Azad Hind Fauz. The INA fought its way right upto the North Eastern part of India and further inspired the people. Our purpose here is not exactly the study of the freedom struggle as such but the constitutional reforms, which went on side by side with the revolutionary ideas. Assam was a part and parcel of both aspects of the struggle, the later being much less active than the former. But the province did not receive the attention it deserved in the study of reforms vis-a-vis the all India historical parameters. Therefore, a detailed study of the evolutionary process of local self-government, legislatures and electoral polity is called for and is expected to fill up the gap.

Assam is referred to in some historical works but the degree of emphasis on the province was scarce. Greater attention was laid on the working of the different sets of reforms practically neglecting the evolutionary aspects of the same, as if the people's representation and participation in the Government and the legislatures emerged over night through certain parliamentary act. It has not been asserted that Assam was an active and ardent partner in the national demand for reforms with the object of finding a legitimate role and place in constitutional evolution. The people of Assam were as conscious as those of the other provinces to bring her in the purview of reforms. In every stage of the demand, Assam played its role. We have studied this in detail.

First Chapter of the book gives a glimpse into Assam's history from ancient time to 1947. The next Chapter begins with the study of the Raj of the East India Company, traces its termination and India's absorption into the British Empire and ends with the Government of India Act 1935. Special attention has been given to the essence of constitutional governance namely, people's right and participation therein.

During the later half of the nineteenth century, the principal issue was the development of Panchayats in the rural and semi-rural areas and Municipalities and Local Boards in urban and semi-urban areas respectively. These systems nurtured the principles of local self-government and were the harbingers of the next phase of reforms in Assam along with the rest of India. The Ripon Plan faced strong opposition from the official quarters in Assam but ultimately the basic concept of local self-government namely Panchayats, Municipalities and Local Boards evolved along with the elective principles. These have been elaborately studied in Chapter 3.

The last Chapter gives a detailed account of the evolution of Assam Legislatures in three different phases and consisting of only nominated members, majority nominated and other members elected and finally only elected members. Elections were, however, held on a very restricted franchise granted to an infinitesimal section of the people. By the last constitutional reforms under British rule, the Government of India Act 1935, franchise was no doubt considerably extended but the vast majority of the people did not have the benefit till the elections of 1952 under the Constitution of free India. For the first time in the history of this province, a bicameral legislature was provided. The Assam Legislative Assembly or Lower House was a wholly elected body without any official bloc. The upper House or Assam Legislative Council was partly elected on indirect franchise, naturally limited, and partly nominated, maintaining official majority. All these features have been studied in detail.

1

ASSAM IN A NUTSHELL

Section I
PHYSIOGRAPHY, ETHNIC AND LINGUISTIC COMPOSITION

Assam, one of the constituent units of the People's Republic of India, is situated in the north-eastern corner of the country between 24° - 28°N and 89°-97°E with an area of 78438 square kilometres, almost a third of what it was before 1947. The depletion was the result of repeated political reorganisation and creation of new states. The population of the territory was 26638407 according to the Census of 2001. It is bounded on the north by Bhutan and Arunachal Pradesh and on the east by Burma (Myanmar), Nagaland and Manipur. The states of Mizoram, Tripura and Meghalaya lie to the south. Assam is also co-terminous with Bangladesh along the southern frontiers and is connected with West Bengal and the rest of India through a western corridor 28.8 kilometres long. The rivers Brahmaputra and Surma - Barak divided the state into two valleys named after them till independence. Though the latter rivers flowed through the two districts of Sylhet and Cachar respectively, these were given the common name of Surma Valley of which the town of Sylhet was the most important administrative centre. Since independence Cachar has been known as Barak Valley.

The Surma Valley

Sylhet, which was an extension of the vast Gangetic plains, is now in Bangladesh except a small part which partition left with Assam. The district was bounded on the north by Khasi and Jaintia Hills. It had Cachar on the east, Lushai Hills and Hill Tipperah in the south and the Bangladesh district of Mymensingh in the west.

Northern part of the Cachar district emerges from the Assam range of hills but southern Cachar is like the Gangetic plains. The district is bounded on the north by Jaintia Hills and Naga Hills. Manipur lies to the east, Lushai Hills to the south and Sylhet to the west. The Barak rises in the 2995 metre high Japro in the Kohima Hills. Flowing south west through Manipur for one hundred eighty kilometres within two mountain ranges, it turns first to the north and then to the west and enters the plains af Cachar. At Bhanga in the district of

Karimganj, it divides into two streams named Surma and Kushiara. Traversing the whole district of Sylhet these unite again into a single stream. Proceeding southward it ultimately merges into the "greatest river complex of the world" that flows into the Bay of Bengal.[1]

The Brahmaputra Valley

The Brahmaputra or Assam Valley has two physical divisions. Upper Assam lies between the Eastern Himalayas and the Patkai - Naga - Barail ranges on the east and south and is under "cover of a blanket of alluvium". Lower Assam is situated between the Himalayas in the north and the Meghalaya Plateau in the south and is more fertile than the former. The valley as a whole extends from Sadiya in the north-east to Dhubri in the west covering a length of 1300 km with an average width of 120 km.

The river Tsangpo originates in western Tibet at a height of 5100 metres about 100 km south east of the Manasoravar and east of mount Kailash. Flowing for about 1250 km through Tibet it takes a sharp hairpin bend from the south-west-north-east course to north-east -southwest. Then cutting a deep gorge through the peaks of Namelu Bowrah and Gylla Perse and after taking on the waters of the Dihing, Debang and Lohit rivers, it descends to the plains of Assam near Sadiya. Henceforth it is known as Brahmaputra . Meandering mightily through all the districts of the valley and dividing it into north and south bank territories, it flows into the Padma in Bengal. The valley's present physiography owes its origin to the aggraditional work of the river and its tributaries.[2]

Assam is truly called an anthropological museum. "Assam's culture has never been Assamese culture as understood in the narrow sense of the term; it was and is a composite culture." Being situated on one of the migration routes of human races, her people became an admixture of races which brought with them their specific cultural traits. Negritos, Australoids, Mongoloids, Tibeto-Burmans, Aryans and Non-Aryans, Hindus, Muslims and other non-Hindus, tribals and non-tribals "contributed to its origin and development."[3]

It has not yet been possible to ascertain exactly when in the remote past Assam was first peopled. We also do not know "who those people were, where they came from and whither they have gone." But there is no doubt that this easternmost corner of India received its share of human migration from the east to India "though in much lesser proportion than the racial elements entering the country from the west." Some of them "peopled the land, gradually moved towards the east and the remnants ... passed out of the country over Assam and the hill ranges."[4]

There were four lines of communication, three over land and one along rivers, between Assam and Bengal through which it was connected with the rest of India. The water route connected the two territories through Goalpara via the Jenai river from Jamalpur to the Pabna river reaching the Ganges. The journey required twenty five to thirty days to reach Calcutta through the Sundarbans. One of the land routes passed from Goalpara through Bogra, Rangpur,Dinajpur, Malda, Murshidabad and Calcutta. The second line of land communication connected Goalpara, Singimari and Jamalpur, to Dacca. The third one linked up Guwahati, Ranigaon, Nongkhlow, Mawphlang and Chera connecting Kamrup, Khasi Hills and Sylhet. The non-tribal populations of Assam consist of the Ahoms, Assamese Caste Hindus, Bengali Caste Hindus, Scheduled Castes, Bengali and Assamese Muslims,

Nepalese, Marwaries and tea garden labourers from northern and southern India. They speak Assamese, Bengali, Hindi, Nepali and Tamil group of languages.

The tribal people are broadly divided into the following groups:

Hill Tribes - Dimasas, Garos, Hmars, Kocharis, Karbis, Kukis and Nagas.

Plain Tribes - Burmans, Bodo- Kacharis, Hajongs, Kacharis, Mechs, Mishings, Lalungs and Rabhas.

Recent times witnessed a regression of the process of amalgamation because the various ethnic elements in the population began vigorously to assert their distinctive identities. They are no longer satisfied with the linguistic identification as Assamese. However, Assam remains predominantly Tibeto-Burmese as large segments of the people belong either to that stock or owe their origin to its union with other elements. Therefore, the ethnic and cultural composition of Assam today is very complicated.

Section II
A SKETCH OF POLITICAL HISTORY

Sylhet

Sylhet was a part of the ancient " Pratyanta Desha". The Kingdoms of Gour, Laur and Jaintia emerged there in early times and flourished till the thirteenth century during which contact with the Muslim rulers of Bengal began. Starting with Gour or Sylhet proper, which was conquered by Sikandar Bakt and Shah Jalal in 1384, the territory except Jaintia soon passed to the Muslims and during the rule of Akbar the Great formed a part of Bengal and continued so. Till 1765 it was ruled by a succession of Amils under the Nawab of Dacca and upto 1874 remained a permanently settled unit of the 15th Division of Bengal. The last Hindu ruler of Laur embraced Islam. Bengali language and culture flourished in the district. In order to make Assam into a viable Chief Commissioner's Province, Sylhet was transferred to Assam in 1874. In a way that was the first Partition of Bengal. [5]

Cachar

In ancient times Cachar also was a part of the " Pratyanta Desha". Dimapur in the present state of Nagaland was the seat of the Kachari or Hedamba Kingdom. Like Sylhet, it also formed part of the Mughal empire and till 1765 remained under the rule of Amils. In the sixteenth century, repeated Ahom onslaughts compelled the Kacharis to migrate to North Cachar and establish their capital at Maibong. In 1706, these people were suppressed by the Ahom King Rudra Singha who ruled from 1696 to 1714 and they settled in the plains of Cachar with Khaspur as their capital. Further, repeated incursions and invasions of the Manipuris, Jaintias and Burmese caused the rapid decline of the Kingdom. The East India Company intervened in the Kachari - Manipuri conflicts in 1762 thus beginning their contact with Cachar which remained politically unstable till 1830. [6]

The first Anglo-Burmese war of 1824 was ended by the Treaty of Yandabo, 24 February 1826 which facilitated the British imperial expansion into North East India. The Kachari King Govinda Chandra was murdered in 1830 as a result of internecine conflicts and the territory was informally taken over by the English. But by Lord William Bentinck's

Proclamation of 14 August 1832 it was annexed to the British dominion. At first the territory was administered by a Superintendent under the Agent to the Governor General but Later it was placed under the Dacca Division of Bengal. North Cachar was transferred in1854 to Nowgong district of Assam by Lord Dalhousie. The rest of the district remained in the Dacca division till 1874 in which year, like Sylhet, it was transferred to Assam for the purpose stated above. Linguistically and culturally Cachar has been a part of Bengal.

Goalpara

Goalpara was originally a part of the district of Rangpur in Bengal and was permanently settled. The Koch race had established its military supremacy there early in the sixteenth century under its King Biswa Singh. His son Naranarayana waged successful wars against the Kingdoms of Cachar, Jaintia, Sylhet and Tripura. But even before his death the Koch Kingdom faced disintegration. His nephew, Raghu Rai, claiming to be the ancestor of the Bijni royal family in lower Assam, established his authority over Goalpara, Darrang and Kamrup. The seventeenth century witnessed repeated conflicts between the Ahoms and the Mughals for military and political supremacy over Assam. The latter wrested the eastern Koch country or the district of Goalpara and Kamrup from Parikshit, son of Raghu Rai, in 1614. The Goalpara territories were included in the Bengal Subah of the Mughal Empire in 1639. It formed part of the Muslim dominion till 1765.

After the English obtained the Dewani of Bengal, Bihar and Orissa, Goalpara continued to be a frontier outpost. Considerable trade was carried on from there as well as Jogigopha on the opposite bank of the Brahmaputra between the European merchants and the Assamese. In 1826 Goalpara was made a district and attached to the Assam Division of Bengal. In 1866 the eastern Duars were annexed by the British after the Bhutan war. Along with Goalpara the entire area was included in the Bengal Commissionership of Cooch Behar. The following year it was placed for judicial purpose under the Judicial Commissioner of Assam. The territory, however, remained with the province of Bengal continuously from 1639 to 1874. The same year, like Sylhet and Cachar, Goalpara was transferred to Assam. During these two and half centuries it became a constituent of Bengali culture and majority of its people cosidered Bengali as their mother tongue. Along with Sylhet and Cachar, Goalpara was also brought under Assam Chief Commissionership in 1874. The Assamese had only a marginal presence in the district. Primary education continued to be imparted in Bengali till 1947. Then overnight the people became Assamese. In this connection, a veteran Communist leader, Phani Bora said in a Press Conference at Gauhati on 24 may 1954,

> *The Assam Government, through their official and non-official agents forcibly sealed off all Bengali Schools in Goalpara district denying safeguards of the Bengalee's cultural and linguistic rights. Such imperialist and reactionary actions of Assam Congress Government were responsible for encouraging disintegrating elements in Assam.*

The Brahmaputra Valley

In ancient times Assam was known as Pragjyotisha and in early medieval times as Kamarupa. The present day Assam was a part of ancient Pragjyotisha mentioned in

Ramayana and *Mahabharata*. The *Vishnu Purana*, *Kalika Purana* and *Yogini Tantra* contain information regarding the territory's early traditions. It was ruled by Kings called Danava Asura suggesting their non-Aryan origin. The first epigraphic reference to Kamarupa was found in the Allahabad Pillar Inscription of Samudra Gupta. But the Chinese pilgrim Hiuen Tsang who visited Kamarupa during 642 - 643 A.D. left an authentic account of the area which at that time was a strong and prosperous Kingdom under Bhaskara Varman of the Varmana dynasty. Its area was about 1700 miles "in circuit". Winningham was induced by Hiuen Tsang's account to conclude that Kamarupa then included the whole Brahmaputra Valley, Bhutan and Cooch Behar. [7]

Political history of Pragjyotisha - Kamarupa began with the Varmana dynasty which ruled over the territory for about three centuries, from the middle of the fourth to the middle of the seventh. Pragjyotishpura (Gauhati) was its capital. It was followed by the Salastamba dynasty founded in 650 AD by Avanti Varman, a close relative of Bhaskara Varman. Their rule lasted till the end of the tenth century. Tyaga Singha was the last King of the line. Then came the Palas under Brahmapala in 990 and their regime lasted for one hundred fifty years. The last King of the line was Jayapala who died in 1138. Vaidyadeva, a General of the Pala King of Pundravardhana or north Bengal, Kumarapala, established a new line of kings in Kamarupa. [8] Towards the end of the 12th century Kamarupa was conquered by Lakshman Sena, King of Bengal, who defeated Vallabhadeva. Vaidyadeva's other "successors are not definitely known."[9] The emergence of Muslim power in Bengal affected Kamarupa in the form of repeated invasions between 1206 and 1257.

At the time of Bakhtiyar Khalji's invasion of Assam in 1206, Rai Prithu was the King of Kamarupa. He is claimed to have defeated Bakhtiyar. A second invasion of 1427 led by Sultan Ghyias Uddin, Governor of Bengal, was also repulsed successfully by Prithu. He was overthrown and killed by Nasiruddin, son of Iltutmish and Governor of Bengal. After the death of Prithu, "Kamarupa was probably for some time a Vassal State of the Sultans of Delhi". [10] North Gauhati or Kamarupnagar was then the capital of Kamarupa. During the rule of the last King of the line, Sandhya from 1250 to 1270, Tughril Khan Malik Yuzbeg, the Turkish Governor of Bengal invaded Kamarupa in 1257 but he was defeated. Shortly after Yuzbeg's invasion Sandhya shifted his capital from north Gauhati to Kamatapur situated in Goalpara. From that time the Kingdom of Kamarupa came to be known as Kamata or Kamarupa - Kamata. The kings were known by the appellation of Kamateswara or Kameswar (Lord of Kamata).

This Kingdom was smaller than that of ancient Kamarupa and included only Goalpara and Kamrup territories of present Assam as well as some parts of Pundravardhana and Mymensingh. In fact, since the fall of the Pala dynasty in the twelfth century, "the political sway of ancient Kamarupa had been shrinking gradually", so that by 1200 A.D., the "rule of Kamarupa - Kamata Kings became limited, to all intents and purposes, to Kamrup and Goalpara, i.e., Western Assam."[11] Sandhya's successors continued to rule over Kamata till the third quarter of the 15th century during which period Kamarupa was free from Muslim invasions. But in 1498, the Kingdom of Kamata "was destroyed" by Hussain Shah, the Nawab of Gaud. But as he was "compelled" to leave Kamata in the face of revolt of petty local chiefs called Bhuyans, the Kotch tribe curved out a principality for itself under the leadership of Haria Mandal. They reached prominence under one of Haria's sons, Biswa

Singha who brought the whole stretch of territory from "Karatoya in the west to Barnadi in the east under his sway." [12]

Though the Koch Kings from Biswa Singha to Naranarayan and Chila Rai fought relentless wars against the Ahoms, who had already come to Assam, on occasions attaining victory, the Kingdom had to be divided by 1581 to satisfy rebel claimants into two parts, the western one being known as Koch Behar and the eastern part as Koch Hajo. The last king of Koch Hajo, Parikshit was "carried away to Delhi " by the Mughals under Jehangir who agreed to restore him to his kingdom on payment of rupees four lakhs, but he died on his way back. Koch Hajo was annexed to the Mughal Empire. Koch Behar also came under the Mughals and later became one of the hundreds of tributary states of the British.[13] Despite repeated invasions beginning with Bakhtiyar Khalji and ending with MirJumla in 1662 the Muslims had short lived successes but could not conquer Assam. The achievement was left to the English East India Company.

The most important event of history of the 13th century Assam was the invasion of the Ahoms. Members of the Shan Tribe of the Tai family of human race had established a powerful Kingdom in upper Burma, called Maulang. Prince (Chao Lung) Sukapha, brother of the king, left Burma in 1215 due to family hitches and after years of adventures and wanderings in the Patkai Hill ranges, led an invasion of the upper Brahmaputra Valley in 1228, i.e., immediately after the second Muslim invasion. Sukapha soon established his authority over the local residents who were the Chutias, Marans and Barahis. In dealing with these subdued tribes, he adopted a "policy of appeasement and conciliation." [14] He and his followers married local women. The Shans' exemplary "courage", their large heartedness and the amiable treatment won "great admiration" from these people. It is these tribes which found Sukapha and his people "unequalled" and " unparalleled or Ahom or Asom".[15]

Sukapha and his successors followed a policy of conquest and expansion. Rudrasingha or Sukhrungpha who ruled from 1696 to 1714 completed the conquest of the whole of the Brahmaputra Valley.[16] Assam had been under Ahom rule for nearly six hundred years. But from 1769 internecine conflicts of leaders and rival claimants to the throne as well as repeated rebellions of the Maomarias sapped the vitality of the Ahom imperial power that led to political chaos and instability. The situation was fully exploited by the East India Company to annex Assam to their possession within a few years of the first Anglo-Burmese war.

Section III
BRITISH INTERVENTION AND ANNEXATION

Berthalomeo Plaisted, a Surveyor of East India Company in Bengal pioneered the writing on Assam following Tavernier's account. Another officer, Major James Rennel, called the father of Indian Geography, was appointed Surveyor, Government of Bengal in 1764. He surveyed the Assam frontier and traced the course of the river Brahmaputra upto the Bengal border.[17] James Mill of the Ostend East India Company was the first to attempt at establishing trade relations with Assam. Ahom King Siva Singha allowed him only to do so but not to stay here. Robert Clive, during his second Governorship of Bengal, 1765-1767, through his Society of Trade, tried to explore the commercial possibilities but the Board of Directors did not give the necessary permission. They, however, asked the third Governor Cartier, 1770-72, to collect more information in the matter.[18]

During that period, Ahom power was declining and there was political instability which hindered the Company's efforts. Series of rebellions and depredation along the Assam borders followed the death of King Rajeswar Singha in 1780. His successor, young Gourinath, was compelled to leave his capital Gorgaon and flee to Gauhati where also he was practically beseiged by his opponents. From there he sought the help of Lord Cornwallis, Governor General of Bengal, asking for a batallion of sepoys at his own cost. In response to his appeal Capt. Welsh was sent to Assam with two missions, namely, expulsion of the 'bandits' and restoration of Gourinath to authority.[19]

Welsh reached Goalpara on 8 November 1792 at the head of six companies of 360 sepoys belonging to the 27th Native Infantry Battalion. By the end of December, Gauhati was recovered by a combined fleet of the East India Company and the king. Welsh assured Gourinath of his restoration to Gorgaon. By January 1793, Assam was rid of the depredators as they surrendered. By that time the Ahom Kingdom had been overburdened with an hierarchical structure. An "opium addict", the king under the influence of the "crafty priests" and "flattering dependants" safeguarded only their interests. This created great discontent among the people and rapidly eroded his authority. Cornwallis reminded the Captain of his second mission, i.e., restoration of Gourinath. But the latter wrote that it would not be possible without interference with the management of the territory and wanted necessary permission for the purpose.[20]

Without waiting for the Governor General's consent, Welsh unilaterally decided to purge the royal court by swiftly removing the vested influences. He obtained popular support by a proclamation issued in Bengali and Assamese asserting the innocuous objects of his expedition. He further assured them of protection against tyranny, oppression and injustice. Though resentful of Welsh's intervention, the Ahom king had to dismiss all his unfaithful officials and grant general amnesty to rebels. Cornwallis now advised the officer to assure the subjects that the Company would no longer abandon them to "so ferocious and sanguinary tyrant" as Gourinath. As the king was vacillating in taking proper actions against subversive elements, Welsh did so and brought them under control.

The Ahom king was made to sign a secret commercial treaty with the Company on 28 February 1793. It was "a reciprocal and entire liberty of commerce between the subjects of Bengal and Assam for all singular goods and merchandises" of a good number. However without the permission of the two contracting parties, no European would be allowed to fix a residence in Assam. The Company simultaneously raised its armed strength ostensively to maintain peace and tranquillity which was pre-requisite to the success of the treaty. In addition to opening of trade and commerce between Bengal and Assam, the treaty gave the Company enormous political advantage by establishing its contact with a territory lying just outside the frontiers of Bengal which had already become the centre of expansion of the British power.

Sir John Shore succeeded Lord Cornwallis as Governor General of Bengal in 1793. Under the concept of the policy of neutrality he wanted to know from Capt. Welsh whether his continued presence in Assam with an army was beneficial and in keeping with the Company's intention. He also wanted a detailed report on the various aspects of his relation with the Ahom king. The reply was that "support of the most respectable natives of Assam" was with the Company. Further, withdrawal of its troops and cessation of English presence would be disastrous to both Assam and the Company's trade. This was so because there were continuous troubles due to personal rivalries of leaders and their conflicting interests which made the king's position precarious. Despite all this, however, Shore decided, in January 1794, to withdraw and Welsh had to leave Assam in July. Gourinath died on 17 December 1794. His successor Kamaleswar Singha now led a more decadent monarchy. In view of the same old internecine quarrels, confusion and anarchy, he had to request the English repeatedly for further assistance with troops, arms and ammunition.[21]

The next Governor General, Lord Wellesely from 1798 to 1805 followed a different policy. He helped Kamaleswar with men, money and material and enabled him to establish his authority giving Assam a period of sixteen years' comparative peace despite ambitions of rival pretenders to the throne. He was succeeded by his sixteen year old brother Chandrakanta Singha who ruled for ten years. His Prime Minister Purnananda Burgohain managed to appropriate to himself the state power. However, the vitality of the Ahom Kingdom further decayed due to continuous court intrigues and a new factor which was repeated Burmese invasions, actually invited by disaffected aristocrats like Badan Chandra Phukan. The new invaders established their power in large areas of the Brahmaputra Valley between 1821 and 1824 and King Jogeswar Singha had to accept their authority.

The East India Company under Lord Almherst's Governor Generalship could not silently accept the Burmese advance towards their Bengal frontiers. This resulted in the first Anglo-Burmese war which started in 1824 and ended with the defeat of the Burmese and the Treaty of Yandabo, 24 February1826. This had two immediate results. Firstly, the British victory not only pushed the Burmese out of Assam but also signalled the establishment of the Company's undisputed supremacy over the land even without a formal conquest. Secondly, there remained the least possibility of resistance to their expansion. They had, however, given a solemn assurance to the people which read,

> *We are not led to your country by the thirst of conquest, but are forced, in our own defence, to deprive our enemy of the means of annoying us. You may, therefore rest assured that we will never consent to depart until we exclude our foe from Assam and re-establish in that country a Government adapted to your wants and calculated to promote happiness of all classes.*[22]

A degenerate Ahom monarchy, however, could no longer protect Assam, far less the Bengal - Assam border.

After Yandabo, the East India Company followed a two-fold policy with respect to Assam. On the advice of David Scott, Political Agent to the Governor General, Civil Commissioner of Rangpur and Agent, North East Frontier, they annexed western Assam without any pretension pending a general settlement with a tributary King at a later date. At the same time, on the recommendation of T.C. Robertson, Agent to the Governor General, Assam was organised into five districts, namely, Darrang, Kamrup, Lakhimpur, Nowgong and Sibasgar under a European Principal Assistant endowed with the triple power of a Collecter, a Judge and a Magistrate. Again on the advice of Scott, the Company installed Purandar Singha as the King of eastern or upper Assam in 1833. Purandar had to sign a treaty with Robertson agreeing to pay an annual tribute of fifty thousand rupees. But soon the arrangement failed. In 1838 the Ahom king expressed inability to rule and eastern Assam was annexed to the British territory on 31 July 1839. The newly formed districts were constituted into a Commissioner's Division of the Bengal Presidency. In 1854, the Governor General was authorised by the Company's home authorities to appoint officers designated Chief Commissioners, to administer territories under his control. However, the Brahmaputra Valley districts as mentioned above remained under the "umbrella" of the Bengal Presidency till the administrative reorganisation of 1874.[23]

Section IV
EARLY RESISTANCE TO BRITISH RULE

(a) The Ahom Loyalists' Disaffection

The Assamese ruling sections soon realised that the British Raj had come to stay despite their innocuous pre-war assurance of allowing an Ahom monarchy to continue. The new rulers took quick economic and administrative measures to consolidate their freshly acquired position. This was done through permanent establishments under European officers with overriding powers and discretions. This alerted some of the chiefs not only in Assam but also in the neighbouring areas. There were repeated uprisings of various group leaders like Gomdhar Konwar, Peali Phukan and Rupchand. They had either vested personal interests or wanted to serve the cause of this or that scion of the Ahom royal family. But these failed because of superior British strength, lack of real popular enthusiasm and the disunity amongst the rebels even in the face of a common danger. By the close of the 19th century the whole of north-east India was captured and controlled by the British.

(b) Peasant Uprising

The spirit of resistance took a new form with the progress of the Company rule. The new Government had started new periodic taxation and random increase in land revenue, sometimes to the extent of one hundred per cent. The tax-net included houses, licences and income demanding payments in cash. This only resulted in a deplorable economic crisis in the life of peasants and the burden was too much for them. Even the Board of Directors of the Company in 1832 had expressed the view that

> ......*the dreadful extortion had beggared the ryots and reduced large portion of Assam waste in which upto our conquest such a thing as jungle was hardly to be seen.*[24]

Yet the authorities in Assam did not pay heed to the condition of the peasants who constituted the bulk of the population. The peasants in the districts of Kamrup, Nowgong and Sibsagar, especially in areas namely Rangya, Bajali, Pathacharkuchi, Phulguri and Pathureaghat, organised themselves under the Raj Mels or People's Assemblies. There began public demonstrations of resentment against the Government policy. Peasants in large numbers met the officers and petitioned them to redress their grievances. But the latter made only show of force which dissatisfied and angered the victims. The Raj Mels decided not to pay taxes. The police occasionally resorted to firing, killing some of the demonstrators and imprisoned their leaders. Though the uprisings were ruthlessly suppressed the contemporary

Indian Press considered these as "open rebellion against the Government."[25]

(c) The Revolt of 1857

Establishment of the Company's rule did not improve the social, economic and political conditions of Assam. Secondly, the final replacement of the Ahom monarchy with English supremacy disillusioned the upper stratum of society which had eagerly welcomed the new masters who had assured freedom after the Anglo-Burmese war. They now thought of the status quo ante bellum to restore themselves at least to their earlier status. They realised that it was not possible under the new regime which was much more disciplined and determined to consolidate their new-found power. The aristocrats began to look for an Ahom protege who could facilitate the restoration of their lost glory. Purandar Singh died in 1846. His successor passed away shortly after accession. The next prince, Kandarpeswar was an eleven year old boy who could not be put up even as a symbol of royalty. However, an altogether unexpected person, Moniram Dewan, began to think of putting him on the throne.

Moniram was the son of Ram Dutt Barkataki, the erstwhile Chief Adviser to the Company's administration. A young man during the Anglo-Burmese war, Moniram had welcomed the British victory as a pious act of rescuing Assam from the Burmese menace. He had also prayed for their "uninterrupted and undiminished sovereignty" for ever. He had also helped the Company in the suppression of the uprisings. All this impressed the authorities and he was made the Sheristadar - Tahshildar of the division by Captain Neufvile. He proved himself an able and loyal administrator by reorganising and rejuvenating the finances of the territory. But when the British took over upper Assam and introduced their own revenue system, Moniram not only lost much of his property and income but also his status as Englishmen became all powerful. Out of frustration, he now veered round to the thought that only the old Ahom royal family could save the country. He criticised the British and became intimate with Kandarpeswar, now of age, and advocated the cause of his restoration to royalty. A.J. Moffat Mill was sent from Bengal in 1853 to study in detail the different aspects of their newly acquired dominion and to submit a detail report on it. Moniram pleaded with him for restoration of Kandarpeswar but Mill outright rejected the idea. Dewan joined hands with a Calcutta lawyer, Madhu Mallik and met the Lt. Governor of Bengal early in 1857 but was shown cold shoulders.

In the meantime the revolt of 1857 had started and was spreading over different parts of Northern India. Bahadur Shah was proclaimed Emperor by the rebels. All these events gave Moniram the inspiration for rising in support of Kandarpeswar with accomplices, namely Madhu Mallik, Peali Barua and Sheikh Formud Ali. Some of the Ahom nobles and the people gave the combination some support. But the English with a far superior intelligence network and a very well -organised army soon crushed the plan. All the three planners along with Kandarpeswar were betrayed by their own countrymen to the British. Moniram and Peali were hanged on 26 February 1858 at Jorhat. The pretender to the throne, arrested on 9 September 1857, was detained in Alipur Central Jail, then he was shifted to Burdwan and finally to Gauhati. He lived as a pensioner of the British Indian Government till death in 1880. Following the general amnesty of Queen Victoria in 1858, the other accused condemned to life term in jail were let off.

Some people from different classes had participated in the revolt. But it was not a popular uprising as such because "there were some nebulous frontiers where conflicting interests of different groups met and mingled together." Moniram only tried to utilise the loose support against the British. "Essentially it was a feudal upheaval." He was a rebel out of expediency. There was a common thread of anti - British feeling but in Assam it was "killed in its embryonic stage."[26]

Section V
REORGANISATION — CHIEF COMMISSIONERSHIP 1874

The new rulers of Assam had been only temporarily disturbed by the happenings since Yandabo. But the common man remained a silent spectator because royalty and aristocracy had always kept him aloof. British rule, even though aiming at exploiting the economic resources of Assam, had some how brought back a sense of peace and security. But the tagging of Assam with Bengal, as mentioned earlier, was destined to create some problems. It was impossible to reconcile the geographical, linguistic, ethnic and cultural diversities of the Bengal Presidency as a whole. It became difficult to administer an area of 190000 square miles of territory with a population of 62335217. Moreover, European Planters occupied a "unique position" and had to be given special considerations. These problems were being discussed by the authorities for quite some time.

The Governor General Lord Northbrook took a number of important decisions. By his Proclamation No. 379 of 6 February 1874 he took over the management of Assam Division, the adjoining districts of Garo Hills, Khasi Hills, Naga Hills, South Cachar and the district of Goalpara. By another Proclamation of 7 February, he constituted these areas into Chief Commissionership of Assam headed by Col. R.H. Keatinge, V.C., C.S.I., and Bombay Staff. The new administrative unit was big but had a meagre revenue potential. Therefore to ensure its economic viability, two proclamations No. 2343 and 2344 were issued on 12 September. The first severed the district of Sylhet from Bengal and placed it under his charge. The second provided for administration of the district "by attaching the same to the Chief Commissionership of Assam"

The term Assam which originally stood for Assam proper, i.e., the erstwhile Ahom territory alone and later for the whole of the Brahmaputra Valley that was made a Commissionership, was now further extended to Bengal. The inclusion of Cachar, Goalpara and Sylhet in the Chief Commissioner's domain was a fact of tremendous social, economic, political, linguistic and cultural significance. A movement for re-union with Bengal soon began in all the three districts. By 1920, the agitation in Goalpara petered out. Sylhet and Cachar people were on the whole united for their demand for re-union.

After the Lahore Resolution of the All India Muslim League, there was a complete reversal of opinion of the Hindus and the Muslims of the Surma Valley. The League's demand for inclusion of the whole of Assam by 1946 in the Eastern Zone of Pakistan was now supported by the Sylhet Muslims except those of the Jamiat-Ul- Ulema - E -Hind. The Hindus who had all along been more vocal for reunion now became ardent advocates of retention in undivided India. The final solution came through the Mountbatten Plan of June 3, 1946 which through a so called referendum pushed almost the whole of Sylhet to East Pakistan.[27]

The demographic and linguistic profiles of the new province are depicted below:

TABLE 1 : Demographic and Linguistic Profiles of Assam 1874 (Census of 1871)

Brahmaputra Valley	Population in 1871 Plain Districts	Population after Reconstitution	Language
Darrang	235300	235300	
Kamrup	561681	561681	
Lakhimpur	121267	121267	
Nowgong	256390	256390	
Sibsagar	296589	296589	
Total	1471227	1471227	Assamese majority
Surma Valley Plain Districts			
Sylhet	1719539	1719539	
Cachar	205027	205027	
Total	1924566	1924566	Bengali majority
Goalpara (in Bengal)	444761	444761	Bengali majority
Total	2369327	2369327	Bengali majority
Total new Province (1874)		3840554	Bengali majority

It would be seen from the Table that the population of the Surma Valley exceeded that of the other Valley by 453339. Even the population of the Sylhet District only was more than the population of the five districts of the Brahmaputra Valley. Sylhet, Cachar and Goalpara together had 2369327 people, i.e., 898100 more than the Brahmaputra Valley. In other words the Assamese constituted 38.30 per cent of the provincial population. Vast majority of the remaining people were Bengalees. This drastic alteration of the demographic, ethnic and linguistic profiles soon created the pernicious Assamese - Bengali rifts which continued till 1947 and the legacy still plagues Assam's life.

The following Table gives us an idea of the Non- Muslim and Muslim components of the new province:

The Table shows that while in the Brahmaputra Valley, non-Muslims accounted for 94.15 per cent of the population, Muslims constituted only 5.9 per cent. With the inclusion of Sylhet, Cachar and Goalpara in the reconstituted province, the non- Muslims formed 71.24 per cent and the Muslims 28.76 per cent. This was a drastic alteration in demography. This had far reaching impact on the electoral process which started four decade later as Muslims with increasing number due to migration played important and often dominant role in Assam politics.

TABLE 1.1 : Non - Muslim and Muslim populations of Assam 1874 (Census India 1871)

	Non-Muslin	Percentage	Muslim	Percentage
Brahmaputra Valley Plains				
Darrang	221441	94.1	13859	5.9
Kamrup	515858	91.8	45823	8.2
Lakhimpur	117441	96.9	3826	3.1
Nowgong	246324	96.1	10066	3.9
Sibsagar	283970	95.7	12619	4.3
Total	1385034	94.15	86193	5.85
Surma Valley Plains				
Sylhet	865408	50.3	854131	49.7
Cachar	130666	63.7	74361	36.3
Total	996074	51.75	928492	48.25
Goalpara	354845	79.8	89916	20.2
Total Surma Valley and Goalpara	1350919	57	1018408	43.00
Total New Province	2735953	71.24	1104601	28.76

As the Bengalis had the benefit of earlier English education, they naturally became the instruments and beneficiaries of the British imperial administration everywhere in the Bengal Presidency, more especially in the new province of Assam. But it must be noted that the policy making powers were vested only in the English bureaucracy. The fact having been either ignorantly or motivatingly missed by most writers on Assam history, distortions followed leading to the alienation of the Assamese and Bengalis though they have been living together for more than a century and a quarter.

In their own interest, Government of Bengal had in 1831 unilaterally and unjustly replaced the Assamese language by Bengali. No doubt Assamese was restored to its legitimate status by the time of the reorganisation but the inter-community alienation persisted.

A psychological fear developed in the minds of the Assamese who would be happy to part at least with Sylhet. There also arose the questions of the diversities of the two physically isolated parts of the province. The Hindu-Muslim question added fuel to the fire. Assam's life was very much influenced by these factors and the conflicts ramified into education, employment, land settlement, election to legislatures and what not. The Partition of Bengal in 1905, the creation of the province of Eastern Bengal and Assam and the Morley - Minto Reforms aggravated the conflicts. The Congress- League tangle during the freedom struggle completed the alienation of the communities. Those seriously discordant dispositions of the communities and the valleys coloured the political consciousness even though the people were equally exploited by the alien rulers.

Truly speaking, the history of Assam between 1874 and 1947 had been the history of those conflicts. The Sylhet Referendum was planned and executed partly as a remedy. But the same maladies dominate Assam history even today. With the expansion of the colonial power and the development of plantation economy and industry like tea, an almost closed society in Assam was face to face with importation of labour force, traders and rising middle class. In the professional fields like clerical jobs, education, law and medicine, the Bengalees occupied dominant positions under the British administration.

Section VI

PARTITION OF BENGAL AND CREATION OF EASTERN BENGAL AND ASSAM PROVINCE

Governor General Lord Curzon Partitioned Bengal in 1905 ostensibly to facilitate a more efficient administration. But its consequence was much greater and far reaching. Though the Muslims had reasons to be happy with a majority in the new province, neither the Bengali Hindus nor the Assamese were satisfied, though for different reasons. The former treated the action as a sinister design of the English to strangle their spirit of nationalism by separating their kith and kin. They vigorously opposed Partition and started a movement which was characterised by an intense spirit of Swadeshi and Boycott of the British. The new spirit led to the cult of violence against them and spread to other parts of the country. The echo reached Assam also though for a short while.

The Assamese reacted in a threefold manner. The Jorhat Sarbajanik Sabha supported Partition provided Assam's interests were safeguarded. The Assam Association felt that it was an annexation of Assam to Bengal and the Assamese would be elbowed out of all spheres of life by Bengalees. It therefore demanded immediate restoration of Assam to its previous status. A comparatively young group of Assamese was inspired by revolutionary ideas for a short time.[28] This could not produce any mass upsurge in the Brahmaputra Valley as in Bengal. The Muslims were happy because with a majority of their population in the new province of Eastern Bengal and Assam with its capital at Dacca, they expected their interests to be more protected. They were further inspired by the Lt Governor Sir Bamfylde Fuller who publicly declared the Muslims to be a "favourite wife."

The response in the Surma Valley varied with the two communities, Hindus and Muslims. Though they had earlier been united in their objective of reunion, now a dichotomy appeared. The Muslims would have a political advantage and so a section supported Partition. Anti-Partition Agitation therefore had a much greater appeal to the Hindus who accounted for forty five per cent of the population. The Brahmaputra Valley, in addition to the small section of people supporting it, lacked co-ordinated leadership and organisation. But the Surma Valley Conference spearheading the Movement could boast of the great orator and leader Bipin Chandra Pal. His stirring speeches "emitted burning flame of patriotism and their rays illumined the other valley too"[29]

The Bengalees succeeded in forcing the English to unsettle the "settled fact" of Partition in 1912. Assam got back her earlier geographical and administrative structures as a Chief Commissioner's province outside the Bengal Presidency. The annulment of Partition pleased the Assamese Hindus in particular. The Hindus of Sylhet felt betrayed being tagged to Assam again. They felt like a "golden calf" which was sacrificed in 1874 to the alter of the idol called the province of Assam.[30] These happened again in 1912. They could not foresee that they would be the same calf for a third time through the so called Referendum of 1947 and the crafty inclusion of almost the whole district in East Pakistan. Assam remained a Chief Commissionerate till it was made a Governor's Province in 1921 under the Dyarchy plan of the Montagu -Chelmsford Reforms and continued so till 1947.

Section VII
Political Awakening and Freedom Struggle

We have seen how Assam had been under the administrative umbrella of Bengal from 1826 to 1874. But along with the rest of the country, especially Bengal, Assam also witnessed some cultural and political resurgence. This came under the patriotic and guiding spirit of a small but determined and devoted band of English- educated westernised liberal Assamese gentry in intimate contact with Bengal where renaissance was taking place. The time soon arrived when the political tumult originating in Bengal and other parts of India could not leave Assam untouched.

In view of the geographical, administrative, linguistic, ethnic and cultural diversities, political awakening in the province was not uniform. Further, valley and community questions also influenced the process. Till the Khilafat and Non-Co-operation Movement, there was no political organisation in the Brahmaputra Valley. The Jorhat Sarvajanik Sabha founded in 1884 was the forum for expression of public opinion on contemporary topics of interest. Ryot Sabhas and Kisan Sabhas existing in some places had no central organisation and these ventilated only local grievances independently of one another.

The first ever public organisation of the Valley to take up political issues was the Assam Association formed in 1903. Till the emergence of the Congress organisation there, the Association claimed and partially commanded the confidence of the people and played a vital role in bringing Assam under the purview of the Montagu-Chelmsford Reforms. After its 17th Session held at Tezpur in December 1920, it adopted the Congress programme of Non-Co-operation. The Assam Association was then officially suspended or allowed to be defunct. [31] The Assam Provincial Congress Committee was formed on 5 June 1921, that is, almost a year after the Non- Cooperation Movement had started.

Muslim Organisations of the late nineteenth century were the Assam Valley Mohammadan Association, Shillong Muslim Institute and Anjuman Islamias which looked after the community's interest till the end of Dyarchy. The Assam Provincial Muslim League was founded in 1928 under the guidance of the Surma Valley Muslims. Since then till 1947, this organisation was the sole spokesman of the community, particularly in the Surma Valley and could master support in the Brahmaputra Valley after Sir Muhammed Saadulla joined the Muslim League in 1937 and more particularly, after the adoption of the Lahore Resolution.

Hindus of Sylhet were generally represented by the Surma Valley Conference "which was the precursor of the Congress, stirred the depth of the Surma Valley and initiated the cult of nationalism", Cachar having little voice of its own till late twenties. However, this association could not enlist any noticeable Muslim support in either valley. Other Muslim organisations appeared on the scene, namely Surma Valley Muslim Federation and Mohammedan Defence Association. Till the formation of the Provincial Congress Committee, Brahmaputra Valley's voice was heard in the Indian National Congress through the Bengal

Provincial Congress which also controlled the Surma valley. This arrangement continued till independence.

The Anti-Partition Agitation

The most important factor which made any widespread movement in the Brahmaputra Valley impossible was the absence of any well organised public opinion. The formation of a new province as well as the vast expanse of cultivable waste lands attracted the attention of the Muslims of Eastern Bengal, particularly of Mymensingh, the majority of whom were landless labourers and agriculturists. Their kith and kin in Bengal part defended their cause and so supported Partition as being in the same province would help them utilise the waste land easily. They were also inspired by a new sense of political importance that accrued to a majority. Further, the cult of nationalism was characterised by intensely Hindu tinges like Rakhibandhan, Bande Mataram Song and teachings of the Geeta which failed to attract the Muslims much. Last but not the least, the Muslims of both Eastern Bengal and Assam could "rely as firmly as ever on British justice and fair play for the appreciation of its loyalty and the safeguarding of its interests."[32] This was evident from the particular provision for separate electorate for Muslims under the Morley – Minto Reforms of 1909.

The Armed Revolution

It is generally accepted that Partition of Bengal gave rise to "extremism" and underground revolutionary activities. According to Assamese writers, "the Swadeshi Movement which originated in Bengal early in the present century, at last took on the nature of terrorism which could not allure the peace loving people of Assam."[33]

The Khilafat and Non-Cooperation Movements

The beginning of the Non-Cooperation Movement in Assam can be traced to March 1920. By that time, Gandhi's manifesto had embodied a definite course of action for the redressal of Muslim grievances with respect to Khilafat. It also elaborated his doctrine of Non-Violent Non-Co-operation. This imparted an impetus specially after the return of the Assam delegates from the Congress Session and the Students' Conference held at Nagpur. The initial stage was characterised by public meetings held all over the province. The speakers emphasized the need of implementing the programme of propagation of Swadeshi and restoration of the Khilafat. They pointed out the evils of British rule. Issues like eviction of Nepalese, discontent of tea-garden labourers arising out of the planters' racial hatred and economic exploitation through low wages, retrenchment and dismissal of labourers, mass exodus of workers from thirteen Surma Valley tea gardens and police atrocities were raised.

The Assam Association, the Surma Valley Conference and the Surma Valley Muslim Conference separately adopted the programme towards the end of 1920. These organisations, however, ceased to function as the provincial branches of the Indian National Congress and the Central Khilafat Committee took charge of the Movement. But the two valleys remained under two different Provincial Congress Committees. The unanimity of the Surma

Valley organisations eroded soon after their resolutions were adopted. Government claimed that leading Hindus and Muslims regretted that those conferences should have been held at all and they particularly "deplored the folly of Bipin Chandra Pal having been invited." Some prominent loyalists of both the communities, the Anjumans and the Local Boards were opposed to the idea of Boycott.[34]

Conflicting social, economic and linguistic interests of the two valleys and the communities which had been agitating the leaders since the formation of Assam Chief Commissionership in 1874 could not be reconciled even though there was a common anti-British objective. A strong religious overtone prevailing between the Hindus and the Muslims despite absence of open hostilities in respect of the Movement hindered its progress. Absence of one single co-ordinated central authority either in the valley or at the provincial level was another obstacle to united action. This was particularly important as the bulk of the province's population was Hindu.

Though there was a considerable interest in the Brahmaputra Valley, it failed to observe the first August 1920, the inaugural day of the Khilafat Movement. However the Non-Co-operation aspect held sway there as the overwhelming Hindu majority population had less concern for the Khilafat. In the Surma Valley, on the other hand, the Khilafat issue received greater support in view of its majority of Muslim population. A serious deficiency of the Movement was that no single person could command respect of both the valleys and the communities. As a result only sectional leadership developed amongst the various ethnic and religious entities of the people. This is a dominant legacy even today in all spheres and aspects of Assam's life.

The boycott of educational institutions, Law Courts and Legislatures was the most exciting aspect of the Non-Co-operation Movement. Of the Triple Boycott Scheme most attractive was the first one. About ten per cent of the total enrolled student population, both male and female, in three hundred thirty four Middle English, Middle Vernacular and High Schools and three Colleges in the province withdrew from their institutions when the "Strike was rife", i.e., during 1920- 1921. Next year enrolment fell by about twelve per cent and attendance by twenty one per cent. The students also played the leading role in picketing shops, selling liquor and foreign cloth. Students' procession formed an important element of the Movement. The initial enthusiasm did not take long to diminish. The Government gave students a specific time limit after which most of them returned to their classes.

The establishment of National Schools was another important aspect of the programme. Twentyfour such schools were established in the Brahmaputra Valley and sixteen in the Surma Valley with public support. About one thousand three hundred students joined those schools. Most of the schools disappeared soon after the dissipation of the Movement. But a significant consequence of student participation was that for the first time a select band of young men swearing allegiance to the cause of India's emancipation appeared on the political scene. Khaddar became a symbol of sacrifice and devotion to the country's cause.

Due to vigorous propaganda of the non-co-operators all over the province, the Government suffered heavy losses on land revenue, excise, stamp and forest duties and choukidari taxes. The consumption of liquor, opium and ganja came down by 49.8%,

35.8% and 24.4 % respectively. The most widespread item of the programme was the boycott of hats (markets) for prevention of essential supplies to garden labourers under European planters and Government officers to bring them to their knees. In this respect both Hindus and Muslim united.

The Movement gained strength and momentum towards the end of 1921. The AICC's Civil Disobedience call of 4 and 5 November, though not implemented in Assam, created a stir in the province further inspiring the non-co-operators in their propaganda. Organisations like the Assam National Volunteer Corps consisting of Congress and Khilafat workers, Santi Sena and Sevak Sampradaya worked simultaneously. Nearly seventy thousand young men joined the organisations. Further, the third Jamiat-Ul-Ulema-E-Hind Conference and thirtysixth Session of the Indian National Congress held at Sylhet and Hyderabad respectively renewed the pledge of Non-violent Non-Co-operation and made the Movement in Assam more vigorous. The Movement was admittedly tarnished by some amount of violence and intimidation in different places. Volunteers challenged the police and forcibly rescued the persons arrested. In some places, threat, social ostracism and boycott of pro-goverment elements became widespread.

Government adopted an elaborate policy to contain the Movement, namely, restraint on the Press, organised counter-propaganda against Gandhi and Congress and persecution and repression of its supporters. As the native Press criticised Government atrocities and published critical articles written by Congressmen, the authorities imposed fines, demanded security deposits, seized copies of publication and sentenced editors and printers to imprisonment and fines. They also appointed loyalists for counter propaganda in urban and rural areas through public meetings and pamphlets condemning Gandhi and Congress and assuring the people that if the movement was withdrawn Swaraj would be established.

Further, the Congress Khilafat Volunteer Corps, Santi Sena and Sevak Sampradaya were declared unlawful associations under Section 16 of the Indian Criminal Law Amendment Act 1908. The whole province was brought under operation of the Prevention of Seditious Meeting Act 1911, the Press Act, the Police Act and Section 144 of Cr.P.C. was invoked vigorously. The deployment of Assam Rifles in demonstration marches and punitive expeditions and suppression of labour participation became the regular features of Government action. Houses of Khilafatists, Congressmen and their offices were searched, records seized or destroyed and buildings demolished and properties were forfeited. Workers were fined, imprisoned and ill-treated in Jails. European tea planters were utilised to suppress the tea garden labourers.

On 5 February 1922, the police fired upon a procession of about 3000 peasants at the Chouri Chaura village of Gorakhpur district of Uttar Pradesh. When their ammunition ran short the policemen took shelter in the Police Station. The agitated and angry crowd attacked and burnt the Police Station killing 22 policemen. Gandhi was altogether upset at the violence and unilaterally decided to suspend the entire Movement forthwith. Though the movement failed, its significance should not be lost sight of. Participation and suffering of large sections of the people imparted to it the character of an upheaval. Further, the events hurled Assam into the vortex of the national politics. The upsurge of the Movement continued to inspire successive generations of the people of Assam as elsewhere.

The Period of Parliamentary Politics 1921 – 1937 Congress a Divided House

The Montagu-Chelmsford Reforms had introduced Dyarchy in 1921. It came into force despite Congress opposition and non-co-operation. Division appeared among Congressmen regarding participation in election and Council Entry. One group under the leadership of Deshabandhu Chitta Ranjan Das, V. J. Patel, Hakim Ajmal Khan and Pandit Motilal Nehru wanted to take part in the elections to enter the Legislatures and wreck Dyarchy from within. Other Congressmen like Chakravarty Rajagopalachariar, Kasturiranga Ayangar and Pattabhi Sitaramayya favoured complete boycott of elections. In June 1922 therefore, the AICC appointed the Civil Disobedience Enquiry Committee under Hakim Ajmal Khan to consider and report whether Civil Disobedience in some form or any other measure could be adopted and whether the party should participate in the elections.

The Committee made an assessment and reported that the country as a whole was not prepared for any Civil Disobedience Movement. As regards Assam, the consensus gathered during the Committee's itinerary was that no full- fledged agitation was feasible in the Brahmaputra Valley. Similar conclusion was drawn by the Central Khilafat Enquiry Committee which visited the province about the same time. Congress Committees were, however, given the liberty of launching such Movement on a limited nature on their own responsibility.

On the question of Council Entry, the leaders were almost equally divided, one group favouring Das's view and the other supporting Gopalachariar. The fight between pro-changers and no-changers, as they were called, reached its climax at the Thirtyseventh Congress Session of December 1922 held at Gaya when a clear schism appeared in the party. The delegates rejected Das's resolution for Council entry. He resigned presidentship in the Session itself. The Congress Khilafat Swarajya Party was born on 7 January 1923 with Das as President and Motilal as General Secretary. The Delhi Congress of 1923, however adopted a face saving compromise formula. It permitted individual Congressmen of Swarajya Party to contest the elections and enter the Councils.

The majority of witnesses before the Civil Disobedience Enquiry Committee had opposed non-co-operation and civil disobedience. In Gaya Congress, the Brahmaputra Valley delegates led by Tarun Ram Phukan, APCC President and including Faiznur Ali, supported Chittaranjan. Phukan and most other non-co-operating lawyers joined the Swarajist group and returned to the bar. They formed the Assam Branch of the party on 25 July 1923 and decided to contest the Municipal Election. Tarun Ram Phukan, Rohini Kumar Choudhury and Gopinath Bordoloi were elected President, General Secretary and Assistant General Secretary respectively. Bishnu Ram Medhi, Dhaniram Talukdar, Jadav Chandra Das and Kamahkyaram Barua became members. This led to acute differences in the Assam Congress and Phukan was compelled to resign. Kualadhar Chaliha, Nabin Chandra Bordoloi and Hem Chandra Das were elected President, General Secretary and Assistant General Secretary respectively. Despite the opposition and boycott of the Congressmen in general, Dyarchy came into operation in Assam as there was no dearth of co-operators. Four elections were held under the scheme and the Assam Legislative Council functioned till the elections of 1937.

The Civil Disobedience Movement

The Madras Congress Session of 1927 had declared complete independence as India's goal. The Congress boycotted the all-white Simon Commission. This imprudent act of the Government provided a rallying ground for nationalists of all shades and created a universal indignation in the country. But the Calcutta Congress Session of 1928, in a volta face, adopted a resolution demanding Dominion Status on the basis of Nehru Committee Report. The resolution affirmed that if the Government failed to grant Dominion Status, the party would launch a Non-violent Non-Co-operation Movement for attainment of full independence. During the following year of waiting the Government made the trifling offer of a Round Table Conference. In the Lahore Congress Session of December 1929 a resolution was adopted reiterating the earlier demand of complete independence. It was further decided to observe 26th January 1930 as the Independence Day all over the country.

Conflicting views of Congress in Assam made it impossible for them to project a clear reaction to the Lahore resolution. However, till the celebration of Independence Day, the differences were not expressed in public. But soon the facade of unity and supremacy of the old guards disappeared. In the Surma Valley, there was unanimity for full implementation of the Lahore resolution. The party High Command asked all its representatives in central and provincial legislatures to resign forthwith and boycott all future elections. The AICC was directed to launch a Civil Disobedience Movement which would start with an 'independence' pledge. Accordingly, the Swarajists in the Assam Legislature Council also resigned.

The Assam Provincial Congress was a divided house so far as the Lahore Resolution on resignation and Council boycott were concerned. Tarun Ram Phukan APCC President, Gopinath Bordoloi and Rohini Kumar Choudhury openly opposed that part of the Civl Disobedience Programme. In the Surma Valley, despite differences, unanimity was reached on the issue. Gandhi's 241 mile Dandi March, which started on 12 March 1930 for violation of the Salt Laws was the beginning of the countrywide Civil Disobedience Movement. However, some of the elder leaders like Tarun Ram Phukan, Kuladhar Chaliha and Nabin Chandra Bordoloi were not willing to lead the Assam Congressmen. The old guards resigned on 27 January 1930.

Bishnu Ram Medhi and Muhammad Tayyabulla became the President and Secretary respectively of the APCC to "...to take Assam to the path of struggle..." Here again the Congressmen and the Swarajists differed. Some of the latter who earlier resigned, re-entered legislatures through bye elections. They also pleaded that Assam was not yet prepared for the Civil Disobedience Movement. The Congress asked them to resign but they went a step further by resigning from Congress itself. In the meantime the Movement was gathering momentum. In April 1930, the first batch of Satyagrahis left Sylhet for Noakhali and Midnapur for breaking Salt Laws. Students and other volunteers held meetings and processions, campaigned against payment of taxes, violated prohibitions under Section 144 Cr.P.C., courted arrest and boycotted schools and colleges. In this connection, the Hindu - Muslim divide was evident. A prominent Muslim League leader and President, Assam Provincial Muslim League, Munawar Ali said, "we condemn Civil Disobedience Movement in no unmistakable terms, so also we condemn some of the Bureaucratic methods which have been adopted for its suppression. We condemn some of their methods and not the end".[35]

The progressive unrest and student participation alerted the Government. The result was the famous Cunningham Circular of May 1930. J.R. Cuningham, Director of Public Instruction asked the heads of educational institutions to obtain from the pupils and their guardians an undertaking to abjure all political activities and to obey the rules and authority of the Education Department. But instead of suppressing the students, this step further incensed anti- British feelings and they took active parts in the various aspects of Civil Disobedience including agitation against the Circular. Repressive measures of the rulers resulted in the imprisonment and other forms of punishment of hundreds of workers, but they remained undaunted and implemented the programme in right earnest.

The British Government's declaration to hold a Round Table Conference at London with loyalists and excluding Congressmen caused further resentment. The Congress refused to recognise any such Conference and Assam witnessed "series of demonstrations and processions" held in defiance of prohibitory orders. Government repression only strengthened the anti- British sentiment. However, the first phase of the Movement ended without achieving the cherished result. Two months of deliberations of the first Round Table Conference also failed to bear fruit. In pursuance of the Gandhi- Irwin Pact of 5 March 1931, the Congress decided to suspend the Civil Disobedience Movement.

The Government agreed to invite the Congress representatives to the Second Round Table Conference which started on 7 September 1931 and was attended by Gandhi as its sole representative. But he returned home empty handed. The Congress Working Committee decided to resume the Movement on 1 January 1932. The Government adopted a tough attitude and affected arrest and imprisonment of a large number of Congressmen. The events of 1932-33 ran much on the same line as in the earlier years. But the national feeling was now more intense and more determined. The repression was ever so much more ruthless and the peoples' sufferings were much greater. In Assam the response was very enthusiastic. Three items of the programme received the greatest attention namely, boycott, non-payment of taxes and hoisting of the National Flag. More than a thousand persons including eight women were prosecuted and imprisoned.

The Congress condemned Ramsay MacDonald's Communal Award of 1932 but Gandhi could not devise any thing better than that. The party agreed to reservation of double the number of seats suggested by Macdonald as well as the benefit of a separate electorate for Depressed Classes. The British Government accepted the formula which came to be called Poona Pact. The Civil Disobedience Movement in fact petered out as Gandhi adopted diversionary strategy. His "purification fast", resolve to devote himself to the upliftment of the Harijans, removal of untouchability and individual Satyagraha replaced the Movement after his release from jail on 8 May 1933. In Assam the fourth Independence Day was observed in a lack -luster manner only in Nowgong and Sylhet. Emphasis was now laid on social reconstruction rather than independence. The Movement was officially terminated on 20 May 1934.

The Congress now accepted parliamentary form of Government and methods of agitation for remedy to the Indian political problem. Between the Non-Cooperation and Civil Disobedience Movements, Assam witnessed some new dimensions of people's awakening in the form of peasant movements, working class struggle, Plantation labourer strike, agitation against Governments' Opium Policy, popularisation of Khadi, anti - untouchability, spread of communism and revolutionary terrorism especially after Bhagat Singh's martyrdom. These factors however, disappeared with the Civil Disobedience Movement.

The Period of Provincial Autonomy

Mainly on the recommendation of the Simon Commission, the British Government unilaterally decided to replace Dyarchy in the provinces by 'Autonomy' and to establish a Federal Government at the centre. The Government of India Act 1935 was passed by the British Parliament for the purpose. Elections were held in February 1937. In Assam the Congress emerged as the largest single party in the Legislative Assembly. Earlier the Congress High Command had decided not to accept Government responsibility in provinces wherein it could not obtain electoral majority. This left the field open for Sir Muhammad Saadulla who formed a Coalition Cabinet on 1 April 1937. His team consisted of his supporters, the Muslim Party, United People's Party and the Progressive Party. The Saadulla Government started functioning amidst strong opposition and antagonism of the Congress which observed the Assembly's inaugural day as Anti-Constitution Day.

The period from 1937 to 1947 witnessed intense parliamentary activities, though often of a shady character, aimed at petty political gain for the Congress and the Muslim League. No issue was discussed without a communal and racial tinge and vehemence. The League's ambition had already crystalised into an attitude of separatism for which the fear of Hindu and Congress domination were greatly responsible. The Congress under leadership of Gopinath Bordoloi entered the Assembly with the noble ideal that his party's "... policy is more important than winning the seats and capture of fictitious majority in the legislatures". But it ended with the ignoble scramble for such majority and political power in the form of defection and tricky toppling of Cabinets.

The Provincial Muslim League, the main contender for power in Assam, had started its parliamentary career in an humble way with four members only. But by 1938, it consolidated the Muslims under its control with 33 out of 34 Muslim members who rallied round it under the leadership of Sir Saadulla. With short breaks totalling to less than two years, Saadulla was the Assam Premier and dominated the political scene from 1937 to 1946. The entire tenure of his office was characterised by Hindu- Muslim bitterness centering round land settlement, Line System, Grow More Food Scheme, Provincial Census of 1941, Anti-War Satyagraha and Quit India Movement. The Muslim League's demand for inclusion of Assam in East Pakistan is well known.

The Anti-War Satyagraha

The Viceroy's offer of expansion of his Council with the addition of more Indian members to it and his offer of August 8, 1940 promising setting up of a representative Indian body to frame a new constitution did not appeal to the Congress. The party had declared in March 1940 that "nothing short of complete Independence would be acceptable to the people of India". It was decided to launch a Civil Disobedience Movement for the purpose without of course, fixing any programme. However, a few days later, Gandhi formulated the Anti-War Satyagraha Plan in protest against the Government's unilateral declaration of India as a belligerent in the Second World War. The Muslim League's Lahore Session of 20 March 1940 also adopted the disastrous resolution demanding the creation of a sovereign Muslim home- land called Pakistan on the basis of Two Nation Theory.

As Assam was a Hindu majority province, its opposition to British war efforts was natural. But the Muslims were more concerned with the safeguarding of the interests of the community vis-à-vis the Hindus. The Assam Provincial Muslim League by a resolution of 18 September 1940 agreed to co-operate with the British. The Assam Premier Saadulla joined the Provincial War Aid Committee along with Rohini Kumar Chowdhury from the Brahmaputra Valley and Hirendra Chandra Chakravarty and Abdul Matin Choudhury from the Surma Valley. The Provincial Muslim League gave the Committee whole hearted support and the Saadulla Government donated one lakh of rupees to the War Fund. Eleven Municipalities and Local Boards resolved to contribute to the War Fund much to the criticism of large sections of the people of Assam. The Anti-War Satyagraha had three phases, from October 1940 to December 1940, from January 1941 to March 1941 and from April 1941 to the beginning of Quit India Movement. The programme failed to stir the people as much as the earlier uprisings. But it succeeded in recording a forceful moral protest against the imperial policy of involving India in the war. The Satyagraha was suspended in December 1941 in view of escalation of the war to India.

The Quit India Movement

Early in 1942, war situation worsened for the British through the fall of Burma at the hands of the Azad Hind Fauz of Netaji Subhas Chandra Bose. This national army quickly proceeded to Indian soil. Through the Cripp's Mission of 1942, the British Government offered Dominion Status to the country at the end of the war. But the offer was rejected by the Congress thus closing the door for negotiation. The party now went on a war path and the Working Committee adopted the famous Quit India Resolution on 14 July 1942 which was endorsed by the A.I.C.C. on 8 August. Though the Movement was supposed to be non- violent, it did not remain so as the Government adopted a policy of persecution and repression from the morning of 9 August.

The Movement in Assam, as in other places, was initially peaceful. But soon disruption of military supply bases and postal and rail communications, attacks on Government properties and police stations, sabotage and incendiarism, mail dacoities, establishment of parallel Governments, organisation of Santi Senas and clashes between the public and the police turned the Movement violent despite Gandhi's disapproval. The most interesting feature of the event was the absence of any blue-print of organisation and plan of action. Young workers became the only link between the Congress and the people through their underground organisations. The Quit India Movement failed to compel the Government to leave the country. As observed by a historian,

> *The revolutionary movement which had begun early in the century as well as the non - violent Satyagraha which Gandhi launched in 1920, both came to an end almost simultaneously...The last battle for India's freedom began almost immediately after far beyond her frontier.*

under the leadership of Netaji Subhas Chandra Bose and the Azad Hind Fouz (INA).[36]

The constitutional wrangle for the settlement of the Indian problem was resumed at the end of the Second World War. The Pakistan demand of the Muslim League influenced the Assam Muslims under the leadership of Maulana Abdul Hamid Khan Bhasani and Saadulla who respectively controlled the organisational and parliamentary wings of the Assam Provincial Muslim League. As on All India level so also in Assam, the Hindus and the Muslims presented two opposing fronts, namely, independence of the country as a whole and that with Partition. The views were reflected in the elections of 1946 exposing the complete communal division of the electorate. In the Assam Legislative Assembly, the Congress captured all the 47 General seats and 11 other Special Interest seats while the Muslim League won 31 out of 34 reserved seats, the remaining 3 Muslim Seats going to the Jamiat-Ul-Ulema-E-Hind.

The Cabinet Mission

The Cabinet Mission having failed to secure unanimity of Indian opinions recommended its own plan on 16 May 1946. Its most important provisions were,

i) The immediate establishment of an Interim Government,
ii) A Union of India for the whole country dealing with defence, communication and foreign relations
iii) Compulsory formation of groups of provinces with representation in proportion to their respective share of the population with the right to secede from the groups and the
iv) Formation of a Constituent Assembly of members elected on the method of proportional representation with a single transferable vote and on communal basis.

The Congress and the League accepted the proposal

Assam and Bengal were placed in Group C. That rightly roused strong protests and opposition from the Assam Provincial Congress Committee and other organisations including the Communist Party of India. They were supported by powerful leaders of Bengal, namely, Sarat Chandra Bose, Shyama Prasad Mukherjee, Soumendra Nath Tagore and Biswanath Mukherjee. Opposition in Assam led by Gopinath Bordoloi was one of the main causes of the failure of the Cabinet Mission Plan which was the last move for freedom with some kind of United India, of course with the seeds of Partition. The British Prime Minister Clement Attlee took a momentous decision in favour of "... transference of power to responsible Indian hands" by a date not later than June 1948.

The Mountbatten Plan of 3rd June 1947 clinched the issue of independence by proposing the division of the country into India and Pakistan. With the acceptance of the plan by both the Congress and the League on 10 and 12 June 1947 respectively, the British Government advanced the date of freedom to 15th August 1947. It was decided by the two parties and the Government that in case of Partition of Bengal, a referendum would be held in the district of Sylhet under the aegis of the Governor General to decide whether the people in the district wanted to remain in Assam or go to East Pakistan.

The referendum was held in an atmosphere of intimidation and violence against Hindu voters by the volunteers of the Muslim League and the National Guards before the very eyes of the Government authorities. None of the Central and Provincial Governments, the Assam Provincial Congress Committee, the Central Congress or the Bengal Provincial Congress Committee made any attempts at ensuring peaceful exercise of franchise by all legitimate voters. The authorities also did not allow a large member of non- Muslim voters to exercise their franchise. A mere 6 lakhs of the district's 32 lakh population were entitled to vote. By a fake majority of 55578 votes fate of the district was decided in favour of its inclusion in Pakistan. Thus ended the freedom struggle through a barter system.

REFERENCES

1. Bhattacharjee,K.K., 'Physiography and People of North-East India' in *Social Research*, Shillong, January 1981, p.39.
2. *Ibid*, p.38.
3. Choudhury, Pratap Chandra, *Assam's case Before the State Reorganisation Commission 1955,* pp.17-23 and Rafiabadi,H.N., *Assam from Agitation to Accord*, p.VII.
4. Bhattacherjee, p.39.
5. Bhattacharjee, J.B., Cachar under British Rule in North East India, Chapter I, Guha, Upendra Chandra, *Cacharer Itibritta* (Bengali), Chapter I and Guha, Amalendu, *Planter Raj to Swaraj*, p.27.
6. Bhattacharjee, J.B., Chapter I.
7. Rao, V. Venkata and Niru Hazarika, *A Century of Government and Politics in North East India*, Vol-I (Assam) 1874-1980, p.9.
8. Dutta Pramatha Nath, *Glimpses into the History of Assam*, p. 46.
9. *Ibid*, p.49 and Acharyya, N.N., *A Brief History of Assam*, p.40.
10. Dutta, p.45.
11. *Ibid*, p.81, p. 109, p.111.
12. Acharyya, p.95.
13. *Ibid*, p.99.
14. *Ibid*, p.68.
15. *Ibid* and Dutta, p.82.
16. *Ibid*, pp.153-164 and *Ibid*, pp. 180-188.
17. Bhuyan,S.K., *Anglo-Assamese Relations*, p.62.
18. *Ibid*, p.62 onward.
19. *Ibid*, p.316 onward.
20. *Ibid*, pp.340-341.
21. *Ibid*, p. 389 and Barpujari,H.K., *Assam in the Days of the Company,* p.6.
22. Wilson's Document No.32 quoted in Bhuyan, p.525, p.568.
23. Barpujari, H.K.,(Gen. Ed.), *Political History of Assam*, Volume I, p.29 and Guha, Chapter I.
24. Lahiri, R.M., *The Annexation of Assam*, n.2, p.235, p.255 and Guha, p.2.
25. For details see Guha, pp.11-17, pp.47-56 and Barpujari, pp.101-102,Chapters 5 and 6.
26. Bora, Mahendra, 1857 in Assam, Chapter One, Guha, pp.3-5 and Barpujari, Chapter 5.
27. Kar, M., *Muslims in Assam Politics*,1990, Chapters 6 and 15 for further details.
28. Ibid, pp.264-265.

29. Dutt, K.N., *Landmarks of the Freedom Struggle in Assam*, Reprint 1998, p.45.
30. Pal, Kristodas(Ed.), *The Hindu Patriot*, 7 September 1874, cited in K. Deb's Speech in Assam Legislative Council,1924, Vol.4., p.590 and Guha, p.28.
31. *History of Freedom Movement Record*, cited in Bhuyan, Arun Chandra and Sibopada De (Eds.), *Political History of Assam*, Volume Two, p.14.
32. Gopal, Ram, *The Indian Muslims*, p.337.
33. Sastri, Biswanaarayan and Promode Chandra Bhattacharjee, *This is Assam*, p.16.
34. For details see,
    Government of India File No.59 of December 1920,
    Home Political Fortnightly Report on Assam,
    Assam Secretariat File No. Judicial B., December 1924,
    No.233 – 246.,
    No.Pol.B.March 1921, Nos.350 -354,
    Dutt, K.N, pp.54-55 and
    Kar, M., 'Khilafat and Non-Co-operation Movements in Assam' in Hassan, Mushirul(Ed.), *Communal and Pan-Islamic Trends in Colonial India*, pp.134 – 138.
35. *Assam Gazette*, Part VI A, 1930, pp.1051 – 1065 and Kar, p.282 for details.
36. Majumdar, R.C., *Struggle for Freedom*, Vol. 3, p.679.

2

EVOLUTION OF CONSTITUTIONAL GOVERNMENT IN INDIA

Section I
THE PERIOD OF CHARTERS

"European interests in India have been found to be perennial since classical times."[1] But a group of Portuguese navigators under Vasco de Gama was the first to reach the Zamorin's territory in Calicut on 27th May, 1498. Alfonso de Albuquerque who became the Governor of their affairs laid the foundation of a short-lived domain with his conquest of Goa in 1510 from the Sultan of Bijapur. By the end of the 16th Century the Portuguese became a dominant power over the whole of the Eastern seas. They were followed by the Dutch and the French. We shall not enter into the detailed discussions of this part of Indian history but concentrate on the development of the British power.

The lucrative eastern trade of their European brethren could not but attract the attention of the English merchants. On 31 December 1600, a group of them obtained from Queen Elizabeth a Charter granting exclusive trading rights for fifteen years in the name of the "Governor and Company of Merchants of London trading into the East Indies". The organisation was rechristened the East India Company in 1605. The story of how the scales and weights of these traders became the King's scepters is not our concern here. But we shall only touch upon the salient features of the constitutional development from 1612 to 1935, i.e., from the establishment of their first factory at Surat with the permission of the Mughal Emperor Jahangir to the beginning of Provincial Autonomy. The successive British Royal Charters, most notably of 1661, 1683, 1726 and 1765 gradually...

> *Conferred on it large political powers originally for defensive purposes and to enable it to exercise effective control over its servants, but later on, when it acquired territories in India also, to govern its possessions.*[2]

Between 1612 and the establishment of the first French settlement at Surat in 1667, the East India Company had established its trading centres all along the western and eastern coasts of India upto Calcutta with permission and indulgence of the successive Mughal rulers. Between 1631 and 1680, the Company obtained various commercial privileges which paved the way to its ultimately unchallengeable supremacy in Bengal and its neighbouring provinces. More important of its gains were the Bengal Subedar's Firman of 1631 granting it the unique privilege of trading by making an annual payment of Rs.3000 only. Again in 1656 it was exempted from payment of customs duties. In 1672 the privilege was confirmed. In 1680, Emperor Aurangzeb ordered that "none should molest the Company's people for customs or obstruct their trade", thus further strengthening their position.

Foundation of Calcutta by Job Charnock in 1690 was a further step towards the establishment of British power in Bengal and India. The Fort William, its head quarters, came into existence within a short time. Mughal Emperor Aurangzeb died in 1707. In 1717, Emperor Farruksiyar not only confirmed the Company's duty- free trading rights in Bengal but also gave them the advantage of renting territories around Calcutta, commuted its dues for Surat for an annual payment of Rs.10000 only and made the coins minted by it at Bombay the legal tender throughout his empire. Though the Portuguese, the Dutch and the French were also in the scene, by the end of the 18th Century the English were running far ahead of them. It was from Bengal that the British Indian Empire flourished.

The Age of Parliamentary Control

As the Company prospered, members of the British House of Commons began to feel that instead of Royal Charters, the monopoly of trade should be granted by a Parliamentary Act and in 1691 adopted a resolution to that effect. At the same time the Company's Charter was renewed and that caused an outburst of indignation in the Commons. By a resolution of 1694, therefore, they declared that all the subjects of England had equal right to trade with the East Indies "Unless prohibited by an Act of Parliament". The resolution marked the beginning of Parliamentary control over the Company's affairs as it "Transferred the power of granting monopoly of trade from the Crown to the Parliament..."[3]

The ignoble defeat of Sirajuddaula in the Battle of Plassey in 1757 had made the English the de facto sovereign in Bengal. Mir Qasim's rout in the Battle of Buxar in 1764 was followed by the granting of Dewani of Bengal, Bihar and Orissa to the Company in 1765 by Emperor Shah Alam. This gave it the de jure political supremacy by establishing a sort of Dual Government. The Company was now to be in charge of revenue administration with an army of its own, criminal authority being left in the hands of the incapacitated Nawab. All this opened before the foreign merchants a flood-gate of imperial ambitions which achieved ultimate success through tortuous processes of diplomacy and war. They entered into agreements, open and clandestine, with Indian powers. It could thus be seen that the Company derived its powers from three sources, namely, the British Royal Charters, grant of Dewani and succession to earlier Indian Governments and later Statutes of British Parliament.

All this could not but further attract the notice of the British Parliament. There started an agitation for more government control over the Company's affairs. In 1759, Robert Clive had suggested assumption of royal authority with regard to its acquisitions and the economic benefits derived in India. By 1765, the moot question was whether a private Company was the sovereign over its possessions or should the sovereignty go to the Crown allowing the former only the trade monopoly. The end of the period of Royal Charters was in sight. In 1766 the Parliament constituted a Committee to look into the Company's affairs. Within two years "The British Government started openly interfering... and secured a large share its spoils.[4]

Within the next few years, the Company had to pay the Government a tribute to the tune of £ 40000 for retaining their territorial acquisitions and revenues earned in India. In the meantime its finances depleted with a debt of six million pounds resulting from bribery and corruption among the employees, payment of huge amounts to the Mughals, the Nizam and the British Government, repeated wars with native powers and last but not the least, the Bengal famine of 1770-1772 in which 30 lakhs of people perished. The Company applied to the Government for a loan of one million pounds. On 13 April 1772, Col. Burgyone's resolution in the House of Commons for constitution of a Select Committee of thirty-one members to inquire into the nature and state of the Company and its affairs in the East Indies was accepted. On 26 November the King in his address to the Parliament re-emphasized the "imperative necessity of regulating the affairs" of the Company. The same day, Prime Minister Lord North's proposal for forming a Committee of secrecy was accepted by the House. The reports of the Committees almost unanimously condemned the Company's misrule in India. Series of resolutions were also brought aiming at steps for greater and greater government control over the organization's territories and the economic benefits derived in India.

On 10 May 1773, Burgyone made the following statement to the House of Commons,

1. "...That all acquisitions made under the influence of a military force or by treaty with foreign powers, do as of right belong to the State.
2. "...That to appropriate acquisitions so made to the private emoluments of persons entrusted with the civil or military power of the State is illegal and
3. "...that very great sums of money and other valuable property have been acquired in Bengal from princes and others of the country by persons entrusted with civil and military powers of the State which sums of money and other valuable property have been appropriated to the private use of such persons". No specific decision was taken on Burgyone's contention. But the trend towards government intervention became apparent and added strength to the feelings of the members which were precisely expressed as follows in the Report of the Committee on Constitutional Reforms of a later date. It said,

   The Company's peril of bankruptcy was the immediate cause of Parliament's first intervention, but a more powerful motive was the growing feeling in England, to which the opulence and arrogance of officials returning from India contributed, that the nation must assert the responsibility of seeing that the new and vast experiment of distant and alien race was properly conducted.[5]

The Regulating Act 1773

In 1773, an Act was passed by the Lower House sanctioning a big loan to the Company. But more importantly, Lord North introduced on 18 May, the same year, The East India Company's Regulation Bill that was passed on 10 June by the Commons and on 19 June by the Lords and became the famous Regulating Act, the very first legislative interference of the Parliament into the Company's affairs both in England and India. The Preamble to the Act read,

> *Whereas the several powers and authorities granted by the Charters to the Company of Merchants... have been found, by experience, not to have sufficient force and efficiency to prevent various abuses which have prevailed in the government and administration of the affairs of the said United Company as well of home as in India, to the manifest injury of the public credit, and of the commercial interests of the said Company, and it has therefore become highly expedient that certain further regulations better adopted to present circumstances and condition, should be provided and established. And whereas the electing and choosing of Directors of the said United Company every year, in such a manner as at present prescribed by Charter, has not answered the good purposes intended thereby, but on the contrary, by limiting the duration of their office to so short a time, evidently tends to weaken the authority of the court of Directors ... may it, therefore, please be enacted...*[6]

The main provisions of the Regulating Act are stated below.

The Company's Administration at Home

(a) Election of Directors for four years in place of annual election, on the basis of higher stock holding or property qualification raised from £500 to £1000. This resulted in the disenfranchisement of 1246 share holders of the Company. But the votes of proprietors were increased in proportion to the shares, for example, one vote for property worth £1000, two for £ 3000, three for £ 6000 and four for £10000.

(b) One fourth of the Directors would retire every year and new members elected in their place.

(c) Only the Crown could remove a member on a representation of the Court of Directors.

(d) All papers relating to the Company's Indian revenue would be placed before the Treasury and those of Civil & Military administration of the Indian territories before the Secretary of State.

(e) The Directors were to be kept informed of all affairs of interest of the Company in India.

(f) The Governor General of Bengal and the Governors of Bombay and Madras were required to pay due obedience to the Board of Directors.

The Government of Indian Territories

1. The Governor of Bengal was redesignated Governor General of Bengal with a Council of four members. He could not over-rule the Council but had a casting vote in case of a tie. He also had the power to superintend and control the other Governors, thus ending their political and administrative isolation from Bengal. The members of the Governor General's Council were appointed for five years and could be removed by the king on a representation of the Directors of the Company.

2. The Governors of Bombay and Madras were required to pay due obedience to the Governor General-in-Council. All rules and regulations framed by them would be sent to the Governor General.

3. The Governor General-in-Council was vested with the "whole civil and military government" of the Bengal Presidency and also the ordering, management and government of territorial acquisitions and revenues in Bengal, Bihar and Orissa.
4. The Governor General-in-Council was empowered to make rules, ordinances and regulations for the good order and civil government of the Company's settlement at Fort William and factories and places subordinate to it. The said actions would have to be registered with the Supreme Court.
5. The Supreme Court established under the Act had a Chief Justice and three Puisne Judges. The Court had the power to try civil, criminal admiralty and ecclesiastical cases. Its jurisdiction extended to all British subjects residing in Bengal, Bihar and Orissa and it had both original and appellate jurisdiction. Trial by jury was introduced.

Constitutional significance of the Act

The Act was a landmark in the constitutional history of India for the following reasons.

1. Political nature of the Company was recognised by the British Parliament.
2. This enactment placed the control of the Company's affairs largely in the hands of the British Parliament and Government.
3. The Finance Department and the Secretaries of State of Britain were clearly brought into the picture vis-à-vis the Company's Government both in England and India. It "... gave a definite and recognizable form to the vague and arbitrary powers of sovereignty that had devolved upon the Company."[7]
4. The Company's patronage was greatly curtailed as the Act made the appointment of the first Governor General, his Councillors, the Chief Justice of India and Judges of the Supreme Court at Calcutta. Subsequent appointments would need the Crown's approval.
5. It was the first enactment of its kind to empower a foreign Government in India.
6. It made an "honest attempt towards the unification" of the Company's possessions in India through the Governor General and his Council.
7. It was an attempt at putting to an end the corruption and misrule of the Company's servants.
8. By this Act "...The British nation ... assumed the actual responsibility of the government of the territories won by the servants of the trading corporation."
9. It "altered the constitution of the Company at home, changed the structure of the Company in India, subjected in some degree the whole territories to some supreme control in India and provided in a very efficient manner for the supervision of the Company by the Ministry", thus laying down a definite form of government.[8]

The Amending Act of 1781

In 1781 two Committees were constituted by the British Parliament, one to look into the existing state of affairs of the Company in India and the other to study the administration of justice in the country. This Act was the result of the findings of the Committees and aimed at remedying some of the deficiencies of the Regulating Act. Its more important provisions briefly were:

1. It very much strengthened the position of the Governor General-in-Council vis-à-vis the Supreme Court.
2. It recognised and legalised the legislative powers of the Governor General-in-Council without reference to the Supreme Court.

The Pitt's India Act 1784

The Government of Great Britain was not satisfied with the changes brought about so far in the affairs of the Company. Therefore, in framing a system of Government of India, Prime Minister William Pitt said that it was their duty to see that "though no Charter could or ought to supersede state necessity, still nothing but absolute necessity could justify a departure from the Charter". Further, to remove the deficiencies of the Regulating Act and amend some aspects of its provisions, Pitt's India Act was passed. It provided as follows:

The Home Administration of the Company - A Dual Government

(a) A Board of six Commissioners, popularly called Board of Control was established. The Commissioners were the Chancellor of Exchequer, a Secretary of State and four Councillors, all unpaid.

(b) The Board could issue secret orders to the Company's authority in India through a Secret Committee of Directors. The Board regulated the civil, military and revenue administration of the Company's territorial possessions in India. They were now to have access to all papers, minutes and correspondence etc. of the Company. It could also recall any official appointed by the Directors who remained responsible only for the trading activities of the Company. Obviously the British Cabinet became the ultimate authority over the Company. Thus there was a kind of Dual Government working in England with respect to the organization.

(c) Powers of the proprietors were eclipsed.

The Government of Indian possessions

(a) In this respect, only the covenanted servants of the Company could be appointed Governor Generals.

(b) The Crown was empowered to recall or remove the Company's servants.

(c) The Governor General's Council would now consist of three members. With his casting vote, he could dominate over the Council with the support of one member only.

(d) For the first time the Company's territories in India were called the "territorial possessions of this Kingdom" and the "British possession in India".

(e) The Governor General-in-Council was given full authority and power to "Superintend, direct and control" the Presidencies and Governments thereof in matters of war and peace, application of revenues or forces during war or transaction with country powers".[9]

Constitutional significance of the Act

1. It formed the basis of Indian Constitution till 1858 having virtually transferred the responsibility for Indian Government from the Court of Proprietors to the Board of

Control. The Board became the sole governing power so much so that

...There was nothing which could have been done, previous to the passing of the Act, by the Court of Directors, that the Board of Control had not now the power to do by virtue of the Act.[10]

According to Lord Dundas, "without the whole power of Government, the Board of Control would be a nugatory body". The Court of Directors controlled only the distribution of patronage and management of trade.[11]

2. The Act adopted the principle of placing the Company in direct and permanent subordination to a body representing the British Government and the Directors now played second fiddle to the Government.
3. The Governor General or Viceroy and the Governors became the executive heads of their respective administration. The Governor General had now two masters, the Board of Directors and the Board of Control.
4. According to Sir J. Holland Rose, Pitt's biographer,

   ...while wielding despotic authority in India, the new Viceroy was but an adjunct of the British Constitutional machine. It is perhaps the highest of Pitt's achievements that he saw how to combine two ideals of Governments, the oriental and occidental, in a way that conduced to vigor of action in Bengal and did not impair popular progress at home while investing the real ruler of India with powers far greater than those wielded by Warren Hastings. He subordinated them to the will of the King and Parliament.[12]
5. It finally established a Dual Government of the Company at home; it divided the commercial, political and administrative affairs into two distinct parts-the Directors in charge of commercial affairs and the Board of Control in charge of the rest. However, there was an inherent deficiency in the Act. Lord Palmerston remarked,

   The functioning of government and its responsibility have been divided between the Director, the Board of Control and the Governor General... and among these authorities ... dispatch and unity of purpose can hardly be expected.

Secondly, the long distance and problems of communication gave the Governor General the opportunity to act by evading both authorities quite often. It took two years to get a reply to a dispatch sent to the Home Government from India. Moreover, before a dispatch upon the most important matter could go out to India, "it had to oscillate between the Canon Row (Board of Control's office) and India House (Company's office). It was proposed by one party, altered by the other, altered again by the first and sent back altered to the other". Thus the direction of Indian affairs from London "was a sort of post mortem" because the Governor General might have already acted in his own way.[13] Warren Hastings was succeeded in 1786 by Lord Cornwallis. On his demand as a precondition to acceptance of office, another Act was passed, "empowering the Governor General to override his Council and act on his own responsibility whenever he deemed fit" and whenever the "situation so demanded."[14]

The Charter Act of 1793

The Company's Charter was renewed in 1793 with the following salient features.

1. Its trade monopoly was extended for another twenty years.
2. The Governors were now given the power to override their Councils.
3. It reiterated the Governor General's authority over the Bombay and Madras Presidencies including transactions with a country power or State, declaring war and signing peace, collection of revenue, employment of armed forces and the civil and military administration of their territories.
4. A general statement of the Company's affairs was to be placed before the Parliament.
5. The Permanent Settlement of 1793 was reiterated making the Company the proprietor of their land in Bengal and the settlement was extended to Benaras.
6. Payments of salaries of the members of the Board of Control were to be made out of the Company's revenues.
7. The Governor General and some other officers were not to leave India during their tenure.
8. The Commander-in-Chief of Company's army was not to be a member of the Governor-General's Council at Fort William unless specially appointed by the Directors.
9. The Governor General was authorised to appoint a Vice-President to act during his absence.The net result of the Charter was further concentration of political and economic powers of the Company in the hands of the Parliament. Sir John Shore was appointed Governor General in succession to Cornwallis for five years. The most important development following the Charter Act of 1793 was the extension of the Permanent Settlement to Benaras. Lord Wellesley who succeeded Shore was the founder of the system of Subsidiary Alliance, which constituted the basis of political law, governing the relation between the Company's Government and the native states. Other developments till the next renewal of Charter in 1813 were the establishment of a Supreme Court in Madras, authorization of the Governors and their Councils to make regulations for their territories subject to registration in the Supreme Court (Madras), and the Recorder's Court (Bombay). Laws made for the Company's Courts were not required to get registered. In 1823, a Supreme Court replaced the Bombay Court.

The Charter Act of 1813

1. After extensive scrutiny of the Fifth Report of 1812, the territorial acquisitions of the Company with their revenues were granted to it for another twenty years "without prejudice to the undoubted sovereignty of the United Kingdom... in and over the same." It was also proclaimed that the Government's duty was to promote the interest and happiness of the native inhabitants of India.
2. Vacancies in the offices of Governor General, Governors and Commander-in-Chief were to be filled by the Directors subject to the approval of the Crown, to be signified in writing under the Royal Sign Manual countersigned by the President of the Board of Control.
3. Trade monopoly of the East India Company in India was abolished.
4. Church establishments were permitted in India.
5. The Company would now have to maintain separate commercial and territorial accounts.
6. It laid down the basis of modern Indian education system by authorising the Governor General to spend a lakh of rupees a year for revival, improvement and encouragement

of education and learning and for the introduction and promotion of the knowledge of sciences among Indians.

The Charter Act of 1833

The Indian problem was discussed when England was swept by liberal ideas which led to a number of reforms such as extension of suffrage, abolition of slavery, liberalisation of Press Laws and extension of popular education etc. There was a lot of controversies centering round the Company's affairs. On June 13, 1833, Charles Grant told the House of Commons that two factors "marred the efficiency" of Indian Government. One factor was the "Union of the trader and the sovereign"; the other was the interference from home. Therefore,

> *It was essential to the well-being of India that confidence should be placed in its administration and that as far as possible the intervention of the home authorities should be confined to cases of a strong and extra-ordinary nature ...All that depended on the administration of government in India which ought to be left to the administration there.*[16]

Sir Thomas Munro had written in 1807,

> *The strength of British Government enables it to give its Subjects a degree of protection which those of no native power enjoy. Its laws and institutions also afford them a security from domestic oppression unknown in those states; but these advantages are dearly bought. They are purchased by the sacrifice of independence, of natural character and of whatever renders a people respectable. The natives of British provinces may without fear pursue their different occupations and enjoy the fruit of their labour in tranquility; but none of them can aspire to anything beyond his mere animal state of thriving in peace; none of them can look forward to any share in the legislation of civil or military government of their country.*[17]

Resolutions proposing the renewal of the Company's Charter were placed before the Parliament in June 1833. The following ideas could be gleaned from the observations of some members of the House.

1. The Indian possessions of the Company belonged to the British nation. Therefore, it was "preposterous" to leave the political government of "an immense empire" in the hands of a Joint Stock Company, said Buckingham. Further, according to him, the Company's *interests were merely those of... proprietors of Indian Stock, anxious chiefly to secure payments of their dividend, but when that was attained, having no interest whatever... in the happiness and welfare of the people which was the only legitimate end of all government.*
2. Indians were British subjects. In this connection the Marquis of Lansdowne said,

   ... that their only justification before God and Providence for the great and unprecedented domain which they exercised in India was in the happiness which they communicated to the Subjects under their rule, and in proving to the world at large and to the inhabitants of Hindustan, that the inheritance of Akbar the wisest and the most beneficial of Muhammadan princes, had not fallen into unworthy and degenerate hands.
3. Participation of Indians in their affairs.

The discussion in the House of Lords "centered round" the question of Indians' employment in offices under the British Government in India and participation therein. Wyme said,

The only principle on which the empire could be justly or wisely or advantageously administered was that of admitting the natives to participate in the Government, and allowing them to hold every office, the duties of which they were competent to discharge.

According to Lansdowne, "... to every office in India, every native whatever caste or religion, should be by law equally admissible..."Buckingham suggested,

the admission into Supreme Council in India, of some few representatives of British population in India as well as that of the natives, in order to make a beginning, at least of that system of self-government to which they might advance with all our colonies, as far as possible.

However, Macaulay ruled out the possibility of representative institutions as time was not ripe as yet for that. He said,

In India you cannot have representative institutions. Of all the innumerable speculators who have offered their suggestions on Indian politics, not a single one, as far as I know, however democratic his opinion may be, has ever maintained the possibility of giving, at the present time, such institutions. The destinies of Indian Empire is covered with thick darkness ... It may be that the public mind in India may expand under our system till it has overgrown that system; that by good government we may educate our Subjects a capacity for better government, that having become instructed in European knowledge, they in some future age, demand European institutions. Whether such a day will ever come I know not. But never will I avert or retard it. Whenever it comes it will be the proudest day in English history.

Lord Ellenborough believed that a time would come when Indians could fill even the highest situations in their country. But he did not look forward to a period when all offices in India would be placed in their hands. Therefore he said, "No man in his senses would propose to place the political and military power in India in the hands of the natives."[18]

In this background the East India Company's Charter was renewed for another twenty years on 28 August 1833. Main provisions of the Act were as follows:

1. Administrative and political powers of the Company were to remain till 30 April 1854 "under the Crown" in trust for His Majesty, his heirs and successors, for the service of the Government of India. Thus the East India Company ceased to be a trading body and "became a political Agent for the Crown".[19]
2. The monopoly on China trade and trade in tea was abolished w.e.f. 22 April 1834. The Company was required to close its business with all "convenient speed". A compensation of ninety million pound sterling would be paid to it out of Indian revenues. All debts and liabilities of the Company were to be charged to the same revenues.
3. The constitution of the Board of Control was modified. The Lord President of the Council, the Lord Privy Seal, the First Lord of Treasury, the Principal Secretaries of State and the Chancellor of Exchequer were to be ex-officio members for the affairs of India.
4. The system of licenses for coming to or staying in India or acquiring properties was abandoned, thus opening the country's doors to all British subjects.

The Government of India

1. The Governor General of Bengal was re-designated Governor General of India. His Council was extended by the addition of a law member to the existing three. He was to attend the Council in its meetings related to law making. The Governor General was also the Governor of Bengal ex-officio.
2. The Governor General-in-Council was given the full power of superintendence and control over all the Presidencies, i.e., the entire possession of the Company thereby centralising the administration of its Indian affairs. Thus for the first time we get the name, Government of India.
3. The Governor General-in-Council only was authorised to make laws and regulations for all persons, courts and places within and throughout the whole of the Company's territories. As a result, the Governors of Bombay and Madras Presidencies were deprived of law making authority and came under the Central Government for legislation.
4. The laws made by the Government of India were henceforth called Acts which prior to 1833 were known as (a) Hindu or Mohammedan Law, (b) English Statutes and Common Law, (c) Bengal Regulations, (d) Bombay Regulations and (e) Madras Regulations. Now with administrative centralization also came the legislative centralization.
5. The Control of civil and military administration of the entire territories of the Company were vested in the Governor General-in-Council.
6. The Governor General-in-Council was required to make laws and regulations providing for the prevention and punishment of persons illicitly entering or residing in India.
7. Neither any native of His Majesty's territories nor any natural born subject thereof would be by reason of religion, place of birth, descent, colour or any of them disabled from any place, office or employment under the Company. Despite the generous sentiments expressed as above, however, Indians continued to be excluded from high offices. The net effect of the Act was the uniformity and centralization of political, administrative and legislative powers, uniformity of law and central control over the finances of the country which were treated as a single fund, any expenditure out of which required the authorization by the Governor General-in-Council. All this clearly further strengthened the unitary character of the Government of India. The clause regarding employment, however, did not remove the prohibition, under the Regulating Act, of employment of Indians to high offices. Therefore, the Duke of Wellington observed,

   why was this declaration made in the face of a regulation preventing its being carried into effect? It was a mere deception.[20]

The Charter Act of 1853

As the time for renewal of the Charter approached, there appeared persistent demands both in India and England that,

1. The Dual system of Government of the Company at home be abolished,
2. There should be a Secretary of State for India assisted by a Council of India, partly elected and partly nominated,
3. The Indian Legislature should be distinct from the Executive and should possess a certain amount of popular character without of course defining the term popular,

4. The Governor General should not be allowed to act contrary to his Council's advice and
5. Civil Services should be thrown open to all British subjects through a system of Competitive Examinations to be held in England and appointments were to be made on the basis of merit only.

Democratization of institutions was still a far cry. It would be indicated by the following statement made by the Earl of Derby on 2 April, 1852 while suggesting appointment of a Select Committee of Parliament to inquire into the Company's affairs.

> *The time is far from being come at which anything like popular institutions could be conferred upon any portion of India, but of this I am quite sure that this is your bounden duty in the interest of humanity, of benevolence, and of morality and religion, that as far and as fast as you can do it safely, wisely and prudently, the inhabitants of India should be gradually entrusted with more and more of the superintendence of their own internal affairs under the control of British authority and taught to respect that authority which is vested in the law and which they see judiciously and firmly enforced, temperately enforced also, by the superior British authority, which they may by long habit and practice learn to imitate, and, I would hope, even surpass.*[21]

Thus the stage of apprenticeship was to continue. However, important changes were made both at home and in India by the Charter Act of 20 August 1853 as shown below.

The Home Government

1. The territories and revenue of India "...were to be held by the Company in trust for Her Majesty, Her heirs and successors until Parliament shall otherwise direct." Thus the renewal, unlike the previous ones was not made for any definite period of time.
2. The number of Directors was reduced from 24 to 18; of them six were to be appointed by the Crown. The quorum was fixed at ten to ensure a majority of the Crown nominees.
3. The Court of Directors was deprived of the privilege of patronage as all civil servants of the Company would be appointed through an Open General Competitive Examination and on the basis of merit only. It was open to all British subjects.
4. The position of the Board of Control was made equal to that of the Secretary of State.
5. The Crown's approval became necessary for all appointments of Councillors.
6. The Court of Directors was empowered to create a new Presidency.
7. A Law Commission was appointed in England for codification of Indian laws. It also drafted the Civil Procedure Code and the Criminal Procedure Code.
8. The number of members of the Governor's Council of Bombay and Madras was reduced.
9. These provinces were allowed to retain their armies of course under the control of the Governor General.

The Government of India

1. The Governor General's Council was expanded to make it a separate Legislative Council by addition of six members. They were the representatives each of Bengal, Bombay, Madras and North Western Province, the Chief Justice and a Puisne Judge. The Council would function on the lines of the British Parliament. All laws passed were subject to

the approval of the Governor General who was also empowered to veto any legislation.

2. Some amount of administrative reforms was carried out. The newly annexed Province of Punjab was at first placed under a Board and then constituted into a Chief Commissioner's Province in 1859. Similar arrangements were later made in respect of Oudh, Assam and Burma in 1856, 1874 and 1889 respectively. The provinces of Bengal, Bihar and Orissa were placed under Lt. Governors. They were covenanted Civil Servants with ten years' experience and appointed by the Court of Directors. The Governor General no longer functioned as the Governor of Bengal.

Significance of the Act of 1853

1. The expression "Until the Parliament otherwise directs" was an indication that the Crown might take away the power of the Company and abolish its rule in India. The Government of India Acts of 1854 and 1858 did exactly that.
2. The Legislative Council
   Legislation was for the first time treated as a special function of the Government requiring a special machinery and a special process. This was the beginning of the system of law making through a legislative body. Bills were referred to Select Committees instead of to single persons. Discussion in the legislature, though oral, was made in public. According to some scholars, this Council was the beginning of Parliamentary system in India. However, Sir Charles Wood, the author of the Act had observed,
   Contrary to the intentions of the framers of the Act of 1853, it had developed into an Anglo-Indian House of Commons questioning the Executive and its acts and forcing it lay even confidential papers before it.[22]

He then asserted,

"I do not look upon it as some of the young Indians do, as the nucleus of and beginning of a Constitutional Parliament in India."[23]

The Council showed a spirit of independence by refusing "... to submit legislative projects to the Secretary of State before their consideration in the Council. ... On the other hand, it asserted its right of independent legislation."[24]

The Government of India Act 1854

A further step towards taking over of India by the British Government was taken in 1854. Section 34 of the Act provided as follows:

It shall be lawful for the Governor General-in-Council, with the sanction and approbation of the Court of Directors...acting under the control and direction of Board of Commissioners...from time to time by proclamation duly published, to take under immediate authority and management of the said Governor General of India-in-Council and part or parts of the territories for the time being in possession or under the Government of the said Company and thereupon to give all necessary orders and directions respecting the administration of such part or parts of the said territories or otherwise to provide for the administration thereof, provided always that no law or regulation in force at any such portion of territory shall be altered or repealed except by law or regulation made by the Governor General of India-in-Council.

It was under this provision that Chief Commissionership was created in Assam and other territories mentioned earlier. However, the most serious defects of the Act were that no Indian was associated with legislation and all members of the Council were European Civil Servants and others. In this connection, even seven years later, Sir Bartle Frier advocated the need of inclusion of Indians in the Legislatures so as to do away with

> *... the perilous experiments of continuing to legislate for millions of people with few means of knowing except by rebellion, whether the laws suit them or not.*[25]

Section II
THE GOVERNMENT OF INDIA ACT 1858 – FINAL TAKEOVER

The Mutiny of 1857 brought home to the people of England the insufficiency of earlier enactments for establishment of their authority over India, the " incongruity of the administration of a great empire by a mercantile company" as well as the need of a better government.[26] The Indian feelings with respect to legislation were expressed by Sir Syed Ahmed Khan. He had said,

> *Most men, I believe, agree in thinking that it is highly conducive to the welfare and prosperity of Government – it is essential to its stability – that the people should have a voice in its Councils. It is from the people only that Government can learn whether its projects are likely to be well received. The voice of the people alone can check error in the bud and warn us of dangers before they burst upon and destroy us...This voice, however, can never be heard, and this security never acquired unless the people are allowed a share in the consultations of Government. ... The security of a Government ... is founded on its knowledge and character of the governed, as well as on its careful observance of their rights and privileges. ...The evils which resulted in India from the non-admission of natives into the Legislative Council of India were various. Government could never know the inadvisability of any of the laws and regulations which it passed. It could never hear ... the voice of the people on such a subject. The people had no means of protesting ... or giving public expression to their own wishes. But greatest mischief lay in this that the people misunderstood the views and intentions of Government.*[27]

Further,

> *"... at last came the time when all men looked upon the English Government as slow poison, a rope of sand, a treacherous flame of fire."*[28]

The English view-points could be gauged from some of the statements made in the Parliament in course of debates on a Bill presented for bringing India under direct British rule. In February 1858 Lord Palmerston moved a Bill for better Government in India and abolition of Double Government of the Company in London. But after its second reading the Prime Minister resigned.

Disraeli's motion of 25th March sought to :

1. transfer the Government of India to the British Crown,
2. entrust the Government of India with a separate Minister assisted by a Council of eighteen members, of whom nine would be Crown nominees and others represent commer-

cial bodies of England. Palmerston who now led the opposition criticised the Bill as a laughing stone and it "died of ridicule."

Lord Stanley observed in connection with the proposed Council,

It is intended that the Council should be not merely nominal but real, and that its members should be assistants to the Minister and not a mere screen or pretence. But if the Council were to be a reality, it must possess substantial independence, and not only that, but it must be known to have that character.

According to Willoughby,

Upon the Council of India would mainly depend the good and bad government of the country...The Council, therefore, upon which so much depends, should consist of persons of knowledge, experience and independence.

Gladstone's opinion was as follows:

It is impossible that this house can be perpetually legislating about India. It cannot be perpetually considering from year to year in what manner it can frame and assert on behalf of natives that arrangement of government and administration which shall be well adapted to bring them forward in proportion to their powers in the work of governing themselves ...

About the peoples awakening resulting from the revolts, he observed,

... I confess, I cannot conceive circumstances more unfortunate for the consideration of such a question than the present circumstances of India, when a considerable portion of the natives are still in arms against you, and the concession you make, if too narrow, will fail to satisfy them; while on the other hand, if they are large and liberal they may be ascribed not to your deliberate conviction, but the apprehensions which they may think they have excited.

There was no unanimity about the Indians' rights and privileges and their participation in the governance of the country but there was hardly any difference on the question of British sovereignty over India and the East India Company. On 30th April the Parliament passed fourteen resolutions which formed the basis of the Government of India Act (Act for the better Government of India) of 2nd August 1858. Its provisions are briefly described below.

The Home Government

1. The Act clearly transferred the Government of India from the Company to the Crown of England.
2. India was to be governed by and in the name of the Crown through a Secretary of State with a Council of fifteen members and presided over by him. Eight of those members would be appointed by the Crown and seven elected by the Court of Directors from amongst themselves then existing. More than half of the Council members would be those who had been living and serving in India for more than ten years preceding their appointments.
3. The Secretary of State for India would be responsible to the British Parliament and not to his Council. So in practice, he could even override it.

4. All the territories and the revenues thereof were to be received for and in the name of Her Majesty and applied and disposed of for the purposes of the Government of India alone.
5. The Council of India was to " combine the promptness, the decision, the energy which are the result of undivided authority with the knowledge, the experience and the practice which can only be furnished by a body of men of distinguished talent, who have had considerable acquaintance with the vast and various forms of Indian life".[29]

The Government of India

1. The Governor General was to be appointed by the Crown and the members of their Councils by the Secretary of State of India- in -Council.
2. The Governors were to be appointed by the Governor General with the approval of the Crown.
3. Appointments to Civil Services were to be made through open competition under rules made by the Secretary of State-in-Council with the assistance of the Civil Services Commission.
4. Company's military and naval forces were transferred to the services of the Crown under the same conditions which determined their initial recruitment.
5. Indian revenues were not to be used for defraying expenses of military operations outside Indian frontiers, except for preventing or repelling of actual invasion, without Parliament's approval.

Thus the provisions of Government of India Act were the fundamental laws which governed

(a) the position of the Home Government vis-à-vis the Government of India,

(b) the Secretary of State's relation with his Council and

(c) Parliamentary control over Indian government and administration as a British territory.No radical changes were made in the Constitution till the Montagu-Chelmsford Reforms of 1919.

The Nature of Parliamentary Control[30]

The entrusting of responsibility for Government of India to the Crown was not intended to empower the Secretary of State for India to interfere with the day to day task of administration or to give him all authority for initiatives. " India was to be governed in India." One member in the House of Commons said on 24 June 1858, "If we are to have the details settled here, I am perfectly certain we can have no good government in India." The Parliamentary control over Indian Government and administration under the Secretary of State was very much limited and conditioned as follows:

1. The Secretary of State for India was bound to lay before the Parliament a financial statement "in such form as best exhibited the moral and material progress and condition in India."

2. Involvement of Her Majesty's forces in India would be communicated to both Houses of Parliament within a specified period of time.
3. Except for prevention or repulsion of actual invasion of British possessions or under urgency, the revenues of India could not be utilised for meeting the expenses of army operations beyond the British Indian territories without the consent of Parliament.

Representation of Indians

According to one author,

> *the credit of demanding representative legislature in India goes to Gopalrao Hari Deshmukh (1823-1892), commonly known as Lokhitawadi (advocate of public welfare who was employed in the Judicial Department of the Government of Bombay).*

In the "middle" of the 19th Century, in an article entitled "Reform of the State", in the journal 'Prabhakar', he wrote

> *We send a memorial to the Queen asking for the establishment of some kind of Parliament in India. The Indian Parliament would bridge the wide gulf of separation which exists between the British rulers and the Indian people.*

Main features of his proposal were as follows:

1. Two delegates each from every city and every district should be elected in the Bombay Presidency as directed by the District Magistrates.
2. The representatives must be good speakers, intelligent and statesmanlike as they "would really be the co-sharers of sovereign authority".
3. "in electing representatives, caste, creed or colour should be no consideration".
4. ".... when Parliament of this type would be formed people would be able to distinguish between Democracy and Despotic Rule....."
5. The Governor should preside over the Parliament.

The atmosphere after the revolt of 1857 was " surcharged with suspicion and it was considered inadvisable at that juncture to liberalise the Council and make a statutory provision for the admission of Indians into the Council." Both Lord Canning and the Home Government proposed the idea of setting up a representative legislative body in India.[31] It was therefore decided to frame a new legislature in accordance with the "extreme notions with regard to legislation which prevailed in India." According to Sir Charles Wood, then Secretary of State, the notion of legislation which was "entertained by a native, is that of a chief or sovereign, who makes what laws he pleases." He had "little or no idea of any distinction between the executive and the legislative functions of Government." This was to be the "fabric" of a new Constitution. As regards inclusion of Indians in the legislature, Sir Charles Wood observed that it was

> *...simply and utterly impossible, for you cannot possibly assemble at any one place in India persons who shall be the real representatives of the various classes of the native population of that empire.*[32]

The Council under the Act of 1853 had, according to some Englishmen, "assumed the functions of a petty Parliament" to redress grievances and criticise the conduct of the Executives. But the first Vice-President of the Council had observed that, "It has no jurisdiction, in the nature of the grand inquest of the nation. Its functions are purely legislative and are limited even in that respect. It is not an Anglo-Indian House of Commons for the redress of grievances, to refuse supplies, and so forth."[33] Sir Charles Wood, while moving the Bill for a new Act said, "I have no intention of doing anything to make this Council a debating society".

Lord Grey and Lord Ripon also assured the Upper House that Government would make special provision to ensure that the Council would not assume the functions of a little Parliament. Accordingly, no statutory provision for Indian representatives was yet conceived. But the authorities considered it enough to leave a discretion with the Governor General to admit particularly Indian Chiefs for legislative purposes. They were convinced that Indians then "will no longer feel, as they have hitherto done, that they are excluded from management of affairs in their own country."[34] The assumption of Government by the Crown was to be proclaimed to the Princes and people of India by Queen Victoria on the first of November 1858 in a Special Darbar at Allahabad. The Proclamation was made as scheduled.

Section III
REFORMS CONTINUE

The Indian Councils Act 1861

Having taken over the administration the British Parliament took steps for further consolidation of power through this Act which got royal assent on 1August 1861.Its main provisions were:

1. The number of ordinary members of the Governor General's Council was increased to five, the fifth being a Barrister of five years' standing. Three of them were to be serving in India for ten years.
2. The Governor General was authorised to make rules and orders for transaction of the Council's business in the name of the Governor General-in-Council. Rules so made introduced the portfolio system in India. There would be the President of the Council to officiate the Governor General during his absence with all powers excepting assenting to or withdrawing assent from any law or regulation.
3. He was further empowered to establish, by proclamations, Councils for law making for Bengal, Punjab and North Western Frontier Province.
4. He could create new provinces, appoint Lt. Governors and fix or alter the boundaries of any Presidency or Province. Accordingly the Bengal Council was established in 1862. One third of the Councillors nominated was non-official.

Changes in the Central Legislature

1. The Governor General's Council was enlarged with the addition of not less than six and not more than twelve members, for not more than two years and for "better exercise of

power of making laws and regulations". Half cf the additional members could not be civil or military officers of the Government in India.

2. Without the Governor General's prior approval, no measure could be introduced with regard to public debt or revenues, religious matter, armed forces and foreign relations.
3. The Governor General might give his assent to or withdraw or reserve it for the Crown's decision. The Crown might veto any measure approved by him.
4. The Council was authorised to make laws for all persons, native, British or foreign, in India, all courts of justice, all places and things and all servants of the Government within the dominions of rulers in alliance with the British except in matters affecting the British Constitution and the Parliament's jurisdiction. All such laws required the assent of the Governor General but could be disallowed by the Crown acting through the Secretary of State.
5. The Governor General was authorised to issue Ordinances in case of urgent necessity and valid for a period not exceeding six months and subject to cancellation by the Crown or repeal by a legislative act.
6. Legislative powers of the Presidency Councils of Bombay and Madras were restored. The Governor's Council which was expanded now would have not less than four and not more than eight nominated members besides the Advocate General. Half of the nominees would have to be non-officials. The Council's jurisdiction was limited as in the case of the Central Council. Any law passed by it would require the Governor's assent and could be rejected by the Governor General or the Crown. Laws and regulations made by the Governor's Council could not affect Parliament's jurisdiction and Acts.
7. Legislation by executive orders could no longer be made.

   Though the Act did not very clearly demarcate the spheres of central and provincial legislatures, it was a measure of great constitutional importance as indicated below :

1. It consolidated and in certain respect amended the former Acts of Parliament respecting the constitution and functioning of the Councils, both provincial and central.
2. By restoring the legislative powers of the provinces and associating Indians in the legislative process, the Act took an important step towards decentralisation and sowed the seeds of representative institutions and perhaps some amount of provincial authority.
3. It laid down a 'mechanical frame work' of Constitution of India which remained practically undisturbed for the next sixty years.

The demerits of the Act, however, could not be overlooked. Firstly, the principle of nomination often brought in persons not interested and not actually representing Indian opinion. Secondly, "The functions of these Councils are limited to registering the decrees of the Executive Government and stamp(ing) them with legislative sanction".[35] These were thus mere committees for endorsing government's orders and not debating fora. These were "akin to the durbars which Indian rulers had traditionally held in order to sound their subjects' opinion".[36] Further, the Governor General's power of issuing Ordinances enabled him to make laws to suit his purposes. The presence of Indians in the Councils were not of much importance as they could only be expected to satisfy their appointing authorities. The object of the measure was clearly stated by Sir Charles Wood as he observed,

I am as much as any body can be for the self-government of a colony of British settlers. They can manage their own affairs, and if they misgovern, they suffer and will learn to mend their ways – but such a form of Government seems to be singularly unsuited to India.[37]

While innugurating the Indian Legislative Assembly on 9 February 1921, Lord Chelmsford said that the Act had completed the first phase of constitutional reforms.

The Government of India Act 1869 (Indian Councils Act 1869)

The Home Government

Already the Secretary of State for India came to occupy supreme position vis-à-vis his Council. This Act further strengthened his hands by taking away most of the powers of the Council. Members thereof would now be appointed for ten years only, but in exceptional cases extension for five years could be given. All future vacancies would now be filled by the Crown on the advice of the Secretary of State for India.

The Government of India

This Act expressly authorized the Governor General-in-Council to make laws binding upon native Indian subjects without as well as within the Indian territories under the dominion of Her Majesty.

The Indian Councils Act 1870

It enabled the Governor General-in-Council to promulgate regulations for any part of British India thus virtually restoring the executive power of legislation which had been taken away by the Indian Councils Act 1861.

The Indian Councils Act 1874

The Act empowered the Crown to increase the number of ordinary members of the Governor General's Council to six; the additional member was designated the Member of Council for Public Works purposes. The Crown could diminish the number to five in case of any vacancy except that of the Law Member.

The Indian Councils Act 1892

During the period from 1861 to 1891 the most notable change in the Indian administration was the increase of the legislative power and authority of the Governor General's Council. Then the Parliament authorised him to pass regulations without reference to the legislature. In other words, legislation became a function of the Executive. Thus serious deficiencies remained, namely, absence of people's representation, right to interpolation, independent expression of views and the Government's obligation of explaining its policies to anybody.

The Indian National Congress, in its first Session at Bombay in 1885 had taken up the issues through the following resolution:

> … that this Congress considers the reform and expansion of the Supreme and existing Legislative Councils by the admission of a considerable proportion of elected members

... essential and holds that all Budgets should be referred to these Councils for consideration, their members being empowered to interpellate the executive in regard to all branches of administration.

In the next Session the Congress demanded sizeable increase in the number of members in the Legislative Councils with no less than half of them elected. Further, the elected members of the Governor General's Council should be elected by the elected members of the provincial councils who in turn would be elected by the members of the Municipalities, Local Boards, Universities and Chambers of Commerce. Lord Duffrein, the then Governor General, criticised the Congress as an organisation of only a microscopic minority of literate Indians. He asked,

> *How could any reasonable man imagine that the British Government would be content to allow this microscopic minority to control the administration of that majestic and multiform empire for whose safety and welfare, they are responsible in the eye of God and before the face of civilisation?*[38]

At the same time, however, he also observed,

> *... Among the natives I have met, there are a considerable number who are both able and sensible and upon whose loyal co-operation one could undoubtedly rely. The fact of their supporting the Government would popularise many of its acts which now have the appearance of being driven through the legislature by force; and if they in their turn had a native party behind them, the Government of India would cease to stand up as it does now as an isolated rock in the tempestuous sea, around whose base the breakers dash themselves simultaneously from all four quarters of the heavens.*[39]

Duffrein was not, however, opposed to changes bringing in more Indians into the administration of the Indian Empire, without relaxing "in the slightest degree our grasp of the supreme administration of the country". Further,

> *so long as we hold firmly to this principle and remain alive to our own imperial responsibility, I believe that both with safety and advantage we can give full play to the legitimate and praise-worthy ambition of the loyal, patriotic and educated classes of India who are desirous of taking a larger share than hitherto in the transaction of the public business of their respective provinces.*[40]

The next dose of reforms in the matter of legislation and administration was very much in keeping with these concepts, though not completely satisfying the Congress. The main provisions of the Act are summarised below.

1. Enlargement of Legislative Councils.

   Not less than ten and not more than sixteen members were to be added to the existing strength of the central legislature. The Bombay and Madras Councils could have an additional strength of twenty members each, all categorised into official and non – official, the latter having a majority.

2. Introduction of Elective Elements.

   Certain number of non-official members would be recommended by the local bodies like Municipalities and Local Boards, University Senates, Chambers of Commerce and

Zaminders to the Governor and the Governor General for nomination to the respective councils. Suggestions of members for introducing election was rejected by the Parliament. "The word 'election' was carefully avoided but in as much as every recommendation came to be accepted, it did not differ in any way from election".[41]

Gladstone observed in this connection,

The great question we have before us, the question of real and profound interest – is the question of the introduction of the elective element in the Government of India ... while the language of the Bill cannot be said to embody the elective principle – it is very peculiar language, unless it is intended to pave the way for adoption of that principle.

The Under Secretary of State for India said,

It would be in the power of the Viceroy to invite representative bodies to elect, select or delegate representatives of those bodies and thus by slow degrees, by tentative measure in a matter like this, measure cannot be otherwise than tentative-we might perhaps approximate in some way to the ideal.[42]

Indian opinion on the subject was aired by Surendra Nath Banerjee who also felt that the Act had laid down the foundation of representative government. It is interesting note that men like G.K.Gokhale, S.N.Banerjee, R.B.Ghosh, Pheroz Shah Mehta and Ashutosh Mukherjee could become members.

3. Right to discuss Budget and raise questions of public interests.

   Budgets were to be laid before the Councils for discussion and criticism. They were not to vote to the Budget "... item by item ... but to indulge in a full, free and fair criticism of the financial policy of the Government." Members were allowed to raise matters of public interests and question the Executive as to their administrative action.

According to Chelmsford, the Act had completed the second phase of constitutional reforms.

The Council of India Act 1907

1. It provided that the Council of India at home should not have less than ten and more than fourteen members as the Secretary of State might determine. Majority of the members must have served in British India and not left India more than five years before appointment. Their term of office was reduced from ten to seven years.
2. Under the provisions of the Act the Governor General-in-Council and all officers of India were completely subordinated to the Secretary of State for India and the British Parliament requiring them to obey all orders and directions from England. "In the absence of popular legislative control over the authorities in India, this was the only logical position". About the supremacy of Home Government over the Governor General-in-Council and India, one Secretary of States had said,

   The Government established in India is (from the nature of the case) subordinate to the Imperial Government at Home. And no Government can be subordinate, unless it is within the power of the Superior Government to order what is to be done or left undone, and to enforce on its officers, through the constitutional means, obedience to its directions as to the use which they are to make of official position and power in furtherance of the policy which has been finally decided upon by the advisers of the Crown.

Further, he said,

> *Neither can I admit that it makes any real difference in case if the directions issued by the Imperial Government relate to what may be termed legislative as distinguished from executive affairs. It may be quite essential, in order to carry into effect the views of the Imperial Government, as to the well being of Her majesty's Indian dominions, that a certain measure should be passed into law ... described in common language as executive should be performed.... The Government must hold in its hand the ultimate power of requiring the Governor General to introduce a measure, and of requiring also all the members of his Government to vote for it.*[43]

Disraeli's Government had laid down that.

> *Full legal powers having been entrusted to Her Majesty's Government, Parliament would expect that care should be taken that no policy should be pursued which Her Majesty's Government were unable to defend. If the control they possess were to be in any respect less than complete, the power of Parliament over Indian questions would be necessarily annulled.*[44]

All this would clearly show that the Government of India still remained unitary under the control of the Home Government.

Prelude to Morley-Minto Reforms

All constitutional reforms till 1892 were characterised by the absence of a truly representative and effective Indian presence in legislatures and administration. But such participation alone might in any way influence, alter or modify a decision of a highly centralised Government. Lord Curzon's tyrannical regime as Governor General from 1898 to 1905 further alienated the Government from the people. It ushered in a new political awakening in the form of Anti-Partition Agitation and Swadeshi Movement. The Indian National Congress meeting at Benaras in 1905 under the presidentship of Gopal Krishna Gokhale explained its goal "which had a strong bearing on the events of the day." It said,

> *The goal of the Congress is that India should be governed in the interests of the Indians themselves and that in course of time, a form of government should be attained in this country similar to what exists in the self-governing colonies of the British Empire.*[45]

The immediate demand of the party was the reform of legislatures. The Hindu-Muslim divide made a strong presence in India's political life and the Muslims began to plead for their interests separately.

Following the General Elections of 1905, the Labour Party came to power in England. This was followed by three important changes in governments both in London and India. Lord Curzon was replaced by Lord Minto as Governor General on 19 November 1905. St. John Broderick had to give way to Lord Morley as Secretary of State for India in December. Sir J. Bamfylde Fuller, Lt. Governor of Eastern Bengal and Assam had to resign and L.Hare took his place on 26 August,1906. Now the authorities in both the countries began to give thought to changes in legislatures and government. We may here acquaint ourselves with their perceptions and ideas before entering into the discussion of the forthcoming constitutional reforms keeping in mind that Minto was not very much in favour of Congress demand and reforms.[46]

Morley had no direct personal knowledge of the East. For him India was a world as "vast as it is unfamiliar, the distance and the strangeness are formidable." Minto was also called upon to deal with a difficult situation after his arrival in India on 21 November 1905. This was the result of the Partition of Bengal, a measure originated by Lord Curzon. It is well known that the Bengalees, especially the Hindus, had by then launched the Anti-Partition Agitation. Authorities on the history of our National Movement agree that Partition was the immediate cause of the growth of extremism in Bengal. The Government's policy of repression transformed the agitation into a revolutionary movement. On the other hand the Swadeshi Movement, especially its boycott aspect created a turmoil in the country. The Congress fully supported the Movement in its resolution of 1906 which read,

> *Having regard to the fact that the people of this country have little or no voice in its administration, and that their representations to the Government do not receive due consideration, this Congress is of opinion that the Boycott Movement inaugurated in Bengal by way of protest against the Partition of that Province, was, and is, justified.*[47]

The Hindu-Muslim divide to a certain extent weakened the Movement for some time though ultimately Partition had to be annulled.

Both the new Secretary of State and the Governor General were aware of the loyal elements side by side with the revolutionaries. Minto wrote to Morley on 28 May 1906,

> *We are here a small British garrison surrounded by millions composed of an inflammability unknown to the western world and we must be physically strong or go to the wall.*[48]

In order to avert that danger it was necessary to think of a possible counterpoise. The most effective one, apart from the Council of Princes, was to win over the Muslims to the support of the Government and to undermine the feeling of a growing nationality which was "already doing much to unite the Hindus and Muhammadans in a common cause." It is well known that this spirit of nationalism was developing under the Congress leadership and the atmosphere of Swadeshi and Boycott. It was therefore, necessary to evolve a counterpoise to the Congress aims.

On 11 July 1906, Minto wrote to Morley,

> *Ideas can be combated by ideas and you cannot keep the younger generation away from the Congress unless you have another set of ideas to set up against theirs.*[49]

Morley also realised that repression alone, so long perpetrated by Fuller, would not bring normalcy in India. Therefore, endeavours would have to be made for rallying the loyal elements behind the government. A feeling of unrest existed throughout the country and dissatisfaction prevailed amongst the people of all classes and creeds. But

> *The watchword " sympathy" which seemed to have entered with the new regime had spread like fire. The Muhammadans were the first to formulate and put forward their aspirations.*[50]

Their feelings were estimated by Minto as follows:

> *The Mohammedan population which numbers sixty two millions who have always been intensely loyal resent not having proper representation and consider themselves slighted in many ways, preference having been given to the Hindus.*[51]

The leaders of Swadeshi and Boycott Movement tried to "foster this feeling and have naturally done their utmost to secure the co-operation of the vast community." The younger generations "were wavering, inclined to throw in their lot with the advanced agitators of the Congress and a howl went up that loyal Mohammedans were not to be supported and that agitators were to obtain their demands through agitation."

Before taking any action, however, they wanted to appraise the Viceroy of their grievances through a memorandum. It was the first occasion on which the Indian Muslims acted as a distinct community. The memorandum was finalised by 16 November 1906 and signed by thirty-five prominent Muslim nobles, Ministers of various States, great landowners, merchants and many others of the community. A copy of the document was sent in advance to the Viceroy. Agha Khan, the spiritual head of the Khoja Muslim community was selected to lead a delegation of seventy members to Lord Minto at Shimla on 1 October 1906. It was a "very long but excellent Address" stating their grievances and aspirations. It

1. recognised the benefits conferred by British rule on the diverse races of many creeds who formed the population of this huge continent,
2. expressed gratitude for the personal freedom, the liberty of worship, the general peace and the hopeful future which the British Empire had secured for India,
3. assured the rulers that the Muslims would not like to "embarrass" them at the "present moment",
4. observed that "representative institutions of the European type are entirely new to the people of India"; introduction of those institutions "requires the most earnest thought and care",
5. claimed that any system of representation whether it affected a Municipality, a District Board or a Legislative Council in which it was proposed to introduce or increase an electoral organisation, the Muslim community should be represented through representatives elected by Muslim electors only,
6. pointed out that in many cases electoral bodies as constituted "cannot be expected to choose a Muslim candidate" and if " by chance" they did so, it could only be " at the sacrifice" of such a candidate's views to " those of a majority opposed to his community whom he could in no way represent",
7. claimed that the quantum of Muslim representation should be estimated not merely on the basis of its numerical strength, but " in respect to the political importance of the community" and " the services it has rendered to the Empire." The Muslim League formed two months later echoed the same voice.
8. maintained that the initial rungs in the ladder of self- government were to be found in the Municipal and the District Boards.[52]

Minto read his reply which he had thought out most carefully. According to Lady Minto, " it was impossible to promise too much for fear of offending other communities."

But he made the following policy statement vis-a-vis the Muslims.[53]

1. He appreciated the " just claims" of the followers of Islam and their "determination to share the political history of our empire."
2. "It should be very far from welcoming all the political machinery of the western world among the hereditary traditions and instincts of eastern races...
3. "... the only representation for which India is at present fitted is a representation of communities...and only to a very small extent in that direction.
4. "...I am entirely in accord with you...I make no attempt to indicate by what means representation of communities can be obtained. I am as firmly convinced as I believe you to be, that any electoral representation in India would be doomed to mischievous failure which aimed at personal enfranchisement regardless of the beliefs and traditions of the communities comprising the population of this continent. The great masses of the people of India have no knowledge of representative institutions.
5. " ... The Muhammedan Community may rest assured that their political rights and interest as a community will be safeguarded by any administrative reorganisation with which I am concerned and that you and the people of India, may rely on the British Raj to respect, as it has been its pride to do, the religious beliefs and the national traditions of the myriads composing the population of His Majesty's Empire."

Lady Minto claimed that "... as he spoke in very clear distinct tones, murmurs of satisfaction passed through the audience." Minto observed that the day was " ... very eventful" and " ... an epoch in Indian history." He referred to a letter received from an official the same evening which read ,

> *I must send your Excellency a line to say that a very very big thing has happened today. A work of statesmanship that will affect India and Indian history for many a long year. It is nothing less then pulling back of sixty-two millions of people joining the ranks of the seditious opposition.*

Very much the same view was taken at the White Hall in England. Morley, on receipt of an account of the proceedings wrote to Minto on 26 October 1906,

> *All that you tell me of your Mohammadans is full of interest and I only regret that I could not have moved about unseen at your garden party. The whole thing has been as good as it could be, and stamps your position and personal authority decisively.*[54]

Among other good effects of Minto's speech, Morley observed,

> *...it has completely deranged the plans and tactics of the critical faction here, that is to say, it prevented them from any longer representing the Indian Government as the ordinary case of bureaucracy versus the people . I hope that even my stoutest radical friends will now see that the problem is not quite so simple as this.*[55]

Minto's assurances were the precursors of the separate electorates for Muslims.

The Reforms

Lady Minto wrote that throughout the last six months of 1906, Minto's plan for future policies were developing in a dichotomous perception. According to her,

> *He always distinguished between sedition and legitimate aspirations. He realised that we had come to the parting of ways; that the Indians would have to be recognised and allowed to assist in the governance of the country but that it was equally important to have strong legislation to stop sedition.*[56]

Therefore, a twofold policy was necessary for running the Government, namely, a skillful disruption of enemy forces and a dexterous combination of ruthlessness and affability.

In the words of Minto himself,

> *Before I had been in the country a year, I shared the view of my colleagues that beneath seemingly calm surface there existed a mass of smothered political discontent, much of which was thoroughly justified and due to causes we were called upon to examine.*[57]

Recalling the events he told his Council on 25 January 1910 that the reforms had their "genesis" in a note of his own addressed to his colleagues in August 1906. It was based on the views

> *...entirely I had myself formed of the position of affairs in India. It was due to no suggestion from home.*

He then asserted that whether it was good or bad

> *I am entirely responsible for it.*

Since then Minto was in constant correspondence with Morley. Much of it had not till then been made public.

The process of reforms had been initiated by Minto in August 1906. He appointed a Committee chaired by Sir Aurundel with Sir Dennizel Ibbetson, E.M. Baker and Earl Richards as members, all from his Council. H.H. Risley was the Secretary. The Aurundel Committee was asked to consider the whole question of reforms and to "discover" whether it was possible to give India a Constitution framed on

> *sufficiently liberal lines to satisfy the legitimate aspirations of the most advanced Indians, whilst at the same time enlisting the support of the conservatives and practices of both English and Indian rulers.*

That Constitution would not be

> *...an experimental makeshift, but a working machine representing all interests that are capable of being represented.*

It would also provide for an adequate expression of the sentiments and requirements of the masses of the people, the great agricultural classes who formed two thirds of the entire population of the country.[58] He concluded the address by observing, "...to my mind, there is no answer to be found to the problem unless we call to our counsels the people over whom we rule."[59] But sadly enough this apparently liberal attitude was blown out by the succinct explanation as regards the form of the forthcoming legislatures.

Minto claimed to have "distinctly" maintained that

1. "...representative Government, in its western sense is totally inapplicable to the Indian Empire and could be uncongenial to the traditions of Eastern population,

2. "...that Indian conditions do not admit of popular representations,
3. "...that the safety and welfare of this country must depend on the supremacy of British administration" and
4. "...supremacy can, in no circumstances be delegated to any kind of representative Assembly."[60]

Describing the existing condition in the country and justifying Government's actions he continued,

> *...the progress of the work upon which we have been engaged and in the completion of which we hoped to confer a welcome boon upon the people of India, has been marred by a succession of abominable crimes which have forced my Government into one repressive measure after another...A spirit hitherto unknown in India has come into existence, a spirit opposed to all the teachings of Indian religion and traditions, a spirit of anarchy and lawlessness which seeks to subverse not only British rule but the governments of Indian chiefs, to whom I am so deeply indebted for their loyal assistance. We are called upon to deal with subterranean machinations and methods of assassination and robbery dangerous to the public safety and discreditable to the fair name of India.*[61]

Establishment of the Muslim League at Dacca on 6 December 1906 further consolidated and reiterated the Muslim demand for separate electorate and attracted Minto's attention. In his letter dated 27 February1907 addressed to Morley he observed,

> *The truth is that by far the most important factor we have to deal with the political life of India is not impossible Congress ambition but the growing strength of an educated class perfectly loyal and moderate in its views, but which I think quite justly considers itself entitled to a greater share in the Government of India. I believe that we shall derive much assistance from this class if we recognise its existence and that if we do not, we shall drive it into the arms of Congress cadres to whom it will be forced to look for salvation.*[62]

In March 1907 Minto gave his Council a clearer idea of the forthcoming reforms. He said that " with the object of satisfying the constitutional aspirations of the day," his Government was considering how to give the people of India "wider opportunities of expressing their views". Secondly, there was increasing readiness of the landed and commercial classes to share public life and to render assistance to Government. Thirdly, the growing number of educated Indians desired to have a larger voice in administrative questions. These factors convinced both Morley and Minto that "... it was time to carry to further stage the reforms effected in Lord Landsdowne's days." Morley was obsessed with the idea that the gulf between the two major communities of India was unbridgeable. As to the disturbed condition prevailing in the country, he observed on 26April 1907 in his letter to Minto,

> *... We must use language to convince people that we mean to stand no nonsense and that disorder will extinguish the chances of reforms.*
>
> *Further*
>
> *... No body in the world has better reason for desiring us to suppress the rioters than the moderates among the party (Congress), for they know they will be dished out if disorder prevails.*[63]

However, he suggested to Minto that though not the British Parliamentary institutions, the spirit thereof might be introduced in the Indian administration. But Minto was totally opposed to such a proposition. Even Morley, initially a liberal, backtracked.

The reform proposals of the Aurundel Committee were based on Minto's perception and concepts. The Governor General-in-Council " generally agreed as to the outlines of the reforms" excepting the matters of including an Indian in his Executive Council and the Budget. He thought that " ... on the whole what we have proposed will go far to meet the requirement of the time." The final dispatch containing the reform proposal was sent to the Secretary of State for India on 21 March 1907.Two more dispatches were sent, one on 24August 1907 and another on 10 October 1908. The Governor General and his Council

> *...wanted to check, if possible,... throttle popular views by the reactionary influence of an Imperial Advisory Council consisting of about sixty members of whom twenty were to be Ruling Chiefs and the rest territorial magnates.*[64]

Minto observed that no dispatch " fraught with greater difficulties and greater possibilities has ever left India. It deals with a future no one can foretell."

Minto's covering memorandum to his dispatch to Morley further elaborated the perceptions of the proposed reforms as detailed below.[65]

1. Permanence of British Power

   " No one believes more firmly than I do that the safety and welfare of India depends on the permanence of British administration, but I equally believe that the permanence ... depends upon a sound appreciation of the changing conditions which surrounded it."

2. No Western Type Representation

   " I am no advocate of representative government for India in the western sense of the term. It could never be akin to the instincts of the many races comprising the population of the Indian Empire. It would be a western implantation unnatural to eastern states."

3. Indian History against Popular Representation

   Justifying this contention, he observed, "From time immemorial, the power of the state has rested in the hands of absolute rulers. Neither under Hindu kings nor Mohammedan Emperors had the people any voice in the affairs of State." He quoted Sir Courteney Ilbert in his work on the Government of India that " British authority in India may be traced to a twofold source : it is derived partly from the British Crown, partly from the Great Mughals and other Native Rulers of India."

4. British obligations to Indians

   As heirs to a long series of Indian rulers we are bound to reserve to ourselves the ultimate control over all executive actions and the final decisions in matters of legislation; as trusties of the British principles and traditions we are equally bound to consult the wishes of the people and to provide a machinery by which their views may be expressed as far as they are articulate.

5. Autocracy a Must for India

   He further clarified his views expressed in the forgoing para by saying,

   ...This is not to advocate the introduction of popular representation. The Government of

India must remain autocratic, the sovereignty must be vested in the British hands and cannot be delegated to any kind of representative Assembly.

That was so because , he held, no such Assembly could speak on behalf of the Indian people

so long as the uneducated masses, forming nearly ninety per cent of the adult population, are absolutely incapable of understanding what representative government means and of taking any effective part in any system of election.

6. Constitutional Autocracy the Solution

Not only was Minto not in favour of the spirit of British institutions being brought into action but also he justified autocracy in following manner.The dual origin referred to above might suggest a solution of the problem " consonant both with English ideas with Indian history and tradition." The British Government in India embodied two principles, namely autocracy derived from the Mughal Emperors and the Hindu rulers whose methods they adopted and constitutionalism derived from the British Crown and Parliament. He therefore intended to "fuse" these two principles

into a definite system of government, into what may be called constitutional autocracy which binds itself to govern by rule which admits and invites to its councils representatives of all interests which are capable of being represented and which reserves to itself, in the form of a narrow majority, the predominant and absolute power which it can only abdicate at the risk of bringing back the chaos to which our rule put an end.

Again,

Autocracy was to be maintained by crushing the party which demanded self- government and by conciliating the aristocratic elements and moderate men who will range themselves on the side of the Government and oppose any further shifting of balance of power and any attempt to democratise Indian institutions.

Morley in his Budget speech of 1906 had said,

I should not be taken to indicate for a moment that I dream you can transplant British institutions whole sale into India. You cannot transmit bodily the venerable oak of our constitution, the spirit , the temper, the principles and the maxims of the British institutions. I dot not insist that India should be on the same footing as our self-governing colonies like Canada.[66]

Referring to Gopal Krishna Gokhale's advocacy of national autonomy, self-governing colony and so forth, Morley wrote on 20 June, 1907,

... I regard all this as merely words and phrases for making time or keeping his head above water. I know that to turn India into a Self-governing Colony today is absurd and will not be attempted.

In a derogatory remark he said, "Gokhale as a party manager is a baby, as a party manager or for that matter any politician should never whine. Gokhale is always whining just like the second rate Irishman between Dan O'Connel and Parnell."[67]

He also observed, "Indian ideas! What are they? caste (not exactly labour ideal), purdah, Sattee, child marriage, female infanticide-these are the Indian ideas-what nonsense." Interestingly enough, Minto held a different impression of Gokhale. Before dispatching his reform proposals he wrote to Morley praising Gokhale as very reasonable.[68]

Side by side with these views, however, both Minto and Morley began to think of bringing in Indians to their respective Councils to show their liberal attitude by giving them a share in the government of the country. But at the same time they continued with the repressive measures against the revolutionaries. We need not go into the details which are too well known to be repeated. Morley himself had observed,

> *... if I were attempting to set up a parliamentary system in India or if it could be said that this chapter of reforms led indirectly or necessarily up to the establishment of a parliamentary system in India, I for one, would have nothing at all to with it. I do not believe it will, in spite of the attempts in oriental countries at this moment - attempts which we all wish well - to set up parliamentary government. It is no ambition of mine, at all events, to have any share in the beginning of that operation in India. If my existence, either officially or corporally, were prolonged twenty times longer than either of them is likely to be, a parliamentary system in India is not a goal to which I for one moment would aspire.*[69]

However, he wrote to Minto, "fundamental difference between us, I really believe there is none. Not one whit more than you do, I think is desirable or possible or even conceivable to adopt English political institutions to the nations who inhabit India."

On May 16, 1907, Minto wrote to Morley,

> *The future of British administration in India is a tremendous problem and I agree with you that we need not covet for our descendants the position either of Secretary of State or Governor General. My firm belief is that we can save India from a tremendous convulsion which may result, I know not how, is in recognising the right of the Indian gentlemen loyal at the present moment, to greater share in the government of the country... If we do not do so, we shall ere long have a force opposed to us of a strength of which we had had no experience.*

He again asserted on 6 June 1907 that " India for a long time to come, so far as my imagination could reach, would be the theatre of absolute and personal government."[70]

During the Budget Session of the Imperial Legislative Council 1909, Minto claimed that the policy of Government of India with respect to reforms had emanated from a mature consideration of political and social conditions. But

> *while administrative changes they advocated from being concessions rung from them, have been over and over again endangered by the commission of outrages which could not but encourage doubts as to the opportunities for the introduction of political changes.*

However, he assured the Legislative Council that he had "steadfastly refused" to allow those outrages "to injure the political welfare of the loyal masses of the population of India."

Sir Herbert Risley wrote to Minto that the whole scheme was due to his insight into the general political situation in Asia. Further, if the scheme succeeded in introducing a new spirit and new principles into the Government's dealing with the people of India and thus transformed hostility into cordial fellow service, the achievement would " rank as the greatest that any ruler of India ever had to look back upon."[71] On 17 May 1907

Morley mentioned Minto's five proposals sent through the Dispatch of 21 March. The proposals were discussed in his Council. He observed that " this move in advance has emanated entirely from the Government of India" and not framed in accordance with the instructions conveyed from home. He highly appreciated the Governor General's "initiative" as a good step towards satisfying the present requirement of the British Empire. On 26 November 1908 the "great scheme" was approved by the Secretary of State's Council. Morley wrote to Minto that it was "with uncommon relief yesterday that I wound up the reform proceedings in Council... The Cabinet took the thing on trust having rather urgent business of most domestic moment on their hands."

On 17 December 1908, Morley acquainted the House of Lords with the proposed reforms which he put under several heads. Those were to

1. increase the number of additional members of both central and provincial councils,
2. introduce elections side by side with nomination,
3. allow resolutions or divisions on financial matters by repealing prohibition under the Act of 1892,
4. allow the Legislative Councils to discuss matters of public importance and to make recommendations,
5. enlarge the Executive Councils of Bombay and Madras,
6. extend the power to appoint a member on council to preside over it and
7. create Executive Councils in Lt Governor's provinces and empower them to overrule their Executive Councils.
8. dispense with official majority in the provincial councils.[72]

On 18 December 1908, Morley introduced the Reforms Bills in the House of Lords. Reactions in India were indicated by Lady Minto who wrote that the proposals were received with a "chorus of approval". The reforms, she felt, were "far more liberal than any one anticipated." In this connection it may be noted that the first formal constitution of the Congress was adopted in 1888. Since then and more especially since 1905 the party was making demands for liberalised functioning of legislatures. The party's Madras Session of 29 December 1908 diluted its aim as it adopted the following resolution on the reform proposals.

> *This Congress desires to give expression to the deep and general satisfaction with which the reform proposal formulated in Lord Morley's dispatch has been received throughout the country; it places on record its sense of high appreciation of the statesmanship in the matter and it renders to Lord Morley and Lord Minto its most sincere and grateful thanks for their proposal.*[73]

The broad outlines of the reforms approved by the Secretary of State's Council thus inspired universal jubilation in the country as these did not contain the objectionable provisions which ultimately appeared in the Act. Muhammed Ali Jinnah who supported Surendra Nath Banerjee's resolution quoted above said,

> *I would like to point out that responsibility always brings with it solidity and unless a certain amount of responsibility is thrown on a nation, that nation is bound to creep down. Now that this responsibility has been thrown on us, we should prove to the*

authorities that we are capable of accepting that responsibility. Gentlemen, from a Mohammedan point of view, I join with my Hindu brethren to express out gratitude.

"The Immortal Bill", as Morley called it, was put before the House of Commons in April 1909. It was finally passed on 21 May and with Royal Assent, became the Indian Councils Act of 25May 1909. It came into force with effect from 15November 1909. According to Tara Chand, ninety per cent of the original proposals were recast in the form of the Act. Obviously modified under the conservative pressure, it shattered the hopes of the vast majority of Indians.[74]

However, high appreciation from Hindu leaders was not wanting. We give here one example. Gopal Krishna Gokhale had said in the Imperial Council on 29 March 1909,

> *I think it is safe to say that when in future times the eyes of our countrymen turn back to these days, they will see two figures stand apart from the rest. One will be your Excellency and the other Lord Morley. ...The country owes deep debt of gratitude, to your Lordships, both personally and as the head of the Government of India for this reform...*

Equating Minto with Bentinck, Canning and Ripon he observed that "It is in the company of those Viceroys that your Lordship's name will go down to posterity of India". Morley had called Lord Satyendra Prasanna Sinha one of the "King's equal subjects". Gokhale said that this would "...live in the history of this country...will remain engraved in the hearts of the people."

Further,

> *My Lord, I sincerely believe that your Lordship and Lord Morley have between you saved India from drifting towards what cannot be described by any other name than chaos. For, however strong a Government may be, repression can never put down the aspirations of a people and never will.*

Provisions of the Indian Councils Act 1909
The Morley-Minto Reforms

The Act had eight clauses which laid down the frame work of the reforms. The details were left to be worked out and proclaimed through Regulations. The main provisions of the Act and the Regulations issued under clause 6 of the former are summarised below.

1. Nomination of members of the Legislative Councils

   The Councils, central as well as provincial, had three classes of members, namely nominated officials, nominated non – officials and elected. A substantial official majority was ensured in every Council. The nominated non – official members were expected not to go against the Government. The Secretary of State in his Reform Despatch of 1 October 1908 had written to the Governor General, "Your Excellency's Council in its legislative as well as its executive character should continue to be so as to ensure its constant and uninterrupted power to fulfill the constitutional obligations that it owes and must always owe to His Majesty's Government and to the Imperial Parliament."[75] According to Government, nomination ensured the representation of certain interest groups which would not otherwise be properly represented through election. Such nominations to the Councils were within the absolute power and discretion of the Governor General, the

Governors and the Lt Governors. Nominations required no specific qualification.

2. Separate Electorate for Muslims

While voting in general constituencies side by side with the Hindus, Muslims would vote for electing their own representatives in separate and wholly Muslim constituencies, They were given more seats than they were entitled to on the basis of their numerical strength, by way of weightage.

3. The Electorates

The electorates created under the regulations were classified as

(i) Muslim Electorate as stated above

(ii) General Electorate – this elected the members other than officials and non- officials

(iii) Class and Special Interest Electorates consisted of Presidency Corporations, Universities, Local Bodies, Chambers of Commerce, Port Trusts, Traders, Planters and Landholders.

As regards territorial representation, the authorities held that it was

> *...unsuitable to India as it was a land of diverse races, castes, creeds and sects embracing verying and conflicting interests.*

Further,

> *...representation of classes and interests is the only practicable method of embodying the elective principle in the Constitution of the Indian Legislative Council.*

4. The Imperial Legislative Council

It was expanded and had 60 additional members, of whom 33 would be nominated and 27 elected. The elected seats were distributed as follows :

13 members elected by General Electorate – two each by the non- official members of Bengal, Bombay, Madras and United Provinces,

1 member each by those of Assam, Bihar and Orissa, Burma, Central Provinces and Punjab,

6 members, 1 each by the land holder constituencies of Bengal, Bihar, Bombay, Central Provinces, Madras and Orissa.

6 members by separate Muslim constituencies – 2 from Bengal and 1 each from other Governor's Provinces.

2 members by special electorates-one each by Bombay and Bengal Chamber of Commerce.

In the Governor General's Council, the first Indian , Lord Satyendra Prasanna Sinha was made the Law Member as announced on 24 March 1909. In his Reform Despatch of 1908, Morley had described the purpose of fixing the number 4 in the Executive Council at the Centre to be the inclusion of an Indian. But this was to be done not by statutory provision but by practice and usage.

5. Provincial Councils –Expanded by bringing in additional members.

The following Table gives us an idea of the strength of the Councils under the Act in detail.

Table I : Strength of the Provincial Councils

Legislative Council of	Elected	Nominated Non-Official	Official	Total excluding Head of Govt. and experts
India	25 (27)	7 (5)	36	68
Bengal	26 (28)	5 (4)	20	51 (52)
Bihar & Orissa	21	4	18	43
Bombay	21	7	18	46
Burma	1	8	6	15
Eastern Bengal and Assam	18	5	17	40
Madras	19 (21)	7 (5)	20	46
Punjab	5 (18)	9 (6)	10	24 (34)
United Provinces	20 (21)	6	20	46 (47)

Figures in bracket indicate changes brought about by the Government of India Act of 1912. In Chapter 4, Section III, we have elaborately discussed Assam's representation in the Eastern Bengal and Assam Legislative Council of 1906 and 1910. Of the members therein there was one Assamese to begin with; later five seats were given to Assam of which two were Assamese Hindus, one a Bengali Hindu from Surma Valley and one European tea planter. Out of forty members in the Council in 1910 sixteen were Bengalis twentytwo Europeans and two Assamese. Thus the Muslims of Brahmaputra Valley were unrepresented at first. In 1910 out of five members from Assam one was a Muslim from the Brahmaputra Valley.

6. Executive Councils in Provinces

   Executive Councils were created in the Provinces under Governors and Lt. Governors, the former having four and the latter having two Executive Councillors.

7. Principles of Composition of the Councils

   The composition of the Councils was based on two principles. Firstly a " substantive" though not " overwhelming official majority" was ensured for the Central Legislative Council. Secondly in the provincial councils, official majority was not considered essential because the respective Heads of Government had been given the power to reject or withhold any measure adopted by their Councils. However, the non-official majority did not necessarily mean a majority of elected non-official members, the sole exception being Bengal.

8. Functioning of the Councils

   The Councillors were now allowed to ask questions followed by supplimentaries to the questions on matters of public interests. They could also move and adopt resolutions, which could, however, be overridden by the heads of Governments. In other words neither any adverse resolution nor any criticism had any effect on Government, as there was no responsibility to the people.

9. Voting Qualifications

In Bengal, Bombay and Madras, franchise was confined to membership of local bodies such as Municipalities and District Boards only. In the United Provinces, there were no such restrictions. Property qualification was prescribed along with the minimum age of twenty-three years.

Reaction to Separate Electorates

The moderates in the Congress, whose resolution was referred to, " had ceased to represent the politically conscious India". But even they were disillusioned before the year ended. In the Lahore Session of 27 Dec. 1909, under the presidentship of Pandit Modan Mohan Malaviya, it adopted the following resolution.

That this Congress while gratefully appreciating the earnest and arduous endeavours of lord Morley and Lord Minto in extending to the people of this Country a fairly liberal measure of Constitutional reforms as embodied in the Indian Councils Act of 1909, deems its duty to place on record its strong sense of disapproval of the creation of separate electorate on the basis of religion and regrets that the regulations formed under the Act have not been formed in the same liberal spirit in which Lord Morley's despatch of last year was conceived. In particular the regulations have caused wide-spread dissatisfaction throughout the country by reason of...

(a) "The excessive and unfairly preponderant share of representation given to the followers of one particular religion,

(b) "The unjust invidious and humiliating distinctions made between Muslim and Non-Muslim subjects of His Majesty in the matter of electorates, the franchise and the qualification of candidates,

(c) "The wide, arbitrary and unreasonable disqualification for the candidates seeking election to the councils,

(d) "The general distrust of the educated classes that runs through the whole course of the Regulations,

(e) "The unsatisfactory composition of the non-official majority in the provincial councils rendering them ineffective and unreal for all practical purposes."

(f) "And this Congress earnestly requests the Government so to revise the Regulation as soon as the present elections are over so as to resolve these objectionable features and bring them into harmony with the spirit of the Royal Message and the Secretary of State's despatch last year".[76]

The Hindus in general under the Congress flag resented most of the provisions for separate electorate. Muslims largely under the leadership of the Muslim League were naturally happy. Both in East Punjab and Eastern Bengal and Assam, the Hindus were a minority but no provisions of the Act safeguarded their interests. Contrary to this, in United Provinces, the Muslims accounted for sixteen per cent of the population but had non- official representation in the Council to the extent of thirtyone per cent. The constitutionalists were "sorely disappointed." Malavya devoted the major part of his presidential address to the evil features of the reforms. To him weightage given to the Muslims was the worst feature of the reforms along with the right to take part in the elections through mixed electorate. In Eastern Bengal and Assam also, said Malavya,

> *Hindu candidates for election have failed and Mahomedans have succeeded in obtaining almost every seat, this is protecting the interest of minorities with vengeance, nay, it is a case of exclusion of the majority by a minority. This advantage has, however, been Reserved only to the favoured minority of our Mahomedan fellow subjects.*[77]

Another complaint against those reforms was that while the Muslims could elect their representatives directly, the Hindus could do so only indirectly through Local Bodies. Let us see how the upper class Muslims had reacted.

Interestingly, the provision of separate electorate was criticised by a number of Muslim leaders like Muhammad Ali, Mazhar-ul-Haque and Muhammad Ali Jinnah. They urged upon the Muslim League to oppose its sectional demands " in the interest of national unity" for a year.[78] Hasan Imam, one of the elected members of the Provincial Committee of the Muslim League's First Session at Dacca in 1906, had said in the Lahore Session of the Congress in 1909,

> *I have always been against the representation of communities. I have always been against special electorates of any kind whatsoever. I feel that such of us as have asked for separate electorates or even for separate representation have missed the opportunities that had been presented to them for united action amongst us.*[79]

Dr H. Suhrawardi, a Barrister, observed,

> *The educated section of the Mussalman community was so much disappointed at the composition of the Mahomedan Electors which unfortunately eliminate and exclude educated Muslims from having any effective role in the election that they thought at first that it would be better to allow Khan Bahadurs, Khan Sahibs, Khansamas, Daftaries, Ostagars and Marriage Registrars to have their way and return their own representatives to the Council. Mahomedan Barristers, MA's ,MD's, MB's, PhD's, and other diploma holders of Indian and British Universities have been deprived of the franchise in these days of reforms and progress, while Mahomedan roll – a curious document of historical interest – confers the much coveted privilege indiscriminately on the illiterate. I happen to be the only Mahomedan Barrister whose name by a singular fluke appears on the Mahomedan Electoral Roll of Bengal.*[80]

In the Congress Session of 1910, Nawab Sadiq Ali of Lucknow delivered a "highly important" speech which is quoted in full.

He said,

> *It cannot be denied that, as our new Viceroy so justly observed in Bombay, the grant of special privileges to one community means disabilities to other communities and that in this respect in my humble opinion the Government of Lord Minto went on a wrong track in safeguarding the so called Mahomedan interest in a manner which has excited the just resentment of the Hindus and which, I am sure, is regretted even by a section of sensible*

and fair minded Mahomedans. Separate electorate for Mohamedans, seats in the Councils Reserved ... in excess of their numerical strength are no doubt great allurements for they bring immediate gain to a certain number of Mahomedan gentlemen but in reality they are calculated to do no good to the community at large, for they are sure to alienate the Hindu sympathisers from it, and therefore, as long as the two communities remain divided from each other by sectarian jealousies and animosities, the larger and wider interests of the whole Indian nation are bound to suffer.[81]

The following Congress Resolution (No XV)adopted at the Session indicated its reaction after the implementation of the reforms;

While recognising the necessity of providing for a fair and adequate representation in the Legislative Councils for the Mahomedans and other communities, where they are in a minority, this Congress disapproves the Regulations promulgated last year to carry out this object by means of separate electorates, and ... it urges upon the Government ... the justice and expediency of modifying the Regulations...before another election comes on, so as to remove anomalous distinctions between different sections of His Majesty's Subjects in the matter of franchise and ... the arbitrary disqualifications and restrictions for candidates seeking election to the Council. The Congress also urges the modification of the Regulations, where necessary, relating to the composition of non-official majority in the Provincial Councils, so as to render them effective for practical purposes.[82]

Thus neither the Hindus nor the Muslims were wholly satisfied and happy with the reforms. Despite all these discontents expressed, however, the Muslims generally accepted the policy of reservation and separate electorate. From the Hindu side, there were no signs of agitation. But the demands for election of a non-official majority of members, condemnation of separate electorate, removal of over- representation of Muslims and enfranchisement of people on the basis of academic qualifications continued.

It is interesting to note that as the Act became a fait accompli, some of the Congress stalwarts and prominent individuals appreciated the reforms. Annie Beasant was quoted by Lady Minto as saying, " it is a long time since God gave India so good a gift as Lord Minto. History will do justice some day to the strength which could face the unpopularity of bringing in repressive measures, while not withholding wise reforms."

On a frame containing Minto's picture Beasant had engraved, "He laid in India the foundation of Self-Government within the Empire ." Lord Sinha, the Law Member of the Executive Council was certain that it was owing to Minto's personality that the reforms had been so well received. Discussing the "impossibility of any Indian rule without British participation" he said, " if the English left India in a body, we should have to telegraph to Aden to get them to return. India would be in a state of chaos in a couple of days." Other leaders also had similar views.

Bhupendra Nath Basu who was allegedly leaning towards sedition, commented, " the Viceroy has the power of drawing out the best side of a man, he makes one feel affection for him because he speaks in a friendly spirit and not as if he were the Emperor of India". Rash Behari Ghosh " rhapsodized" British actions when he said,

Clouds are now breaking in blessings over our heads, slaking the perched and thirsty earth. English statesmanship which Lord Morley justly boasted, has never yet failed in

> *any part of the world, has risen to its fullest height in this critical time, and has seized the golden moment, for it knows the season when to take occasion by the head, not to suppress but to guide the new spirit which England has created in India.*

Though British conservatives like Arther Balfour, the leader of his party in the House of Commons, was opposed to the reforms, the radicals like Rutherford and Cotton welcomed the Act as an instalment, though a moderate one, of Self-Government.

Minto himself was very happy on the enactment itself. On 7 June 1909, he had written to Morley "I rejoice with you that the great bill is through. The ship has weathered the storm at home well under your command and we may justly feel pleased. At any rate as you say, "we have got what we wanted" and in India "we have got it with a general welcome too". Further

> ... *things are going very well just now, but the anarchical under-current exists and we can't afford to neglect it for a moment and these pin pricks (criticism of provisions on disqualification suggested with reference to deportees) at home do shake us.*[83]

Giving his experience of Indian reaction to the reforms, he wrote to Morley on 3 February 1910 that despite signs of outrages, there was "... an increasing Indian sympathy with the government." Indian public opinion was making itself felt and he was deeply impressed by the changing political conditions. Minto claimed to have

> *endeavoured to meet them by broadening the representation authorised by the Council Act of 1892, ...and facilitating opportunities of debate by inviting leaders of public opinion to become fellow with us...and by securing representation of those important interests and communities who go to form the real strength of India while at the same time recognising the claims of educational advance.*

He then claimed that the members of the greatly enlarged Council "thoroughly representative of Indian interests" had passed what might be called a "repressive measure", i.e., the new Press Act because they had believed that the measure was "essential for the welfare of this country." In doing so he claimed that "...they have furnished the proof... that increased representation of Indian interests and communities would not weaken, but would vastly strengthen the British administration ..." He congratulated the members for the thoughtful tone of their speeches.[84]

Government took a liberal measure in releasing some deportees. The Governor General said that the action was based upon the belief that the political situation had changed " entirely." He asserted that the political movement of which they were leaders – " seditious as it was" – had "degenerated into an anarchical plot" which could no longer be legitimately included as part of the political agitation. He then observed that "We believe that we are no longer confronted by a political movement such as they inaugurated but are face to face with an anarchical conspiracy waging war against British and Indian communities alike." He believed that "... it will be long before we can exterminate the evil unless these communities agree to work together hand in hand".

Further,

> ...*we must not be surprised if we have more outrages, but there are unmistakable signs that the population generally is getting thoroughly disgusted with the state of affairs and*

that the outrages themselves, if they occur, will be rather in the nature of thuggism than political crimes.[85]

On 15 February 1910, Minto asserted with Morley that " ...at any rate the evident wish to support the government is encouraging." On 7 March 1910, he again told the Secretary of State that he had heard "...On all sides that a better spirit is aboard and that every one feels happier." On 30 March Lady Minto wrote that she had attended the Legislative Council to listen to Minto's Budget Speech. She observed that all the Indian members concluded their speeches by thanking the Viceroy for the "inestimable boon" which the possibility of a debate had given to the enlarged Council. She claimed that "...The wall which of necessity had separated them has been broken down."

Concluding his speech Minto said,

> *...And now gentlemen, as this is the last time that I shall preside over a full Council, I would ask you to bear in mind that for sometime to come there must be much that is experimental in our reforms. It rests upon you to consolidate the work which has been done, to prove yourself worthy of the interests which you represent, to safeguard the moderation and good sense of the Council of which you are members. It is to you that the Executive Government will look for an expression both of official and non-official opinion. It is on your support that they should be able to rely.*

Finally, while leaving for Agra on a tour on 31 March 1910, Lady Minto wrote in her journal about the people's attitude that

> *... they have realised that a genuine movement has been made to give the Indians a share in the government of their country and I think they know that we take a genuine interest in their welfare.*[86]

Interestingly, even a year earlier, i.e., on 2 April 1909, during his visit to Lahore, he was accorded a rousing welcome. Lady Minto wrote,

> *One could almost touch the houses on either side, when every window and balcony was filled with people massed like border of brightly coloured flowers. Had there been any desire to attempt an outrage, nothing would have been easier, but the population were evidently anxious to show their loyalty. Hardly a house was without a welcoming token and many beautiful silken embroideries hung from the windows and mottoes were stretched across the streets. On one of these were written, Ripon, Minto, Morley, England's greatest three India sing their praises till eternity.*[87]

However, the reforms were not so rosy as can be seen from the Report on Indian Constitutional Reforms.

Official Critique of the Reforms

The Report on Indian Constitutional Reforms 1918, made by Englishmen themselves, gave a succinct critique of the Morley- Minto Reforms. Some of the views expressed therein may help us partly to understand the background to the next phase of reforms.[88]

To begin with, the Report observed that the Morley-Minto reforms were essentially of an evolutionary character. They were a natural extension of the previously existing system. "Excessive" claims were made in the enthusiasm of the moment, but in any case these could not justly be described as embodying any new policy. The change was one of degree and not of any kind. These were based on the fundamental principle that the executive government should retain the final decision on all questions although some degree of popular control over Legislation was established in the provinces by providing for small non-official majority. "There is no doubt that these constituted a real and important advance." At first the provisions were received well. The Congress welcomed them and Gokhale spoke of the "generous and fair nature" thereof. But very soon depreciatory criticism began to manifest itself and dissatisfaction steadily increased.

We have referred to the problem which Minto's Government set themselves to solve, for which they hoped to secure the support of the conservatives, the moderates and the aristocrats. The sanguine expectations were, however, short-lived.

> *The nine years of the Morley- Minto Reforms have spent their utility. They are no longer acceptable to Indian opinion.*

Why was it so? The report said,

> *...in the light of experience, official opinion also views them with a critical eye. We judge that this is due in various degrees to the political development brought about by the reforms themselves, to precipitation of democratic feeling caused by the war, to some inherent features of the scheme of reform itself.*

Both Morley and Minto as well as the British Government held the same view on representative government. It was that election only through limited franchise and of the educated upper stratum of the society was the ideal for associating Indians with the British rule. Anything beyond limited constituencies and indirect franchise was unthinkable in India. Nonetheless, they said that the features of the reforms

> *... do constitute a decided step forward on a road leading at no distant future to a stage at which the question of responsible government was bound to present itself.*

Regarding the electoral system the Report commented as follows:

> *No one can deny that as an embodiment of representative principle the present electoral system has great defects. The chief of these are the very restricted nature of the present franchise and except in the constituencies composed of members of some special class or community, the lack of any real connection between the primary voter and the member who sits in the councils.*

Regarding the representation by classes and interests claimed as the only practicable means of embodying the elective principle, Morley and Minto observed that for certain limited interests like Presidency Corporations, Universities, Chambers of Commerce or the planting community, it was an easy task to frame limited electorates. But difficulties arose when it was a question of providing for widespread interests or communities such as the land holding or professional classes or for important minorities, namely the Muslims in many provinces or the Sikhs in the Punjab. As regard separate Muslim electorate, they observed,

> *it is probable that the far reaching consequences of this decision and the difficulties which it would create at a later date were not fully foreseen...*

The residuary constituencies, which formed the only means of representation of the people at large, were constructed of Municipalities and District Boards voting in groups. The deficiencies and unrepresentative character of elections did not fail to attract their reaction.

The Central Legislature

With regard to the central legislature they commented that in the Indian Legislature 18 members were elected to speak on sectional interests and 9 others might be said to represent, however remotely, the views of the people as a whole. The largest constituency, which returned a member directly to the Council, did not exceed 650 persons and most of the constituencies were decidedly smaller. Further, the constituencies which returned the 9 representatives of the people at large were composed of the non-official members of the various provincial councils; and the average number of voters in these electoral bodies was only 22 while in one case the actual number was 9.

The Provincial Legislatures

In the provincial legislatures the members were categorised in a similar manner; those elected directly represented special interests and those elected indirectly by local bodies as electors or by electoral delegates. But in neither case did the constituencies exceed a few hundred persons. If the small class constituencies were ignored, the local bodies, which in a limited sense might be taken as standing for the people at large, enjoyed the best representation and returned 7.4 per cent members for every 1000 electors. Then came the landholders with 3.6 representatives for every 1000 voters followed by the Muslims with 1.3 members per 1000 electors. As regards election by the local bodies it was not only indirect but in cases where delegates were chosen, doubly indirect. In these cases members were themselves elected by constituencies which cast their votes "... purely with reference to personal or local considerations and without any thought of contributing to determine the composition of the legislative councils."

In such circumstances "we are bound to hold that in the one case the non-official members of the provincial councils and in other case the members of the municipal and local boards are for all practical purposes primary voters..." But "there was absolutely no connection between the supposed primary voter and the man who sits as his representative in the legislative council, and the vote of the supposed primary voters has no effect upon the proceedings." Consequently, "... there can be no responsibility upon and political education for the people who nominally exercise a vote. The work of calling into existence an electorate capable of learning the weight of responsible Government is still to come... and the difficulties are great and it is likely to be a work of time."

Thus according to the Report, the reforms of 1909 offered no answer and could offer no answer, to the Indian political problem. Narrow franchises and indirect elections failed to encourage a sense of responsibility to the people generally and made it impossible, except in special constituencies, for those who had votes to use them with perception and effect. Moreover the responsibility for administration remains undivided with the result that the Government found themselves far more exposed to questions and criticism than hitherto; questions and criticism were uninformed by a real sense of responsibility, such as came from the prospect of having to assume offices. The conception of a responsible executive, wholly or partially amenable to the elected councils was not admitted. "Powers remained with the government and the councils were left with no functions but criticism..."

The Report further commented that

> *...The Morley Minto Reforms in our view are the final outcome of the old conception which made the Government of India a benevolent despotism (tempered by a remote and only occasionally vigilant democracy) which might as it saw fit for purposes of enlightenment consult the wishes of its subjects. To recur to Sir Burtle Friere's figure, the Government is still a monarch in durbar, but his councilors are uneasy and not wholly content with personal rule ...*

What did India then have?

> *We have at present in India neither the best of the old system nor the best of the new. Responsibility is the savour of the responsible Government and that savour the present Councils lack.*

Therefore,

> *"our first objective must be to invest them with it. They must have real work to do, and they must have people to call them to account for their doing of it"*[88]

Criticism of the Reforms

The most pernicious provision of the Act was the introduction of separate electorate for Muslims which, among other factors, was a prelude to the Partition of India. The reformers expected to blend Indian autocracy and British constitutionalism for ensuring a predominant and absolute power for the rulers. The authorities anticipated that the autocratic element "in society and the moderate man for whom then there was no place in Indian politics, would range themselves on the side of the Government and oppose any attempt to democratise Indian institutions."

The reforms, therefore did not recognize the principle of responsibility or popular character of the legislatures. Though the underlying idea of the Act was to "really and effectively associate the people of India in the work not only of occasional legislation but of actual every day administration," the reality was far short of expectation. Further, there remained the over-centralisatioon of power in the hands of the Governor General, the Governors and the Lt. Governors. In other words, the absence of decentralization deprived the legislatures of much of their utility and delayed the development of self-governing institutions.

In an emerging national awakening and awareness, desire and demand for reforms formed an integral element of the activities of the political organizations of the day, namely the Indian National Congress and the All India Muslim League. The Morley-Minto reforms had for the first time officially recognized the principle of election, though not uniformly in all the provinces. Further, the preponderance of official and nominated members ensured the official majority in the legislatures. New classes of special interests created and recognized were naturally loyalists. Thus the Council remained a subservient and safe political platform for the Government. The moderate-extremist rift of the Indian National Congress had subsided but the "Revolutionaries continued to be as active as ever if not more virulent" after the Rules under the Act were published.[89]

It was in such an atmosphere of political discontent in India that the First World War broke out. Gandhi, Congress and other political parties made a sort of truce and allowed Government to concentrate their attention on war efforts. At the same time, however, the Congress continued the demand for further reforms and establishment of self-governing institutions.

All said and done, however, the constitutional significance of the Morley-Minto Reforms should not be overlooked. Firstly, the Act marked an important stage in the evolution of representative institution on modern lines. Secondly, though the declared intention of the reforms was not the creation of a parliamentary system of Government, "the Councils did possess the trappings of a parliamentary government without, however, its substance, responsibility".[90]

Inclusion of an Indian in the Viceroy's Council was a significant contribution to the Indianisation of administration through some amount of effective participation of efficient and able persons in the process. According to Lord Morley, the reforms were the "opening of a very important chapter in the history of relationship of Great Britain and India" and "turning of a fresh leaf in the history of British responsibility." Further, "the constitutional autocracy that it set up was bound to find its autocratic side challenged by its constitutionalism and an answer had to be found for that challenge. Autocracy was likely to be overboard."[91]

Lord Chelmsford, in his speech referred to above, said that this Act had completed the third phase of costitutional reforms.

Section IV
THE NEXT PHASE OF REFORMS - DYARCHY

On the outbreak of the First World War the British Government declared India a belligerent. The Indian National Congress led by Moderates such as Gokhale decided to co-operate with the Government in its efforts hoping for "... radical changes in the political situations, which would strengthen its demand for self-government". Even Bal Gangadhar Tilak leading the "extremist" Congressmen declared, "It is the duty of every Indian, be he great or small, rich or poor, to support and assist His Majesty's Government to the best of ability". But the revolutionaries continued their efforts to wrest freedom by armed revolt "... by the Indian army with the help of the powers in enmity with Britain"[92].

With reference to the general political situation we discuss two observations. One of these read, "Indian middle classes showed a general desire to co-operate with the British cause rather than hamper it and their aspirations were limited to what in Pal's words(Bipin Chandra Pal) was an equal co-partnership with Great Britain and her colonies in the present association called the British Empire." According to the other the Indian attitude was "one of bargaining for political reforms as a price for loyalty to the British Crown". But the Muslims in general resented Great Britain's unhelpful attitude to Turkey. However, their younger sections particularly those of the middle classes were "... positively with the mainstream of Indian nationalism.[93]

Interestingly, however, in 1916 the "extremist" and "moderate" Congressmen , Home Rule leaders and the All India Muslim League joined hands and unanimously entered into what came to be called the Lucknow Pact. Its main provisions were,

1. Special or Separate Electorate for Muslims in the Provincial Councils in the following percentage proportions: Bengal 40, Bihar 25, Bombay 33.33,Central Provinces 15, Madras 15, Punjab 15 and United Provinces 30. But there was no provision for such reservation in the Chief Commissioner's Province of Assam. The reasons for its exclusions were perhaps the absence of organised political parties like the Congress and the Muslim League, hence absence of party politics in its Council, the small number of Muslims in the plains of the Brahmaputra Valley which was 355340 as against 2190339 Hindus, constituting only about 6% of the total population of the plain districts as a whole.
2. The Central Legislature would consist of 150 members of whom 120 would be non-officials and one-third of the elected members would be Muslims.
3. Neither a bill nor any part thereof nor a non-official resolution affecting any community shall be proceeded with if threefourths of the members of the community concerned either in the provincial or the central council opposed those measures.
4. Defence, Foreign and Political Affairs such as, war, peace and frontiers would be outside the central legislature's jurisdiction.

The Lucknow Pact was the basis of a resolution adopted by the Congress which read,

> *it is of opinion that the time has come when His Majesty the King Emperor should be pleased to issue a proclamation announcing that it is the aim and intention of British Policy to confer self-government on India at an early date.*[94]

The Lucknow Pact, between the Congress and the Muslim League, by accepting separate electorate accorded categorical recognition to the distinctly different political interests of the Muslim community. This created a friendly atmosphere in the country for a short while. The Home Rule Movement under Anne Beasant and Bal Gangadhar Tilak consolidated the demand for self- rule. Public opinion and demands were crystalised by prominent Indians like Pandit Modan Mohan Malaviya, Muhammed Ali Jinnah, Tej Bahadur Sapru, Srinivas Shastri and Surendra Nath Banerjee in the Memorandum of Nineteen. It demanded, among other things, Indianisation of the Executive Council, widening of franchise, local self-government, provincial autonomy and abolition of the Secretary of State for India Council.

Morley and Minto are always criticised for beginning and perpetuating the Hindu-Muslim divide. But can the Indian National Congress and others shirk responsibility in this regard? The Montagu-Chelmsford Report frequently referred to the communal question. While the authors strongly deprecated the recognition of communal claim to separate representation, they were "constrained" to give effect to it because of the existence of the Pact "by which they felt themselves bound." Fifteen years later, Ramsay Macdonald only extended the League's victory by granting the same right to other communal interests. The Joint Parliamentary Select Committee while considering the proposed Government of India Act of 1935, also accepted the recommendation of the Franchise Committee in respect of the proportional representation of the Muslims based on the Pact.[95]

Lionel Curtis was the leader of Round Table Group, an association of English publicmen, which took interest in Indian problems. At his request, Sir William Duke, a former Governor of Bengal and member of the Secretary of State Council, prepared a memorandum embodying various recommendations including Dyarchy. The Duke Memorandum formed some of the basic principles of the next dose of reforms.

During the period from 1916 to 1920, which preceded the Khilafat and Non-Co-operation Movements, there was a growing political consciousness and demand for reforms. The Home Rule Movement, the Indigo Growers Movement leading to Gandhi's Champaran Satyagraha, the United States President Woodrow Wilson's advocacy of Self-Rule, establishment of the Gaddar Party by the Indian Revolutionaries in that country and the irrepressible vitality of their dedicated activities in India and the Russian Revolution played important roles in arousing Indian aspiration.

In course of the war, Indians were making immense sacrifices and contribution in terms of men, money and material. But the British Government was silent with respect to their actual goal in India. That gave rise to a sentiment that the people of this country had really little to do with or gain from the war. But continued Indian support to the British war efforts was essentially necessary and that certainly put pressure on the Government to make some promises to India. The British Government now adopted strategies for meeting the rising tempo of Indian political awakening and nationalism. The appointment of Edward Montagu as the Secretary of State for India created a sympathetic atmosphere for reforms and hastened a policy declaration. On 20 August 1917, Montagu made the following declaration in the House of Commons:

The policy of His Majesty's Government, with which the Government of India are in complete accord is that of the increasing association of Indians in every branch of the administration and the gradual development of self-governing institutions with a view to the progressive realisation of responsible government in India as an integral part of the British Empire...

In the Calcutta Session of 1917 the Indian National Congress adopted the following resolution as a compromise between the two views. It read,

This Congress expresses its grateful satisfaction over the pronouncement made by His Majesty's Secretary of State for India on behalf of the Imperial government and its object is the establishment of responsible Government in India.

This Congress strongly urges the necessity for immediate enactment of a Parliamentary Statute providing for the establishment of responsible government in India, the full measure to be attained within a time limit to be fixed in the statute itself at an early date.

This Congress is emphatically of opinion that the Congress-League Scheme of reforms ought to be immediately introduced as the first step in the process.

The speech was highly appreciated as the Magna Carta by the moderate Congressmen.

But to the radicals the promise of progressive realisation of responsible government was "unsatisfactory" both in language and substance. The declaration had put to the shelf the Congress demand for early self-government.

In the same speech mentioned above Montagu also said that the British government had decided to take " substantial steps" in the matter. As a pre-requisite to considering what those steps should be, there should be " a free and informal exchange of opinion between the authorities at home and in India." The first strategy in the promised direction was to send Montagu to India for a " personal study of the Indian Political situation." Accordingly he arrived at Delhi in Nov 1917. For six months he discussed the views of the Viceroy, the Government of India, the local governments and suggestions of other representative bodies in the country. Montagu and Chelmsford prepared a detailed Report which they signed at Shimla on 22 April 1918.It was approved by other members of the Montagu Commission, namely, Lord Donoughmore, Sir William Duke, Charles Roberts and Bhupendra Nath Bose on 3 May 1918. The Report laid down the following basic principles of the proposed reforms:

1. "There should be as far as possible, complete popular control in local bodies and the largest possible independence for them from outside control,
2. "The provinces are the domain in which the earlier steps towards progressive realisation of responsible Government should be taken. Some measures of responsibility should be given at once and our aim is to give complete responsibility as soon as conditions permit. This involves at once giving the provinces the largest measure of independence, legislative, administrative and financial, of the Government of India which is compatible with the due discharge by the latter of its own responsibilities.
3. "The Government of India must remain wholly responsible to Parliament, and, saving such responsibility, its authority in essential matters must remain indisputable pending experiences of effects of the changes now to be introduced in the provinces. In the meantime the Indian Legislative Council should be enlarged and made more representative and its opportunities of influencing Government increased.
4. "In proportion as the foregoing changes take effect, the control of Parliament and Secretary of State over the Government and Provincial Governments must be relaxed."The intention of the framers of the reforms was

...to provide a training school for politicians and to test the ability of Indians to profit by their training in the use of Parliamentary methods of Government rather than to confide the welfare of the people into their hands.

The Report was published on 8 July 1918. A summary of the Report on Indian Constitutional Reforms or Maontagu-Chelmsford Report is annexed to this Chapter. (Appendix A)

Reactions to the Report

It was received with a mixed reaction. The main reason was that the demand for self-government had not been conceded and its recommendations were saddled with various limitations. Some moderates like Surendra Nath Banerjee welcomed the scheme as a great political advance. But to Tilak and his group it was entirely unacceptable. Anne Beasant denounced the reforms as " unworthy of England to offer and unworthy of India to accept." The Congress Session held at Bombay in August 1918 condemned the proposals as "disappointing and unsatisfactory." It asserted that the people of India were fit for self- government and that " ...nothing less than self-government within the empire can satisfy the people." The reform proposals discussed in the Imperial Legislative Council on 6 September 1918 caused dissatisfaction. Kamini Kumar Chanda representing Assam demanded the appointment of a Committee for examining and modifying the scheme. He also asserted that "...nothing short of executive responsibility to the Legislative Council would satisfy the Indian public." However, the matter was not pursued any further.[96]

In its Delhi Session in December 1918 the Congress demand was reiterated. It also resolved that "so far as provinces are concerned full responsible government should be granted at once and that no part of British India should be excluded fron the benefit of the proposed constitutional reforms..." One group of the middle class leaders of the National Movement would accept the reforms but another favoured total rejection of the proposals. A third group thought of responsive co-operation. However any open division amongst Congressmen in the issue was yet to come.

Following the publication of the Report on the Constitutional Reforms, the British Government appointed the following Committees to complete the details, namely,

(i) Franchise Committee headed by Lord Southborough,
(ii) The Functions Committee under the presidentship of Richard Feetham and
(iii) The Committee on Home Administration under the Marquess of Crewe.

The Government of India Bill drafted on the basis of the reports of these Committees was referred to a Joint Parliamentary Select Committee after its second reading. It made a number of amendments to the recommendations of the Committees. The Government of India sent to England a despatch dated 5 March 1919 containing their views. On the basis of all these documents the final Bill was drafted and presented before the Parliament on 19 May 1919. The House of Commons and the House of Lords passed the Bill respectively on 5th and 18th December. It received the Royal Assent and became the Government of India Act of 23 December 1919 embodying the Mantagu- Chelmsford Reforms. The existing political situation which will be discussed further subsequently did not deter the authorities from imposing the reforms on India with effect from 3 January 1921.

Provisions of the Act — The Montagu -Chelmsford Reforms
The Government of India

1. The Governor General as before remained responsible to the Secretary of State for India and the British Parliament.
2. He was given an expanded Council to which some prominent Indians would be appointed.
3. **Bicameral Legislature**

(a) The Central Legislature was to consist of the Council of State or Upper House with a tenure of five years and a Legislative Assembly or Lower House with a tenure of three years . The Governor General could extend the life of the latter.

(b) Both Houses could have elected majority of members.

(c) The Constituencies were divided into General, Communal, Provincial and Special categories.

(d) The Governor General was to have the power of veto.

The Provincial Government

(a) The Governor remained supreme with the power of veto.

(b) The sizes of Legislatures were considerably increased and their tenure was three years.

(c) Till the reforms, British India had three Governor's Provinces, four Lt. Governor's Provinces and eight Chief Commissionerships. The Act converted five of the last administrative units into Governor's Provinces which now had a total of eight.

(d) The Council was empowered to make laws for the "peace and good" of the province. But the Governor had the authority and power to deny assent to a legislation, or reject or refer it back to the Council for reconsideration.

The System of Dyarchy

It was in the provincial sphere that the main constitutional changes were brought about. In all of these the Government consisted of two parts: the Governor with an Executive Council dealt with subjects categorised as "Reserved". With a Council of Ministers he administered subjects, quite a large number, prescribed as "Transferred". The Executive Councilors were nominated by the Governor while the Ministers were chosen by him from the elected members of the provincial legislature. Both the Executive Councilors and the Ministers held office at the pleasure of the Governor. He was not a member of the House but was given the right to address it. The Council was, to begin with, Presided over by his nominee; subsequently the incumbent was to be elected by the members of the Council. Appendix A to this Chapter has an illustrative list showing Provincial Subjects. The process of further devolution of subjects was contemplated.

The Franchise and Electorate

Communal electorate introduced by the Morley-Minto Reforms was retained. Franchise was more elaborately defined. Property, Income Tax, Land Revenue payment and academic qualifications determined franchise. Age limit was 21 years for eligibility.

Women were not having voting rights. But if a provincial legislature adopted a resolution in favour of granting them the right, their names would be included in the electoral rolls of that province.

The reforms, though failed to satisfy Indian aspirations, were no doubt an important step towards Indianisation of administration. Under Dyarchy, which might have been bad in principle, the provincial governments with jurisdiction over a large number of Subjects, got a lot of chances and power to work for the welfare of the people. Those powers might be regarded as milestones on the road to self-government despite many lacunae. According to some scholars the reforms "started a constitutional clock which would not stop".[97]

Government's Second Strategy

Simultaneously with the negotiations and debate on a set of reforms, the authorities adopted another strategy to deal with the emerging political situation. They appointed a Committee under Justice Sydney Rowlatt on 10 December 1917 which came to be known as the Rowlatt Committee or Sedition Committee. It was asked to recommend measures for suppressing the rising Indian consciousness, which to them was sedition. The Report gave a further twist to the Hindu-Muslim question. According to it very few Muslims were involved in any of the "conspiracies". The only Muslim movement for the forcible elimination of British Rule "was isolated, weakly supported and mainly due to the remarkable circumstances of the present time. In the mass Indian Muslims may justly claim the credit for the part they have played...."[98]

On the basis of the Report, two Bills were introduced in the Central Legislature. Opposing the Criminal Law (Emergency Power) Bill on 6 February 1919, Kamini Kumar Chanda of Assam said,

> *Now my Lord you are going to give us reforms and side by side with them, and in fact, even before them, you are going to give us this repressive law. Will that pave the ground for the reforms in this country? If this measure is passed, it is bound to create considerable agitation.*

Muhammad Ali Jinnah observed,

> *...it is my duty to tell you that if these measures are passed, you will create in the country from one end to another a discontent and agitation, the like of which you have not witnessed...*

The measures were strongly condemned in different parts of the country. Almost all the one hundred and eightyfive amendments to the Bills moved by the opposition were defeated, all the thirty five votes in favour were cast by Europeans and all the Indians numbering twentyfive voted against the said Bill. It was enacted as Anarchical and Revolutionary Crimes Act of 1919 and came into operation with effect from 26 March the same year. The other Bill was also passed.

The Rowlatt Report and the passage of these Bills turned Gandhi's initially favourable response " into a determined hostility to the Raj." He started an All India Satyagraha on 30March 1919 in order to prepare the country " for resistance to these lawless laws." He also gave a call for a general hartal on 6 April to be followed by Civil Disobedience. Thus, the "considerable" agitation forewarned by Chanda and Jinnah gathered momentum. Imposition of the Acts by the Government hastened ominous consequences which landed on the people. The thirteenth of April 1919 which witnessed the unprovoked Jallianwallabagh massacre was the blackest day in British Indian history. The incident and other repressive measures, instead of breaking the nerves of a subjugated nation raised the anti- imperial fury to a new pitch. "A strange sense of vengeance throbbed the blood" of Indians for whom "the paramount duty was to avenge at any cost the insults inflicted by those who were shorn of all human instincts and animated by nothing better then a naked brutal force."[99] The Congress led the people in a non-violent way to meet the situation under Gandhi's leadership though he became rebellious against the Raj.

Congress Reaction to the Reforms

The Indian National Congress dithered ιo decide clearly whether to accept or reject the reforms. The Amritsar Congress of December 1919 debated the issue and the strategy to be adopted. Differences arose amongst the Congressmen. One group favoured Council Entry and responsive co-operation under Tilak's leadership. Another group led by Deshabandhu Chitta Ranjan Das advocated Council Entry for breaking the government by persistent opposition from within. Others were opposed to it. The Differences were, however, put under the carpet when Gandhi carried the Congress with him and a compromise resolution was adopted in favour of giving the reforms a fair trial as and when these were implemented. But the Congress attitude changed as the publication of the Hunter Commission Report on Jallianwallabagh massacre recording the open appreciation of Dyer's action in England by raising a fund came as a shock.[100]

Muslim Reaction

The Muslims as a community were very much agitated over the British policy of harsh treatment meted out towards Turkey and the Caliphate depriving the country of some of its territories and the Sultan of his authority as the Khalifa, representing God. Following the Versailles Settlement and early in 1920 the Indian Muslims started the Khilafat Movement under the leadership of Ali brothers for recovering the Califate. They joined forces with Congress under Gandhi's leadership. The Central Khilafat Committee decided to launch non-co-operation against the Government, which was characterised by the programme of renunciation of and resignation from honorary posts, titles and membership of Councils, resignation from government service, police and military forces and refusal to pay taxes. The Movement was intensified after the Treaty of the Serves as a part of Versailles Settlement of 14 May 1920. The Central Khilafat Committee then gave a call for an All India hartal on 1 August 1920. There was a short-lived Hindu-Muslim unity though the two communities came closer for different reasons as explained by Gandhi. He said,

> *I claim that with us both the Khilafat is the central fact, with Maulana Mahammad Ali because it is his religion, with me because, in laying down my life for the Khilafat, I ensure the safety of the cow, that is my religion, from the Mussalman knife.*[101]

His active participation in the agitation gave it a new turn and made it a National Movement.

Towards Non-Cooperation of the Congress

The famous Congress resolution on Non-Co-operation was adopted at its Calcutta Session of 4-9 September 1920 by 1886 votes against 884 after a stormy debate and opposition from a section of its leaders. The Thirtyfifth Session of the party was held at Nagpur from 26 to 31 in December 1920 for ratification of the Calcutta resolution. C. Vijayaraghavachariar presided over the Session. Before that the opponents of the Calcutta resolution met secretly. C.R.Das brought 250 delegates from East Bengal and Assam at his own expense of Rupees thirtysix thousand to undo it. But the "spirit of Gandhiji" prevailed and Das's opposition fell through. He himself now "magnanimously" moved the resolution of the day and Lala Lajpat Rai seconded it. Thus Gandhi's opponents were simply overpowered. The Congress constitution was vitally amended at Nagpur. Earlier goal of self- government was replaced by the single clear aim of attainment of Swaraj not necessarily only by constitutional means. Further, Swaraj was now to be attained within the Empire if possible but outside it if necessary. While till then the Congress had favoured only constitutional means, the Nagpur Session permitted the use of all legitimate and peaceful means thus broadening the base of the National Movement.[102]

Side by side with the implementation of the Reforms, another important political development took place. The Non-Co-operation Movement was launched on 1 August 1921 under Gandhi's leadership and with his promise of Swaraj within a year's time. It was a Triple Boycott scheme similar to the Khilafat Movement. We will not enter into the details thereof, but note only that both the Non-Co-operation and Khilafat Movements which at one stage had become one, failed to achieve both the restoration of the Khilafat and the establishment of Swaraj. But the country witnessed a tremendous awakening and there was a persistent demand for further reforms. We separately discussed the development of Swarajya Party and its politics within the Congress itself. The Congress continuously criticised the reforms as inadequate, unsatisfactory and disappointing.

We have referred to the Chouri Chaura massacre and Gandhi's unilateral suspension of the Non-Co-operation Movement. However, due to the Swarajya Party's policy of " uniform, continuous and consistent opposition to the Government" and its determination to "wreck" the reforms " from within", the Governments both at the Centre and the provinces faced repeated defeats. These included rejection of Finance Bills and passing of resolutions demanding the establishment of responsible government in the country. On 7 February 1924, the Indian Legislative Council adopted a resolution demanding an early revision of the Montagu-Chelmsford Reforms.

The Muddiman Commission

As a result of the country-wide criticism the Government considered it politic to "offer a sop to pacify" the nationalists. On 4 June 1924 an announcement was made that the Government of India had decided to appoint a Reforms Enquiry Committee. It consisted of nine members as follows:

1. Sir Alexander Muddiman, Home Member, Government of India – Chairman ,
2. Sir Muhammad Shafi, Law Member,
3. Arthur Froam,
4. Morcrief Smith,
5. Sir Tez Bahadur Sapru,
6. Shivaswami Aiyer,
7. Muhammad Ali Jinnah,
8. R.P Paranjpye and
9. Maharaja of Darbhanga.

The Committee's terms of reference were,

1. to inquire into difficulties arising out from or defects inherent in the working of the Act of 1919 and rules there-under in regard to Central and Provincial Governments,
2. to investigate the possibility and desirability and of securing remedies for such difficulties or defects, consistent with the purposes of the Act,
3. (a) by action under the Act and the rules or

   (b) by such amendments of the Act as appeared necessary to rectify any administra tive imperfections.

The Indian National Congress was not satisfied and kept aloof from the inquiry. Following the AICC's directive of 6-7 March 1925, the Swarajists walked out of all Councils. As a result of their absence, a motion of Jinnah in the Central Legislature on 11 March 1925 criticising the Government for their policy vis-à-vis reforms was defeated.

Members of the Muddiman Committee were sharply divided. As a result its report published on 19 March 1925 consisted of majority and minority conclusions. The former consisted of Muddiman, Froam, Smith and the Maharaja of Darbhanga and the latter of the remaining Indian members. The division centred round the basic question whether the deficiencies and defects could be remedied with or without any radical revision of the reforms. The Chairman's group held that it was too early to undertake a revision and that the working of the reforms could be improved without any alteration of the Act. The minority group on the other hand was convinced that Dyarchy had failed and noted its total breakdown in Central Provinces and Bengal. They agreed with the Government of the former that the Act was "a complex confused system having no logical basis, rooted in compromise and defensible only as a transitional expedient". According to the group, Dyarchy had been given a fair trial and "no minor remedies short of a fundamental remodelling of the Act would provide any substantial result. They further opined that Dyarchy should be replaced by a unitary and responsible provincial Government.[103]

The Central Legislature on Muddiman Report

On 7 September 1925 Muddiman tabled a motion in the Council recommending acceptance of his resolution. Motilal Nehru moved an amendment demanding parliamentary recognition of India's right to responsible Government. He also proposed the convening of a Round Table Conference of Indian political parties to frame a Constitution which would be enacted. The amendment was adopted by 45 votes in favour and 14 against. The Government of India took no action. However, some rethinking in the matter seemed to be on the card even under the Conservative Government of Baldwin in England.

Simultaneously with the working of the Muddiman Committee, an important but not very well known development took place in the Swarajya Party. Its decision to contest the elections of 1923 had enthused the whole country "which seemed to have got over the political inertia brought about by the sudden suspension of the Non-Co-operation Movement". The party's performance, though differing in provinces, "practically routed" the moderates and liberals. Among the victims of defeat were personalities like Surendra Nath Banerjee, Sheshagiri Aiyer, Chintmoni Panigrhai and Hridoy Nath Kunjuru in Bengal, Madras, Bombay and United Provinces and Orissa respectively. The moderates "henceforth ceased to count as an effective factor in Indian Politics" and "forfeited the confidence of educated classes and had no influence upon the masses"[104]

The election results of 1923 brought about a change of attitude among the Swarajists. They had a solid block of 48 members in the Indian Legislative Assembly. Another 24 members constituted the Independent group led by Muhammad Ali Jinnah. The official block consisted of thirty nine members–25 officials and 14 non-officials. Thus a combination of the former two groups could easily defeat the Government. Therefore, "Ere long," there was a coalition generally known as the New Nationalist Party. Thus began coalition politics in the country's struggle for self-rule and freedom. The Swarajists no doubt retained a separate identify but had to "revise its declared policy of uniform, continuous and consistent" obstruction. It now drew up a new programme through which it would throw out Budgets, official resolutions and Bills and support measures necessary for "healthy growth of national life and the constructive programme of the Congress."

The new party adopted the following resolution:

If the Government does not make a satisfactory response to the resolution demanding reforms within a reasonable tine, the Party will be bound to a policy of obstruction and will put the policy into operation at the earliest period when the demands for grant are made by the Government, by refusing supplies provided the party decides by majority of three fourths at a meeting specially to be convened for the purpose ; that the response if any made by the Government is not satisfactory.[105]

The combine achieved notable successes on the floor of the Legislative Assembly but within less than two years the independents changed their mind. On some occasions, either they did not support the Swarajists or sided with the Government.

In January 1925, during the Fourth Session of the Assembly, the Independents adopted the following resolution:

In the event of the party desiring to resort to a policy of obstruction, ... no such decision shall be taken in the Nationalist Party unless the Swaraj and Independent Parties have separately met in the first instance and decided at their respective meetings to make it a party question. If either group does not desire to resort to a policy of obstruction... the Nationalist Party shall not make it a party question. In the event, either group will be free to act as it may determine.[106]

Thus " the definite end of the Coalition" made it impossible for the Swarajists to persue their policy of obstruction. This was "undoubtedly" the main cause of their decision to walk out of the Assembly as directed by the Annual Congress Session of Kanpur in December 1925. They also walked out of the provincial legislatures and remained out after 6 March 1926.

Inside the Swarajya Party

The differences on the question of Council Entry between Gandhi and the Deshabandhu-Motilal group continued. The AICC meeting held at Ahmedabad on 27 June 1924 provided the climax. Gandhi proposed to disqualify for the membership of any Congress Executive Body those who did not subscribe to the Non-Co-operation programme.

Motilal's amendment, saying that the resolution violated the party's Constitution was rejected by 82 votes against 68. Das and Nehru walked out of the meeting. The no-changers carried on with their campaign for the constructive programme. Both groups, however tried to avoid a clear split. Gandhi, Das and Nehru signed the Calcutta Pact on 6 November 1924. According to it the constructive programme of the Congress as well as the promotion of Hindu-Muslim unity would be carried out by the Swarajists as part of the Congress under their own rules and with funds raised and administered by them.

But "ere long" the political view of Das underwent a great change. At Ahmedabad he was opposed to Gandhi's condemnation of Gopinath Saha for murdering a European. He also moved an amendment to the former's resolution and appreciated and respected Saha's self sacrifice. The amendment was lost by 78 votes to 75. On 25 March 1925, he issued a "manifesto condemning unreservedly all acts of violence for political purposes". Secretary of State for India, Birkenhead appreciated Das and requested his co-operation with the Government. Das reciprocated the spirit in a statement issued on 3 April. On 2 May in his presidential address to the Bengal Provincial Conference held at Faridapur (now in Bangladesh), he "defended the ideal of Dominion Status as against independence". He offered co-operation on the following conditions.

> *In the first place, the Government should divest itself of its wide discretionary powers of constraint and follow up by proclaiming a general amnesty to all political prisoners. In the next place the Government should guarantee to us the fullest recognition of our right to the establishment of Swaraj within the Commonwealth in the near future and that in the meantime, till Swaraj comes, a sure and sufficient foundation of such Swaraj should be laid at once.*

Thus Das extended the hand of fellowship to the Government by sacrificing some of the cherished principles of his party. Further, his talk created great discontent among a section of his followers and it was openly talked about that it was the result of a secret negotiation between Das and the Government.The suspicion grew stronger when the Viceroy Lord Reading left for London and it was announced that after consulting him Burkenhead would make an important pronouncement about India. The sudden death of Das on 16 June 1925, however, set all speculations at rest. According to Subhas Chandra Bose "who testifies to the negotiations...",
the death of Das led the British Government to change its mind. The official pronouncement scheduled to be made on 7 July was "suppressed and a non-committal speech" was made in the House of Lords on that date".[107]

On 16 July the party's General Council adopted a resolution "wholly" endorsing the sentiments and the conditions of honourable co-operation with the Government expressed by Das at the Faridpur Conference. The Council regretted that the speech of the Secretary of State was "not only no response" to the late President, but "was calculated to make the chances of honourable co-operation difficult if not impossible". In a letter to Motilal on 19 July, Gandhi reacted by making the following observations:

> *I have come to the conclusion that I should absolve the Swarajya Party from all obligations of the Pact of last year. The result is that the Congress need no longer be predominantly a spinning association. I recognise that under the situation created by the speech, the*

authority and influence of the Swarajya Party need to be increased... This can be done if the Congress becomes a predominantly political body. Under the pact the Congress activity is restricted to the constructive programme mentioned therein. I recognise that the restriction should not continue under the altered circumstances that faces the country. I propose to ask the forthcoming meeting of the AICC to place the whole machinery of the Congress at your disposal.[108]

On the 22nd September 1925, the AICC meeting at Patna adopted the following resolution:

That the Congress now take up and carry out all such political work as may be necessary in the interest of the country and for this purpose do employ the whole machinery and funds of the Congress provided that the work in the legislatures shall be carried on by the Swarajya Party under the Constitution framed by the party and the rules made thereunder subject to such modifications made by the Congress as may be found necessary from time to time for the purpose of carrying out the said policy.

A separate permanent autonomous body was created for the development of hand spinning and Khaddar under a Council of its own and funds, the latter being separated from those available for political purpose. Thus, " the position of the Swarajya Party vis-à-vis the Congress was reversed; the party and its politics now became the concern of the Congress" and the constructive programme was relegated to a separate non-political organisation within the Congress. But very soon the Swarajya Party was split into two opposing groups. The programme of Responsive Co-operation advocated by Tilak inspired one group. But the "majority steadily persued" the old policy of obstruction. In the Annual Session of the Congress at Kanpur on 25 December 1925 Motilal suggested the following directive to the party:

If by the end of February 1926 the Government do not give any satisfactory reply to the demand for constitutional reforms set for them in resolution passed by the Assembly on 18 February 1924, the party will no longer continue the work in the present legislature.

So far as Assam was concerned, in absence of any Government response, the Swarajists in the Council did not attend it. Pandit Madan Mohan Malaviya moved the following amendment to Nehru's resolution.

That the work in the Legislatures shall be so carried on as to utilize them to the best possible advantage for early establishment of full responsible Government, co-operation being resorted to when it may be necessary to advance the national cause and obstruction when that may be necessary for the advancement of the same cause.

Jayakar, Kelkar and Moorje did not subscribe to the policy of the party. Therefore, though Jayakar seconded the amendment at the very outset he "dramatically" announced their resignation from the party. He said that the party must come out of the legislatures altogether or being in " take the last juice out of it by occupying every place of power, initiative and responsibility and would give no quarter to the bureaucracy". The Amendment was lost and Nehru's resolution was carried by a large majority.[109]

The responsivists among Swarajists held a meeting on 23 June 1926 at Calcutta for organising a party within the Congress to carry out their programme. By end of July, a very influential group in the U.P. Legislative Council left the party. On 24 August Lala Lajpat Rai tendered his resignation. At Malavya's initiative independent Congressmen and Responsivists met in a Conference on 11 September at Delhi and formed the Independent Congress Party. On 28 September 1926 a manifesto was issued with its programme based on responsive co-operation.[110]

Congress was further weakened by growing communalism. Some Muslim leaders made the propaganda that they would have nothing to do with the Hindu non-co-operators but would work out the 1919 Act. According to the Hindu Mahasabha, in case the Hindus did not co-operate but the Muslims did so, the former would suffer great disadvantage. The elections to the councils held in 1926 showed that the old Swarajya Party had been replaced by three distinct groups, namely, Swarajist Congress, Swarajist Responsivists and Communalists. It may be mentioned here that the Hindu-Muslim relations had seriously deteriorated between 1923 and 1927 during which no less than 112 communal riots had taken place covering " almost every province" on an increasing scale. About 450 people were killed and 5000 injured.[111]

The 41st Annual Session of the Indian National Congress was held at Pandu (Gauhati) from December 26 to 28, 1926 under the presidentship of S. Srinivasa Iyengar. Despite the divergences, all the groups of Congressmen, the Swarajists, No-changers and Responsivists attended the Session. By this time Gandhi had retired from active politics though only temporarily. Tarun Ram Phukan, Chairman Reception Committee, appealed to him to resume the leadership of the party. Referring to the Congress groups with differing perceptions, he said,

> *Let us hope that the magic influence of this land will enable the fighting groups to settle their differences and make the Hindus and Muhammedans united in love and brotherhood and follow the leadership of the Congress like innocent lambs tended by the gentle shepherd of Sabarmati.*
>
> Further, he advised,
>
> *Let Gauhati Congress decide whether India should be humiliated into co-operation in the hope of getting some favours or that she should stoutly refuse co-operation till her legitimate rights are conceded to.*

The Gauhati Congress refused to accept the Mantagu-Chelmsford Reforms. But abandoning the walk out policy adopted at Kanpur, it decided to follow the older policy namely,

I. refusal of ministership or other official positions,
II. opposition to formation of a Cabinet by other parties until a "satisfactory response was made by the Government to the national demand",
III. throwing out of Budgets, refusal of supplies and opposing repressive legislations.

But the party would move resolutions and support measures in favour of any interest of India and for the protection of the freedom of the person, speech, association and of the press and the consequent displacement of the bureaucracy. "By and large, the proceedings of the Session were dominated by the Swarajists. Tarun Ram Phukan, an Assamese Swarajist was elected a member of the Congress Working Committee. Phukan also became the President and Mohammad Tayyabulla the Secretary respectively of the Assam Pradesh Congress Committee. In the elections of November 1926, 14 Swarajists had been elected to the Legislative Council. Phukan was also reelected to the Central Legislative Assembly. Thus the Swarajists dominated the provincial politics.[112]

We have referred to the communal situation. The political picture was further elaborated and complicated by a resolution of the All India Muslim League adopted at its Delhi Conference of 1 January 1926. It read:

Whereas in view of India's vast extent and its ethnological, linguistic, administrative and geographical or territorial divisions, the only form of government suitable to Indian conditions is a federal system with complete autonomy and residuary powers vested in the constituent states, the Central Government having control only of such matters of common interests as may be specifically entrusted to it by the Constitution;

And whereas it is essential that no Bill, resolution, motion or amendment regarding inter-communal matters be moved, discussed or passed by any legislature, central and provincial, if a threefourth majority of either the Hindu or the Muslim community affected thereby in the legislature oppose the introduction, discussion or passing such Bill, resolution, motion or amendment ;

And whereas the right of Muslims to elect their representatives of the various Indian legislatures through separate electorates is now the law of the land and Muslims cannot be deprived of their right without their consent;

And whereas in the conditions existing at present in India and so long as those conditions exist, representation in various legislatures and other statutory self-governing bodies of Muslims through their own separate electorate is essential in order to bring into existence a really representative democratic Government;

And whereas as long as Musalmans are not satisfied that their rights and interests are adequately safeguarded in the Constitution, they will in no way consent to the establishment of joint electorates whether with or without conditions;

And whereas for the purposes aforesaid, it is essential that the Musalmans should have their due share in the Central and Provincial Cabinets;

And whereas it is essential that representation of the Musalmans in the various legislatures and other statutory self-governing bodies should be based on a plan whereby the Muslim majority in those provinces where Muslims constitute a majority of population shall in no way be affected and in the provinces in which Muslims constitute a minority, they shall have a representation in no case less than enjoyed by them under the existing law;

And whereas representative Muslim gatherings in all provinces in India have unanimously resolved that with a view to provide adequate safeguards for the protection of Muslim interests in India as a whole, Musalmans should have the right of 33 per cent representation in the Central Legislature and this Conference entirely endorses that demand;

And whereas on ethnological, linguistic, geographical and administrative grounds the province of Sindh has no affinity whatever with the rest of the Bombay Presidency and its unconditional constitution into a separate province, possessing its own separate legislative and administrative machinery on the same line as the other provinces of India is essential in the interests of its people, the Hindu minority in Sindh being given adequate and effective representation in proportion as may be given to Musalmans in provinces in which they constitute a minority of population;

And whereas the introduction of constitutional reforms in the N.W.F Province and Baluchistan along such lines as may be adopted in provinces of India is essential not only in the interests of these provinces but also of the constitutional advance of India as a whole, the Hindu minorities, in these provinces being given adequate and effective representation in excess of their proportion in population as is given to the Muslim community in provinces in which it constitutes a minority of population;

And whereas it is essential in the interests of Indian administration that provision should be made in the constitution giving Muslims their adequate share along with other Indians in all services of the State and in all statutory Self-Governing bodies having due regard to the requirements of efficiency;

And whereas, having regard to the political conditions obtaining in India, it is essential that the Indian Constitution should embody adequate safeguards for protection and promotion of Muslim education, language, religion, personal law and Muslim Charitable Institutions and for their due share in grants-in-aid;

And whereas it is essential that the Constitution should provide that no change in the Indian Constitution shall, after its inauguration be made by the Central Legislature except with the concurrence of all the States constituting the Indian Federation;

This Conference emphatically declares that no Constitution by whomsoever proposed or devised will be acceptable to Indian Musalmans unless it conforms with the principles embodied in this resolution.[113]

Section V
STRUGGLE FOR CONSTITUTIONAL REFORMS CONTINUES

The Montagu-Chelmsford Reforms or the new Constitution

survived the attempts of Non-Co-operation Movement to wreck it from within and without the Council Chamber. But it had to work in an atmosphere which destroyed even the slender chance which it possessed, on its own merit, of proving to be a real stage in the evolution of a responsible Government in India as it was represented to be. By a strange irony of fate it was almost a stillborn baby.

But whatever that might be, two features of the reforms cannot perhaps be overlooked. First, the expanded legislatures in provinces with majority of members elected, though on an extremely restricted franchise, had given ample opportunity to legislate on a large number of Transferred Subjects. Though the Governor's position remained unassailable, there were hardly any conflicts in Assam on this account. Even in free

India a Governor has the power to ask the legislature to review legislation. This gave the Council the power to legislate in people's interest. Second, the intention of the Act was "to provide a training school for politicians and to test the ability of Indians to profit by this training in the use of Parliamentary methods of Government rather than to confide the welfare of the people into their hands."[114] However, as the members belonged to the creams of society, the high standard of debates was characterized by facts and figures, dispassionate logic and reasoning . Unlike in free India of recent times where our legislators resort to hooliganism and physical violence, the earlier Houses witnessed sober, useful and constructive debates on matters of public interests.

The Montagu- Chelmsford Report had provided for the appointment of a Commission ten years after the first meeting of the new legislative councils to review the constitutional position both as regards the Government of India and the provinces. Commissioners would be appointed with the Parliament's approval. Similar Commissions would be constituted at intervals of not more than twelve years. There was a national unanimity among the leaders of different political parties for acceleration of the pace of political progress through a revision of the Mantagu-Chelmsford Reforms without waiting for ten years. But the Government steadily refused to concede the demand. Both in England and India the British authorities persistently emphasised the communal and other differences among Indians. However, the process of framing a new constitution " was initiated" under the Conservative Government of Baldwin as Prime Minister and Birkenhead as Secretary of State in 1927. Continued under the Labour Government of Ramsay Mac Donald, it came into operation during the national Government of Ramsay Mac Donald with the support of Baldwin and Samuel Hore.

Birkenhead was skeptical about reforms and believed that the Act of 1919 had " given too much". He wanted to prevent the appointment of the Statutory Commission and the conduct of inquiry by the Labour Party. He wanted " to keep India on the tentherhook of expectation hoping that the clamour for the reforms would subside". He confessed, "Mere antedating the setting up of the Commission means nothing. We can play with time as we want." Two changes in Government of Great Britain during eight years inevitably affected the course of deliberations in England. As early as 7 July 1925, Birkenhed had thrown a challenge to the Indian leaders saying,

> *Let them produce a constitution, which carries behind it a fair measure of general agreement among the great peoples of India. Such a contribution to our problems would nowhere be resented, it would on the contrary, be most carefully examined by the Government of India, by myself and I am sure, by the Commission, whenever that may be assembled.*

The Simon Commission

The British Cabinet, however, decided on 21 July to appoint a Royal Commission consisting of seven members of Parliament, four of them being Government supporters, one a Liberal and two from the Labour Party. On 8 November 1927, the Prime Minister sprang a surprise on the Indian public announcing the decision. Birkenhead, while proposing the Constitution of the Committee in the Parliament in November 1927, repeated his challenge to Indian leaders and said, "I have twice invited our critics in India to put forward their own suggestion for a constitution. That offer is still open."

According to the eminent Indian historian, R.C. Majumdar, the motive behind the Government's announcement was "apparent to everybody". The tenure of the House of Commons would be over in 1929. There was a growing probability that the Labour Party would come to power and would be more sympathetic to Indian demands. They would perhaps "go further in conceding reforms that would be compatible with the vested interests of Britain in India". The Government, therefore, "considered safer" to appoint the Commission forthwith and thus "forestall the Labour Government".[115] The Commission, they decided, would consist of white men only and without any Indian representatives. But they would be associated with the Commission as assesses in the examination of witnesses and deliberate with the Committee. This took the form of the Indian Central Committee and the Provincial Committees to Co-operate with the Commission. The Commission was constituted as follows:

1. Sir John Simon – a Liberal Party Member of House of Commons-Chairman.
2. Burnham, a traveller all over the British dominion.
3. Strathcona – a Member of the House of Lords.
4. G.R.Lane Fox – Lord Irwin's brother-in-law and Conservative M.P.of House of Commons.
5. Edward Codogen – former Secretary to Speaker- Conservative M.P.of House of Commons.
6. Clement Atlee and
7. Vernon Hartshorn – both Labour Party Members of House of Commons.

The Indian Central Committee consisted of

1. Sir Sankaran Nayar – Chairman
2. A.H. Fiom
3. Shivdev Singh Uberoi
4. Nawab Ali Khan
5. Zulifikar Ali Khan
6. Abdullah A.L.Momin Suhrawardy
7. Hari Singh Gour and
8. M.C. Raja.

H.H.F.M.Tyler, was appointed, Secretary to the Commission.

Following were the most important terms of reference of the Simon Commission:

1. to enquire into the system of Government, the growth of education and development of representative institutions in British India and matters concerned therewith,
2. to find out "as to whether and to what extent it is desirable to establish the principle of responsible Government and
3. to extend, modify or restrict the degree of responsible Government.

The Congress Reaction – Boycott

The Indian National Congress in its Madras Session of December 1927 adopted the following resolution:

Whereas the British Government have appointed the Statutory Commission in utter disregard of India's right of self determination; this Congress resolves that the self-respecting course for India to adopt is to boycott the Commission at every stage and in every form.

On 16 February 1928, Lala Lajpat Rai moved a resolution in the Legislative Assembly to the effect that as the scheme of the Commission was unacceptable to the House, it would have nothing to do with it at any stage and in any form. The resolution, supported by an overwhelming majority of elected members, was passed amid the cries of Bande Mataram.

The Nehru Constitution – Its failure

We have referred to Birkenhead's challenge. The Indian leaders now decided to act. Discussion on the main hindrance that was, the Hindu-Muslim question began in a friendly manner. The Madras Session of the Congress took up the matter. It adopted a resolution authorising the Working Committee to consult other political parties and representatives of various interests with the purpose of drafting a Constitution for India. The draft would then be presented before a Special Conference of the AICC, representatives of other organisations and elected members of the provincial and central legislatures. On full approval of the idea by all concerned, such a Conference was held in Delhi on 12 February 1928 with M.A. Ansari in the Chair. Differences now appeared among the Hindu Mahasabha, the Muslim League and the Sikh delegates. The Conference met again on 19 May and appointed a small Committee presided over by Motilal Nehru to consider and formulate the principles of a new Constitution.The members of the Committee were:

1. Sir Ali Imam,
2. Sir Tej Bahadur Sapru,
3. M.S. Aney,
4. Sardar Mangal Singh,
5. Shuaib Quraishi,
6. Subhas Chandra Bose, and
7. G.Pradhan.

The Committee's draft, completed on 10 August 1928 was discussed at the All Parties Conference at Lucknow from 28 to 31 August. It was attended by representatives of 17 parties. The proponents of complete independence had their way and got a resolution adopted nem. con. Another resolution adopted unanimously provided for Joint Electorate without reservation of seats for any community in Punjab provided that the franchise was based on adult suffrage and it was open to reconsideration after two years. Subject to this the Report was adopted with only one dissenting voice. The Nehru Constitution, as it was called, envisaged as follows:

1. A sovereign Bi-Cameral Parliament with a Senate and a House of Representatives with powers analogous to those of the Dominions like Canada, South Africa, Australia and Irish Free State,

2. Federal system with residuary powers vested in the Central Government,
3. Single Chamber Provincial Councils,
4. Mixed joint electorate for the whole of India for the House of Representatives and the provincial legislatures,
5. No reservation of seats in the House of Representatives except for Muslims in the provinces wherein they were in a minority and non- Muslims in North Western Frontier Provinces – such reservation would be in strict proportion of Muslim population in every province where they were in a minority and in proportion to the non-Muslim population in the North Western Frontier Province. The Muslims or non-Muslims, where reservation was allowed to them, shall have the right to contest additional seats,
6. Fundamental rights such as freedom of conscience, profession and practice of religion,
7. In provinces –

(a) no reservation of seats for any community in Bengal and Punjab.

(b) in other provinces – reservation for Muslim minorities on population basis with right to contest additional seats

(c) in N.W.F.P – similar reservation for non-Muslims with right to contest additional seats.

(d) reservation where allowed would be in force for a period of ten years.

The Lucknow Conference decided to place the new Constitution before a representative Convention at Calcutta and it was held on 22 December 1928.

The End of Nehru Constitution

But now, to the Muslim League and a section of the Khilafat Committee led by M.A Jinnah, the formula for communal representation provided in the proposed constitution was not acceptable. Jinnah moved a resolution incorporating the following provisions:

1. The Muslims should have one third representation on the Central legislatures.
2. Bengal and Punjab should have representation on the basis of population for ten years if adult franchise was not introduced.
3. Residuary powers should rest in the provinces and not in the Centre.

An "acrimonious debate" followed. Jinnah's amendments were lost and he walked out in protest. The following day the Sikhs also withdrew from it. On 1 January 1929, the Convention was "Adjourned sine die." Jinnah, Agha Khan and Mohhamad Shafi organised an All India Muslim All Parties meeting on the same date under Agha Khan's Chairmanship. The meeting adopted the amendments of Jinnah. Separate Muslim electorates were demanded both for legislatures and other self-governing bodies. The Conference also demanded the formation of separate province of Sindh and upgrading of the status of Baluchistan and North Western Frontier provinces to that of other provinces. Thus we see that there was hardly any meeting point between the Congress and the Muslim League. Birkenhead's challenge remained unmet and India's constitutional progress remained a dream. "Though Jinnah was defeated at the Convention, the failure of the Nehru Report was a great triumph for him, It also killed the Nationalist Muslim Party formed by Ansari and left the field open for communalists."[116]

Discussions following the publication of the constitution revealed the " all important fact that on the question of immediate granting of responsible Government, the whole of India stood united, the difference being only in respect of details and Hindu-Muslim reconciliation. The sentiment of India's goal of complete independence, which was envisaged in the Madras Congress of 1927, gained ground and Subhash Chandra Bose and Jawaharlal Nehru launched active propaganda for independence. As a result, in the Annual Congress Session of 1928 held at Calcutta, Gandhi moved the following "compromise" resolution which apparently tried to override the Muslim objection and give a sop to the advocates of complete independence. It read,

> *This Congress having considered the constitution recommended by all Parties Conference welcomes it as a good contribution towards the solution of India's communal problems and congratulates the Committee on the vital unanimity of its recommendations and whilst adhering to the resolution relating to Complete Independence..., approves of the Constitution... as a great step in political advance, specially as it represents the largest measure of agreement attained among the important parties in the country.*
>
> *Subject to the exigencies of the political situation, this Congress will adopt the constitution if it is accepted in its entirety by the British Parliament on or before 31st December 1929, but in the event of its non-acceptance by that date or its earlier rejection, the Congress will organise a campaign of non-violent non-co-operation by advising the country to refuse taxation and in such other manner as may be decided upon.*
>
> *Consistently with the above,nothing in this resolution shall interfere with the carrying on in the name of the Congress of the propaganda for complete independence.*

Bose and Nehru "vigorously opposed" Gandhi's proposal. Bose moved an amendment to the effect that the "Congress would be content with nothing short of independence. But it was lost by 1350 votes to 973 votes.[117]

The Muslims were divided into various groups:

1. Shafi Section – followed the traditional line of loyalty to Government and separate electorate for Muslims.
2. Muslim Conference under Agha Khan stood for separate electorate but desired advance towards self -government with sufficient safeguard for Muslim interests.
3. Nationalist Muslims who accepted the Congress ideals and methods. The prominent members were Abul Kalam Azad, M.A. Ansari, Tassadduqe Ahmed Khan Sherwani and Choudhury Khaliquzzaman.
4. The Jinnah group which accepted Dominion Status as India's political goal but laid down conditions in the form of his 14 points for co-operation with the Congress.
5. Jamiat-Ul-Ulema-E-Hind which first co-operated with the Muslim League but then for the rest of the freedom struggle worked with the Congress.

Jinnah had drafted the 14 points for the Muslim League Conference in March 1929 but his effort to get these adopted failed due to the division mentioned above. The Conference was adjourned. He now circulated the points which formed the basis of the future constitution acceptable to the Muslims. These further elaborated his proposed amendments to the Nehru constitution.

1. Federal Government at the Centre with subsidiary powers vested in the provinces.
2. Uniform measure of autonomy for all provinces.
3. Representation in all legislatures and elected bodies on the principle of adequate and effective representation of minorities in every province without reducing the majority into a minority or even equality.
4. No less than one third Muslim representation in Central Legislature.
5. Communal and separate electorate to continue, but it would be open to any group or community at any time to abandon its separate electorate in favour of joint electorate.
6. Any territorial redistribution shall not in any way affect the Muslim majority in Bengal, Punjab and the North Western Frontier Provinces.
7. Full religious liberty, that is, liberty of belief, worship, observance and propaganda. Association and education shall be guaranteed to all communities.
8. No Bill or resolution or any part thereof shall be passed in any legislature or any elected body if three fourths of the members of any community in a particular body opposed such a measure on the ground that it would be injurious to its interests.
9. Separation of Sindh from Bombay Presidency.
10. Reforms in NWFP and Baluchistan on the same footing as in other provinces.
11. Adequate share to the Muslims along with other Indians in all services of the State and Local Self-Government Bodies having due regard to the requirement of efficiency.
12. Adequate safeguards to the protection of Muslim culture and their education language, religion, personal laws and Muslim Charitable institutions and for their due share in the grants in-aid given by the State and the Local Self-Government Bodies.
13. One third Muslim Ministers in Central and Provincial Cabinets.
14. No change in the Constitution except with the concurrence of the States constituting the Indian Federation.The adjourned meeting of the Muslim League was summoned again at Delhi on 28 March 1929. Jinnah repudiated the Nehru Constitution and laid down the 14 points as the minimum demands of his community.

These were not acceptable to Congress. All these developments could not deter the work of the Simon Commission. It had visited India twice. The first visit lasted from 3 March to 31 March 1928 and the second from 28 October to 4 April 1928. In June 1929 the Labour Party came to power in England. Lord Irwin, the Viceroy, went to London to apprise the new Government with the political situation in India. On his return to Delhi on 31 October1929, he declared that he had been directed to state clearly that the natural issue of India's constitutional progress was the attainment of Dominion Status.[118]

Under pressure from the Conservatives, the British Government declared on 5 November 1929 that Dominion status would come about in the future and not immediately. Just as the Viceroy's announcement had roused a lot of enthusiasm among the nationalists, the second one frustrated them and caused serious discontent. However, for seeking a clarification in respect of the full-fledged Dominion status, Gandhi met Irwin on 29 December. Irwin was non-committal. The Congress ultimatum of 1928 mentioned earlier also went unheeded. Therefore, the Lahore Congress of 29-31 December 1929 unequivocally declared complete Independence as its goal and set the country astire. It also directed the Congress legislators and various Government Committees to resign their seats forthwith and to abstain from future elections. The second important decision was to observe 26 January 1930 as Independence Day. A new Working Committee met on 2 January 1930 and issued an Independence Pledge which read,

> We believe it is the inalienable right of the people...to have freedom and enjoy the fruits of the their toil...Purna Swaraj or Complete Independence.[119]

The pledge was solemnly taken in gatherings all over the country. The Civil Disobedience Movement as mentioned in Capter1, was launched by Gandhi through his Dandi March which lasted from 12 March to 6 April 1930.

The Simon Commission Report was published on 7 June 1930. Its chief recommendations were the following:

1. The new Constitution should as far as possible contain within itself provision for its own development.
2. Ultimate Constitution of India must be federal including not only British India but also the princely States.
3. Bicameral Central Legislatures – the Lower House to be called Federal Assembly should be enlarged and elected by provincial Councils. The Upper House, the Council of States, should remain much as it was.
4. The Governor General's Council should not include the Commander-in-Chief of the Army and he should not sit in the legislature.
5. The Governor General should select and appoint members of his Council. He should be the actual and active head of the Government and in some matters his powers should be enlarged. The Commission did not recommend responsibility at the Centre.
6. High Courts should be under the administrative control of the Central Government.
7. The functions and membership of the Council of the Secretary of State should be reduced.
8. Burma should be excluded from the Constitution.
9. Presence of British troops and British Officers in Indian regiments was essential for many years.
10. Full Autonomy to provinces including the Department of Law and Order but the Government should on the administrative side be given overriding powers in matters like internal security and safeguarding of all communities.
11. Retention of separate electorate.
12. The provincial councils should be enlarged.
13. Creation of provincial funds ensuring adequate resources without infringing their autonomy.

Simon also suggested the convening of a Round Table Conference of leaders after the publication of its Report. Thus, the Commission did not even recommend Dominion status. Further, it strengthened the Government with overriding powers. As such, the Report was universally condemned.

Following the Lahore Congress Session, Government adopted repressive measures, declared the Congress illegal and arrested the prominent leaders of the party. Similar action was taken against the Working Committee members, several other leaders, both of the party and its allies, by a Notification dated 23 December 1930. We have referred to the Civil Disobedience Movement. Undeterred by that, the British Government decided to hold a Round Table Conference in London, which was inaugurated by King George V on 12 November 1930. They did not invite the Congress to the Conference. Fifty Seven Indians were selected at random to attend the Conference. On 20 September the Government of India sent a dispatch to London as a preliminary to the discussions. It was in general in agreement with the Simon Commission's recommendation.

Gandhi-Irwin Pact

It may be noted here that for almost a year since the launching of the Civil Disobedience Movement, the Government and the Congress were not in any official contact or negotiation whatsoever. As the first Round Table Conference heralded no progress in arriving at any agreed solution of India's constitutional problem, two steps were taken by the Government in Delhi and London. On 17 January 1931 Irwin "prepared the ground for a rapprochement". On that day, in the Legislative Assembly he urged the Congress to steer a course of negotiation. On 19 January the Round Table Conference was adjourned sine die.. In his concluding speech the Prime Minister defined his Government's policy in the following statement:

> *The view of His Majesty's Government is that the responsibility for Government of India should be placed upon Legislatures, central and provincial, with such provisions as may be necessary to guarantee, during a period of transition, the observance of certain obligations and to meet other special circumstances, and also with such guarantees as are required by minorities to protect their political liberties and rights.*
>
> *His Majesty's Government has taken note that the deliberations of the Conference have proceeded on the basis accepted by all parties that the Central Government should be a Federation of all India embracing both the Indian States in a bicameral legislature.*
>
> *With a legislature constituted on a federal basis, His Majesty's Government will be prepared to recognise the principle of responsibility of the Executive to the Legislature.*
>
> *Under existing conditions the subjects of Defence and External Affairs will be Reserved to the Governor General and arrangements will be made to place in his hands the powers necessary for the administration of those Subjects. Moreover, as the Governor General must, as a last resort, be able in an emergency to maintain the tranquility of the State and must similarly be responsible for the observance of the constitutional rights of the minorities, he must be granted the necessary powers for these purposes.*
>
> *The Governors's Provinces will be constituted on a basis of full responsibility. Their Ministries will be taken from Legislature and will be jointly responsible to it. The range of provincial subjects will be defined so as to give them the greatest possible measure of Self-Government. The authority of the Federal Government will be limited to provisions required to secure its administration of Federal Subjects and so discharge its responsibility for Subjects defined in the Constitution as of all India concern.*
>
> *In such statutory safeguards as may be made for meeting the needs of the transitional period, it will be a primary concern of His Majesty's Government to see that the Reserved powers are so formed and expressed as not to prejudice the advance of India to full responsibility for her Government.*

It was the duty of the communities to come to an agreement among themselves. The Government will continue to render what good offices it can help to secure that end, as it is anxious not only that no delay should take place in putting the new Constitution into operation but that it should start with the goodwill and confidence of all communities concerned.

The policy declared "undoubtedly marked a considerable advance over the recommendations of the Simon Commission...everything depended upon the attitude of the Congress. The Congress alone could deliver the goods and thus determine whether new British Policy would bring peace in India and carry her constitutional progress one stage further". The party reacted sharply. On 21 January 1931 the Working Committee meeting at Allahabad adopted a detailed resolution on the subject. It refused to give any recognition to the Conference and regarded the statement of policy "... as too vague and general to justify any change" in the Congress policy. The country was, therefore advised to carry on with the Civil Disobedience Movement with "unabated vigour."[120]

On 22nd January the Working Committee received a telegram from Sapru and Sastri who had attended the RTC. They requested the party to defer a decision. Publication of the resolution was put off to 25 January. This was followed by the Governor General's statement lifting the ban on the party and releasing its members from prison. The purpose of this action was to give the Working Committee full opportunity to discuss the Prime Minister's Policy Statement.

Twentysix Non-Congress invitees to the Round Table Conference returned to India on 6 February and appealed to the Congress to reconsider its decision and requested Gandhi to meet the Governor General. He complied with the request and met Irwin on 17 February. Their discussion continued till 5 March 1931. The Congress Working Committee met that day, At 2-30 AM, Gandhi came back with a draft settlement to place before the expectant members of the Working Committee "who had kept a whole night vigil". He asked them for a unanimous support for a view either rejecting the whole settlement or part thereof. The first three paragraphs of the agreement are quoted and the rest are summarised below.

1. "Consequent on the conversation that have taken place between His Excellency the Viceroy and Mr. Gandhi, it has been arranged that the Civil Disobedience Movement be discontinued, and that with the approval of His Majesty's Government, certain actions be taken by the Government of India and Local governments.
2. "As regards constitutional questions the scope of future discussion is stated with the assent of His Majesty's Government to be with the object of considering further the scheme for the constitutional Government of India discussed at the Round Table Conference. Of the scheme there outlined, Federation is an essential part, so also are Indian responsibility and reservations or safeguards in the interests of India , for such matters, as for instance, defence, external affairs, the position of minorities, the financial credit in India and discharge of obligations.
3. "In pursuance of the statement made by the Prime Minister in his announcement of the 19th of January 1931, steps will be taken for the participation of the representatives of the Congress in the future discussions that are to take place on the scheme of constitutional reforms".

The agreement further postulated to

a. "Undo" the sufferings of individuals,
b. withdraw the Emergency Ordinances,
c. Release all Satyagrahis and withdraw pending cases against them,
d. remit the fines still due,
e. restore properties still with the Government,
f. adopt a liberal policy for reappointment of Government employees and village officials who applied for the same,
g. allow peaceful picketing for furtherance of consumption of Indian goods or against consumption of intoxicating liquor or drugs subject to the condition that boycott of British goods would not be a "political weapon".

The Pact was endorsed at the Annual Congress Session held at Karachi on 29 March 1931. Surprisingly, despite the fact that the pact clearly laid down the acceptance of British control over such matters as defence, external affairs and financial credit of India etc., "the Congress desires to make it clear that the Congress goal of Purna Swaraj remains intact". R.C. Majumdar criticised the Congress and Gandhi in the following words: "This all important clause (para 2) which practically gave away the whole Congress case was agreed to by Gandhi without the knowledge, not to speak of the previous approval of the members of the Working Committee in Delhi, although they were kept informed of the progress of negotiation from day to day". The Civil Disobedience Movement was suspended. The prisoners, except those charged with violence were released.

Nehru reportedly reacted adversely saying that

> *clause 2... with its reference to safeguards etc. gave me a tremendous shock. I was wholly unprepared for it. I said nothing and then we all retired...The question of our objective of Independence also remained. I saw in the clause 2 of the settlement that even this seems to be jeopardised. Was it for this that our people had behaved so gallantly for a year...? There appeared to me to be no middle way.*

Again, according to Majumdar

> *it will be clear to any unprejudiced mind, as it was to Nehru, that the Congress not only gave up the demand for Independence or Dominion Status, but definitely and substantially receded from the position they had taken up at the conference with the Viceroy on 23 December 1929 which led to the non-recognition of the first Round Table Conference and precipitated the Civil Disobedience Movement. The Congress also went back upon its resolution of 21 January 1931.*[121]

After the Pact

The Congress Session of 29 March 1931 was held under the shadows of execution of Bhagatsing, communal riots and increasing agitation of the Scheduled Castes for separate electoral rights. As regards the first, a compromise resolution was adopted. It read that the Congress "...while dissociating from and disapproving of political violence in any shape or form, places on record its admiration of the bravery and sacrifice..."

Lord Irwin's term of office came to an end and he was replaced by Lord Willingdon who took charge on 17 April 1931. Despite the Pact, the new Viceroy adopted a policy of confrontation. Gandhi warned that if repression continued, the Civil Disobedience which had been suspended would be resumed. To contend Gandhi's allegation of repression the Government maintained that the " Local governments have been scrupulous in carrying out the obligations imposed on them by the pact." They brought counter charges against Congress workers. After a prolonged correspondence Gandhi requested the Home Secretary to the Government of India to appoint Boards of Inquiry in different provinces, each with an officer and a Congress nominee to conduct an inquiry into the allegations on either side. The Secretary declined point blank Gandhi's request. Similar was the fate of his request for appointment of a permanent board of arbitration to decide the question of interpretation of the Agreement.

As regards the communal problem with particular reference to the Muslims, Sikhs and Hindu minorities in some provinces, the Congress devised a formula. On 20 July 1931 the Working Committee issued a long statement described in official history as its "magnum opus." In practical suppression of the Lahore Resolution, the Committee offered a Scheme of Communal Settlement. Some of its provisions are given below.

1. (a) The article in the Constitution relating to fundamental rights should include a guarantee to the communities concerned of their cultures, languages, scripts, education, profession and practice of religion and religious endowments.
   (b) Personal laws shall be protected by specific provisions to be embodied in the Constitution.
   (c) Protection of political and other rights of minority communities in the various provinces shall be the concern and within the jurisdiction of the Federal Government.
3. (a) Joint electorates shall form the basis of representation in the future Constitution of India.
   (b) For the Hindus in Sindh, the Muslims in Assam and the Sikhs in the Punjab and the North –West Frontier Provinces, and for the Hindus and Muslims in any province where they were less than 25 per cent of the population, seats shall be reserved in the federal and provincial legislatures on the basis of population with the right to contest additional seats.
7. Sind shall be constituted into a separate province provided that the people of Sind were prepared to bear the financial burden of the separated Province.
8. The future Constitution of the country shall be federal. The residuary powers shall vest in the federating units, unless, on further examination, it is found to be against the best interests of India.

   There was hardly any positive response from the Muslims or the Government, thus leaving the problem unsolved.[122] A new problem appeared on the scene and created a stalemate.

Section VI
THE SCHEDULED CASTE PROBLEM AND GANDHI-AMBEDKAR CONFLICT

We referred to separate electorate for Muslims in local bodies and legislatures and its further ratification and under the Lucknow Pact. The July formula just detailed protected the interests of Sikhs in Punjab and Hindu minority in some of the provinces. By that time however, the Hindu society dominated by Caste Hindus had virtually split. B .R. Ambedkar had become the undisputed leader and spokesman of the Scheduled Castes and made forceful demand for separate electorate for them. The issue had come to the forefront in the Ist Round Table Conference. But it failed to solve the problem. We will restrict our discussion of the matter during the period from the Gandhi-Irwin Pact to the Poona Pact i.e., 5 March 1931 to 25 September 1932.Their conflict centered round Ambedkar's demand for separate electorate as a minority for the Depressed classes as Muslims, Sikhs, Christians, Anglo-Indians and Europeans. On Gandhi's invitation the two leaders met on 14 August 1931. Ambedkar told the former that because of him the Congress had formally recognized the problem of the untouchables but " it failed to do anything for their uplift". Further,

> *Hindus have not shown a change of heart... we would believe neither the Congress nor the Hindus , we believe in self- help and self-respect...History tells us(that) the Mahatmas, like fleeting fantoms, raise dust, but raise no level-why should the Congressmen oppose our movement and dub me as a traitor?... Owing to the promptings of my conscience I have been striving to win human rights for my people without meaning or doing any harm to this country.*[123]

Gandhi wanted to dissuade him from demanding separate political rights for the Depressed Classes. He was strongly opposed to their political separation from the Hindus as it would be "absolutely suicidal". Ambedkar then "...left the hall, his face beaming with a fiery resolve to fight out the issue with all his might and to win human rights for his downtrodden people." The interview thus ended in a "grim atmosphere."[124] To oppose Gandhi was a daring act. Doing so was "to incur permanent displeasure" and "create undying bitterness". But "the die was cast. The spark of opposition was ignited" and the interview "sounded the beginning of a war" between the two stalwarts. Interestingly, Gandhi thought that "Ambedkar is not a Harijan". Till he went to London he thought "...he is some Brahmin who is taking deep interest in Harijans, and, therefore, talked intemperately". About the possibilities of Gandhi's help for the cause Ambedkar observed,

> *In a conference of one hundred and twenty-five members, we are two but rest assured that we will move heaven and earth for the sake of your welfare. I had a talk with Gandhiji this afternoon. At present he cannot do anything to promote your interests. We must stand on our own feet and fight as best as we can for our own right, so carry on your agitation and organise your forces. Power and prestige will come to you through struggle.*[125]

The Second Round Table Conference started on 7 September 1931. As a part of the Gandhi-Irwin Pact, the Government invited the Congress to participate in the deliberations. They also deputed 106 other "distinguished Indians." Gandhi attended the Conference as the sole representative of the party. He left India on 29 August and reached London on 12 September. The main task of the Conference was entrusted to two large committees on federal structure and Minorities. Gandhi was a member of both. He asserted the Congress demand for full responsible Governments at the centre and the provinces. He emphasized that the Congress was a national party and not merely a party organisation and represented also the Native States. He also "claimed that the Congress not only represented all India but also was its only proper representative since the non-Congress Indian delegates had not been chosen by the people but by the Government".

The Conference reached consensus on three following important aspects of reforms.

1. Completion of the structure of Federal Judiciary and Federal Legislature.
2. Distribution of financial resources between the central and provincial Governments and
3. The mode of accession of the Native States to the Federation.

But the most outstanding feature of the Conference was the unending debate on the communal problem. No agreement could be reached in the matter mainly due to lack of harmony among Indian delegates and an "obstinate reluctance of the conservatives to part with real power in India".

The other reasons were,

1. Differences over the Hindu-Muslim and Scheduled Caste questions centering round separate electorate.
2. Despite the Lahore Resolution, Gandhi was now willing to accept Dominion Status with federal responsibility. Ambedkar agreed with him but the Muslims were opposed to the proposition.[126]

In his first speech on 15 September 1931, Gandhi ruled out the Scheduled Castes' demand for separate electorate. He made the usual Congress claim of representing all Indian classes and interests including the Depressed Classes. He justified the claim by asserting that "... the removal of untouchability was a plank on the political agenda of the Congress." He never considered the Scheduled Castes separately from the Hindus dominated by the Brahmins and upper castes. This claim to Congress supremacy of spokesmanship of the non-Muslims of India continued right upto 1946. In this connection Jawaharlal Nehru's letter of 6 October 1946 addressed to Mohammad Ali Jinnah may be of interest. He wrote,

> *We are willing as a result of the elections (1946) to accept the Muslim League as the authoritative representative organisation of an overwhelming majority of the Muslims of India and as such in accordance with democratic principles they have today the unquestionable right to represent the Muslims of India, provided that for identical reasons the League recognises the Congress as the authoritative organisation representing all non- Muslims and such Muslims who have thrown their lot with the Congress.*

Gandhi also asserted that

> *the Congress has reconciled itself to special treatment of the Hindu-Muslim-Sikh tangle. There are historical reasons for it but the Congress will not extend that doctrine in any shape or form to the untouchables. I have not yet quite grasped what Dr Ambedkar has to say, but of course the Congress will share the onus with Dr. Ambedkar of representing the interests of the untouchables.*

Therefore, he declared that he would "most strongly resist" any further special representation.

In the meantime, some minorities except Sikhs and Depressed Classes had reached an agreement, the 'Minorities Pact' on representation "under the guidance and due approval of the British Government". Ambedkar desired an agreement with Gandhi

> *...whereby a certain number of seats should be reserved in the legislatures for the Depressed Classes on the basis of a common electorate for all sections of the Hindus.*

But Gandhi was opposed to such a compromise. Ambedkar joined the 'Minorities Pact' and was assured of both a number of seats and separate electorate. Subhas Chandra Bose observed later,

> *There is no doubt that if Gandhiji had made a settlement with Ambedkar, the terms would been much better than the terms of the Poona Pact in September 1932 after the historic fast of Mahatma.*

When Gandhi came to know about the Minorities Pact, he "devised a scheme to isolate the untouchables." His plan was to "buy out the Musalmans by accepting their demands, which Gandhiji was not in the beginning prepared to agree and which were rejected by the Congress, Hindu Mahasabha and even the Simon Commission", on the condition that the Muslims withdrew their support to the demand of the untouchables. The agreement was actually drafted on October 6, 1931 and it was named "Draft of Gandhi-Muslim Pact". Gandhi's negotiation with the Muslims and the Minority Committee was considered by Ambedkar to be a "mischievous move." So he said,

> *I would like to say one word before we adjourn. As regards your suggestions that while these negotiations are going on, members of the other minority communities should prepare their case, I would like to say that so far as depressed classes are concerned, we have already presented our case to the Minorities Sub Committee last time.*

Representatives of Muslims, Depressed Classes, Anglo-Indians, a section of Indian Christians and Europeans informed Gandhi of their agreement which they formally presented for consideration of the Committee. In his speech on 13 November 1931, while chairing the meeting, MacDonald "officially appreciated" that the Minorities Pact embodying these assurances was accepted by 115 million people. Gandhi claimed that Congress represented 85% of the whole population of India. He would accept MacDonald's arbitration provided it related to Muslims and Sikhs only. But "Gandhiji saw the snake in the grass and decided to set his foot down on it." He said,

> *Let this Committee and let the whole world know that today there is a body of Hindu reformers who are pledged to remove this blot of untouchability. We do not want to register on our census untouchable classified as a separate class. Sikhs may remain as such in perpetuity, so may Mohammadans, so may Europeans. Will untouchables remain untouchable in perpetuity? I would rather that Hinduism died than that untouchability lived.*

Therefore, with all his regard for Dr Ambedkar and for his desire to see untouchables uplifted he said,

... I must say that the great wrong under which he has laboured and perhaps the bitter experience that he has undergone have for the moment wrapped his judgment... it hurts me to have to say this, but I would be untrue to the cause of the untouchables which is as dear to me as life itself, if I do not say it. I will not bargain away their rights for the kingdom of the whole world ... it will create division in Hindustan ... I do not mind untouchables if they so desire being converted into Islam or Christianity. I cannot possibly tolerate if there are two divisions set forth in the villages. Those who speak of the political rights of the untouchables do not know their India ... and therefore I want to say with all the emphasis that I can command that if I was the only person to resist this thing I would resist it with my own life.

In his concluding speech he said,

I can understand the claims advanced by other minorities, but the claim advanced on behalf of the untouchables is the unkindest cut of all. It means the perpetual bar sinister. I would not sell the vital interests of the untouchables even for the sake of winning the freedom of India. I claim myself in my own person to represent the vast mass of untouchables and I claim that I would get, if there was a referendum of untouchables, their vote and I would top the list.[127]

Interestingly however, in the 9th Session of the Depressed Class Conference held at Gurgaon on 31 October 1931, Ambedkar had been given full support for his demand for separate electorate. President of the Conference, M.C. Rajah claimed that their people constituted 30 per cent of the Hindu population. Moreover, the Minority Report of the Muddiman Reforms Inquiry Committee, the Nehru Committee and the Simon Commission had agreed to separate constituencies and representation of the Depressed Classes. The claim of Gandhi was outright rejected by the leaders of that class. Their view was succinctly represented by the General Secretary, Depressed Class Institute who wrote in 'Janata' dated 9th January 1932, that the claim of Gandhi :

... that he represented the Depressed Classes and not Dr Ambedkar is an insult not only to Dr. Ambedkar but also to these millions of the so called untouchables in the country who looked upon Dr. Ambedkar as their foremost and trusted leader. Leadership cannot be imposed, it must be accepted by those on whose behalf it is claimed.[128]

In course of the Conference MacDonald realised that no agreed solution would come through the deliberations of the Minority Committee. He therefore suggested the adjournment of the Conference sine die. with effect from 11 December 1931. He asked the members to put to him a "signed" request to settle the communal question and "pledge themselves to accept his decision." Gandhi was a signatory to the request. However, Ambedkar did not sign the document as he felt that "the demand of the untouchables was so reasonable that no arbitration was necessary." Gandhi returned to India empty-handed on 28 December 1931. The Labour Government of Great Britain had given way to the Conservatives who now led a National Government. Macdonald continued as Prime Minister.

The new Government abandoned the policy of reconciliation with the Congress. Wedgewood Ben, the Secretary of State was replaced by Sir Samuel Hore. We have referred to Wilingdon's policy of confrontation which now continued with a renewed vigour. Gandhi told the Governor General that if repression of people continued the Civil Disobedience Movement would be resumed. This had no effect on the Government. The Congress Working Committee in a resolution on 1 January 1932 observed that any further co-operation with the Government was "utterly impossible unless the Government policy is radically changed." Further, "... In the event of satisfactory response not forth coming, the Working Committee calls upon the nation to resume Civil Disobedience including non-payment of taxes".[129]

The Government response was more reprehensible. During 2nd and 4th January they issued five Ordinances (and another five between February and July) for crushing the Movement. The "weapon having been fashioned", its operation began on 4 January 1932. All Congress organisations were put under a blanket ban. A large number of partymen was indiscriminately arrested and sentenced. They included Gandhi, Nehru, Rajendra Prasad, Rajagopalachariar, Ansari, Azad, Mufti Kifayat Ullah and many others. Thus began the second phase of the Civil Disobedience Movement. Gandhi was put in the Yervada Jail.

The Communal Award

We have referred to Macdonald's proposed mediation on the communal question. Ambedkar's determination to secure separate electorate for the Scheduled Castes continued unabated. While Civil Disobedience Movement was continuing in full force despite the unabated fury of Government repression, "Gandhi side-tracked the whole campaign by raising a side issue" i.e., the question of Depressed class representation. Even Nehru was annoyed at this. Gandhi anticipated that separate electorate for Depressed Classes was on the card. Therefore, on 11 March 1932, he wrote to the Secretary of State for India, Sir Samuel Hore, that in that case he would resort to fast unto death. Further, he asserted

> *I hold that separate electorate is harmful for them and for Hindus whatever it may be from purely point of view. So far as Hinduism is concerned, separate election would simply vivisect and vivisect and disrupt it.*[130]

Ambedkar decided to go to London again to represent his case to the British authorities. He addressed the All India Depressed Class Congress at Kamtee near Nagpur. In reply to the welcome address he said that he was "the most hated man in Hindu India." He was called a traitor and destroyer of Hinduism and the greatest enemy of the country. However he was confident the when that "dust settles down" and the proceedings of the Round Table Conference were dispassionately considered by historians, the Hindus would acclaim his services to the nation. Even if they did not, his great satisfaction would be that the Depressed Classes had implicit faith in his work and undivided devotion to his mission to die for their cause. Further, he would not budge an inch from his "righteous cause" for "the violent and disparaging criticism" of his detractors. The Session ended by declaring that it stood by Ambedkar and the Minorities Pact.[131] On 26 May 1932 Ambedkar left India and reached London on 7 June. He met British officials and Ministers and "passionately and with confidence for success" pleaded for separate representation for his people. He then submitted a detailed memorandum to the Cabinet. Before Ambedkar left London, Macdonald had formulated a scheme of communal settlement and signed it on 14 August. The leader reached India on 17th August and the very same day the Communal Award was pronounced.

The most important provisions of the Award are summarised below:

Para 1. It was clearly stated that the communal question would not stand on the way of constitutional reforms.

Para 9. "All members of the Depressed Classes so entitled under the ordinary electoral qualifications will vote in a general constituency. In addition since it is improbable that members of the Depressed Classes would under present conditions secure adequate representation in the legislature by this means alone; it is provided that some special seats shall also be assigned to them. These seats will be filled by election from special constituencies in which only members of Depressed Classes residing in these areas will be entitled to vote. Members of Depressed Classes will thus be allowed two votes, one in a general constituency and one in a special constituency while members outside them will vote in general constituency only. The separate Depressed Class Constituencies, however, are a temporary device, designed to safeguard the community until its present social and educational disabilities have been, to some extent, made good and His Majesty's Government intend that the new constitution shall provide for their compulsory abolition after 20 years if this has not been previously affected with the agreement of the parties concerned by the means afforded in the Award itself." The Award was based on the British theory that India was not a nation but a congeries of racial, religious and cultural groups, classes and interests. It accorded recognition to the following minorities and similar interests.

1. Muslims
2. Depressed Classes
3. Backward Classes
4. Indian Christians
5. Anglo Indians
6. Europeans
7. Sikhs
8. Commerce and Industry Classes
9. Landholders
10. Labour and
11. Universities.

Distribution of seats in the Legislatures was made in such a manner that no section of the people could by itself form a stable Government. As an example, we may give the composition of the Lower House of the Federal Legislature. It consisted of 250 members distributes as follows:

Hindus 105, Muslims 82, Depressed or Scheduled Classes 19, other groups and interests 44.

Muslims constituted almost 33 per cent of the total strength of the House. In his letter of 21 August 1932, Ambedkar wrote to Samuel Hore that he was not prepared for so unjust a treatment of the Depressed Class as was accorded to them. His main objection to the Award was that it was not applicable to Punjab and that para 9 limited the special constituencies to a period of twenty years. Demanding clarification of the position of the Depressed Classes after twenty years he asked,

> *Are they to have joint electorates and reserved seats after 20 years of separate electorates? ...We have never surrendered our right to special or separate constituencies...it is unthinkable that our need for special political protection as a safeguard against the evil of untouchability vanish in the next 20 years, a thing which had not happened within last two thousand years. I am therefore unable to see my way to make the Depressed Classes accept the Award.*

He also observed that while revision in the electoral arrangements for other communities would be made with their consent, the provision for the Depressed Class would be ended without their consent. He therefore demanded the same right with others. On September 9, 1932 Hore expressed regret on Ambedkar's insistence and observed, "our sympathies were all with the Depressed Classes. At the same time we realise the extreme danger of appearing to vary at all on the communal decision. We intend, however to give the Depressed Classes the fullest possible run that we can within the terms of the communal decision". Further, he assured that their case would " continue to receive advocacy not less effective than what has marked the discussion of the last two years". The Award " was ...the fairest decision the Government could have made, if it did not yield to Gandhiji's point of view, it had to remember that Ambedkar was the accredited leader of the untouchables" and that between Gandhi and Amebdkar there had been no rapprochement.

Gandhi was not prepared to concede. He had therefore suggested a scheme to Ambedkar. Under that Depressed class candidates might stand in general electorate as against other high caste Hindu candidates. If such a candidate was defeated and obtained a verdict that such defeat was due to his belonging to the Depressed class, Gandhi would advise the winner to resign. Then the defeated candidate or another of his class would again contest the election and the process would go on. Ambedkar had rejected the scheme and said that he could not leave so important a question as the protection of his people to convention and understanding. The "Mahatma is not an immortal person nor Congress, assuming that it is not a malevolent force and is not to have an abiding existence." Further,

> *There have been many Mahatmas in India whose sole object was to remove untouchability and to elevate and absorb the Depressed class but every one of them has failed on his mission. Mahatmas have come and Mahatmas have gone. But the untouchables have remained untouchables.*

Ambedkar also felt that Gandhi was not prepared to concede anything to the Depressed Classes by way of securing their representation in the legislature, that was the stand taken by him in the Second Round Table Conference.[132]

Gandhi's Fast unto Death – the Poona Pact

We have referred to Gandhi's threat of fast unto death. Immediately after Macdonald's pronouncement he decided to act. On 18 August 1932, he wrote to the Prime Minister from the Yervada Jail informing of his decision to launch his programme of fast with effect from 12 noon of 20 September. He said,

> *... the fast shall continue till the British Government on its own or under pressure of public opinion revise their decision and withdraw the scheme of communal electorates for the Depressed Classes.*

MacDonald's reply dated 8 September asserted that " Under the scheme the Depressed Classes remain part of Hindu community... and that the British Government has no intention of severing Depressed Classes from Hindu Community" But Gandhi started his fast as announced.

Ambedkar knew the significance and magnitude of the crisis generated by Gandhi's decision to fast. It put him to an unenviable position. People from all corners of the country now appealed to him to reconsider the issue. In a statement to the Press, he said,

> *So far as I am concerned I am willing to consider anything but I am not willing to allow the rights of the Depressed Classes to be curtailed in any way.*

In another statement he observed,

> *It passes my comprehension why Mr. Gandhi should stake his life on the issue arising out of communal question which he, at the Round Table Conference said, was one of comparatively small importance and was only an appendix to the book of India's constitution and not its main chapter. It is also a painful surprise that Mr. Gandhi should single out special representation of Depressed Classes in the Communal Award as an excuse for his self-immolation.*

According to the Viceroy,

> *The essence of Mr. Gandhi's plan clearly is by a sedulous fostering of popular compassion for him in suffering to overwhelm a group of people who have not been able to accept his views regarding a matter which primarily affect them.*[133]

Ambedkar added that Gandhi knew what would have happened to his life if he had resorted to a fast unto death against separate electorates of Muslims and others or if he had gone on a fast unto death against the British Government for immediate independence. Gandhiji had never threatened a fast unto death against untouchability. He called the fast a political stunt. The Scheduled Caste leader considered the Award as a launching pad for the development of his community.[134] However, Ambedkar, who had been, at the beginning the subject of criticism as a " "monster, traitor and hireling", now became the saviour of Gandhi. Louis Fisher wrote that

> *If any body could have contemplated with equanimity the death of Gandhi, Ambedkar was the man... He must have derived sweet pleasure watching them (Hindus) courting him in order to save their Mahatma.*[135]

Ambedkar felt that "all eyes turned to me as the man of the moment or rather as the villain of the peace". He however, asserted, " I will never be moved by these methods. My decision stands, if Mr. Gandhi wants to fight with his life for the interest of the

Hindu community, the Depressed Class will also be forced with their lives to safeguard their interests." He even rejected the appeal of M.C. Raja, another representative of the community to accept joint electorate with reservation of seats.

A Hindu leaders' Conference was held on 19 September 1932 at Bombay. Modan Mohan Malavya presided over it. Ambedkar, an invitee, was called upon to speak first. He said that it was very proper that everybody should try to save the precious life of Gandhi. But for saving his life, he could not be a party to any proposal that was against the interests of his people. Chimanlal Sitalbad said that Gandhi had no personal objection to reservation of seats for Depressed Classes. Ambedkar observed that he was on the horns of a dilemma and said,

> *I tell you I shall not be deterred from my pious duty and betray the just and legitimate cause of my people even if you hang me on the nearest lamp post in the street. You better appeal to Mr. Gandhi to postpone his fast for a week and then seek for the solution of the problem.*

Gandhi reaffirmed his determination to eradicate untouchability saying,

> *I want, therefore, a living pact whose life giving effect should be felt not in the distant tomorrow but today and therefore, the pact should be sealed by an all India demonstration of the touchables and untouchables meeting together not by way of a theatrical show, but in real brotherly embrace.*[136]

Tez Bahadur Sapru gave a scheme under which primary and secondary elections would be held for a limited number of seats. He also said that the system while maintaining the principle of joint electorates would enable the Depressed Classes to choose their own candidates. Ambedkar and Dr. P.G. Solanki welcomed the proposal but demanded a much larger share of seats than the Award had promised. Gandhi objected to Sapru's plan as he thought that it would again divide the untouchables into two parts, one panel group and the other which would come by direct election. He suggested panel system for all seats.

Ambedkar and Solanki met Gandhi on 22 September. The former told Gandhi, "I have made my concession by accepting joint electorates. Your offer to accept primary elections for all seats is very kind." On 23 September in a Conference of about 25 leaders at Malaviya's place, Gandhi's suggestion for extension of Panel System for all seats was unanimously accepted and the number of candidates to constitute the panel was fixed at four. Next the problem of distribution of seats was solved. Ambedkar had demanded the Panel System for ten years, extendable by five years at the end of which a referendum of Depressed Classes would deal with the questions, namely, merger of electorates, retention of Panel System and the demand for separate electorate. Gandhi wanted referendum after 5 years but Ambedkar insisted on ten years. Ultimately the leaders agreed to leave the matter of time limit to be decided by mutual agreement in future. Gopalachariar communicated this to Gandhi who found the agreement "excellent". Gopalachariar and Ambedkar exchanged their pens and signed the agreement along with Malaviya and M.C. Raja. This came to be known as the Poona Pact.

On 25 September, the Conference chaired by Malavya " ratified the agreement arrived at Poona". Mathuradas Vasanji had moved the resolution which was supported by Sapru and Ambedkar. He observed that had Gandhi taken the same attitude at the Second Round Table Conference, it would not be necessary for him to go through the ordeal. The Conference also adopted a resolution drafted by Gandhi regarding removal of untouchability. The agreement was endorsed by other political parties.

Gandhi would not break his fast unless the agreement was accepted by the British Cabinet "unconditionally in toto". Urgent telegrams were sent to British Prime Minister urging immediate action. After prolonged deliberation extending to mid-night, the Cabinet agreed to substitute their earlier decision by the Provision of the Pact. Simultaneous statements to that effect were issued both in England and India on the morning of September 26. The British Government in its statement also expressed satisfaction over the agreement. It said that the scheme agreed upon by the Hindus and the Depressed Classes would be recommended to the Parliament for adoption of the clauses of the agreement in place of the provisions of clause 9 of the Award. Gandhi broke his fast at 5-15 the same evening thus bringing an end to the Hindu-Scheduled Caste tangle. The provisions of Poona Pact were incorporated in the Govt of India Act of 1935.

Text of the Poona Pact is summarised below :

1. There shall be seats Reserved for the Depressed Classes out of general electorate seats in the Provincial Legislatures as follows:

Madras 30, Bombay with Sind 15; Punjab 8; Bihar and Orrisa 18; Central Provinces 20; Assam 7; Bengal 30; United Provinces 20; total 148.

These figures were based on the total strength of the Provincial Councils, announced in the Prime Minister's decision.

Election to these seats shall be by joint electorates subject, however, to the following procedure :

2. All the members of the Depressed Classes, registered in the general electoral roll in a constituency, will form an electoral college, which will elect a panel of four candidates belonging to the Depressed Classes for each of such Reserved seat, by the method of single vote; the four persons getting the highest number of votes in such primary election shall be candidates for election by the general electorate.

3. Representation of the Depressed Classes in the Central Legislature shall likewise be on the principle of joint electorates and Reserved seats by the method of primary election in the manner provided for in Clause 2 above, for their representation in the Provincial Legislatures.

4. In the Central Legislature, eighteen per cent of the seats allotted to the general electorate for British India in the said Legislature shall be Reserved for the Depressed Classes.

5. The term of primary election to a panel of candidates for election of the Central and Provincial Legislatures, as herein-before mentioned, shall come to an end after the first ten years, unless terminated sooner by mutual agreement under the provision of Clause 6 below.

6. The system of representation of the Depressed Classes by Reserved seats for

Clauses 1 and 4 shall continue until determined by mutual agreement between the communities concerned in the statement.

7. Franchise for the Central and Provincial Legislatures for the Depresses Classes shall be as indicated in the Lothian Committee Report.

8. There shall be no disabilities attaching to anyone on the ground of his being a member of the Depressed Classes in regard to any elections to local bodies or appointment to the Public Services. Every endeavour shall be made to secure fair representation of the Depressed Classes in these respects, subject to such educational qualifications as may be laid down for appointment to the Public Services.

9. In every province, out of the educational grant, an adequate sum shall be earmarked for providing educational facilities to the members of the Depressed Classes.

After the Poona Pact, "expectedly the orthodox Hindus opposed the Reform, surprisingly Ambedkar too started a propaganda against the Poona Pact." Gandhi was "so much perplexed by these developments". He suddenly made up his mind to go on another fast for 21 days and began it on 8 May 1933 in the Yervada Jail. On the same night Government released him from jail and shifted him to Poona. He wanted to create an atmosphere in the country for advancing the Harijan cause. He advised the Acting Congress President to suspend the Civil Disobedience Movement and asked the Government to release the Congress workers from jails. The Viceroy, Willingdon declined to do so unless the Movement was temporarily suspended. The Congress did so.[137] The party officially terminated the Movement on 24 May 1934.

Section VII

LAST PRE-INDEPENDENCE REFORMS – GOVERNMENT OF INDIA ACT 1935

We have referred to the Second Round Table Conference, the failure of which led to the resumption of the Civil Disobedience Movement. Undeterred by this development the British Government continued its efforts to formulate another set of Constitutional Reforms. The Third Round Table Conference was convened on 17 November 1932. Fortysix delegates were chosen by the Government. The Congress was not represented. The main business of the Conference was the consideration of the reports of Luthian Committee, Percy Committee and Davidson Committee set up earlier dealing respectively with franchise, finance and States. After prolonged discussions and on 15 March 1933, the Government published a White Paper. It contained the general features on the basis of which the forthcoming constitution was to be formulated. The document was more or less based on the Simon Commission recommendations except with regard to a deferred scheme of Federal Central Government subject to participation of a certain number of Native States.

The most noticeable feature of deliberations of the Session was a substantial change in the attitude of the rulers of Indian States who seemed to have lost enthusiasm over federation. Further, there was less enthusiasm or optimism among Indian members as regards a satisfactory settlement than was the case a year before. There was unmistakable sign that the attitude of the New British Government dominated by the Conservatives was far less sympathetic than before. The Conference ended on 24 December 1932 without any final agreement. But the authorities carried on with their plan. On 27 March,1933 a Joint Select Committee of Parliament chaired by Lord Linlithgo consisting of 16 members each of both Houses was appointed to consider the reforms outlined in the White Paper. The Indian delegation consisted of 28 members of whom 21 hailed from British India and 7 from the Native States. They took part in the deliberations and examined witnesses. The exercise lasted for 18 months. The final report was submitted to Parliament in October 1933 and published on 22 November 1934. It recommended, amongst other things, indirect election to the Federal Upper Chamber of the Indian Legislature, extension of separate electorate and empowered the Parliament to abolish bicameral legislatures.

The Government of India Act 1935

The net outcome of deliberation of the three Round Table Conferences, the White Paper and the Report of the Joint Select Committee was a Bill introduced in the Parliament on 19 December 1934. After some amendments, the Bill was passed in the House of Commons in June 1935. With Royal Assent received on 2 August it became the Government of India Act of 1935, the last British effort to keep India under bondage. It came into operation with effect from 1April 1937. The Act was a very lengthy document containing 321 Sections and 10 Schedules. Its main provisions are summarised below. Some other details can be seen in the AppendixB to this Chapter.

SUMMARY OF PROVISIONS

The Home Government

The Council of Secretary of State for India was abolished. Instead he had now advisors whom he could ignore. He still controlled the Governor General and remained responsible to the Parliament. The Home Government alone could bring about any amendment to the Constitution. "The Indian Legislatures were given the power to express by resolutions to His Majesty's Government their intention of a constitutional change…"

The Government of India -Diarchy at the Centre

All subjects of administration were divided into three lists namely Federal or Central, Provincial and Concurrent. The Federal Subjects such as Defence, External Affairs, Ecclesiastical affairs and Tribal Affairs were administered by the Governor General with the help of three Executive Councilors appointed by himself. Other Central Subjects were administered by him with the help of a Council of Ministers responsible to the bicameral legislature.

The Governor General

The Governor General was the pivot of the new constitution. "It was he who gave unity and direction to its various diverse and often conflicting elements… he was expected to keep the ship of the state on an even keel and to protect the British vested interests."[59] Though ordinarily he acted on his Council's advice, he could ignore them when performing his special responsibilities which included the preservation of peace and tranquility in the country, safeguarding the interests of minorities and the financial stability of the empire in India. Further, he could act in his discretion in the matters of defence, external affairs, tribal areas, appointment of Council of Ministers, issuance of Ordinances and Federal Budget etc. Above all he could suspend the Constitution. He had the authority to summon, address and prorogue the Federal Legislatures.

Bicameral Central Legislature

It consisted of two Houses, namely Federal or Legislative Assembly and Council of State. The former having a tenure of five years was elected directly on restricted franchise on territorial and communal basis. The latter was elected indirectly by the members of provincial legislatures and was a permanent body, one third of its members retiring every three years. Members from the Indian Native States were nominated by the rulers. Legislation by these bodies was restricted to Central and Concurrent Lists of Subjects. The Act established a Federal Court with both original and appellate jurisdiction over the whole of India subject to the control of the Privy Council sitting in London.

Allocation of seats to the British territories is shown in Appendix B to this Chapter. Details of the Bicameral Legislature of Assam and its representation in the Central Legislatures are furnished in Chapter 4.

The Provinces : Provincial Autonomy

The most significant provision of the Act was the institution of Provincial Autonomy though it was not intended to establish a full-fledged responsible Government in view of the Governor's extra ordinary power under section 93 of the Act. This Section empowered him to suspend the provincial part of the Constitution and take over its administration, the Ministers holding office during the Governor's pleasure only. However, abolition of Dyarchy was a great step forward in constitutional development in the country.

The Provincial Legislatures

The Provinces of Assam, Bengal, Bihar, Uttar Pradesh, Bombay and Madras were given bicameral legislatures, namely Legislative Assembly and Legislative Council. Orissa, Punjab, Sindh, Central Provinces and North Western Frontier Provinces had only the Legislative Assembly. All members of the assembly were directly elected, through restricted and communal franchise, for five years. The Council with members elected indirectly had a life of nine years but one third of members thereof would retire every three years. The provincial legislatures with a five year tenure could pass laws on subjects under provincial and concurrent lists, the central Acts having preponderance with respect to the latter. Dyarchy was abolished at the provincial level.

Only the provincial part of the Act of 1935 came into force on 1 April 1937. Dyarchy at the Centre did not materialise as the native rulers did not agree to it. Both the Congress and the League participated in the elections and formed Governments wherever they could. On the question of India's participation in the Second World War, the Congress Ministries resigned between 27 October and 16 November 1939. Seven of the 8 provinces went under Governor's rule between 30 October and 10 November. In Assam a Muslim League Coalition Cabinet under Sir Syed Muhammad Saadulla took office for the second time on 17 November 1939. He remained the Premier till the elections of 1946 with a short break of 8 months.

The British War Cabinet of Winston Churchill made a Draft Declaration which among, other things, proposed the formation of an elected body charged with the framing of a new Constitution for India at the end of the War. For negotiation with the Indian leaders Sir Stafford Cripps, the Lord Privy Seal and Member of the War Cabinet, reached Delhi on 23 March 1942. In a Press Conference on 29 March, the proposal was made public. But the Congress Working Committee rejected it on 11 April. Mainly on its objection to any British control over the country and the Muslims League's opposition to the creation of a single free Indian Government, the Cripp's proposal failed to solve the problem.

The General Elections held in Britain in 1945 changed the Government's attitude with the formation of the Labour Government under Clement Attlee. He declared the British resolve to solve the problem. The process of framing of a new Constitution of the Indians, by the Indians and for the Indians began with the Interim Government and the Constituent Assembly formed in 1946. The interim Government was in fact an expanded Executive Council of the Governor General formed on 2 September 1946. But the Congress-League tussle remained unresolved. On the latter's refusal to participate in the Constituent Assembly, the Congress demanded the resignations of its representatives in the Interim Cabinet, complicating the situation further. The British Prime Minister Attlee decided to transfer power to "responsible Indian hands" by a date not later than June 1948. Lord Wavell, the Viceroy was replaced by Lord Mountbatten who took charge in March 1947. In course of his deliberations with the leaders, he found no agreed solution of the problem . Then came the fateful Mountbatten Plan of 3 June 1947 which envisaged the partition of India into two sovereign states of India and Pakistan. In terms of the Plan and the Indian Independence Act passed in the British Parliament on 18 July 1947, the Indian National Congress and the All India Muslim League divided the country into India and Pakistan at midnight of 15 August 1947. The new Constitution of free, though truncated, India came into force on 26 January 1950. The federal idea of free India's Constitution had emerged in the Round Table Conferences. This was also embodied in the proceedings of the All India Muslim Conference held at Delhi on 1st January 1926. According to the Party,

> *...in view of India's vast extent and its ethnological, linguistic, administrative and geographical or territorial divisions, the only form of Government suitable to Indian conditions is a federal system with complete autonomy and residuary powers vested in the constituent states, the Central Government having control only of such matters of common interest as may be specifically entrusted to it by the Constitution...*

After Independence the framers of our constitution, " untrammeled by any restrictions imposed by external authority, borrowed many things" from the concept of Provincial Autonomy embodied in the last Constitutional Act under the British rule.[138]

REFERENCES

1. Sen, Sailendra Nath, *History of Modern India*, 2nd Revised Edition, p.2.
2. Anand, C.L., *Constitutional Law and History of India*, Sixth Edition 1990, Introduction, p.i.
3. Bhagwan, Vishnu, *Constitutional History of India and National Movement*, p.4.
4. *Ibid*, p.11.
5. *Report on Indian Constitutional Reforms* 1918, p.17,and Anand, p.91.
6. Rai, B.C., *Constitutional History of India and National Movement*, Details of Regulating Act 1773.
7. Bhagwan, pp.2-23 and Anand, p.9 onward.
8. Lyall, *British Dominion*, p.131, quoted in Bhagwan, p.22.
9. Bhagwan, p.23.
10. Anand, p.20.
11. *Ibid*.
12. Bhagwan, p.32.
13. *Ibid*, p.37 and Anand, p.24 onward.
14. *Ibid*, p.38.
15. Hansard, Vol. XXVII, p.1317 quoted in Anand, p.25 onward.
16. *Ibid*, p.27.
17. *Ibid*, pp.27-28.
18. Hansard, 3 Series, Vol. XIX, p.169.
19. Ibid and Roy, N.C. and A.K. Sinha, *A History of India*, p.512.
20. Anand, p.48 and Roy and Sinha, p.513.
21. Hansard CXX, p.559.
22. Quoted in Bhagwan, p.24.
23. *Ibid*.
24. Mahajan, V.D., *India Since 1526*, 7th Edition, p.266.
25. Mahajan, V.D., *British Rule in India and After*, p.296.
26. Majumdar, R.C., *A Brief History of India*, Diamond Jubilee Edition 1986, p. 248.
27. Graham, Major, *The Life and Work of Sir Syed Ahmed Khan*, pp.26-27.
28. Sen, p.112.
29. Hansard, Vol. CL, 2046 quoted in Anand, p.48.
30. *Ibid*, p.53.
31. Majumdar Bimanbehari, *Indian Political Associations and Reform of Legislature (1818 - 1918)*, p.32 and Hansard, Vol. CL., 2046 uoted in Anand, p.65.
32. *Ibid*, p.63
33. *Ibid*.
34. Ibid, pp. 63-64.
35. Subramania Aiyer's speech at the Indian National Congress 1885, quoted in Bhagawan, p.72.
36. Coupland, R., *Indian Problem*, p.56.
37. Sen, p.113.
38. Bhagwan, p.74.

39. Anand, p.72.
40. *Ibid*, pp.72-73.
41. Punniah, K.K., *The Constitutional History of India*, p.112.
42. Anand, p.75.
43. *Report on Indian Constitutional Reforms 1918*, pp.22-23.
44. Anand, p.59.
45. Bhagwan, p.84.
46. Majumdar, Bimanbehari, p.371 onward, and Chand, Tara, *History of the Freedom Movement in India*, Volume Three, Third Reprint, p .389 for details.
47. Majumdar, Bimanbehari, p.372.
48. *Minto Papers*, Minto to Morley and Chand, Tara, p.365.
49. Mary, Countess of Minto (Lady Minto), India Minto and Morley-Compiled from the correspondence between the Viceroy and the Secretary of State, with extracts from her journal 1905-1910- Minto gave Morley this quotation without citing the source, p.99.
50. *Ibid*, p.45.
51. *Ibid*, October I, 1906.
52. *Ibid*, Summarized from Minto's reply to Agha Khan Delegation of October 1, 1906.
53. *Ibid*.
54. *Ibid*, p.48.
55. *Ibid*.
56. *Ibid*, p.97.
57. *Ibid*, p. 371.
58. *Ibid*, p.110.
59. *Ibid*, Lady Minto's Journal dated 25 January 1910, p.371.
60. *Ibid*, p.372.
61. *Ibid*.
62. *Ibid*, p.104.
63. *Ibid*, p.104.
64. Majumdar, Bimanbehari., p.371.
65. Mary Countess of Minto, p 110 onward.
66. *Ibid*.
67. Chamberlain, A., *Politics from Within*, pp.59-60 quoted in Chand, Tara, p. 359.
68. Mary, Countess of Minto, p.109.
69. Hansard, CXCVIII, quoted in Chand, Tara, p.79.
70. Mary, Countess of Minto, p.132.
71. *Ibid*, p.221.
72. Majumdar, R.C., pp.372-373.
73. Ibid, p.373 and Congress Secretariat (pub), Report of the Indian National Congress (RINC) 1908, pp.113-120 for further details.
74. Majumdar, Bimanbehari., pp.373-374, RINC 1908, pp.113-120, and Chand, Tara, Chapter on Morley-Minto Reforms for further details.

75. Anand, p.78 and Bhagwan, p.87.
76. Majumdar, R.C., (Gen. Ed.), *History and Culture of the Indian People* Vol.XI, pp.140-141.
77. Majumdar, Bimanbehari., p.376.
78. NCERT (pub), India's Struggle for Independence, Visuals and Documents, January 1988, p.44.
79. RINC 1909, p.58 quoted in Majumdar, p.377.
80. Ibid, quoted in Majumdar, p.378.
81. Ibid, 1910 pp.84-93 quoted in Majumdar, p. 381.
82. Ibid, p.90 quoted in Majumdar, p.380.
83. Mary, Countess of Minto, p.421, p.298, Natesan, G.A., *The Indian National Congress*, 2nd Edition, Part II, p.127, Chand, Tara, p.368 and Mary, Countess of Minto, June 7, 1909..
84. *Ibid*, Journal 3 February 1910.
85. *Ibid*, p.372 onward for details.
86. *Ibid*, pp.389-390.
87. *Ibid*, pp.289-294.
88. *Report on Indian Constitutional Reforms*, paras 2,3,9, 74, 79, 81and 83.
89. Majumdar, p.375.
90. Punniah, p.136.
91. Ibid.
92. Tahmankar, D.V., *Lokamanya Tilak*, p.210 quoted in Barpujari, H.K., (Gen.Ed.), *Political History of Assam*, Volume One 1826-1919, p.212.
93. Bipin Chandra Pal's Speech in England, 1911, quoted in Guha, Amalendu, Planter Raj to Swaraj, p.109.
94. Natesan, p.180 and Allana, G, (Ed.), Pakistan Movement, Historic Documents, p.26.
95. Indian Central Committee Report (Simon Commission), para 62, pp.116-122.
96. Barpujari, p.215-216, Anand, p.205 onward for details.
97. Mahajan, V.D., *Modern Indian History*, Seventeenth Edition 1990, p.312.
98. *Rowlatt Committee Report*, pp.173-174, p.182
99. Majumdar, R.C.(Gen.Ed.), Vol.XI, p. 42 and Bhuyan, Arun Chandra and Sibopada De (Eds.), *Political History of Assam*, Volume Two, 1920-1939, p.1
100. *Gazetteer of India,* Vol.II, October 1973, p.540.
101. *Young India*, 20 October 1921, quoted in Majumdar, R.C., *History of the Freedom Movement in India*, Vol,3, p.64.
102. Gupta, D. C., Indian National Movement and Constitutional Development, 3rd enlarged Revised Edition, p.100 and Bhuyan and Sibopada De, p.15.
103. Reforms Enquiry Committee (Muddiman Committee), Report of the Minority, Indian Annual Register (IAR), 1935, Volume I, p.38 and Guha, p.160.
104. Majumdar, R.C.(GEN. Ed.), Vol.XI, pp.390-391.
105. *Ibid*, pp.391-392.
106. *Ibid*, p.392.
107. Bose, Subhas Chandra, *The Indian Struggle*, p.109, p.110 quoted in Majumdar p.415.
108. Majumdar, p.415.
109. *Ibid*, p.416.

110. *Ibid*, p.417.
111. *Indian Statutory Commission Report* (ISCR), Vol.1 p.253, Vol.XIV Part I, p.XIV, p.264 and p.106 for further details.
112. Bhuyan and Sibopada De, p.112, Majumdar, pp.259-260 and Gupta, p.117.
113. ISCR, Vol.II, Appendix VII, pp.84-85.
114. Majumdar, p.372 and Chand, Tara, Volume, 3 pp.465-468.
115. *Ibid*, p.454.
116. Sitaramayya, B.Pattabhi, *History of the Indian National Congress*, Vol.I, p.318, Majumdar, pp.457-458, p.530 for details, Bakshi, S.R., *Gandhi and Hindu-Muslim Unity*, Jinnah's speech on Nehru Committee's Recommendations on Hindu-Muslim Problem at the Calcutta Convention of 22 December 1928, pp.90-97.
117. *Ibid*, p.461.
118. *Ibid*, pp.116-117, pp.529-530, p.540.
119. *Ibid*, n.2, pp.330-331, quoted in Bhuyan and Sibopada De, p.139.
120. Sitaramayya, pp.424-425 for full text.
121. Majumdar, p.483, p.487.
122. *Ibid*, p.490.
123. *'Navjug'* Special Number, 13 April 1947 quoted in Sharma, Kusum, *Ambedkar and the Indian Constitution*, p.129.
124. Keer, Dhananjay, Dr. Ambedkar, *Life and Mission*, p.168, quoted in Sharma, p.130, and the *Diary of Mahadev Desai*, Vol.I, p.52 quoted in Sharma, p.130.
125. *Ibid.*
126. *Ibid* and Majumdar, p.497.
127. Chander, Jog Parvesh, *India Steps Forward* p.274, Bose, p.221, Sharma, p.151, 131, RTC II, *Minorities Committee Proceedings*, November 13, 1931 quoted in Sharma, p.132 and Tendulkar, D.G., Mahatma, Vol. III.
128. *'Janata'*, dated January 9, 1932, quoted in Sharma, p.132.
129. Sitaramayya, Vol.I, pp.866-869.
130. *Templewood Collection*, Microfilm, quoted in Sharma, p.134, Majumdar, pp.520-521.
131. Sharma.
132. *Ibid*, p.156, Button, Glorney, *Tragedy of Gandhi*, p.308 quoted in Sharma, p.138, Chand, Tara, p.182.
133. File No. 31/113/32 – Poll 1932 KW Home Pol., p.3 quoted in Sharma, p.138.
134. *Ibid*, pp.138-139.
135. Fischer, Luis, *The Life of the Mahatma*, p.312.
136. *The Times of India*, September 21, 1932 and Sharma, p.140.
137. Tendulkar, p.169., Sharma, pp.140-145, Appendix I.
138. ISC Report, Vol. 2, Appendix VII, pp.84-85 and Banerjee, Anil Chandra, *The Constitutional History of India*, 1977, Preface to the book.

APPENDIX A

Report on Indian Constitutional Reforms 1918
Summary of Recommendations

Parliament and India Office **Paras**

1. The Control of the Parliament and the Secretary 291
   of State for India to be modified 292
2. Salary of Secretary of State for India to be transferred to Home Estimates 294
3. The House of Commons to be asked to appoint a Select Committee for Indian Affairs 295
4. A Committee to be appointed to examine the report on the present constitution of the Council of India and on the India Office establishment 293

The Government of India

5. The Government of India to preserve indisputable authority on matters adjudged by it to be essential in the discharge of its responsibilities for peace, order and good government 266
6. A Privy Council for India to be established 287

The Executive

7. To increase the Indian elements in the Governor General's Executive Council 272
8. To abolish the present statutory maximum for the Executive Council and the Statutory qualification for the seats 271
9. To take power to appoint a limited number of members of the legislature to a position analogous with that of Parliamentary Under Secretaries in Great Britain 275

The Legislature (Central)

10. The present Legislative Council of Governor General to be replaced by a Council of State and a Legislative Assembly 273
11. The Council of State to consist of 50 members excluding the Governor General who would be the President with power to nominate the Vice-President 277
    Of the members-21 to be elected 29 to be nominated by the Governor General 277
    Of the nominated members, 4 to be nominated officials. Not more than 25 including a member of the Executive Council to be officials 278
    Life of each Council – 5 years 278
    Governor General-in-Council to frame regulations as to qualifications of membership of the Council of State
12. The Legislative Assembly to consist of 100 members of whom two thirds to be elected and one third to be nominated 273
    Of the nominated members not less than one third to be non-officials
    The President of the Assembly to be nominated by the Governor General 275
13. Official members of the Council of State to be eligible for nomination to Assembly 277
14. Governor General to have power to dissolve either or both houses

Procedure for Legislation

15. Government Bills

A. Ordinarily to be introduced and carried through the usual stages in the assembly; and if passed by the Assembly, to be sent to the Council of State. If the Council of State amend the Bill in a manner which is unacceptable to the Assembly, the Bill to be submitted to a Joint Session of both Houses, unless the Governor General-in-Council is prepared to certify that the amendments introduced by the Council are essential to the interests of peace and order or good government inlcuding in this term sound financial administration in which case the Assembly not to have power to reject or modify such amendments. But in the event of leave to introduce being refused or the Bill being thrown out at any stage, the Governor General-in-Council also to have the power in cases of emergency so certified to introduce the Bill in the first instance in and to pass it through, the Council of State merely reporting to the Assembly. 279

B. Private Bills
To be introduced in the Chamber of which the mover is a member and on being passed by that Chamber to be submitted to the other. Differences of opinion between the Chambers to be settled by means of joint Session.
If however a Bill emerges from the assembly in a form which the Government think prejudicial to good administration, the Governor General-in-Council to have power to certify it in the terms already cited and to submit it to the Council of State, the Bill only to become law in the form given to it by the Council 280

16. Resolutions to have effect only as recommendations 284
17. The Governor General–in-Council and the Crown to retain their respective powers of assent, reservation and disallowance 283
18. The Governor General to retain his existing power of making ordinances and the Governor General 276
in Council his power of making Regulations 283
19. Nominated Official members of the Council of State of the Legislative Assembly to have freedom of speech and vote except when Government otherwise directs 275
20. Any member of the Council of State or the Legislative Assembly to be entitled to ask supplementary questions. The Governor General not to disallow a question on the ground that it cannot be answered consistently with the public interest, but power to be retained to disallow a question on the ground that the putting of it is inconsistent with the public interest 286
21. Rules governing the procedures for the transaction of business in the Council of State and the Legislative Assembly to be made in the first instance by the Governor General-in-Council. The Legislative Assembly and the Council of State to be entitled to modify their rules subject to the sanction of the Governor General. In each case such modification not to require the sanction of the Secretary of State-in- Council and not to be laid before Parliament 286
22. Joint Standing Committees of both Houses to be associated with as many departments as possible. The Governor General-in-Council to decide with which department Standing Committees may be associated and the Head of the Department concerned to decide what matters to be referred to the Standing

Committee. Two thirds of each Standing Committee to be elected by Ballot
by non-official members, one third to be nominated by the Governor
General- in- Council 285

The Provinces

23. The Provincial Government to be given the widest independence from superior
control in legislative, administrative and financial matters which is compatible
with the due discharge of their own responsibility by the Government of India 189

24. Representative Government in the provinces to be attained first by the devaluation
of responsibility in certain subjects called hereafter 215
the Transferred Subjects (all other subjects being 218
called Reserved Subjects) and then by gradually 219
increasing the devolution by successive stages 238
until complete responsibility is reached 260

Provincial Executives

25. The Executive Government in a province to consist of Governor and Executive
Council, a minister or ministers nominated by Governor from the elected members
of the Legislative 214
Council and an additional member or members 268
without portfolio 220

26. The Executive Council to consist of two members 218
– one of whom will be Indian 218
Reserved Subjects to be in charge of the Governor
and the member of the Executive Council

27. Minister or Ministers to be appointed for the
term of the Legislative Council and to have charge 218
of Transferred Subjects 219

28. The additional member or members to be appointed by the Governor from
among his senior officials for purpose of consultation and advice only 220

29. The Government thus constituted to deliberate generally as a whole but the
Governor to have power to summon either part of his Government to deliberate
with him separately on Reserved Subjects. Decision on Reserved Subjects and on
supply for them in the provincial Budget to rest with the Governor and his
Executive Council, decisions on Transferred Subjects and the supply 219
for them with the Governor and the ministers 221

30. Power to be taken to appoint a limited number of members of the Legislative
Council to a position analogous to Parliamentary Under Secretary in Great Britain 224

31. In each province an enlarged Legislative Council with a substantial elected majority
to be established. The Council to consist of Members elected on as broad a
franchise as possible, Nominated including (a) official and (b) non-official members
and Ex – officio members. The franchise and the composition of the Legislative
Council to be determined by regulation to be made on the advice of the Committee
described in paragraph 53 by the Governor General-in-Council 225
with the sanction of the Secretary of State and 232
laid before the Parliament 233

32. Governor to be President of the council with power to appoint a Vice–President 236

33. Governor to have power to dissolve the Legislative Council 254

34. Resolutions except on Budget, to have effect only as recommendation 237
35. Non- official members to have freedom of speech and vote except when Government otherwise directs 233
36. Any member of the Legislative Council to be entitled to ask supplementary questions 236
37. The existing rules governing the proceedings for transaction of business to continue, but the Legislative Council to have power to modify them with the sanction of the Governor
38. Standing Committees of Legislative Council to be formed and attached to each department. These Committees to consist of members elected by the Legislative Council, of the Heads of Departments concerned and a member or the Minister would preside 235
39. Legislation on all subjects, normally to be passed in the Legislative Council. Exceptional procedure
is provided in the succeeding paragraphs 252
40. The Governor to have power to certify that a Bill dealing with the Reserved Subject is essential either or for discharge of his responsibility for the peace and tranquility of the province or any part thereof or for the discharge of his responsibility for his subjects. The Bill will then, with his certification, be published in the Gazette. It will be introduced and read in the Legislative Council after discussion on its general principles, will be referred to a Grand Committee to refer to Government of India whose decision shall be final, the question whether he has rightly decided that the Bill which he certified was concerned with a Reserved Subject. The Governor not to certify a Bill if he is of opinion that the question of enacting of the legislation may be safely left to the Legislative Council 252
41. The Grand Committee the Composition of which may vary according to the subject matter of the Bill to comprise from 40 to 50 per cent of the Legislative Council. The members to be chosen partly by election by ballot, partly by nomination. The Governor to have power to nominate a bare majority (in addition to himself) but not more than two thirds of the nominated members to be officials 252
42. The Bill as passed in the Grand Committee to be reported to the Legislative Council which may again discuss it generally within such time limit as may be laid down, but may not amend it, except on the motion of a member of the Executive Council or reject it. After such discussion the Bill to pass automatically, but during such discussion the Legislative Council may record by resolution any objection felt to the principle or details and any such resolution to be transmitted with the Act, to the Governor general and the Secretary of State 253
43. Any member of the Executive Council to have the right to challenge the whole or any part of a Bill on its introduction or any amendment, when moved, on the ground that it trenches on the Reserved field of legislation. The Governor to have the choice then either of allowing the Bill to proceed in the Legislative Council or of certifying the Bill, clause or amendment. If he certifies the Bill, clause or amendment, Government may either decline to allow it to be discussed or suggest to the Legislative Council an amended Bill or clause or at the request of the Legislative Council refer the Bill to a Grand Committee. 254
44. All provincial legislation to require the assent of the Governor and the Governor General and to be subject to disallowance by His Majesty 254

45. The veto of the Governor to include power to return for amendment 254
46. The Governor General to have power to reserve provincial Acts 254

Finance

47. A complete separation to be made between Indian and provincial heads of revenue 200 201
48. Provincial contribution to the Government of India to be the first charge on provincial revenue 206 256
49. Provincial Government to have certain powers of taxation and borrowing
50. The Budget to be laid before the Legislative Council. If the Legislative Council refuses to accept the Budget proposals for Reserved Subjects, the Governor in-Council to have power to restore the whole or any part of the original allotment on the Governor's certifying that for reasons to be stated such restoration is in his opinion essential either to the peace or tranquility of the province or any part thereof or to the discharge of his responsibility for Reserved Subjects. Except in so far as he exercises his power, the Budget to be allotted so as to give effect to resolutions of the Legislative Council. 256
51. Local Self-Government 188
    Complete popular control in local bodies to be established as far as possible
    Modification of Provincial Constitution
52. Five years after the first meeting of the new councils the Government of India to consider any applications addressed to it by a provincial Government or a provincial Legislative Council for the modification of the list of Reserved and Transferred Subjects. In such cases the Government of India with the sanction of the Secretary of State to have power to transfer any Reserved Subject or in case of serious mal-administration to remove, to the Reserved list any subject already transferred and to have power also to order that salary of the ministers shall be specifically voted each year by the Legislative Council. The Legislative Council to have the right of deciding at the same or any subsequent time by resolution that such salary be specifically voted yearly

Preliminary Action – Separation of Indian from Provincial regarding Transferred Subjects

53. A Committee to be appointed, consisting of a Chairman appointed from England, an official and an Indian non-official. This Committee to advise on the question of the separation of Indian from provincial functions and to recommend which of the functions assigned to the province should be Transferred Subjects. An official and an Indian non-official in each province which it is at this time examining to be added to the Committee 238
54. A second Committee to be appointed consisting of Chairman appointed from England, two officials and two Indian non-officials, to examine constituencies, franchises and the composition of the Legislative Council in each province and of the Legislative Assembly. An official and non-official in each province to be added to the Committee 225
55. The two Committees to have power to meet and confer 225
56. A Commission to be appointed ten years after the first meeting of the new

Legislative Council to review the constitutional position both as regards the Government of India and the provinces. The names of the Commissioners to be submitted for approval of Parliament. Similar Commissions to be appointed at intervals of not more than twelve years 261

57. To establish a Council of Princes 306
58. The Council of Princes to appoint a Standing Committee 307
59. The Viceroy in his discretion to appoint a Commission consisting of a High Court Judge and one nominee each of the parties to advise in case of disputes between States or between a State and Local government or the Government of India 308
60. Should the necessity arise of considering the question of depriving a Ruler of a State of any of his rights, dignities or power or debarring from succession any member of his family, the Viceroy to appoint a Committee to advise, consisting of a High Court Judge, two Ruling Princes and two persons of high standing nominated by him
61. All States possessing full internal powers to have direct relations with the Government of India 310
62. Relations with the Native States to be excluded from transfer to the control of provincial Legislative Councils 310
63. Arrangements are to be made for joint deliberation and discussion between the Council of Princes and the Council of States on matters of common 278
interest 311

The Public Services

64. Any racial bars that still exist in regulations for appointment to the public services to be abolished 315
65. In addition to recruitment in England where such exists, a system of appointment to all the public services to be established in India 316
66. Percentages of recruitment in India with definite 316
rate of increase to be fixed for all those services 317
67. In the Indian Civil Service the percentage to be 33 of the superior posts, increasing annually by 1 per cent until the position is reviewed by the Commission 317
68. Rates of pay to be considered with reference to the rise in the cost of living and the need for maintaining the standard of recruitment. Incremental time scale to be introduced generally and increments to continue until the superior grade is attained.
Maximum of ordinary pension to be raised to Rs 6000/- payable at the rate of I.s.qd.to the rupee with special pension for certain high appointment. Indian Civil Service Annuities to be made non- contributory but contributions to continue to be funded. Leave rules to be reconsidered with a view to greater elasticity, reduction of excessive amounts of leave admissible, and concession of reduced leave on full pay. The accumulation of 318
privilege leave upto four months to be considered 321
69. A rate of pay based on recruitment in India to be fixed for all public services, but suitable allowances to be granted to persons recruited in Europe or on account of qualifications obtained in Europe and the converse principles to be applied to Indians employed in Europe 322

Conclusion of Montagu and Chelmsford

We have only one more word to say. If anything could enhance the sense of responsibility under which our recommendations are made in a matter fraught with consequences so immense, it would be the knowledge that even as we bring our report to an end for greater issues still hang in the balance upon the battle fields of France. It is there and not in Delhi or Whitehall that the ultimate decision of India's future will be taken. The liberty of the world must be won before our deliberations over the liberalizing of Indian political institutions can acquire any tangible meaning. We can not close this document more fittingly than with the prayer, which we know all India echoes, that the principles of justice and freedom may be saved to the world by the splendid endurance and self sacrifices of His Majesty's and the allies armies.

REPORT ON INDIAN CONSTITUTIONAL REFORMS 1918

Illustrative List 1 Showing Provincial Subjects

pp.232-235, paras 212-213, 238-240

1. Taxation for provincial purposes
2. Borrowing on sole credit of provincial Revenue
3. Financial work on behalf of the Government of India, i.e., 4. collection of Income tax etc. subject to any restriction of Government of India
4. The appointments, conditions of service and control of all provincial services Subject to any existing privileges enjoyed by those in service now
5. Maintenance of law and order
   i. Administration of criminal justice
   ii. Police including Railway police
   iii. Prisons
   iv. Criminal Tribes
   v. Working of Particular Acts
   vi. Poisons
   vii. Gamblings
   viii. Dramatic performance
   ix. Coronors
6. Land Revenue Administration, Assessment and Collection of revenue, Maintenance of procedures of revenue collection
7. Agriculture
8. Forest and Forest products
9. Fisheries and connected Industries
10. Public works
11. Education
12. Medical and Sanitary
13. Local Self- Government
    Rural and Urban-viz. Provision for public health, safety and convenience, construction of local authorities-Municipal rates, taxes, loans, roads, bridges, ferries tolls, markets, ponds, fairs, exhibition, parks, open space, museums, libraries, art galleries, reading rooms, building regulations, disorderly houses, lodging houses, sarais, hackney carriage,

registration of carts, nuisance, water supply, prevention of fires, regulation for sale of foods and drink, smoke nuisance, disposal of the dead, bathing and washing places, warehouses, drains and sewers, control of animals, surveys for municipal purposes, advertisements and anything dealt with in existing municipalities or local self-government Acts, and also any other matters declared by the Government of India to be included in Local Self Government

The question of reserving to the Executive Council the powers of suspending defaulting local bodies to be considered

14. Franchise, electoral law, organization of constituencies
15. Civil Justice
16. Excise
17. Scheduled Districts
18. Land acquisition
19. Industrial matters, electricity, petroleum, explosive mines, Geological Survey for minerals
20. Co-operative Credits
21. Business concerns
22. Government Press, Stationary and Printing
23. Statistics-provincial purposes
24. Inter-provincial emigration and immigration
25. Protection of wild birds and animals and cruelty to animals
26. Assessment and recovery of provincial Government demands
27. Escheats and unclaimed property
28. Management of Charitable Endowments
29. Motor Vehicles

Item Nos. 3,5(I-V), 10,11,12,14 vide para 225, eventually provincial part of 15,18,20,21,22,24,25 and 29 Subject to Government of India's control

APPENDIX B

First Schedule to Government of India Act 1935

PART I

Composition of the Federal Legislature

Representatives of British India–General Qualification for Membership–Franchise qualifications

A person shall not be qualified to be chosen as a representative of British India to fill a seat in the Federal Legislature unless he

a. is a British Subject or the ruler or Subject of an Indian State which has acceded to the Federation and
b. is, in the case of a seat in the Council of State, not less than thirty years of age and in the case of a seat in the Federal Assembly, not less than twenty five years of age, and
c. possesses such, if any other qualification specified in or prescribed under this part of the Schedule as may be appropriate in his case provided that the Ruler or a subject of an Indian State which has not acceded to the Federation,
    i. shall not be disqualified under sub-paragraph of this paragraph to fill a seat

allotted to a province if he would be eligible to be elected to the Legislative Assembly of the province

ii. in such cases as may be prescribed shall not be disqualified under the said sub-paragraph (a) to fill a seat allocated to a Chief Commissioner's province

2. Upon the expiration of the term for which he is chosen to serve as a member of the Federal Legislature, a person if otherwise duly qualified, shall be eligible to be chosen to serve for a further term

The Council of State Allotment of Seats

3. Of the 156 Seats in the Council of States to be filled by the representative of British India, 150 seats to Governors' Provinces, Chief Commissioners' Provinces, European' Anglo- Indian, Christian and 6 seats to be filled by persons chosen by the Governor General in his discretion

Qualification for Voter

6. (1) No persons shall be entitled to vote at an election to fill a Sikh seat or a Muhammadan seat in the Council of State unless he is a Sikh or a Muhammadan as the case may be
   (2) No person who is or entitled to be included in the electoral roll of a territorial constituency in any province for the election of persons to fill a Sikh seat or a Muhammadan seat in the Council of State shall be entitled to vote at an election to fill a general seat therein allotted to that province
   (3) No Anglo-Indian, European or Indian Christian shall be entitled to vote at an election to fill a general seat in the Council of State
   (4) qualification for persons to vote in territorial constituencies shall be such as may be prescribed
7. Nothing in the two last paragraphs applied to British Baluchistan
8. In any province to which a seat is to be filled up by a representative of the Scheduled Caste is allotted, a person to fill that seat shall be chosen by the members of these Castes who hold seats in the Chamber or as the case may be either Chamber of the Legislature of that province
9. In any Province to which a seat Reserved for women is allotted, a woman to fill that seat shall be chosen by the persons, whether men or women, who hold seats in the Chamber or as the case may be, the Chambers of the Legislatures of that Province
10. Persons to fill seats allotted to Anglo – Indian, European and Christian communities shall be chosen by the members of Electoral Colleges consisting of such Anglo – Indians, Europeans and Indian Christians as the case may be, as are members of the Legislative Council of any Governor's Province
11. A person shall not be qualified to hold a seat in the Council of State unless
    In the case of a seat allowed to a Governor's Province or a Chief Commissioner's Province, he is qualified to vote in a territorial constituency in the province at an election of a member of the Council of State
12. The term of office of a member in the Council of State

Subject to the provisions of 13,14,15 and 16, the term of office of a member shall be nine years (remainder period of a predecessor only to be covered by one elected for the remainder

13. Upon the first constitution of the Council of State, persons shall be chosen to all the seats allotted to Governors' Provinces, Chief Commissioners' Provinces and communities, but for the purpose of securing that in every third year, one third of the holders of such seats shall retire, one third of the persons first chosen shall be chosen to serve for three years only, one third shall be chosen to serve for six years only and one third shall be chosen to serve for nine years, and thereafter in every third year persons shall be chosen to serve for nine years, the seats then becoming vacant in consequence of the provision of this paragraph
15. The persons chosen upon the first constitution of the Council to fill the Anglo-Indian seat shall chosen to serve for nine years; of the seven persons chosen to fill the European seats, three shall be chosen to serve for three years, one shall be chosen to serve for six years only and three shall be chosen to serve for nine years Of the 2 Indian Christians, one shall be chosen to serve for three years only and one shall be chosen to serve for nine years
16. Upon the first constitution of the council of State two of the persons to be chosen by the Governor General shall be chosen to serve for three years only, two for six years only and two for nine years

The Federal Assembly

17. Allocation of Seats – Representatives of British India
18. (iii) There shall be in the federal Assembly 4 seats not allowed to any province; of which there shall be in the seats to be Filled by representatives of Commerce and Industry and one shall be a seat to be filled by a representative of Labour
19. Subject to the provisions of the next succeeding paragraph, persons to fill the seats in the Federal Assembly allotted to Governors' Province as general Seats. Sikh seats or Muhammadan seats respectively, voting in the case of a general election in accordance with the principle of proportional representation by means of the single transferable vote

Women Seats

21. ...there shall be for British India , an electoral college consisting of such women as are members of the Legislative Assembly of any Governor's Province, and the person to fill a women's seat allotted to any particular province shall be chosen by the members of the electoral college.

    Rules relating to the conduct of election by women's electoral college shall be such as to secure that of the nine women's seats allotted to Provinces, at least two are held by Muhammadan and at least one by an Indian Christian

Anglo Indian European and Indian Christian

22. Three separate electoral colleges to chose their respective members.

Commerce and Industry, Land holders and Labour

23. Shall be chosen by
    (a) Chambers of Commerce and Similar organisations.
    (b) Land holders
    (c) Labour
    (d) In the case of one of the non- provincial seats which are to be filled by representatives of Commerce and industry, by such Associations as Chambers of Commerce, another by Federated Chambers of Commerce, third seat by Commercial bodies in North India.
    (e) Non- provincial seat for Labour – voting in all as may be prescribed

24-25. Chief Commissioner's Province-Coorg-he shall not be qualified to vote in a seat in the Federal Assembly unless ... he is qualified to hold a seat of the same class in the Legislative Assembly or in the case of Coorg, the Legislative Council of that province.

26.(1)Definition of European, Anglo-Indian , Indian Christian, Scheduled Caste formerly known as Depressed Classes ... prescribed.
Native of India -
Any person born and domiciled within the dominion of His Majesty's in India or Burma of parents habitually resident in India or Burma and not established there for temporary purpose only.

Sixth Schedule
Part IX Assam

General requirement as to residence –

1. Place of residence – within the constituency for inclusion in the electoral roll – ordinarily living in the constituency or he has family dwelling and occasionally occupies it.
2. Qualifications dependant on taxation –qualified if in the previous financial year either was (a) assessed to income tax or (b) municipal or cantonment rates or taxes to an aggregate amount of no less than two rupees or in Sylhet Municipality of no less than one rupee eight annas or to a tax of no less than one rupee in a small town or in the district of Cachar or the district of Goalpara to a tax not less than eight annas under the village Chowkidari Act 1870.
3. Qualifications dependent on Property
   A person shall be qualified to be included in the electoral roll of any constituency if in the constituency, he either

(a) is the owner of land, the land revenue of which has been assessed or is assessable at no less than seven rupees eight annas per annum or
(b) is liable to pay a local rate not less then eight annas per annum.
(c) throughout a previous financial year or previous Bengali year held from a land lord land in any of the following districts that is to say Lakhimpur, Sibsagar, Darrang, Nowgong or Kamrup or in the Garo Hills, and paid to the land lord rent

to the value of not less than seven rupees eight annas in respect of that land. Provided that for the purpose of this paragraph land situate and local rates levied in the districts of Sylhet, Cachar and Goalpara shall be left out of account.

Educational qualifications

4. Also qualified to be included in the electoral roll for any territorial Constituency – passed the Middle Leaving School Certificate Examination or any other examination prescribed equivalent.
   Qualification by reason of Service in His Majesty's forces
5. Service in His Majesty's Service-also be qualified if he is retired, pensioned or discharged officer, non- Commissioned Officer or soldier of His Majesty's regular military forces or the Assam Rifles.

Additional Qualification for Women

6. A woman shall be qualified (territorial Constituency) if she is a pensioned widow or pensioned mother of a person who was an officer, non- Commissioned officer, or soldier in his Majesty's regular military forces or Assam Rifles or literate as prescribed.
7. A husband qualified for inclusion for the purpose of para 6.
   - (a) a retired, pensioned or discharged officer or non- commissioned officer of regular military forces or Assam Rifles.
   - (b) was in the previous financial year assessed to income tax.
   - (c) in the previous financial year assessed in the constituency in respect to municipal or cantonment rates or tax
     - i. in the Nowgong Municipality – not less than two rupees or
     - ii. in Sylhet Municipality – not less than one rupee eight annas
     - iii. elsewhere in the province not less than three rupee's
   - (d) assessed in the previous financial year to a tax not less than rupee in a small town.
   - (e) in the districts of Sylhet, Cachar and Goalpara in the previous financial year to a tax not less than one rupee under the village Chowkidari Act 1870 or
   - (f) elsewhere in the said districts owner of a land in the constituency, the land revenue on which has been assessed or assessable at not less than fifteen rupees per annum or
   - (g) is liable to pay a local rate in the constituency of not less than one rupee per annum.

Application necessary for enrolment in certain cases

8. For the purpose of Para 6 of this Schedule (i.e., women), application for or on behalf for inclusion to be made – no person can be included in the electoral roll without application
   Special Provisions as to Seats Reserved for Women

9. Shall apply to any constituency specially formed for the election of persons to fill the seat Reserved for women, no man shall be included in the electoral roll for the constituency or be entitled to vote in any election therein.

Special Provision as to Shillong

9A. In the case of any territorial constituency comprising any part of Shillong, any reference to this part of this Schedule to the "Constituency" shall be constructed as including a reference to so much of the areas under the jurisdiction of the Shillong Municipal Board and the Cantonment Authority as is not part of British India, and any reference to municipal cantonment areas or taxes shall be constructed as including a reference to any such rates or taxes assessed by or paid to the Board or that authority in the exercise of any jurisdiction exercised by them in relation to areas outside British India.

Special Provision as to Backward Areas and Backward Tribes

10. No person who is entitled to vote in the election of a person to fill any of the seats to be filled by representatives of backward areas or backward tribes or is entitled to be included in the electoral rolls for any constituency formed for the purpose of filling any seat shall be included in the electoral rolls for any territorial constituency in the provinces other than any constituency specially formed for the election of persons to fill the seat Reserved for women.

Interpretations

11.(i) In this schedule in relation to Assam small town means notified area constituted under Chapter XII of Assam Municipal Act 1923

Local rate – assessed under Assam Local Rates Regulation 1879

Rent includes rent in kind or partly in kind or partly in cases

Head of a family or land – Joint holders if the proportion of the joint property, payment or assessment which corresponds with his share therein would be sufficient for him to be qualified if he held it separately

Clause 18

Federal Legislatures

To consist of His Majesty represented by Governor General and two Chambers-Council of State and House of Assembly referred to as the Federal Assembly.

Council of State – a permanent body – one third retiring every 3 years – consisting of 260 members – 104 representing Native States and 156 representing British India

Federal Assembly – tenure 5 years – consisting of 375 members – 125 representing Native States and 250 representing British India.

Provincial Legislatures

Two Chambers in Assam, Bengal, Bihar, Bombay, Madras and United Provinces

Single chamber in Central provinces and Berar, North Western Frontier Provinces,

Orissa and Sindh.

Where there were two Chambers, one was designated Legislative Council, other Legislative Assembly.

Single Chamber Legislature was designated Legislative Council.

ALLOCATION OF SEATS – BRITISH INDIA

1. COUNCIL OF STATES

Sl No	Province or Community	General Seats	Scheduled Caste	Sikh	Muslim	Women	Total
1	Assam	3	-	-	2	-	5
2	Bengal	8	1	-	10	1	20
3	Bihar	10	1	-	4	1	16
4	Bombay	10	1	-	4	1	16
5	Central Provincial and Berar	6	1	-	1	-	8
6	Madras	14	1	-	4	1	20
7	N.W.F. Province	1	-	-	4	-	5
8	Orissa	4	-	-	1	-	5
9	Punjab	3	-	4	8	1	16
10	Sindh	2	-	-	3	-	5
11	United Provinces	11	1	-	7	1	20
12	Ajmeer & Marwar	1	-	-	-	-	1
13	Anglo- Indian	-	-	-	-	-	1
14	British Baluchistan	-	-	-	1	-	1
15	Coorg	1	-	-	-	-	1
16	Delhi	1	-	-	-	-	1
17	European	-	-	-	-	-	7
18	Indian Christian	-	-	-	-	-	2
	Total	**75**	**6**	**4**	**49**	**6**	**150**

In this House, 150 members came from British India. Of them 75 were elected from General Seats allotted to eleven major provinces and four minor ones. Muslims had 49 seats in eleven provinces, and British Baluchistan had only one Muslim member. Sikhs had representation only in Punjab. Scheduled Classes remained very much unrepresented .Six members were chosen by the Governor General at his discretion.

ALLOCATION OF SEATS — BRITISH INDIA

2. FEDERAL/LEGISLATIVE ASSEMBLY

Sl no		General seats	General Reserved (SC)	Sikh	Muslim	Anglo-Indian	European	Indian Christian	Women	Commerce & Industry	Land-holders	Labour	Total Seats
1	Assam	4	1	–	3	–	1	1	–	–	–	1	10
2.	Bengal	10	3	–	17	1	1	1	1	3	1	2	37
3.	Bihar	16	2	–	9	–	1	1	1	–	1	1	30
4.	Bombay	13	2	–	6	1	1	1	2	3	1	2	30
5.	Central Province & Berer	9	2	–	3	–	–	–	1	–	1	1	15
6.	Madras	19	4	–	8	1	1	2	2	2	1	1	37
7.	N.W.F. Province	1	–	–	4	–	–	–	–	–	–	–	5
8.	Orissa	4	1	–	1	–	–	–	–	–	–	–	5
9.	Punjab	6	1	6	14	–	1	1	1	–	1	–	30
10.	Sindh	1	–	–	3	–	1	–	–	–	–	–	5
11.	United Provinces	19	3	–	12	1	1	1	1	–	1	1	37
12.	Ajmeer & Marwar	1	–	–	–	–	–	–	–	–	–	–	1
13.	British Baluchistan	–	–	–	1	–	–	–	–	–	–	–	1
14.	Coorg	1	–	–	–	–	–	–	–	–	–	–	1
15.	Delhi	1	–	–	1	–	–	–	–	–	–	–	2
16.	Non-Provincial or India as a whole	–	–	–	–	–	–	–	–	–	–	–	4
	Total	**105**	**19**	**6**	**82**	**4**	**8**	**8**	**9**	**8**	**7**	**10**	**250**

3

LOCAL BODIES AND ELECTIVE PRINCIPLES IN ASSAM

Having noted the evolution of a system of governance, we proceed to study the people's role therein. This involves tracing the emergence of a democratic principle, i.e., elective representation. It is now recognized that local institutions constitute the strength of free nations. A nation might establish a system of free government but without those institutions it could not have a spirit of liberty. Men like Lord Ripon were also convinced of the value of local government as a training ground for politicians. "They were gratified" when it appeared that local government experience found an important place in the first Legislative Councils and indeed "this result was in large measure guaranteed" by establishing municipalities as constituencies for the indirect elections to the provincial legislatures.[1]

Assam's acquaintance with such a system evolved over a long period of experimentation with democratic concepts like Panchayats, Municipalities and Local Boards. At the beginning these bodies were mere government appendages but gradually developed representative character with elective principles. Many of the later day legislators were men who had made their names in local government and were rooted in politics thereof. Between a quarter and a third of them came to state politics with a District Board or municipal background. It was no less interesting that seventy-five per cent of the Chief Ministers of Assam had their political background in the Guwahati Municipality. However, it was not the traditional landed proprietors but the new westernised professional classes, especially lawyers, who went to the provincial councils through local bodies. For example out of the 43 members elected by municipalities between 1862 and 1909, 40 were lawyers.[2]

During the second decade of the twentieth century, local leaders gave their allegiance to the District Committees "...and local government, instead of serving as a school of political education, became a mere annexe to the national political stadium". But there was no doubt that those institutions were the "Political Seminaries" for future legislators[3]. Though they were not directly elected democratically for a long time, their choice was the precursor of electoral system for local government and legislature. Therefore, a glimpse into the process will help us understand the evolution and development of parliamentary politics in Assam. We begin with the grassroot level organisations, the Panchayat, and discuss mainly the electoral aspects of the different local bodies.

Section I
ELECTED PANCHAYAT SYSTEM

According to Dr. V. Venkata Rao who pioneered the study of Local-Self Government in Assam, the beginning of the system could be traced to the principle of local taxation for local purposes. This was embodied in the Bengal Regulations of 1813 which were applicable to Bengal only. Following the treaty of Yandabo, Assam became a part of that Presidency but the regulations were not operated in this part. The Village Chowkidari system was in force in the districts of Cachar, Goalpara and Sylhet. These territories became part of Assam after the creation of a Chief Commissioner's Province, in 1874. Immediately before the reorganization attempts at improving the Village Panchayats were made but were vetoed by the Governor General on the ground that the time had not arrived for the creation of the machinery for the administration of villages. In the Brahmaputra Valley, other than Goalpara, no village system was recognised by the British Government. Between 1826 and 1856, various steps were taken to develop Panchayats in Bengal. The Act of 1856 authorised the Government to extend the system to any bazar, town and suburb with a Police Station. But the Act was not extended to any part of that valley. Under the Village Chowkidari Act of 1870, a District Magistrate was allowed to "appoint" a Panchayat in any village consisting of more than sixty houses. The Act also permitted the continuation of the government – appointed Gaoburhas in the Brahmaputra Valley except in Goalpara and the Chowkidari Panchayats in that district as well as the Surma Valley districts of Sylhet and Cachar. But in appointing a Panchayat, "... wishes of the residents must be consulted". A Panchayat might be formed also on petitions from villagers.

During the next forty years, until the subject was taken up by the Royal Commission on Decentralization, 1907, nothing meaningful was done in Assam in this respect. The Commission had concluded that

> ... the scant success of the efforts hitherto made to introduce the system of self-government was largely due to the fact that it was not built from the bottom.
>
> *Therefore,*
>
> ... the foundation of any stable edifice which shall associate the people with the administration must be the village.

In 1912, Assam was reconstituted into a Chief Commissionerate after its stint as Eastern Bengal and Assam. During that period "the rural population had indirectly elected representation in all local bodies which were committees appointed by Government "but in a perverted manner". The government – appointed village headmen called Gaoburhas elected village representatives to local bodies "despite increasing public protests".[4] Chief Commissioner Sir Archdale Earle was in agreement with the Decentralization Commission on various aspects of its recommendations but differed on the status of Panchayats. He would not accept the view that those bodies should be under the control of Deputy Commissioners. He suggested that only when a Panchayat performed the duties relating to village police, civil and criminal justice and matters not concerned with local bodies, the Deputy Commissioner concerned should head it. But when such a body dealt with subjects delegated to it by a Local Board, it should be under the control of the Board.

The Assam Local Self-Government Act of 1915 established Village Panchayats. But most of the members of the village authorities were nominated. The Act did not "educate the ordinary villager in the principle of Local Self-Government and that was one of the causes of its failure". The Assam Rural Self-Government Act of 1926 provided, for the first time, that each village should have a village authority consisting of nine members, all of whom could be elected by adult franchise. The voters' qualifications were, residence within the panchayat area, possession of property and payment of tax. Thus adult franchise was obviously extremely limited because a few persons possessed those qualifications. The Act of 1915 had provided for nomination as well as election of panchayat presidents. In 1918, there were 80 Village Panchayats and sixty of these had non-official elected heads. Others were nominated non-officials. By 1926 all the Presidents were non-officials. Out of 228 such incumbents, 145 were elected by the members and 83 non-officials were nominated by the Deputy Commissioner.

The Act of 1926 made it statutory for the panchayat presidents to be elected by the members themselves. The object of the Act, according to Dr.Rao, "was to provide a machinery so that villages might undertake the management of their own affairs and thereby develop a capacity for self-helf".[5] Thus the Act was Assam's earliest acquaintance with elective principle. Those provisions of law may be called the " inspirations" for encouraging popular demand for election. However, with further development of local bodies "... the village panchayat is out of the picture; its members evidently stay in the villages...".[6]

But the Act completed the introduction of Panchayat System in Assam. The term of office of a Panchayat Committee was three years under the Acts of 1871, 1915, 1926 and 1948. Further development in this regard took place only after independence of India and we shall not here enter into that stage of Panchayati Raj in the country.

Section II
ELECTED MUNICIPAL SYSTEM

The earliest attempts at introducing municipal government were made in the Presidency towns of Calcutta, Madras and Bombay through the Acts of 1840, 1841 and 1845 respectively. This was done mainly for assessment and collection of taxes, maintenance of sanitation and repairing of roads etc. in those towns. The expenditure was met from the money raised by assessment on inhabitants; in other words local taxation for local purposes was introduced. This was done through representatives in the form of Justices of the Peace who were employees of the East India Company and the British residents of those towns. But as they did not take much interest in the work, the Chief Magistrates therein gradually took over the responsibility.

The preceding narration would show that there was nothing like popular participation and so the question of their representation did not arise. Series of other Acts were passed between 1840 and 1858 for better assessment and collection of local rates as well as conservancy in these towns which were gradually transformed into Corporations. Government appointed the Municipal Commissioners. Elective principles were introduced during the later half of the nineteenth century. Half the number of Commissioners was elected by the rate payers and the rest represented various interests like trade and commerce. The Chairman of a Corporation was its Chief Executive and highly paid Government servant. By 1918, the three Presidency towns had approximately a uniform system of government. These bodies were given limited franchise and electorate. A strong system of financial and administrative management was ensured under complete government control.[7]

The over-all situation in the newly acquired British dominion in Assam was succinctly pictured by a scholar who is quoted below at length.[8]

> *The period from 1826 to 1873 was a period of transition for Assam's pre-capitalist economy into its colonial phase. British capital penetrated the economy and started building an infrastructure to sustain the exotic capitalistic set-up. Collaborating traders, bankers, lawyers and clerks from other Indian provinces came as camp-followers ...The economy was monetised. ...The closed society was exposed to immigration of labour, new skills... Marwari trader-cum-money lenders monopolized the internal trade as agents of the British trading houses of Calcutta, who in turn worked for their metropolitan counterparts in London. Bengali clerks, doctors and lawyers, with the advantage of their early initiation to English education and the British Indian administrative system, monopolized government jobs and professions.*

However, these people had no say in policy or decision making. Further,

> *... the new-born ricketty Assamese intelligentsia of the period found itself to be an insignificant minority in the urban sector. Towns of Assam were still permanent camps of government servants and traders or were just glorified villages where non-indigenous elements constituted the over-whelmingly dominant section.*

He goes on to say,

> *This situation of a complete lack of urbanisation, alongside of the pre-capitalist production relations, was not, and could not be rapidly altered by the new set-up. Super-imposed as it was on a semi-tribal, semi-feudal society of petty producers, the new plantation economy – subjugated to foreign capital and linked with immigrant usury and merchant capital – could not bring in a radical transformation within the local society itself.*

Under these circumstances, the extent of urbanization "...was practically nil. The incipient Assamese middle class that was coming up was extremely small, week and unconsolidated as a class".

Such a society and the new plantation economy created by Europeans as owners of hundreds of squire miles of "inaccessible sprawling tracts," subsequently converted into hundreds of tea gardens, had little meeting grounds. The European tea planters and land holders, being interested in their own economic prosperity only were "keen" on the development of their estates through better communication and diversion of public funds towards that end. Being the "chief body" of non-officials, they were asked by

Government to participate in the local committees which were set up for the purpose. Those committees had neither any representative character nor popular participation in any form for a long time.

In the non-Presidency towns the first attempts were made at introducing municipal government under the Bengal Act of 1842. It provided that inhabitants of any town in the province except Calcutta could establish a Municipal Board. But that required the consent of two thirds of the householders of a town. Further it provided for levy of direct taxes. It was not applied to any place in Assam. The Act was replaced by another in 1850 which was applicable to the whole of British India. A great significance of this legislation was the empowerment of provincial governments to implement it after satisfying themselves that the inhabitants of a town demanded a municipality. In other words, the provision was permissive and not a compulsive one. Further, a town in which a municipality was established would have a Committee consisting of a Magistrate and such a number of Commissioners as determined by the Governor-in-Council. The Board would have the power to levy and collect any tax, the Commissioners being personally responsible for utilisation of funds. The act was forwarded to the Commissioner of Assam with the following observation:

> *...The President in Council is desirous of exercising extreme caution in giving effect to the provisions of law. The law cannot be put into force without the consent of the local government and the President-in-Council trusts that the consent will never be given except upon the fullest and careful inquiry which it may be possible to make. Local officers with best intentions may frequently be more zealous than prudent. Their recommendation for the introduction of the Act should always therefore be received with caution and should not be acted upon until the statements upon which their recommendations are founded shall have been carefully and minutely scrutinised.*

The First Municipality

On petition from 113 of the 3000 inhabitants of "Guahatee" dated 11 June 1852, the first Statutory Municipal Board was established there on 1 January 1853 with only three nominated European members as election was expressly prohibited. In October 1853, fifty inhabitants of the town submitted a petition to the Government pleading that 80 of the earlier applicants had no social status and therefore the Board should be abolished. Though the petition was rejected, no other municipality was established in Assam under this Act. But it paved the way to establishment of a large number of such bodies in the non-Presidency towns. But as the Commissioners were mostly nominated, there was hardly any democratic elements and progress in the development of Local Self-Government in the Assam part of Bengal Presidency. However, the proceedings of the Gauhati Municipal Board recorded "election" held from 8th to 13th March 1858. Two persons secured equal number of votes and both were appointed Commissioners. The records of subsequent years did not refer to any election. Perhaps " some kind of informal election was adopted to elicit public opinion about the popularity of the candidates."[9] The Board's main function was the determination of persons and properties to be taxed for raising money.

The next step towards establishment and development of municipalities was the District Municipal Improvement Act of 1864. It empowered the Lt. Governor of Bengal to introduce the Act according to his discretion in any town, to determine the jurisdiction of a Board to appoint Chairman and Vice-Chairman, to nominate Commissioners and to determine the tax to be levied on houses and landed properties. The amount so collected had to be spent for maintenance of police force and improvement of sanitation. The Government of India requested the Assam Commissioner to name places wherein the Act could be implemented. At the same time they advised that this should be done gradually and in more populous towns excluding agricultural villages.

There followed a long debate on the question.[10] Hopkinson, Commissioner of Assam, opposed the very idea pleading that social condition here was not conducive to the implementation of the Act. According to him, even Gauhati was nothing more than a permanent camp of government officials whose butlers and followers constituted the town's people and so the Act should not be implemented there. But the Government of Bengal argued that

> *As a matter of policy it is very desirable to encourage in the residents of towns, a habit of Local Self-Government...and of relying upon their own exertions and resources instead of looking to the Government...*

Even admitting that the local condition was not sufficiently advanced the Government held that such an argument could not apply to places which had for quite some time been civil and military stations, with a sizeable mercantile community, both natives and Europeans, and did not differ from such places in Bengal. "Least of all does it apply to a town in which a Municipality under the Act of 1850 has existed for many years and still exists". It was therefore a question whether the more complex and efficient system embodied in the Act of 1864 should replace the Act of 1850 in Guwahati. Further, they claimed that the "ancient police system was strictly municipal and that people were capable of dealing with their own affairs and municipal feeling was deeply rooted in them"

Hopkinson refused to accept the arguments in favour of extension of the Act to Assam. Denying the existence of any municipal concept in ancient Assam, he held that "... no Assamese has the faintest tradition" of such a policy; therefore the applicability of such institutions to Assam should not be made from analogy but on "its own merit". Further, he said, "I humbly think, such will not be found". According to him there were no places in Assam rising to the considerations of towns. For example,

> *...The resources of Tezpur were found to be insufficient lately to provide a dinner for the officer commanding the station ... its bazar would not furnish fish or fowl or butcher's meat of any kind.*

Even in Gauhati,

> *... there is not a carpenter's shop, not a boat builder, nor a mason, nor a tanner, nor a shoe maker. The bulk of the population of Gauhati are out in the fields cutting and bringing in their rice.*

Despite his opposition, however, Gauhati was recognised as a Municipality in 1865 under the said Act. It was during Lord Mayo's Governor Generalship from 1869-1872 that some real progress was made in the direction of Self-Government. His resolution of 1870 dealing with decentralisation of finances referred to the necessity of further steps to bring local interests and supervision to bear on the management of funds devoted to education, sanitation and public works. By that time "confusing systems of Municipal Government with several independent Statutes" were there. In 1871 a Bill was proposed for consolidating the existing laws. It provided for classification of Municipalities into Class I and Class II, appointment of Commissioners, imposition of Municipal taxes, provision for elementary education and formulation of budget. The Bill was vetoed by the Governor General-in-Council. However, some amendments were made in the existing laws as follows[11]

i) Election of some Municipal Commissioners. But it must be noted that such election was extremely limited and based on property and tax qualifications.
ii) Concentration of real power in the hands of Chairmen who were also Magistrates.
iii) Authorisation of Vice-Chairmen to exercise the powers of the Chairmen during the latter's absence. This practically made the former the "real heads" of all Municipalities except those at the headquarters of the Magistrates.
iv) Delegation of all or any of the Chairmen's powers to the Vice-Chairmen.

In 1872 another attempt was made to bring all the existing laws under a single Act. It provided as follows.

1. Creation of three classes of municipalities – Class I, Class II and Class III, based on annual tax rates on building. All bigger towns would be under the first two classes while the little rural towns would come under the third.
2. Election or nomination of Commissioners, the strength of a Board being ten members of whom 7 would be elected and 3 nominated.
3. Appointment of Ward Committees for election of Commissioners.
4. Official Chairmen but elected Vice-Chairmen.

The Bill took four years for enactment in the form of Bengal Municipal Act of 1876 which was adopted in Assam in 1878. Under this Act, the urban areas were divided in to four classes. Those were

1. Class I – Gauhati.
2. Class 2 – Dhubri, Dibrugarh, Goalpara and Sylhet.
3. Station Committees-Habiganj, Sibsagar, Silchar and Shillong.
4. Unions – Balaganj, Golaghat, Jorhat and Sunamganj.

Balaganj, Habiganj, Silchar, Sunamganj and Sylhet were in the Surma Valley and others in the Brahmaputra Valley.

The Ripon Reforms

Lord Ripon, Governor General of India from 1880 to1884, called the "father of Local Self-Government" in India, "provided the starting point of a new outlook" in this regard in the form of Government of India Resolutions of 1881 and 1882. The salient features of the proposed reforms are enumerated here.[12]

1. "It would be hopeless to expect any real development of self-government if the local bodies were subject to check or interference in matters of detail". So Ripon urged "the fullest liberty" to the local authorities. He believed that the previous attempts "were nullified" by official interference.
2. As regards changes and expansion of Local Self-Government,
   It is not primarily with a view to improvement in administration that this measure is put forward and supported. It is chiefly desirable as an instrument of political and popular education. In the beginning there will doubtless be many failures calculated to discourage exaggerated hopes and even in some cases to cast apparent discredit upon the practice of self-government itself.
3. As the task of administration was "... yearly becoming more onerous" with the country's progress, "...it becomes imperatively necessary to look round for some means of relief; and the only reasonable plan open to the Government is to induce the people themselves to undertake ... the management of their own affairs".
   He believed that there was gradually growing all over the country an intelligent class of public-spirited men and "it was not only bad policy but sheer wastage of power to fail to utilise them".
4. Authorities should control Local Self-Government from "without" and not from within and not dictate anything.
5. Members of local bodies should be elected if there was demand from the people and wherever possible. The system of election should be left to the provincial government to encourage men of character to take up municipal responsibility, titles like Rai Bahadur and Khan Bahadur should be conferred on selected persons.
6. Election should be extended to small Municipalities in some form or other.
7. The Municipal Commissioners were permitted to elect their Chairmen.
8. The bodies should not consist of Government employees. Non-officials should constitute one-half to two thirds of the total membership of a local body.
9. District or Sub-divisional Officers need not be the Chairmen of those bodies because so long as they remained the Chairmen, there would be little chance for the non-official members to gain political experience. Those officers "would occupy a dignified position if they remained out side the Board". Therefore he suggested non-official Chairmenship.
10. Municipal area should be divided indo wards for the purpose of election of Commissioners thus extending the principle to the lowest levels of residents.

The Bengal Municipal Act of 1884, which had been the result of Ripon's efforts, was adopted by the Assam Government in 1887. We have already referred to the Act of 1876. Thus this province had two separate sets of municipalities, one set each under the Acts since 1887. The Act of 1876 was retained as it provided for Station Committees and Union Committees and the Government of Assam wanted to retain the Committees wherever these existed. Both remained in operation till 1923 and "did not differ from each other in essential principles". Under the Acts, normally Commissioners were nominated but with special permission of Government, "could also be elected." Under the first Act the District Magistrate or the Sub-Divisional Officer was "ordinarily" to be the Chairman, though any other person was also held eligible for such appointment. "Despite the accent of Ripon Reforms on an elected Chairman," the second Act allowed the Commissioners to elect their

Chairman or the Municipal Board to request the Government to appoint him.

The First Municipality with Elected Commissioners

In 1882, the rate payers of Sylhet applied for the introduction of election in the town. The Chief Commissioner "...had great pleasure in directing that all the Commissioners to be appointed to that Municipality shall henceforth be elected". Thus Sylhet had the "Unique distinction of being the first municipal board" to consist of only elected Commissioners. The Chief Commissioner also advised the Deputy Commissioners to consider extension of the elective principle to other municipalities.

By that time persistent demand for reforms, particularly election of Chairmen and reduction of tea planters' representation in proportion to their share of revenue went on. A lengthy debate which followed in official circles was characterised by divergent views on the elective principle.[13] Ripon favoured election in some form or other in "towns of any considerable size" and its extension more cautiously and gradually to smaller municipalities. Sir Charles Elliot, Chief Commissioner between 1881 and 1885 was "extremely anxious" to introduce the elective system in the local authorities not only because of the Government's decision but because "the principles set forth in the resolutions of His Excellency-in-Council thoroughly commended themselves to his judgement as sound and wise."

Some of the officers, however, opposed Ripon reform, Local Self -Government as well as election on the characteristic plea that people were not sufficiently advanced to understand the significance of election. Others favoured either direct or indirect election. The Commissioner of Assam Valley, William E. Edward for example, observed in 1882 that the soil of the Brahmaputra Valley was not " fertile enough for Local government institutions to flourish" because the Assamese were devoid of "those business like habits which are so needful to make a man a useful member of any committee to which he may be appointed."

Further,

> *We do not wish to give the people power to elect men who are not respectable or who if respectable are not educated or who, if both respectable or educated, have no capacity for business. If then, we wish to prevent electors form electing unfit candidates for the Boards, we must have a system for election subject to Government approval or the Government selecting the candidate and the people electing what the District officer selects. This will be little or no advance upon the present system by which the Deputy Commissioner nominates and the Government appoints.*

Again, according to him

> *Educated Assamese gentleman of active business like habits are not (so) numerous as to allow the people a very large field for selection. They may be counted on fingers in any district; and it is scarcely worthwhile to introduce the elective system into any district which affords little or no opportunity for the people's elective propensities supposing they have got any.*[13]

Ward was also opposed to election of any kind, direct or indirect as well as election or appointment of a non-official Chairman.

The Chief Commissioner favoured experimentation and asked the Commissioner to follow suit in Sibsagar "because the people of Sibsagar showed greater interest in this matter" as evident from the resolutions adopted in their public meetings.In one of their resolutions, they suggested that the authorities should invite application for membership of the Boards to be decided by a Committee.It should be chaired by the Deputy Commissioner with four Indian members. The Committee would select and recommend them to the electorate for selection or election. The proposals of those meetings were circulated to all the Deputy Commissioners in the Assam Valley for considering the introduction of election. The Deputy Commissioner, Sibsagar recommended the proposal. But as that Town Committee was "not a representative body", the officer was instructed by Government to "call upon the principal communities to elect their representatives. Thus came into existence communal representation in Sibsagar Town Committee"[14]

Between 1882 and 1900, six Municipalities were allowed to elect their Commissioners. By 1915 the system was extended to eleven of the nineteen Boards and by 1919, it was in force in all, except Shillong. The slow progress of elective system can be guessed from the fact that in 1885, there were 59 elected Commissioners out of 125. In 1901, 53 out of 144 Commissioners were elected. Even in 1913, ten out of nineteen Municipal Boards had no elected members. In both the years Europeans constituted one-fifth of the total strength. As to having elected Chairmen, despite such permission in several Municipalities,

> *... caution was exercised, under pressure, by the Municipal politicians themselves. They would rather forego the honour than offend their ambitious district officers who were the real makers of Rai Sahabs and Rai Bahadurs.*[15]

Except Sylhet since 1887, "Everywhere else, for about three decades, since the Ripon Reforms, the District Magistrates or the Sub-Divisional Officers continued to retain Chairmanship at the ostensible request of the Boards themselves".[16] This was perhaps due to indifference of the people entitled to participate in the functions of the Boards.

In this connection, we may note that in 1853, the Europeans constituted 100 per cent of all local authorities. In 1885 their strength came down to 20 per cent. As a consequence of the reduction of numbers of Europeans and officials, their influence over the Boards disappeared. Also there was a rapid Indianisation. Indians formed only twenty per cent of the total strength in 1885 but by 1940, 277 out of 293 Commissioners or more than 90 per cent were Indian. In 1905, the Government decided to introduce election in the Station Committees also with the exception of Shillong even though such a Committee existed there since 1880. It was decided by the Chief Commissioner that in Shillong, candidates informally elected by rate payers would be formally appointed Commissioners subject to Government approval.[17]

In 1893, the question of election in the Shillong Station Committee was mooted. But the Chief Commissioner, William E. Ward opposed it. He said,

> *The population (Shillong) is composed of entirely distinct sets of people-sets whose interests and feelings are so very different that the members of one of the sets could hardly be expected to accept as their representative a member of another set. There are European*

Civil Officers, Khasis, the Bengali Sylhet clerks, Muhammadans ... and a sparkling of Assemese. The only chance of our getting a Municipality to work smoothly is to get upon the Board at least one representative of each leading sect while recognizing the European official character of the station by making European influence dominant. Every such consideration points out to the necessity of filling the Municipal Board by nomination rather than by trusting to the hazards of an election. And in a place so purely official, nomination is not felt even by the theoretical radicals to involve an invasion of popular rights. I would not therefore pursue the question of election further because we are not likely to get decent Commissioners by an elective system.[18]

The arguments were obviously untenable as all towns had composite populations. Clearly, therefore, only maintenance of European domination inspired such opposition.

The debate was concluded only in 1920 when the Government decided to introduce election in the town. But there was a problem. Under the matriarchal system of the Khasis, house property almost invariably stood in the name of women who constituted about fifty per cent of the rate payers who were eligible to vote. But under the Bengal Municipal Act of 1884 women were denied the right to vote. The application of that rule would naturally deprive a majority of Khasis of the right to elect their representatives. So the rule was amended to include women in the electoral rolls. Thus the Khasi women were the first to get the right to franchise. However less than ten per cent of the rate payers had the right to vote due to the prescribed high property qualification.

Elected Chairmen and Indianisation

Right upto 1912 Municipalities in Assam except in Sylhet had ex-officio European Chairmen. Parasuram Khound, an Assamese honorary magistrate was the first non-official Indian to be elected Chairman of the Dibrugarh Municipality on 11 April 1912. Thus a beginning was made in Assam for Indianisation of this office. However, "European pressure" compelled Khound to resign within a month. Almost after a year on 15 February 1913, Radhanath Changkakati became the second non-official Indian to be elected Chairman of the same Municipality. The Silchar Municipality similarly elected another non-official Indian in 1913.[19]

Curiously enough, way back in 1888, Gauhati was allowed to elect Chairman but it had "refused so long to avail itself" of the opportunity. Only on 26 March 1913 Manik Chandra Barooah became non-official elected Chairman of that Municipality. Bhubhan Ram Das, an Ex-Member of the Eastern Bengal and Assam Legislative Council succeeded him in 1915. Mon Mohan Lahiri, a Bengali lawyer and "small capitalist" became Chairman in the like manner in Tezpur Municipality on 4 December 1916. By 1918, thirteen Municipal Boards had non-official elected Chairmen. The Assam Municipal Act of 1923 completely did away with official appointment to the post. Another significant development was extension of the "provisions for separate electorates" in Municipal elections though the Chief Commissioner had earlier opposed it and observed in connection with the Local Boards, "Taking the province as a whole I am inclined to think that the need for communal representation is not urgent and it would be good to avoid it if possible."[20]

In addition to communal representation for Muslims which was obviously in terms of the Morley-Minto Reforms, the electorate was catergorised into four other classes, namely, planters, headquarter residents, mercantile and rural members, the representatives being elected by the respective groups. By 1921 the right to vote was extended to all those who were voters for election of members of the Assam Legislative Council and resident in the circle concerned for twelve months preceding the elections. In other words, the electoral rolls of the Council were adopted for Local Government elections. Between 1923 and 1926 further modifications were made in the electoral rolls in general. But the most important and progressive step was the removal of gender disqualification entitling women to vote. The second reformed Legislative Council of Assam met on 24 March 1924. Sadananda Dowerah of Dibrugarh, an Independent member and supporter of the Swarajya Party, moved a resolution on 25 March recommending franchise for women and their rights to contest elections. The official block opposed the move. But with the support of others including Muslim members, the resolution was adopted. Sex disqualification was abolished by the Government Notification of 24 November 1924. However, women were not allowed to contest elections till 1928. The Act also made the following provisions.[21]

1. All Municipal Boards were allowed to elect one of their own Commissioners a Chairman except in case of Shillong.
2. In case a Board was not willing to elect a Chairman, it might request the Government to appoint a non-official. But the Vice-Chairman had to be elected by the Commissioners. In 1924 except Shillong, all the Chairmen were elected non-officials.

The Act of 1923 was amended in 1931 and 1932. The first one authorised the Government to nominate a Chairman during a vacancy for a part of the tenure on a casual vacancy. The second amendment authorized the Commissioner of Division to do so, the ostensible purpose in both cases being avoidance of administrative inconvenience.

Section III
CONSTITUTIONAL STRUCTURE OF A MUNICIPALITY

The Act of 1850 had not specified either the number of Commissioners or the proportion of official to non-official members. The Municipal Improvement Act of 1864 which repealed the Act of 1850, prescribed the minimum strength of a Board to be seven members in addition to three ex-officio, without, however, fixing the number of nominated non-officials, thus clearly keeping the field open for Government's domination. The District Magistrate would be the Chairman of a Board. The District Towns Act 1868, applicable to small towns, laid down that one third of the total strength would be officials, the others might be official and ex-officio members, the minimum number of them being five. It also provided for appointment of Ward Committees, each consisting of three persons who might be outsiders. In the Goalpara Town Committee formed under that provision, the ex-officio members were Treasury Officer, Superintendent of Police and Chief Medical Officer and seven others nominated by the District Magistrate.

The Bengal Municipal Act of 1876 which replaced the existing rules, reduced the categories of Municipalities to first and second classes only. The strength of officials was cut down from one third to one fourth. The minimum strength of a first class Board was fixed at seven and the maximum at thirty. A second class municipality would have a minimum of four and a maximum of twenty Commissioners. Those other than ex-officio might be elected or nominated partly or wholly. The Ward Committees were not required to consist of Commissioners meaning thereby that these were somewhat extra-constitutional Committees. The Bengal Municipal Act of 1884, adopted in Assam in 1887, brought about radical changes in the composition of Municipal Boards as enumerated below.

1. It completely eliminated the official elements from the Boards but resumed the right to appoint supernumerary members.
2. The minimum number of Commissioners was raised from 7 to 12, the maximum remaining unchanged.
3. Two thirds of the total number of Commissioners had to be elected and one third nominated. Thus the elective principle, now made preponderant, was the most significant provision of the Act. It was a great leap forward for the elective principle in the Boards. Of the nominated members, not more than one fourth could be officers thus lowering down the official influences.
4. In case of failure of election of the prescribed number of Commissioners the Government might nominate members to fill up the vacancies.

The Royal Commission on Decentralization

The Royal Commission on Decentralization was formed in 1907 under the Chairmanship of Hobhouse, to look into, among other questions, the one of decentralization of local bodies. Its recommendations, directly related to election, nomination and appointment of Chairmen, Vice-Chairmen and Commissioners, i.e. composition of the Municipalities, are given below.[22]

1. A majority of members should be elected.
2. Chairman of a Board would ordinarily be a non-official.
3. An officer should not chair more than one Municipal Board.
4. Experts Committees on various matters relating to the functions of Municipalities could be appointed even though they might not be Commissioners.
5. Contested election should be decided by a Civil Court of Law.

By the time of submission of the Commission's recommendations, the Government of Assam realised that existence of two types of Municipalities as already mentioned was "administratively inconvenient". Moreover, these Acts were "obselete and incomplete" in many respects. They decided to remedy the deficiencies. Therefore, though the Government accepted the Commission's recommendations except the last one, they adopted a resolution in 1914 proposing that,

1. Small towns should be governed by a separate Act.
2. Charimen and Vice-Chairmen of the Town Committees would be appointed by Government in the first instance but later these office bearers and Commissioners would be elected. Under the Bengal Municipal Act of 1884, Section 10, it was necessary for a municipal area to have a population of 3000 and a density of 1000 per square mile. Further, three fourths of the adult population were to be non-agriculturists. Though

these rules were generally taken into consideration while establishing municipalities, the Government of Assam found these to be obstacles in some cases. Similar restrictions were not imposed in other provinces. Therefore the authorities felt the necessity of greater discretion in this regard. They agreed to follow the general principle of election of non-official Chairmen and a substantial majority of Commissioners, but wanted the power to appoint these incumbents.

All these suggestions were incorporated in the Assam Municipal Act of 1923, which also brought about other under-noted important changes.

1. The minimum strength of a Board was raised to ten, the maximum remaining as before.
2. The number of Commissioners was based on population of a municipal area.
3. No official but supernumerary members could be appointed. They were allowed to participate in the proceedings but not to vote.
4. Number of nominated members was reduced from one third to one fifth of the total strength. The Government of course continued to exercise control over the Boards through its nominees as well as its power of audit and inspection. In course of the Non-Co-operation Movement the Government's authority was not much slackened. In one Municipality all non-official members resigned together due to disagreement with the Chairman on the question of Gandhi's visit to that town.

Even 14 years later in 1937, in the Assam Legislative Assembly constituted under the Government of India Act 1935, two attempts were made by non-official elected members in both houses at abolishing nomination. Hem Chandra Datta, member of the Legislative Council moved the Assam Municipal (Amendment) Bill seeking to do away with the system and making election of Commissioners by rate payers statutory. Of the ten elected Hindu Members nine voted for the amendment. But all the six Muslims en bloc and two nominated Hindus voted against the motion. Rajendranath Barua sought to refer it to a Select Committee of the Assembly. Ninetythree out of one hundred five members attended the Session. As expected, after introduction of separate electorate the voting was of course on communal line and the planters sided with the Government.[23]

Franchise

The word franchise originally meant a privilege, which every citizen could not have. It was, therefore, natural that to begin with, it would be limited to the upper stratum of the society. Till 1882, there was no election in local bodies and so there was no question of voting. As we noted earlier, Indians had no right to vote and franchise was given only to European tea planters in all the tea districts of the province and they elected their own representatives. The qualifications for franchise varied from time to time and place to place. This on occasions created anomalous situations as the variations made one person eligible to vote in one place and made him ineligible in another. Prior to 1882 there was nothing like right to vote in local bodies. However, the same year, Sir Charles Elliot, Chief Commissioner of Assam, enforced the following set of common criteria for franchise.[24] Only male adults with the following qualifications were allowed to vote.

1. Payment of Municipal Tax varying between rupee one and a half and rupees three.
2. Receipt of a monthly salary or a monthly pension of Rs.20 to 50.

3. Residence in a municipal area for twelve months preceding an election.
4. Pleaders.
5. Bachelor Degree holders.
6. Jurors or Assessors.

Uniformity of franchise qualifications throughout the province was made statutory by the Bengal Municipal Act of 1884 prescribing the following criteria which of course limited the right to adult males as before.

1. Persons residing in a particular municipal area for twelve months precedings an election and paying a tax of Rs.3 per annum.
2. Income tax payers.
3. Graduates and licentiates.
4. Pleaders.
5. Muktears in receipt of a monthly salary of Rs.50.

The Municipal Act of 1923 modified the franchise qualifications by

1. removing sex – distinction for voters.
2. introducing uniform tax payment amounting to Rs.2 per annum.
3. making managers of companies and occupants of building or lands with a monthly rental value of Rs.50 or more eligible to vote.

However property qualifications still remained hindrances to adult franchise as late as 1963. Thus this right was a privilege of an infinitesimal section of residents.

The Tenure of a Municipal Board

Under the Bengal Municipal Acts of 1850, 1864 and 1868, the tenure of a Board was one year. The Bengal Municipal Act of 1876 extended it to three years making the Boards permanent bodies. Th retirement rule was not applicable to supernumerary members. In 1893 the three-year term without requiring annual retirement was enforced and it continued till 1950. The Act of 1857 laid down a four-year term and empowered the Government to extend it by two years, not more than one year at a time. Later the Government postponed election by unlimited periods. The tenure of a Board began with the first meeting of an elected body and ended for all Commissioners at the same time.

Voting by secret Ballot

Till 1915, no electoral roll was published. Obviously the system of voting by secret ballot had to take a long time to evolve. After the introduction of elective principle in local bodies as detailed earlier, the question of voting through ballot papers arose. To begin with, open ballot papers were used. In 1880, for instance, in municipal areas, each voter was given a ballot paper containing the names of candidates. He mentioned the name of the candidate of his choice therein, signed the papers and submitted these to the Chairman before a fixed date. He would then declare the results. In some cases, electors were asked to go to the municipal office to record their votes in the ballot papers there. It was in 1924 that for the first time, the Government of Assam prescribed a set of rules for voting by secret ballot. A Municipal Board would appoint one of its

Commissioners as Presiding Officer. A Committee of five Commissioners would conduct elections in a Ward. A voter put a cross mark against the candidates of his choice on the ballot paper, Folded it and put it in a ballot box thus completing voting by secret ballot.

The foregoing discussion must have shown that development of Municipalities and progress towards democratization and Indianisation with the introduction of elective principle took nearly 75 years in Assam and passed through the following stages.

1. The era of official nomination and Local Committees.
2. Nomination and election of officials only as Commissioners.
3. Only election of non-official Commissioners.
4. Nomination of Chairmen.
5. Partly election and partly nomination of Chairmen.
6. Only election of Chairmen by Commissioners.
7. Nomination of Vice-Chairmen.
8. Election of Vice-Chairmen or nomination.
9. Only election of Vice-Chairmen.
10. Only rate payers' franchise.
11. Adult franchise.
12. Franchise for women.
13. Women's right to contest election.
14. Separate electorate for Muslims and Class interests.
15. Indianisation of Municipalities.

The introduction of elective principle was almost simultaneous with the process of Indianisation. The importance of Municipalities and Local Boards in the composition of the provincial legislatures will be revealed subsequently.

Section IV
ELECTED LOCAL BOARD SYSTEM

The Committee System

"Rudimentary beginnings of Local Boards had the same history" as those of Municipalities. In 1858 there were "ferry funds" in almost every district for construction of roads and bridges. Small District Committees consisting of nominated official and non-official members administered the funds. Europeans were in majority in the Bodies except in Goalpara and Kamrup wherein tea interests were minimal. In 1860 the net proceeds of those funds were merged into an Amalgamated District Road Fund. There were also other district level authorities for looking after various aspects of welfare such as Improvement Committee, School Committee and Charitable Dispensary Committee etc. By the time Assam was constituted into a Chief Commissionership, the districts were "littered with" a number of other funds such as Reserve Fund, Road Fund, Primary School Fund and Miscellaneous Improvement Fund etc, administered by Committees. The District Committees consisted of not less than six members. There were also Branch Committees at Sub-Divisional levels with three members each, both categories being nominated by the Chief Commissioner on the recommendation of Deputy Commissioners. Their functions were the preparation of Budget and allotment of funds.[25]

In 1875 the Deputy Accountant General pointed out the administrative inconvenience caused by the existence of so many funds, accounts and committees in one and the same place and suggested the formation of a single fund for all the purposes. The Chief Commissioner accepted the suggestion and a District Improvement Fund was constituted with four separate subordinate funds. Further, the constitutional structures of the Committees also varied from place to place and so confusion of a multiple of committees and funds still remained. The same year the Chief Commissioner tried to introduce local taxation for local purposes but the Bengal Government rejected his suggestion. The planter community was also dissatisfied. Therefore they recommended only one committee performing all the local functions. Despite protests against the proposal all committees were abolished and replaced by only one Committee in each of the eight plains districts under the provisions of Local Rates Regulations of 1879. Thus for the first time Local rates for Local purposes were levied. Members of the Committees were as before, appointed by the Chief Commissioner on the recommendation of Deputy Commissioners. Atleast one third of them was to be resident non-officials.

Though the Regulations were introduced in all the plains districts, conditions differed from place to place and that was the reason for success of the working of the rules in some and failure in other districts. Sylhet was "unique in many respects. It was a district with small proprietors, permanently settled, thickly populated, education tolerably general and acquaintance with public law greater". Further, the people were "well aware of their rights and were fond of asserting these by joint action, ... So the Committees in the district functioned successfully". In Cachar the situation was equally favourable as inspite of their deficiencies, the tea planting community "constituted nearly the whole of the intelligentia of the district" and dominated the committees. Of the other six districts only Jorhat and Sibsagar, the Centers of Ahom administration, contained an intelligent and fairly well educated class which evinced interests in working of Local Boards. The social and economic conditions in the remaining districts were unfavourable for development of Local Self-Government. Under these unequal and unfavourable circumstances, therefore, those District Committees did not work "satisfactorily". These were dominated by Europeans and became the instruments through which their interests only were served and so the Indian members lost interest.[26]

In 1881 the Government of India made the following suggestions to the provincial government for reform of the Local Boards.

1. Increase of non-official members from 50 to 66 per cent.
2. Decentralisation of certain services and revenues entrusting their functions to the Local bodies. The Chief Commissioner opposed the suggestion on the plea of dirth of education, resources and intelligence or influential gentlemen' suitable to work on the Committees or Boards at the district level. Therefore, he wanted those committees to be only consultative. But the Government of India insisted that these should be endowed with real powers and functions. Accordingly the Chief Commissioner deprovincialised certain services, revenues and functions and allotted these to education, public works and medical services. That resulted in the increase of the powers and functions of the District Committees. Following this the Government of India or Ripon Resolutions of 1881 and 1882 were received.

The resolutions contained the following guidelines and provisions.

1. Local Government should be an instrument of political and popular education "...even at the risk of temporary period of administrative in-efficiency".
2. There should be a network of local authorities.
3. Jurisdiction of the committees should be so limited as to enable a member to understand Local language and Local interests.
4. District Officers should not head the Committees.
5. Non-officials should be Chairmen of the committees and as far as possible they should be elected.
6. Non-official members should have a majority and they should be elected by rate- payers wherever possible.
7. Number of official members should be limited to one third of the total strength.
8. The Chief Executive Officer of a district should keep a watch over the proceedings of the Bodies and the performance of their duties without exceeding their powers.

Divergent and opposing views were put forward by the provincial officers. William E.Ward did not consider the Brahmaputra Valley suitable for Local government institutions. He observed,

Not only are the respectable Assamese of this Division, as a rule, insufficiently educated, they are also by nature devoid of that energy, activity and those business like habits which are so needful to make a man a useful member of a committee to which he may be appointed. All this, I have no doubt, will pass away in time but we have to deal now with the existing facts.

Naturally, he also opposed any system of election, either direct or indirect. Therefore he insisted on appointment of members of the District Committees by the Deputy Commissioners. Ward also wanted that the committees should be headed by them or in their absence, by the Sub-Divisional Officers. Thirdly, his demand was the appointment of a non-official Vice-Chairmen who should be

Selected from the most intelligent of the members who would transact a good deal of business under the supervision of the Chairmen and would thus go through a course of training which might qualify him for election to the office of Chairman....[27]

Replacement of District Committees by Local Boards

As in the case of Municipalities so also the Local Boards, the Assam Government's decisions "much watered down" the Ripon proposals through their resolution of 17 November 1882. It decided as follows.

1. In the plains, nineteen Sub-Divisional Local Boards were established.
2. The district level Committees were abolished.
3. The Deputy Commissioners would be the Chairmen of the Local Boards.
4. Each Board would consist of a minimum of 8 members and a maximum of 24 – and at a later time 10 to 30 members – of whom 3 or four would be ex-officio members.
5. In all the important tea districts, a minimum of fifty per cent of the non-official resident members must be elected by the tea-planters, every Tea Estate having one vote.

6. All other non official members, i.e. Indians, would be elected or else nominated by the Chief Commissioner except in Kamrup, Sibsagar and Sylhet where they had to be elected as before.
7. Boards so constituted would be permanent bodies, one third of the non-official members retiring every year, thus making these Boards permanent bodies like the Municipalities. Later the term of office of members was increased to three years.
8. An official could be elected Chairman. In that case, the Vice-Chairman might be a non-official. The former, however, had only a casting vote.

"Heavily loaded" with ex-officio and elected European planter members these Local Boards functioned with some modifications till 1915. That the composition of the Boards was undemocratic would be evident from the facts and figures that follow. In 1883, there were 300 members in 16 Sub-Divisional Local Boards, of them 75 were planters' elected representatives and 45 were official members. These percentages were much higher in the tea districts. "In most of the Local Boards, therefore, Europeans, acting in coalition with the Indian official members, constituted the majority". Twenty years afterwards, i.e., in 1903 also there were 364 members in nineteen Local Boards. Of them 133 were elected, most of them by tea planters, 60 ex-officio and 171 nominated. Again, of the total membership, 132 or 36 per cent were Europeans and their domination continued for a long time[28].

On 3 September 1898, Sir Henry Cotton, Chief Commissioner of Assam, submitted detailed proposals to the Government of India for reforms which are summarised below:

1. Area of a Local Board remained as before.
2. A Board would consist of 9 to 18 members.
3. Ex-Officio element should not exceed one fourth of the total membrship.
4. Representation of tea planters should remain as it was under Sir Charles Elliot. He had decided that in important tea Sub-Divisions, half the number of non-officials would be representatives of tea planters. Cotton, therefore, suggested the allotment of five seats each to planters in the districts of Cachar, Darrang, Lakhimpur, Nowgong and Sibsagar, two seats each to Karimganj and Sunamganj and four each to Habiganj and North Sylhet.
5. Only the tea planters' representatives would be elected and others would be nominated by the Deputy Commissioners. However, election would be allowed to continue in Kamrup, Sibsagar and Sylhet as it existed since 1882.He would not extend election any further as it did not work satisfactorily.
6. Every Board would have non-official preponderance.
7. Formation of Joint Committees in each district with two non-official representatives of each Sub-Divisional Board of a district but these Committees "would not be district committees in disguise".
8. Elaborate procedures, audited accounts and the machinery for the purpose would be developed.
9. Each Board would have a Sub-Divisional Fund which remained under the control of that Board.

There was a detailed discussion on Cotton's proposals. But in the mean time the creation of a new province of Eastern Bengal and Assam came to the forefront. The Central Government pointed out that the issue of Partition affected the entire position with regard to the reform of Local Self-Government. In the event of transfer of some of the Bengal districts to Assam, two sets of rules and local bodies would come into existence. While the Bengal part of the new province would have only the District Boards under the Bengal Act, the Assam part would have a system of Local Self-Government based on Local Boards in which District Boards had no place. In other words, in one province there would be two Acts for the same purpose. Therefore the Centre decided to maintain status quo of the existisng system in Assam. Cotton was succeeded by Sir Bamfylde Fuller who became the Lt. Governor of Eastern Bengal and Assam. Formation of the new province and appointment of Fuller "ended in smoke" Cotton's efforts for reforms. Fuller introduced some changes of a "reactionery character" which among other things retained the official dominance over local government institutions.

Royal Commission on Decentralisation

The Viceroyalty of Lord Curzon "witnessed excessive centralization of power". The Curzon-Fuller combination thus thwarted the development of local Self-Government. Lord Morley, Secretary of State for India was "alarmed at the process of centralisation that was taking place". Therefore, the Royal Commission on Decentralisation as mentioned earlier was appointed. Its Report was submitted in 1911 and Government took another four years for its consideration. We need not enter into the details of the Report as " practically most of the recommendations of the Commission were rejected and only the minor ones were accepted". Thus "... the labour of four years and the enormous expenditure on the Commission went waste" so far as Assam was concerned.[29] Assam was reconstituted into a Chief Commissionerate following the Annulment of Partition in 1912.

We have already referred to European domination over the Local Boards. Considering the relative share of the planters' contribution to local rates and their numerical strength as a community which were the criteria for allocation of seats, their share remained disproportionately high keeping the Boards under their clutches for a long time. For example, in 1912, they paid Rs.92669 only as local rates whereas other ratepayers paid Rs.539401. Yet they had 82 elected members as against 57 who represented the latter. They had 21 times their share of seats in North Lakhimpur, 27 times in Mongaldai, 5 to 6 times in Jorhat, Golaghat, Sibsagar and Tezpur, 3 times in Dibrugarh and Silchar, 25 times in Nowgang and 40 times in Gauhati. Except the last they outnumbered the other rate payers in all the Local Boards. The planters justified this with the plea that they represented the resident tea labour population of 570000 in 765298 acres of plantation enclaves in the Brahmaputra Valley. "They also linked their claim to the 16 million pound sterling British investment in the tea industry without which Assam would not have developed at all.[30]

Manik Chandra Baruah, Padmanath Gohain Barua, Kamini Kumar Chanda, Tarun Ram Phukan and Muhammad Saadulla, members of the Assam Legislative Council which came into being under the Morley-Minto Reforms brought the matter before the House. They tried to expose the planters' strangle-hold over the "so called rural self-government" and demanded a change in favour of an elected system. They also demanded legislation regularising the Local Boards which were functioning under Executive Orders since 1882. But democratization of Local Self-Government with a broad based franchise "... was not amongst the ostensible purposes" of the Government or the Indian leaders. Also,

> *Nor was the political movement of the day committed to such a principle. The articulated demand was for elected representation of only educated and propertied classes in all local bodies so that they could, within certain limit, influence the decision making process at the local level.*

Manik Chandra Baruah agreed with the Government that Local Boards "need not be necessarily a representative body of all sections and interests". Tarun Ram Phukan had observed, "It will be taking the life of these bodies if we are to restrict their power as regards the appointment of a non-official Chairman". He was the Secretary of the Assam Association which was "decidedly of opinion that property qualification is the only qualification which should be recognized in forming the electorates". However, he maintained that "There ought to be a well understood principle of allotment of seats according to the amount of payment of Local Rates...".

In course of debate on the Assam Local Self-Government Bill in 1914-1915, the Indian members placed arguments on the demand through proposals for amendments but without success. The European and planter members emboldened the Government to declare that they were not willing to accept local rate as the only criterion for allotment of seats. The members also raised the question of introducing the system of election of Chairmen by the Board Members except in a few special cases permitted by the Chief Commissoner. Chanda moved an amendment to the proposed Local Self-Government Bill in 1915 to provide for statutory election of all Chairmen and was supported by Saadulla and Phukan. However, it had to be withdrawn in the face of stiff European opposition.

"Government's intention was to provide a system under which rate payers would elect their own representatives to the village authorities, village authorities to the Local Boards and Local Boards to the provincial Legislative Council." But there was no such village authority in the Brahmaputra Valley other than the appointed Gaoburahs. Therefore "The provisions of the Bill were self – defeating".[31] In the Surma Valley and Goalpara districts there existed the Chaukidari system. Chanda made a proposal for making the village authorities plural and elected bodies. But the motion was lost. He and Gohain Barua also brought up a motion to make representation of various sectional interests proportionate to their respective contribution towards land revenue or local rates as far as possible. But the motion was lost. Chanda said "pathetically" on 15 March 1915,

> *as our proceedings commenced and as the discussions... were taken up one by one, the process of evaporation of our hope commenced and by the time the voting on Clause 37 was taken, it reached almost a vanishing point.*[32]

The Bill was passed almost in its original form without any division at the final stage and became the Assam Local Self-government Act of '1915. Gohain Baruah expressed gratitude to the Chief Commissioner for giving the Local Boards a legal status,

" the first seminaries for political education for us in this country."But other members in the Council did not consider the Act as a great boon to the province.[33] The main provisions of the Act were as follows:

1. Election of non-official majority of Members.
2. Election of non-official Chairmen. But a Board could request the Government to appoint one.
3. Election of non-official Vice-Chairmen.
4. Salaried government officials could not contest for election as Vice-Chairmen.
5. The Boards were allowed to constitute committees with persons who were not members. A committee might have an unspecified number of members.

We have referred to over-representation of European tea planters. The last attempt at curbing their undue share and influence was made by G.S.Barua on 12 January 1918 in the Legislative Council through a resolution. "Hs speech on this occasion was one of the best in the Council's annals." He criticized their lack of local knowledge and, except in the matter of communication, also local interests. Further he said, "The claim of tea planters…is intrinsically based on their being agriculturists and payers of local rates and my point is that their representation should be proportionate to the local rates paid by them". Baruah was supported by members like Muhammad Bakt Majumdar, Romani Mohan Das, Saadulla and others. They pointed out that the planters had a share of nominated seats in addition to their elective ones. In a "division forced upon the House", all the nine Europeans voted against the resolution and eight out of nine Indians supported it. On 3 January 1921 a revised set of rules was issued. The proportion of elected to total members was raised considerably. Thus by 1924, out of 300 members of the Boards, in the province, 264 were elected. It took another fifteen years to complete the process of election of members and Chairmen of the Local Boards.

Section V
CONSTITUTIONAL STRUCTURE OF A LOCAL BOARD

We have seen how the District Committees were replaced by Local Boards at Sub-Divisional level in 1882. Till then one third of the District Committee members was nominated ex-officio. Others were appointed or elected. The strength and composition of the Committees varied from time to time. Under the Local Rates Regulations of 1879, such bodies consisted of no less than six members of whom two were non-officials In 1882, a Sub-Divisional Local Board had a minimum of 8 and maximum of 24 members. In 1883 Assam had 19 Local Boards, all having non-official but nominated majority; only the tea planters' representatives were elected.

We have referred to Cotton's suggestion for reconstitution of Local Bodies. He had also suggested reduction of member from 24 to 18. The Local Boards were allotted four seats in the legislature, two each to the Municipalities and Local Boards with their own electorates. Each of the valleys had one seat on territorial basis..[34] No change was possible in the new province of Eastern Bengal and Assam from 1905 to 1912. Only the Assam Local Self-Government Act of 1915 prescribed the following composition of the Local Boards.

1. Minimum number of members of a Board would be 12 and maximum 20.
2. Chairmen would be appointed as before.
3. There would be four ex-officio members, namely, Deputy Commissioner, Executive Engineer, Civil Surgeon and Deputy Inspector of Schools. In case a non-official was appointed Chairman, an Extra Assistant Commissioner would be an ex-officio member in place of the Deputy Commissioner.
4. Nomination of members was to continue. In case the required number of members was not elected, the vacancy would be filled by nomination. But while nominating non-official members, "the Commissioner of Division had to take into account the claims of several communities which are not adequately represented by means of election".[35] In any case, the Boards would have a non-official elected majority.
5. Elected members were classified as planters, head quarter residents, mercantile and rural representatives. Each member of the first three groups was elected by their own electorates while the general electorate would choose the fourth group. In 1920, the number of ex-officio members was reduced to two who were the Civil Surgeon and the Deputy Inspector of Schools.

In 1924, a Legislative Council Committee was constituted to suggest amendments to the Act of 1915. Most of its recommendations were included in the Assam Local Self – Government (Amendments) Act of 1926. It made the following changes :

1. The membership of a Local Board was fixed at 16, both elected and nominated, the latter not exceeding one fifth of the total strength of the Board.
2. The elected seats would have to be distributed in such a manner that " every community and every locality could get its due" in proportion to its numerical strength in the population, the area and the local rates paid.[36]
3. Elected members were now classified as Non-Muslim or General, Muslim and Planters, thus enforcing separate electorates for Muslims. The Government could nominate supernumerary members to a Board, those being allowed to participate in the proceedings but without franchise.

Elected Chairmen and Vice- Chairmen

Under the Local Rates Regulation of 1879, Deputy Commissioners were the Chairmen of District Committees. A Senior Extra Assistant Commissioner headed the Head Quarters Committee as Vice-Chairman. Sub-Divisional Officers chaired the Branch Committees. A Vice-Chairman was appointed by the Chief Commissioner. Lord Ripon had suggested that Chairmen, as a rule should be elected non-officials. Chief Commissioner, Sir Charles Elliot supported Ripon and held that Deputy Commissioners and Sub-Divisional Officers should not preside over the Head-quarters and Sub-Divisional Boards. For administrative convenience, an Indian Extra Assistant Commissioner might be attached to the respective Board. But the Commissioner of Assam Valley, William E.Ward as well as the Deputy Commissioners of Darrang, Goalpara, Kamrup and Sibsagar opposed Elliot's proposal. They "emphatically" opined that a Deputy Commissioner's participation in the administration of a Local Board was "indispensable". Ward wrote,

> *It is essential I think, for some tome to come that the Deputy Commissioner should be the Chairman ... But they need not have a vote; it would be sufficient if they guided*

without necessarily influencing the deliberation of the Board... The transaction of business and the carrying out of all resolutions must necessarily rest with ... the chairman of the respective boards. The proposal to have a non-official chairman... is one which I cannot recommend for the present though we may possibly be able to see our way to this hereafter.

He further elaborated his opposition to election observing,

Indeed I think we may accept it as a fact that no native, even European would accept the post if offered to him except under a mistaken apprehension of the duties which would be required of him.[37]

As regards the non-official Vice-Chairman, he maintained the same view as in the case of Municipality that the incumbent should be appointed as a probationer under the Deputy Commissioner.

Sir Charles Elliot now changed his mind and supported his subordinate officers. He argued that the European members of the Boards,

... by their greater force of character and stronger interest in the objects of expenditure would be likely, in the absence of some official arbitrator to overbear the native element ... The presence of the district officer or the sub-divisional officer, therefore, is not so likely as it perhaps is elsewhere to stifle discussion and check free expression of opinion.

He therefore permitted the appointment of an official Chairman if the local officials felt it " absolutely necessary." That Chairman would have only a casting vote. Where the Chairman was officially appointed, the Vice-Chairman should be a non-official as suggested by Ripon.[38]

Cotton had suggested that a Local Board Chairman could be appointed or elected but a Vice-Chairman must be elected by the Commissioners themselves. But the proposal " met with a premature death" due to the creation of Eastern Bengal and Assam. The Decentralisation Commission had recommended the continuation of the policy of official appointment of Chairmen. One of its arguments was that in case a non-official one was appointed, the Deputy Commissioner or the Sub-Divisional Officer would lose contact with the general interests of the area concerned and the executive would become " a mere tax gatherer and repressor of crime." Secondly, the Chairman had to have a detailed knowledge of the various needs of the district which presumably a non-official incumbent would not have. A lengthy debate followed.

District officers and European members of the Assam Legislative Council held that a non-official Chairman would not be able to devote enough time to perform his duties. Secondly, the existence of village authorities made it imperative to have official Chairmen as they would have both local Board and administrative functions. The latter could be performed by the executive alone. Thus a dual control could be exercised only by the Deputy Commissioner or the Sub-Divisional Officer. The Chief Commissioner, though agreeing with this view, suggested the appointment of a non-official as a Chairman provided that either of those officers was appointed the Executive Officer. But this was opposed by his own Secretary. Also a member of the Council opposed the proposal and observed, "... I am yet to come across a single individual who could do the necessary work as efficiently as the district officer".

Another member said that a non-official Chairman with his own avocation might not "move out" but an official Chairman moved about constantly and therefore was in a better position to know the needs of the localities. According to a third Councillor,

> *There is no real demand for a non – official Chairman of the Local Boards in Assam... A few people mention it now and then for the most part, I think, because they are under the impression, it shows enlightenment to do so more than because they have any real dissatisfaction.*

Those views were opposed by a vast majority of non-official members. One view was that " there were frequent accusations that the Deputy Commissioner almost always favoured the planter members of the Local Board". Secondly, the Boards being dominated by the European planters with easier access discouraged Indian non-official members, mostly lawyers and businessmen, to express their views "freely and fearlessly." But their most substantial view was that "there can be no local self –government if the people were not trusted to manage their own affairs." Further, "if one wants to swim, one must get into water". These arguments seemed to have influenced the Government.[39]

The Local Self- Government Bill had first contemplated official appointment of Chairmen. But the Act of 1915 removed that rigidity and allowed appointment of non-official Chairmen as well as election by the members with the permission of the Chief Commissioner. But the election of Vice- Chairmen was made statutory. The same year Chief Commissioner Archdale Earle allowed Gauhati and Silchar Local Boards to elect Chairmen. The Commissioner of Surma Valley, W.J.Reid selected Silchar for the experiment. He also suggested that the Deputy Commissioner would not be a member of a Board after the election of a non-official Chairman. The idea was supported by the Deputy Commissioner of Sylhet but opposed by P.R.T. Gordon, Commissioner of Assam Valley Division. It had to be abandoned "... because of alleged opposition from the concerned Local Board itself." By 1920 the Local Boards at Barpeta, Dhubri, Goalpara, North Sylhet and Sunamganj where permitted to elect non-official Chairmen.The permission was extended to all by 1921.[40]

That even public opinion had not yet crystalised into the demand for election was evident from the fact that the Dhubri Local Board with a non- official majority of members opposed the proposal. Thus despite some favourable opinions the system of official appointment continued. In 1920, a resolution was moved in the Legislative Council proposing introduction of election of Chairman by the Board members themselves. By that time "opposition to a non-official Chairman had begun to crumble down". The Assam Government now allowed the Local Boards of Barpeta, Dhubri, Goalpara, North Sylhet and Sunamganj to elect their own Chairmen. But the Deputy Commissioners continued to chair the bodies in Dibrugarh, Gauhati, Jorhat, Nowgong and Tezpur. Sub-Divisional Officers were at the head of Golaghat, Habiganj, Hailakandi, Karimganj, Mangaldai, North Lakhimpur, Sibsagar and South Sylhet. Whereas all but one Chairman were officials in 1921, 13 out of 19 of them were non-officials by 1923.[41] Another progressive step was taken in 1921 allowing all Local Boards to elect non-official Chairmen with prior permission. As a result, the number of non-official incumbents rose from 5 to 13 by 1924-25. The Local Boards of Golaghat, Hailakandi and Nowgong requested the Government to fill up the posts.

The Act of 1926 made the following provisions with regard to election:

1. Chairmen should ordinarily be a non-official elected by the members from amongst themselves. But two thirds of the members of a Board, however, might request Government to appoint a Chairman.
2. Government was given the authority to nominate a Chairman if a Board failed to elect one within the time stipulated.
3. The Government could appoint a Chairman if a Board was constituted after suspension.

By 1928, fourteen Local Boards had elected non-official incumbents, the number rising to seventeen by 1936, excluding only North Lakhimpur and Tezpur. By 1946 all the Chairmen were elected. Thus the Local Boards, like the Municipalities, took almost the same time to evolve the elective principle with regard to the Chairmen.

The Franchise

Like the Municipalities, the voters' qualifications varied from time to time and place to place. In 1883, adult males with the following qualifications were allowed to vote.

1. Residents and or owners of property in the circle concerned.
2. Holders of landed property paying tax varying from Rs 10 to Rs 20 per year.
3. Holders of 20 bighas of rent free land.
4. Payment of municipal tax not less than Rs 2 per annum.
5. Holder of a house with a rental value of Rs. 50.

During Sir J.Bamfylde Fuller's regimes as Chief Commissioner of Assam and Lt. Governor of Eastern Bengal and Assam, there was a debate on the question of franchise for Gaoburhas only. The Commissioner of Assam Valley, P.G. Melitus wanted the right for rate payers. But Fuller implemented his own view.

As village headmen were "practically the servants of the Government, they tried to secure the election of Government nominees or persons acceptable" to the latter. They were also not educated people. Some times they voted for the " highest bidder." Above all, restriction of franchise to them " resulted in the exclusion of the best men from the Local Boards". In 1909, the Commissioner of Assam Valley, Gordon, suggested the extension of franchise to all persons paying local rate of Rs. 100 per annum. In 1909 the citizens of Jorhat also made a similar request to Sir Charles Bailey, the Chief Commissioner. Bailey favoured the proposed liberalisation. But the Secretary to the Government, Local Self-Government Department, Kershaw, remarked,

> *Although the present system of the electorate is exceedingly restricted and excluded many who ought to have a voice in the election of rural members, it is doubtful whether Assam Valley is ripe for the introduction of anything in the nature of the system suggested and still more doubtful whether if it were introduced, it would be anything more than a form.*[42]

The Finance Secretary wanted extension of the right to vote also to citizens paying Rs. 50 as settlement holders and Rs.100 as landholders, title holders, pensioners drawing Rs.50 a month and Jotedars paying Rs.250 a year. However no action was taken in this regard.

In 1912, Sir Archdale Earle, Chief Commissioner, proposed voting rights along with Gaoburahs to

1. Every male 21 years old,
2. Resident or owner of property in a circle and paying local rate of Rupee one,
3. Income Tax assesses,
4. Pensioners,
5. Mauzadars,
6. Mandals and
7. Pleaders and Mukters.

But the Commissioner of Assam Valley, Hennikar opposed these proposals which would considerably liberalise and broaden franchise. The main thrust of his objection was that such a step would extend franchise too widely. He therefore wanted to restrict the right to tax payment of Rs.25 and removal of the "invidious distinction" made between lawyers and other professionals like doctors.However, Earle proceeded no further in this regard.

In 1915, three classes of voters were there for election of members; first, adult residents of Headquarters Station who were voters in municipal elections, second, outside the municipal areas, the right was given to

a) adult male residents in towns for at least 12 months proceeding an election and paying no less than one rupee as Local rate in the previous year,
b) persons paying Income tax,
c) persons with a pass in Intermediate Examination of a University.

The third category of voters included those who elected rural area members. They were again classified into three groups.

1. In the districts of Cachar, Sylhet and Goalpara, members of the Choukidari Panchayats,
2. Members of the village authorities where they existed and
3. Gaoburhas in the districts of Darrang, Kamrup, Lakhimpur, Nowgong and Sibsagar.

According to one author, "a by product" of the Non-Co-operation Movement, launched in the last quarter of 1920, " was perhaps the immediate official action to expedite the reformation of the local bodies". For this purpose, a revised set of rules under the Local Self-Government Act of 1915 was introduced on 3 January 1921. The Local Board franchise was extended and made identical with that of the Assam Legislative Council. But thereby the principle of separate electorate for election to the Local Boards was also for the first time adopted through the Government's rule making authority.[43]

In 1915 the Local Boards had the seats and electorates as shown below.[44]

Distribution of seats and Electorates constituency-wise.

Categories	1915 No. of seats	Electors
1. Head Quarters Stations	19	9065
2. Rural areas	88	10068
3. Mercantile Interests	19	2554
4. Tea planters	82	126
Total	208	21813

There were 7 Local Boards in the Surma Valley and 12 in the Brahmaputra Valley. For 126 elective sits for Indians in the first three categories there was an electorate of 21687 or in other words 172 voters on an average elected one member. One hundred twenty-six planters elected 82 members, their franchise being based on plantation acreage; in other words less than two of them elected one member. While a Head Quarters Station representative was elected by 477 voters, every rural representative was elected by 115. The average electorate for a mercantile member was 135. Next we give the composition of the Boards in 1918.[45]

No.of Local Boards.	Total Seats.	Elective.	Nominated	Ex-Officio	Elected Indians	Elected Tea Planters.
19	323	202	121	NA	120	82

Both in 1915 and 1918, the elected tea Planters had the same strength. The total strength of the Boards in 1918 decreased by 24 members. Elected seats came down by 6 and nominated members increased by 29. The strategy to maintain dominance of Europeans, ex-officio and nominated elements was sustained, though apparently Indians were in a majority. The former categories constituted "no less than two thirds of the consolidated membership" of all the Boards. In 15 of these their concentration was still higher.[46] The proportion of elected to total membership fell by three per cent. In 1920 franchise was extended to persons entitled to vote in the elections of members to the Legislative Council. In other words ultimately the electoral rolls incorporating separate electorate for Muslims were adopted. Other qualifications included 12 months' residence in the area concerned preceding election and payment of local rate of rupee one.

In 1920, all adult persons eligible to get registered as voters for the election to the Legislative Council were allowed to vote in local body election. That enlarged the earlier electorate to 202704 voters or nearly by nine times. But it should be noted that according to the Census of 1911, Assam's population in 1920 was 6074803. Thus even the increase could not enlarge the electorate to more than 3.33 per cent of the total population of this province.

The composition of Local Boards in 1922 is shown here.[47]

No.of Local Boards.	Total Seats.	Elective.	Nominated	Ex-Officio	Elected Indians	Elected Tea Planters.
19	380	264	69	47	NA	NA

Sixty nine per cent of the seats were elective and far exceeded the total strength of the nominated ex-officio members whose share was 31 out of every hundred. They accounted for 44 per cent of the elected members. The break up of Indian and European members was not traceable but the latter could not have been less than 82 i.e. as it was in 1915 and 1918.

In 1927, the composition and constituencies were revised in the light of the principles laid down by the Local Self-Government Act of 1926 and the rules made thereunder. The Act had provided that elected seats of the Boards should be distributed in such a manner that every community and every Locality could get its due proportion to its strength in the population and the contribution it made by way of tax payment. Thus three factors namely, communal, territorial and economic, came into force simultaneously. The next set of figures gives us the picture elaborately between 1926 and 1927.[48]

Distribution of Constituencies Valley, Community and Interestwise

	Before Revision 1926				After Revision 1927			
	General or Non-Muslims	Muslims	Planters	Total	General or Non-Muslims	Muslims	Planters	Total
Brahmaputra Valley	100	29	51	180	133	45	54	232
Surma Valley	39	35	31	105	52	60	32	144
	139	64	82	285	185	105	86	376

There was an increase in the total strength of the Boards by 32 per cent. The percentage in the non-Muslim and Muslim constituencies were 33 and 64 respectively. Valley-wise seats increased by 29 and 37 per cent respectively. Comparative shares of different categories of constituents are shown here.

Percentage of seats

	Before Revision	After Revision
General or Non-Muslim.	48.77	49.20
Muslim.	22.45	27.92
Planters.	28.77	22.87
	99.99	99.99

Percentage-wise the increase in General or Non-Muslim seats was negligible. The Muslims gained by nearly 6 per cent and at the cost of tea planters' share.

Tea Planters' Franchise[49]

A tea planter's franchise qualification was based on the acreage of his tea estate. No one with a garden of less than 100 acres was entitled to vote. The method of determining the number of vote is shown hereunder.

1. Above 100 acres and upto 1000 acres – 1 vote for every 100 acres.
2. 1001 to 2000 acres – one more vote for every 250 acres.
3. 2000 acres and above – one more vote for every 500 acres.

In other words, a holder of 1000 acres of tea land had 10 votes. One having 2000 acres would have 14 votes which would increase in case of bigger areas of the gardens.

This formula continued till 1905. Sir Bamfylde Fuller heading the new province of Eastern Bengal and Assam laid down the following rules for the purpose.

1. Holder of a garden of 100 acres and no less than 500 acres – 1 vote.
2. More than 500 and less than 1500 acres- 2 votes.
3. More than 1500 acres – 3 votes.

This rule was in operation even after the Assam Local Self-Government Act 1915 came into operation.

"The minimum acreage fixed to entitle a planter to the right to vote also indicates that it was done with a view to eliminate square planters who were mostly Indians".

Only Superintendents, or Managers or Assistant Managers could cast the votes allotted to their respective gardens. This arrangement continued till the Constitution of free India came into operation.

Under the Monley-Minto Reforms two representatives of the local bodies, elected on extremely limited franchise, were sent to the Council through nomination by the Lt. Governor during the Eastern Bengal and Assam regime and by the Chief Commissioner after the reconstitution of the province in 1912. The seats were territorially distributed and 19 Local Boards elected 217 members. Of them 89 were planters, 57 rate payers and others were nominated. The valley-wise numbers were not traceable. The number of votes each Local Board was entitled to was, as in the case of Municipalities, determined on the basis of annual income. In 1920, the voters for election to the Legislative Council also became eligible to vote in the Local Board election. In other words, separate electorate was introduced in the Boards. This arrangement continued till 1952 when, under the Constitution of Indian Republic, adult franchise was introduced and special seats for tea planters were abolished.

The Tenure of a Local Board

Under the Local Rates Regulations of 1879, a Local Board's tenure of office was two years. In 1882, it was extended to three years, one third of the members retiring every year, thus making the Boards permanent bodies like the Municipalities. The Local Self-government Act of 1915 retained the said tenure beginning on 1st April of the year concerned. But it no more required the annual retirement as mentioned above. So all the members of a Board remained in office for the full term after election. Between 1853 and 1920, 19 Local Boards and 12 Municipalities evolved in the province . Of these 12 and 9 were situated in the Brahmaputra Valley and 7 and 3 in the Surma Valley respectively. While the Local Boards were of the same status, Municipalities were, at the beginning, put under different categories.

The rules for Secret Ballot System of voting were prescribed by the Government of Assam in 1924.

REFERENCES

1. Jones, Moris, *Parliament in India*, pp.118-119 and Mahahjan, V.D., *British Rule in India and After*, pp.545-554.
2. Hugh, Tinker, *The Foundations of Local Self-Government in India, Pakistan and Burma*, p.58n, Rao,

V.Venkata, *A Hundred Years of Local Self-Government in Assam 1860-1960,* p.183.

3. Guha, Amalendu, *Planter Raj to Swaraj.* p.100.
4. *Ibid*, p.98.
5. Rao, p. 30.
6. Jones, p.119.
7. Mahajan, pp.545-547 for details.
8. Guha, pp.25-26.
9. Rao, p.211.
10. *Ibid*, pp.33-35.
11. *Ibid*, pp.39-40.
12. *Ibid*, pp.42-43 and Guha, p.30.
13. *Ibid*, pp.211-213, File No. 1784 Home A, 2 Nov. 1882 cited in Guha, p.32.
14. Rao, p.214.
15. Guha, p.32.
16. *Ibid*.
17. Rao, p.216.
18. *Ibid*, p.215.
19. Guha, pp.94-95.
20. Rao, p.76.
21. Rao and Niru Hazarika, *A Century of Government and Politics in North-East India,* Vol. 1, Assam, p.109, and Rao, pp.139-142.
22. Rao. pp. 45-48.
23. Bhuyan, Arun Chandra and Sibopada De(Eds.), *Political History of Assam*, Volume Two 1920-1939, p.348.
24. Rao. pp.221 – 222.
25. Guha, pp.24-25, Rao, pp. 51-55.
26. *Ibid*, pp.57-59.
27. *Ibid*,pp.62-63, File No.1784 Home A, 2 Nov. 1882.
28. Guha, p.31, Rao, pp. 63-65, p.167.
29. Rao, pp.77-78.
30. *Assam Legislative Council Proceedings* (ALCP), 15 March 1915, speeches by Government Members.
31. *Eastern Chronicle* (Sylhet), 5 December 1914 and 9 December 1914, ALCP, 1913, 1914, 1915, Guha, pp.96-100 for details.
32. ALCP 1915, No.2, p.84, quoted in Guha, p.98.
33. *Ibid*, *Gohain Barua's speech*, p.116, Guha, p.99 and p.147 for details.
34. Guha, p.82, and Rao and Niru Hazarika, pp.114-115 for details.
35. Rao. pp.143-146.
36. *Ibid*, p.145, Guha, p.147.
37. Rao, p.113.
38. *Ibid*, pp.113-114.
39. *Ibid*, pp.114-117 for details.

40. Guha, p.100.
41. *Ibid*, p.147.
42. Rao, pp.224-226 for details.
43. Guha, p.147.
44. Rao, p.226.
45. *Ibid* (1973), p.195 and Rao (1963), p.226.
46. *Ibid* (1963), p.226, Guha, p.100.
47. Guha, p.147.
48. Rao (1963), p.146.
49. *Ibid*, pp.227-228.

4

EVOLUTION OF LEGISLATURES AND ELECTORAL POLITICS

Section I
Assam's First Ever Taste of legislature

A large part of India's struggle for freedom from British rule centred round the demand for constitutional reforms. The process of law making by directly elected people's representatives evolved through different phases. The process began with the growth of legislatures under the provisions of various Indian Councils Acts as described earlier. Since the Treaty of Yandabo till 1854, Assam was under the direct control of the Governor General of India who administered the territory through an Agent and Commissioner. For the next twenty years it was a division of the Bengal Presidency under a Lt. Governor appointed in terms of the Indian Councils Act of 1853. The creation of a new province of Assam in 1874 was followed by vesting of administrative powers in the Chief Commissioner who ruled with the approval of the Secretary of State for India.

In theory, all portions of British India, which were not included in a Governorship or a Lt.Governorship, were under the immediate authority and management of the Governor General-in-Council. He could issue all necessary orders and directions for administration. A Chief Commissionership was "therefore still regarded as a delegate of the Governor General who might resume or modify such powers" as he had himself conferred. In official terminology, Chief Commissionerships were Generally referred to as " local administration rather than local governments. But in practice the powers entrusted to them were nearly as wide as those of a Lieutenant Governor". With the creation of Legislative Councils in Assam and Central Provinces, any distinction in administrative methods tended to "disappear".[1]

Laws for Assam were made in three ways. First, the Imperial Legislative Council enacted laws applicable to the whole of British India. Second, Regulations were proclaimed by the Government of India on the proposals of the Chief Commissioner approved by the Governor General. Third, under the provisions of the Scheduled Districts Act of 1877, applied to Assam the same year, the Chief Commissioner was empowered to adopt any law in force elsewhere in the country with the Governor General's consent. Thus there was neither any question of people's representation nor law making by the Indians for the Indians. The Indian Councils Act of 1861 and also of 1892 had empowered the Governor General of India to create new provinces and legislatures though without any trace of parliamentary form of government. However, the provisions allowed some persons to be chosen by indirect election on extremely limited franchise and then recommended to the Governor General for nomination as members of those legislatures. Such recommendations could be rejected without showing any reason.

By 1892, the process of Partition of Bengal and creation of a new province in Eastern India had already started. The same year Foreign Department of the Government of India suggested the transfer of Chittagong Division of Bengal to Assam. Sir Henry J.S.Cotton, Chief Commissioner of this province (1896-1902), advised the inclusion of Dacca and Mymensing districts also in it. "The Planters, in particular, desired a redrawing of the provincial boundaries with a view to having the port of Chittagong and the plantations of North Bengal and Assam in one and the same province". Lord Curzon became the Governor General of India on 6 January 1899 and held office till 19 November 1905. During his visit to Assam in 1903, the Europeans "put into his head" the idea that "if Chittagong was tagged to Assam and developed as an outlet to the sea", the prohibitive cost of transport of tea could be substantially reduced. A further advice from the Chief Commissioner, Sir J. Bamfylde Fuller, was the "administrative necessity" of enlarging the size of Assam without which "no" senior civilian was likely to opt for it.

> *These considerations were... buttressed by the European Civilians' general desire to aim a blow at the Bengali middle class – the mainstay of the rising Congress movement, and dislocate it in a vital part of its sphere of influence. The creation of a Muslim majority province on the flank of Bengal, which would take care of all these considerations thus, became a political necessity.*[2]

The scheme was mooted by Curzon and the full text of the Government of India's resolution was published in the Gazette of India on 12 December 1903.There were protests and demonstrations all over Bengal. Sir Alexander Frazer, Lt.Governor of Bengal pointed in his note of 7 February 1904 that

> *... Bengal is very densely populated, that Eastern Bengal is the most densely populated portion, that it needs room for expansion and that it can only expand towards the east. So far from hindering national development we are really giving it greater scope and enabling Bengal to absorb Assam.*[3]

Assam's reaction to such a scheme was not at first favourable. The Assam Association, till then practically the only spokesman of the Assamese population, apprehended that

> *...by the proposed territorial change the historic name of Assam will be obliterated for ever, her language suffer and the removal of the seat of government to a place outside Assam proper and further away from the geographical centre will necessarily make her lose the amount of care and attention which it at present receives from the government.*[4]

While the Association as a whole was opposed to reorganization by transferring the Chittagang Division and the districts of Dacca and Mymensing to the new province, some of its branches like Dibrugarh and Gouripur were not averse to such expansion. The former suggested that "Chittagong may be added to the advantage of Assam".

According to the latter, if territorial redistribution was necessary at all "for the efficient Government in Assam" and to lighten the "excessive burden of Bengal Government", it would be better effected by annexing Rangpur, Kuch Behar, Jalpaiguri and some parts of Bogra district to Assam". The inhabitants of those districts, according to the Gouripur Branch, were "identical in race, religion and language with those of lower Assam which is contiguous with them". However, the decision to create a new province had a different perception behind. Sir Herbert Risley, Home Secretary to Lord Curzon, succinctly defined it in a note dated 6 December 1904 as he wrote,

> *... One of our main objects is to split up and thereby weaken a solid body of opponents to our rule.*[5]

Obviously, the opponents were the Bengalees.

The Hindu-Muslim divide played its role in favour of Curzon. Three factors helped him win the Muslims to his support. Firstly, " All positions of powers could be reached by Indians under the given colonial set up were practically monopolised by the caste Hindus in Bengal," clearly by virtue of their earlier initiation to English education. Secondly, "the mainstream of Indian nationalism" was heavily "loaded" with "the assertion of Hindu might" and "Hindu spiritual content". Thirdly, the prospect of Muslims outnumbering the Bengali Hindus in the new province had its appeal to the Bengali Muslims. It was not, therefore, difficult for the Governor General to win over a major section of the Muslim landlords and middle classes to his " Operation Partition" and Assam's merger with Eastern Bengal or vice versa as the Assamese and the Bengalis looked at it respectively. Indeed, the seeds thus sewn developed in no distant future into the vexatous "Bengali-Assamese conflict" for a second time since 1874. Perhaps realizing this, Sir Henry Cotton, a former Chief Commissioner of Assam and President of the Congress Session of 1904 condemned the plan as "the most arbitrary and unsympathetic evidence of irresponsible statesmanship".[6]

As regards Curzon's scheme; R.C. Majumdar wrote,

> *In East Bengal, the Muslims, politically less advanced and more loyal to the British than the Hindus, would be in a majority, while in Bengal, the Bengalis would form a minority by inclusion of Bihar and Orissa. Thus the Bengalis would be divided from their kith and Kin; the Bengali Hindus, hated and dreaded by Curzon for their advanced political ideas, would form a minority; and a thin wedge would be driven between the Hindus and Muslims of Bengal.*[7]

Interstingly, despite the Assam Association's apprehension mentioned earlier, some individual prominent Assamese were not against the scheme of reorganization. Manik Chandra Baruah, the front rank leader of the Assam Association was prepared to accept it provided eighty per cent of vacancy in Government job were reserved for local candidates. Jagannath Barooah, leader of the Jorhat Sarvajanik Sabha also "expressed similar view". The new province was reportedly going to be named North Eastern Province. Thus it appeared that there was a possibility which created a justifiable fear of the name Assam being obliterated. Padmanath Gohain Barooah, Editor of 'Assam Bani' repeatedly pointed to the fact. He "diffidently accepted" the proposed arrangement as a "settled fact" but at the same time made a plea for retention of the word Assam in the nomenclature of the new province. He also appealed to both the leaders to take up the issue with the authorities but neither of them responded in view of their support to the scheme as mentioned earlier. However, finally the Government named the reconstituted province as Eastern Bengal and Assam, thus ending for the time being its separate existence as a Chief Commissioner's Province.[8]

Curzon's scheme was revised and finalised in utmost secrecy without caring for public opinion and reaction, especially in Bengal. The Secretary of State for India approved it on 9 June 1905. Announcement made in the House of Commons to this effect was flashed to India on 6 July 1905. On 1 September the Royal Proclamation embodying his assent informed the people that the creation of a province, named Eastern Bengal and Assam would come into force with effect from 1 October 1905. It consisted of all the six districts of the Brahmaputra Valley, two of the Surma Valley, thirteen of Eastern Bengal and three native States thereof. Dacca was the capital of the province with a clear Muslim majority. Bengal was partitioned in the face of the fiercest opposition that the government had since 1857. Sir J. Bamfylde Fuller, Chief Commissioner of Assam was promoted to be the Lt. Governor of the province.

Eastern Bengal and Assam had a Legislative Council of its own consisting of fifteen members, all nominated by him. Only local bodies were allowed to recommend, by election on extremely limited non-territorial franchise, some names to the Lt.Governor for nomination as Council members. But such recommendations were not mandatory on the Lt. Governor who could reject these without any explanation. His acceptance was again subject to the Governor General's assent. Under the prescribed procedure, such a Council for a large population could not satisfy the leaders of all communities and parts of it, particularly because two thirds of the members were always Europeans. Only interest groups were represented and only the Eastern Bengal part had three Muslim nominees in the House. Therefore, it was no surprise that Assam part remained unrepresented in the Council for the first four years of its tenure. From the point of view of development of legislative polity, the nomination era, which began with the new province, continued till 1912, when direct election on restricted franchise was introduced. The new Council had its first Session on 18 December 1906. On petition from the Assam Association, two seats were allotted to this part of the province. One of the seats was to be filled by local bodies as mentioned above; the other went to the European tea planters who elected their representative from amongst themselves, that is, through a kind of separate electorate. Manik Chandra Baruah was the first Assamese to be elected in February 1909 and nominated by the Lt. Governor. Barooah did not miss his "very first opportunity" in the Council on 6 April 1909 to declare on behalf of the Assamese people "loyal devotion" to the British crown as was the usual ritual in those days. The subsequent sections throw light on the working of the Council.

Section II
ANTI-PARTITION AGITATION

The influence of nationalism on the Anti-partition Agitation and the intense Boycott and Swadeshi Movement all over India is now recognized. Confidential Reports of the Intelligence Department of Bengal Government reveal that the Movement had assumed an All India character towards the end of 1905 and spread over different provinces with varying degrees of intensity. In Assam, instead of a united stand, several trends were noticeable between the two valleys and the two communities, Hindus and Muslims. Manik Chandra Baruah, one of the founders of the Assam Association which afforded political tutelage to the educated Assamese generation of the Brahmaputra Valley, was now opposed to the tagging of Assam with Eastern Bengal, considered as "annexation". In his maiden speech in the Council, he recapitulated the early days of British rule during which "our best interests were sacrificed". Further, by Partition " Assam has suffered most", he lamented.

Lt. Col. P.R.T. Gordon, Comissioner of the Assam Valley Division publicly "warned against the danger of Assame language being crushed and the Ahoms and Assamese Hindus being elbowed out of all employment by the people from Eastern Bengal". Taking the cue form Gordon, Baruah said that "the partition in its present shape was a mistake". He, therefore, appealed to the Government for protection of Assamese interests " as a minority community". He also complained that "while only 10 per cent of the province's total revenue should have come from Assam, it was actually contributing one third. Thus contrary to common belief, Assam was being taxed more heavily than Eastern Bengal". He was all praise for the planters and observed,

> *The Planting Community have been pioneers of progress and enlightenment in Assam. Their example has stimulated a number of my countrymen to follow an independent and honourable profession, and I am glad and thankful to say that at the present moment, though their number is small, there are some Assamese tea planters, who are doing a lucrative business and occupying a much coveted position, and that with the brighter prospects of the industry their number is sure to increase.*

However, a young educated section of Assamese like Ambikagiri Roy Choudhury, Bishnu Ram Medhi and others "seem to have come under the spell of anarchism for sometime". The Muslim community of the Valley was very small and so could hardly influence polity.[9]

The Surma Valley presented a slightly different picture. Both the Hindus and the Muslims had long been struggling together for transfer of the district of Sylhet to Bengal since amalgamation with Assam in 1874. Similar agitation was also witnessed in Cachar and Goalpara at a later stage. But the creation of the new province in 1905 generated in Muslim minds a sense of political importance derived from a numerical majority and they considered it to be a boon. But to the Hindus, that was a vile conspiracy to strike at their newly aroused nationalism. However, Assam was much less in turmoil than Bengal and the "settled fact" could not disturb the Brahmaputra Valley very much. The initial euphoria of the Anti-Partition Agitation and Hindu – Muslim unity was soon replaced by a rift which embittered their relation. Thus we can see that the Agitation could not take a deep root in the Brahmaputra Valley and only the Hindus of Sylhet and Cachar were under its influence.

An Assamese writer said that Bepin Chandra Pal's stirring speeches before the Surma Valley Conference " emitted burning flames of patriotism, and their rays illuminated the other Valley too". Two others, however, claimed that the Movement did not affect the " peaceloving" Assamese. According to another scholar, " Even the little agitation that was experienced was out of tune with the collaborationist outlook of the Assam Association inside and outside the Council". This was evident from the fact that there were no enrolled Swadeshi volunteers in the districts of Darrang, Lakhimpur and Nowgong. Figures of other districts were also not available.[10] Now we revert to our main concern, the development of Assam legislature.

The discussion on constitutional reforms which went on simultaneously with the furious debate on the creation of the new province "raised high hopes" among the Assamese that their "legitimate aspirations" would be fulfilled. This at least gave them a chance to demand the annulment of Partition which was " a sine qua non" for remedy of the maladies of Assam which had been aggravated by her " amalgamation with the districts of Bengal". Raja Phabhat Chandra Barooah and Manik Chandra Baruah, President and Secretary respectively of the Assam Association along with Calcutta residents, namely, Lalit Chandra Nayak, Kamala Kanta Das and Ram Prasad Das submitted a Memorandum to the Secretary of State for India. They complained that Partition had "reversed" the whole process of development, which was set in motion since Assam's separation from Bengal in 1874. Therefore, they demanded that

> *... the present partition be withdrawn and that a government and a council be appointed for the whole of Bengal (old and new) including Assam, and Assam be placed under a separate Commissioner with a separate service, but reserving a seat for an Assamese in the Council and that its administration should be assimilated with that of Sind. Such an arrangement would be the most convenient to the people of Assam and would be in harmony with popular opinion of the province.*[11]

The representation was "a far cry in wilderness" as the Secretary of State was not prepared to unsettle the settled fact. The long-standing demand of the Surma Valley districts of Sylhet and Cachar as well as the district of Goalpara for transfer to Bengal also remained unfulfilled. Thus Assam accepted the Partition and re-organization without much well organized and powerful opposition. As a result, this part of the province also remained unrepresented in the Eastern Bengal and Assam Legislative council as stated earlier. The first Assamese in it since 1909 could not achieve much in the Council.

The legislatiure had two phases of existence. The first was under the Curzon Plan from 1 October 1905 to 14 November 1909 governed by the Indian Councils Act of 1892. The second phase under the provisions of the Indian Councils Act of 1909 or the Morley-Minto Reforms began on 15 November and ended on 14 November 1912, i.e., the annulment of Partition. Fuller's regime was characterised by a policy of divide and rule. In one of his interviews, he remarked that he had two wives and the Muslims were his favourities.[12] Thus he went a step further in fulfilling Curzon's dream. He also found in Assamese Hindus as well as the Muslims "a counterpoise to the expansion of the Bengali Hindus. Seemingly based on a sense of justice, this menoeuver was sure to bear bitter fruits in the context of the divide and rule policy". Interestingly enough, Fuller claimed that he had opposed the "present form of partition". But his activities proved the hollowness of the claim. The Monley-Minto Reforms had a dual face, namely repression and concession. The Lt.Governor adopted the former in advance and let loose "unbridled coercion". He humiliated and insulted respected leaders, ruthlessly punished teachers and students, even flagging them besides imposing fines and rusticating many of them.

Lord Minto had written to Lord Morley on 29 Marth 1906 that he was "alarmed" and he was not "at all pleased with what he gathered about Fuller's doings". Morley replied,

> *I cannot but read in Fuller's utterances a most stupid misconception of the prevalent policy...Partition was a disagreeable pill and Fuller had guilded the pill with worm wood.*

On 16 May 1906 Gokhale said in England that "there is no hope of peace till he (Fuller) is relieved of his duties". However neither Morley nor Minto deviated from the policy of divide and rule. On 12 January 1906, Minto had "firmly refused to reverse the policy of his predecessors in this matter"in his reply to the Indian Association's address. However, Fuller had to go. His resignation was accepted on 3 August 1906. L.Hare succeeded him on 20August but the same policy was continued.[13]

Now, how far was the Council in its first phase a people's representative organization? what were the rights and privileges of the members vis-a-vis matters of public interests? How far could the Council influence, alter or modify the executive decisions in favour of the people? First of all, the basic function of a legislature, law making, was not within its jurisdiction. Secondly, the members could hardly have a voice of their own; in other words, they had to remain loyal to the executive and therefore any dissenting voices or opinions were hardly recorded. The Council was saddled with an unassailable official monopoly and enjoyed no power worth mentioning. This was also evident in respect of other basic tenets of a legislature. Let us take the case of provincial budget. Formulated long ahead of the Session by the executive, it would be first submitted to the Government of India. After thorough checking and often alteration in the Finance Department, it would be included in the Indian Budget for discussion in the Imperial Legislative Council. Then only the extracts relating to the province would be discussed in the Council. However, the latter could not pass any resolution in any way effecting the Budget. Formal questions could be put with prior notice but no supplementaries were allowed.

In view of the nominated official majority, no adverse motion or resolution could be adopted. Thus even if a matter of public interest came to the Council, the discussion and debate had "hardly anything more than an academic interest." These were "pious wishes" which the members had no power to carry out. The official majority could vote down any attempt contemplated to assert Indians' right to mould the Council's working in the interest of the country. Thus the members' rights, powers and responsibilities were altogether circumscribed and the Council, subordinated to the executive, was reduced to a mere advisory body. But even their advice could be rejected or ignored outright by the Lt.Governor without showing any reason and with impunity.

Rai Bahadur Sitanath Roy, a Zamindar Member from Eastern Bengal, who acclaimed himself as a loyalist "to the backbone," said in the Council on 7 April 1907,

> *...It is of utmost importance, both in the interest of the government and the governed ...that all the Councils should be reformed and enlarged and a potential and substantial voice allowed to the people in the legislation and in the management of the finances of their country. The tax payer who pays the piper should have a voice in the tune.*

Section III
IMPLEMENTATION OF THE MORLEY-MINTO REFORMS

The circumstances, factors and backgrounds leading to the Monley-Minto Reforms embodied in the Indian Councils Act of 1909 were elaborately discussed in the previous Chapter. We could see that there was a peaceful acceptance of the reforms. In such an atmosphere, the newly emerging Assamese leadership could not isolatedly raise their heads against the measures. Under the provisions of the Act, the Eastern Bengal and Assam Legislative Council was expanded to consist of 42 members including the Lt.Governor. Assam's share of seats was raised from two to five. In exercise of the powers conferred by section 6 of the Act, the Governor General-in-Council, with the approval of the Secretary of State-in-Council proclaimed regulations for constituting the central and provincial legislatures by nomination and election of additional members to the respective Houses.[14] Details are given in Appendix 1 to this Chapter. We shall devote our attention to the implementation of the provisions vis-à-vis Assam. So far as nomination was concerned, two guidelines were prescribed.

1. The Central Legislative Council
   ... it shall not be lawful for the Governor General to nominate so many non-official persons under these regulations that the majority of all the members of the council shall be non-officials.
2. Provincial Councils
   ... it shall not be lawful for the Governor or Lieutenant Governor, as the case may be, to nominate so many officials under these regulations that the majority of all the members in the Council shall be officials.

Thus while the central legislature would have official majority, provincial legislatures were given non-official majority. In 1910 Executive Councils were provided for the Lt.Governors' provinces. One of the most important provisions was the introduction of separate electorate. It is interesting to note that when Christians, Sikhs and Europeans (and later Scheduled Castes and Tribes) elected their own representatives, there was hardly any public reaction. But the provision for separate electorate for Muslims raised a hue and cry.

Composition of the Eastern Bengal and Assam Legislative Council (1909-1912) is detailed below.[15]

A.	Nominated members – Not more than 17 to be Officials and one must represent the Indian Commerce	22
B.	Nominated experts either officials and or non-officials	2
C.	Elected Members – Categories	
	(i) by Municipal Commissioners	3
	(ii) by District and Local Boards	5
	(iii) by Landholders	2
	(iv) by Muslim community	4
	(v) by Tea Industry	2
	(vi) by Jute Industry	1
	(vii) by Commissioners of Chittagong Port	1
		42

The two experts were not counted for the total strength of the Council, which was, therefore, forty. The elected members numbering18 would be recommended by the respective authorities to the Lt. Governor who would nominate them to the Council. There was no case of his rejection of any recommendation in the Assam part of the province.

Election Procedures

1. Municipalities

For the election and nomination of members from these constituencies, the municipalities were divided into four groups, namely, Dacca, Rajshahi, Chittagong and Surma Valley and Assam Valley together . Dacca and Rajshahi Divisions would elect one member each. The third and fourth Divisions would elect one member alternately, Chittagong and Surma Valley having the first priority.

2. District and Local Boards

The District Boards in Dacca, Rajshahi and Chittagang Divisions were allotted one seat each. The Local Boards in the Surma Valley and the Assam Valley would elect one member each.

3. Land holders

One seat was to be filled up by the Dacca and Rajshahi Divisions alternately. The other member would be elected by the landholders of Chittagong and Surma Valley (excluding Hill Districts) Divisions alternately. But Dacca and Chittagong had the first right of election. The district of Goalpara was deemed to be included in the Surma Valley and Hill Division.

4. Muslim Community

The Muslim representatives were to be elected by the following groups of Divisions :

1. Dacca.	1
2. Chittagong excluding Chittagong Hill tracts.	1
3. Rajshahi.	1
4. Surma Valley and Hill Districts excluding Hill Districts and Assam Valley excluding Garo Hills.	1

The Surma Valley and Assam Valley would elect one member alternately, the former having the first right of election. The qualified Muslim electors were required first to elect Delegates who in turn elected their representatives for recommendation to the Lt. Governor. Election of Delegates was held on the basis of quota for Divisions and Districts as shown below.

Division & Districts		No. of Delegates to e elected
I. Surma Valley		
Cachar	-	1
Sylhet		5
		6
II. Assam Valley		
Darrang	-	1
Goalpara	-	1
Kamrup	-	1
Lakhimpur	-	1
Nowgong	-	1
Si sagar	-	1
		6
III. Dacca		
Dacca	-	7
Mymensing	-	12
Faridpur	-	5
Bakerganj	-	7
		31
IV. Rajshahi		
Rajshahi	-	5
Dinajpur	-	4
Jalpaiguri	-	1
Rangpur	-	6
Bogra	-	3
Pa na	-	5
Malda	-	2
		26
V. Chittagong		
Chittagong	-	4
Tipperah (Tripura)	-	6
Noakhali	-	4
		14

Total num er of Delegates was 83. Thus the Muslim representatives were also chosen y indirect election y separate electorate.

5. Tea Industry

Assam Branch and Surma Valley Branch of the Indian Tea Association and the Duars Planters' Association were to elect three persons as shown elow.

Assam Branch 4 votes -	1
Surma Valley Branch 4 votes-	1
Duars Planters' Association 2 votes.	1
Total 10 votes	3 Mem ers

Of these three persons elected, two would be chosen by the Lt.Governor for nomination.

6. Jute Industry

The representative of this class was elected by the Narayanganj Chamber of Commerce. Any person not ineligible under the Regulations could be elected.

7. Port of Chittagong

The Commissioners of the Port elected their representative.

The five Assam seats as mentioned earlier were distributed as follows:

1. Local Boards	
Surma Valley	1
Brahmaputra Valley	1
2. Municipalities Province as a whole	1
3. Muslim Delegates of both valleys alternately, Surma Valley having the first right of election	1
4. Tea Planters Province as a whole	1
	5

Thus so far as Assam part of the province was concerned, the elected members were classified into four groups whereas in Eastern Bengal part there were seven groups. The Assam Valley Muslims remained unrepresented, to begin with. The new Council had its first session on 4 January 1910. According to the members' list on that day there were 21 Europeans including one from Assam (tea planter), 16 Bengalis including one Hindu and one Muslim from the Surma Valley and two Assamese Hindus, namely Manik Chandra Baruah and Rai Bahadur Bhuban Ram Das. Syed Abdul Majid represented the Surma Valley Muslims. Name of the Surma Valley representative of Local Boards could not be traced. There was only one nominated non-official member from Assam, namely, Raja Prabhat Chandra Barua, a "son of the soil, more at home in Bengali rather than Assamese" and he hailed from Goalpara.

The Council proceedings revealed that "due to lack of rapport between Eastern Bengal and Assam, (or in other words between the Bengalis and the Assamese), the handful of members from the latter region had practically no role to play". They had to look forward to the administration for support "rather than to the body of non-official members" for any issue of importance to their part of the province. However, the addition of three Assamese members following the expansion of the Council " emboldened" them to "plead more forcefully" Assam's needs, said an Assamese historian. But the details of their achievements were not traceable.[16]

Franchise for Local Bodies Election for Nomination.[17] Municipalities

The number of votes to which a Municipal Board was entitled was determined on the basis of its annual income, and not individual Commissioners, as shown below:

Annual income of	Rs.5000 and less than Rs.10000	–	1 vote.
" "	Rs.10000 and less than Rs.50000	–	1 vote.
" "	Rs.50000 and less than Rs.80000	–	4 votes.

For every additional income of Rs.3000 or part thereof in excess of Rs.80000, one additional vote.

District and Local Boards.[18]

Annual income not exceeding Rs.10000	1 Vote
Every additional income of Rs.10000 or part thereof.	1 additional vote

Thus the impersonal franchise in respect of the two sets of Local Bodies was highly discriminatory and unequal.

Qualification for Candidates

A person could be nominated as a candidate for election if he

1. had a place of residence within the Division concerned and "such practical connection with it as qualified him to represent it",
2. was a member of the District Board in that Division or
3. had served as a member of the Board for a period of two years or
4. his name was entered in the electoral rolls of the landholders entitled to elect a member to the Legislative Council of the province.

Muslims

The Muslim members elected by the votes of Delegates as stated earlier had to be chosen by Muslims alone qualified to vote and having the following qualifications:

1. Place of residence within the electoral area a must.
2. Title conferred by Government or recognised by it or
3. Holder of Kaiser-e-Hind Medal or
4. Ordinary or Honourable Fellow of the Calcutta University or
5. Graduate degree holder of United Kingdom or
6. Honourary Magistrate or
7. A pass in Madrassa Final Examination or
8. Teacher in any High School or College under Calcutta University or
9. Registrar of Marriages or
10. Holder of any property or permanent land tenure, estate or share thereof or
11. Payment of land revenue not less than Rs.50 in the Assam Valley Division or
12. A jotedar in Goalpara district with an annual payment of rent not less than Rs.200 or
13. Payment of Income Tax not less than Rs.1000 or
14. Pensioners getting no less than Rs.50 a month.

An elector had only one vote even if he had more than one qualification.

In connection with representation and electorate, two views of the Government of India are worth quoting. In course of deliberations on the reform proposals, it maintained that territorial representation was

> *Unsuitable to India as it was a land of diverse races, castes, creeds and sects embodying varying and conflicting interests.*

The present reforms, however, distributed seats on territorial basis to a certain extent. However, as before, the authorities maintained that

> *...representation of classes and interests is the only practicable method of embodying the elective principle on the constitution of the Indian Legislative Councils.*

They were particularly interested in strictly maintaining the status quo vis-à-vis the representation of Muslims. During those discussions, Morley had suggested election of representatives through proportional representation on single transferable vote by Electoral Colleges. He had said,

> *... Electoral Colleges should be formed containing a certain number of Muslims and non-Muslims in certain proportions and this Electoral College be called upon to elect the number of members.*

But the government rejected his proposal saying,

> *...the proposal so far as it relates to the Muhammadans was in direct conflict with the undertaking given by the viceroy to the Muhammadans on 1 October 1906 and approved by the Government of India with the approval of the Secretary of State.*

In this connection a little digression may be of interest and so we quote an Indian historian. According to him, Mohammad Ali Jinnah "did not consider separate electorate on the communal award as an ideal arrangement, for, he would replace these by something better". Again,

> *...the activity of Jinnah in the Legislative Councils showed that with one exception, viz, the communal problem, he and his party hardly differed from the Congress on national politics.*[19]

However, this difference alone decided the future of free India.

Character and Functioning of the Council

Discussion in the previous Chapter showed that the establishment of a truly representative parliamentary system of government was not at all the aim of these reforms. In the new Council, eighteen members were elected on the basis of communal and sectarian considerations. So unity was hardly possible especially in the absence of any specific programme and electoral politics. Though a non-official majority was prescribed, in practice there was a "European majority, all nominated Indian members forming its trail". However, the functioning of the Council was somewhat liberalised. The members were allowed to discuss the Budget which was no longer a monopolistic prerogative of the executive. The draft provincial Budget after a thorough scrutiny by the Government of India was discussed by a Finance Committee of the Provincial Council with half of the members elected. The Committee's views were considered before finalisation of the Country's Budget as a whole and its presentation in the Imperial Legislative Council. Then the Provincial Council was allowed to move resolutions on the Budget. Resolutions on other matters were also allowed. These resolutions were however, recommendatory and not mandatory. Supplementaries were also permissible relating to the original questions put only by the member concerned.

"No nation – building activities could ever be undertaken at the Council's initiative under such a rigid financial system", said an Assam historian. Though the reforms were "rightly spurned by the Congress movement of the day", no dissatisfaction was reflected in the Assam leaders' expression. Rather, Manik Chandra Baruah was highly appreciative of the reforms. He told the Council on 6 April 1909 that "the people of Assam considered the reform scheme to be their Magna Carta of rights and privileges". According to Amalendu Guha, "Perhaps the sole cause behind his wonderful perception" was the fact that, in response to an address presented at Guwahati on behalf of the Assam Association, Sir Charles Bayley had held out "the hope that the Assamese would receive their representation on a sure footing in the reformed legislature".[20]

Section IV
THE SETTLED FACT UNSETTLED - ASSAM LEGISLATIVE COUNCIL 1912-1920

The Eastern Bengal and Assam Legislative Council had a short span of three years so far as Assam was concerned, as seen in section I. During this period, important political developments took place both in England and India. Lord Morley resigned as Secretary of State and was replaced by Lord Crewe, a former Privy Seal and Liberal Party leader, on 7 November 1910. Lord Minto was succeeded by Sir Charles Hardinge, who was then permanent Under Secretary of State, on 23 November 1910. Despite Minto's claim of glorious victory in enforcing the reforms, anti-British feelings had taken a violent turn particularly on the issue of Partition of Bengal. Though Minto and Morley had earlier asserted that Partition would not be annulled, the former had told Surendra Nath Banerjee, "...if my country was divided in the way your province has been, I should feel as you do".[21] Despite the authorities' adamant attitude and the ruling team's lack of "brilliance" of its predecessors, a rethinking on the subject started obviously in view of the turmoil in Bengal. King Edward died in May 1910 and King George V succeeded him.

The new Secretary of State initiated the process within two months of taking office. On 27 January 1911, he wrote to Hardinge,

> *When I saw His Majesty last Monday, the 22nd January, and we discussed the various topics on which I telephoned to you, we reopened the question... with the exordium that I probably should think him quite wrong, but that more than anything else, he had set his heart upon doing something which would, to some extent, satisfy that section of opinion in India which regarded partition as a mistake.*[22]

Obviously with the King's approval, Crewe made the following suggestions to Hardinge:

1. Reconstitution of Bengal from Lt. Governor's Province to that under a Governor like Bombay and Madras.
2. Shifting of Capital of British India from Calcutta to Dhaka (Dacca) or elsewhere.
3. Creation of an Imperial Enclave in Calcutta under the direct control of the Governor General.
4. Rectification of the Partition of Bengal.
5. Reconstitution of the provinces of Assam, Bihar and Orissa.
6. The rectification of partition should be announced by the new King at his Coronation Durbar to be held at the Delhi on 12 December 1912 as he was "strongly in favour of it in principle".

Hardinge did not like to give any opinion of his own at that stage. So he consulted several officials in responsible positions. As all of them were strongly opposed to such action, he "declared the scheme to be impracticable". He wrote to Crewe that the question "had ceased to excite" any real public interest and enthusiasion and that the agitation was "dying". Moreover, "it would be breach of faith with the Muslims who would regard it as a Hindu triumph and a blow to the Muslims all over India". He would not agree to the status quo "ante Curzonium". Advising abandonment of the idea he said, "I prefer to bear the ills we have than to fly to others that we know not of".

The Governor General also wrote to the King's Private Secretary, J.Bigge, that the reversal of the policy would be regarded in India as a concession to clamour and would be a severe blow to the loyal section of the Indian people. The idea was dropped for the time being.[23] But within six months or so Hardinge's view of the matter changed altogether. What were the reasons for the volte face?

Sir John Jenkins was the Home Member in the Governor General's Council and responsible for security in India. He held very strong views upon the urgency of transfer of Capital to Delhi. That step, he thought "would be a bold stroke of statesmanship which would give universal satisfaction and make a new era in the history of India..." With this scheme, the Annulment of Partition of Bengal and other changes in the administration of the provinces concerned were to be associated. Jenkins also wanted these changes to be announced in the Coronation Durbar.

Hardinge wrote,

> *During the later months (of 1911), it was brought home to me that if there were to be peace in the two Bengals, it was absolutely necessary to do something to remove what was regarded by all Bengalis as an act of flagrant injustice without justification. There was at the same time a feeling of expectancy aboard that something could be done at the time of the Durbar to remove the injustice and I appreciated the fact that if nothing were done, we have to be prepared for even more serious trouble in the future than in the past in Bengal.*

He also took a dig at the Bengalis and felt that.

> *... the presence of the Legislative Assembly in Calcutta created an undue and inevitable Bengali influence upon the members which was detrimental to their legislative impartiality and presented a field for intrigue in which the Bengalis excelled. All these aspects of the situation in Bengal were most unsatisfactory and were a constant source of anxiety for me for which I did not then see the remedy.*

Further,

> *It was Sir John Jenkins...who in a letter to me dated the 17th June 1911 sent me a Memorandum, which caused my views to materialise into a definite policy.*[24]

Hardinge now prepared a secret Memorandum for the members of his Council. "The principal points" of that document were:

1. The transfer of British India's Capital from Calcutta to Delhi.
2. The creation of a United Bengal into a Presidency with a Governor-in-Council appointed from England.
3. The constitution of Bihar and Orissa into a Lt. Governor's Province with a Legislative Council and Capital at Patna and

4. The restoration of Chief Commissionership of Assam with a Legislative Council of its own. The Capital was to be at Shillong. Curiously enough, the same members of his Council who had rejected the scheme of Crewe, now gave their unanimous consent to the "more comprehensive proposal". The Governor General now sent the proposals to the Secretary of State. In his letter to him on 13 July 1911 Hardinge wrote that the political power of the Bengalis – " the born agitators as they were" had not been broken and they would never cease to agitate "until they have attained a modification of the partition". In his letter of 7 August 1911 Crewe assured the Governor General of "entire support and full authority to proceed." He also agreed that the first announcement would be made at the Imperial Durbar. Both the Secretary of State's Council and the British Cabinet approved the proposals in November 1911.[25]

At the Delhi Durbar on 12 December, King George V declared,

1. "the creation at as early a date as possible" of a Governorship-in-Council for the Presidency of Bengal,
2. of a Lt.Governorship in Council, administering the areas of Bihar, Chhotanagpur and Orissa and
3. of a Chief Commissionership of Assam.

The administrative changes redistributing the territories of pre-Partition Bengal were made through three proclamations issued on 22 March 1912. Then an Act to this effect was passed by the Government of India on 25 March. Finally, the Government of India Act of 1912 of the British Parliament received the Royal Assent on 25 June 1912. This completed the enactments for Annulment of Partition and administrative reorganization of the provinces concerned as announced by the King. The Annulment of Partition and reconstitution of territories were given effect in the following manner:

1. Assam was separated from Bengal and re-constituted into a Chief Commissioner's Province with Capital at Shillong. Its geographical area consisted of the earlier eight plains districts, Khasi and Jaintia Hills and Garo Hills. The arrangement came into effect on 7 April 1912. The province for a second time in its history was under the immediate control of the Governor General of India as on the earlier occasion.
2. The rest of two Bengals were constituted into the Province of Bengal under a Governor placing it on the same footing as Bombay and Madras.
3. Bihar, Chhotanagpur and Orissa together became a Lt. Governor's province with capital at Patna.
4. Executive Council was created for Bihar and Orissa.
5. Central Provinces became a Chief Commissionerate with effect from 13 November 1913.
6. British India's capital was shifted to Delhi comprising the Imperial City and its immediate neighbourhood and placed under a Chief Commissioner's administration.

The State entry into the new Capital was scheduled for 23 December 1912. A long procession started from the Railway station. It was headed by a number of elephants carrying Lord and Lady Hardinge, the rulers of princely States and Senior Government officials. In Chadnichak, some one hurled a bomb at Hardinge's carriage. He was badly wounded and fell unconscious on the pavement. A servant holding the State umbrella was killed. After regaining consciousness and still on the pavement, Hardinge directed that the programme be continued. A senior member of his Council read out his address. Thus ended the Partition of Bengal. To Lord Hardinge "belongs the credit of undoing a great wrong to Bengal".[26]

The Assam Legislative Council 1912 – 1920

The fourteenth of November 1912 was a red letter day in the History of British rule. That day for the first time the province was given a Legislative Council of its own. It started functioning in January 1913 and lasted till 3 January 1921, the date of implementation of the next set of reforms under the Government of India Act 1919 or the Montagu-Chelmsford Reforms. We now proceed to study the various aspects of the Council and begin with its composition. The Council consisted of 25 members of whom 14 were nominated and 11 elected on extremely restricted franchise. The nominated members were categorized as follows:

Nominated Members

(a)	Chief Commissioner, Ex-Officio President, nominated by the Governor General	1
(b)	Officials nominated by the Chief Commissioner-maximum.	9
(c)	Non – officials nominated by the Chief Commissioner.	4
		14

The nominated members of both categories were mostly Europeans. Apparently the non-officials and elected members together constituted a non- official majority in the council. But in practice, the Europeans including the elected tea planters together out-numbered the Indians. Further, the nominated members were naturally expected to be loyalists. Even among the elected members, in absence of electoral politics or parties, there could hardly by any unity. "Besides, the nomination of Indian members, too, was skillfully manipulated if necessary, to maintain the parity". The four nominated officials included one representative each of the Ahoms, Railway workers, Zaminders and Commerce.

Elected Members

The elective seats, classified under four groups or constituencies were allotted on the basis of Valleys or territories, interest groups and separate electorate for Muslims as shown in the Table.

Table 1 : Distributi n f Elective Seats

	Surma Valley	Assam Valley	Total Seats
1. Muslim	1	1	2
2. Local Bodies			
(i) Municipalities	1	1	2
(ii) Local Boards	1	1	2
3. Landholders	1	1	2
4. Tea Planters	1	2	3
Total	5	6	11

Of the eleven seats 4 went to Bengalis, 4 to Assamese and three to Europeans. Of the Assamese and Bengalees, six were Caste Hindus and two Muslims, one Bengali and one Assamese. Clearly the Caste Hindus dominated the scene by virtue of their numbers and socio-economic status. The tea planters were given more than their share on the plea that they were the principal investers of capital and contributed a big share of the provincial labour force. It is important to note that both nomination and election were characterised by all round check and balance of the Indian elements. It was therefore, no surprise that European and Government dominance continued unbroken in the four Councils under the Act, though the Swarajists who entered the second Council earned a name for themselves through their opposition to Government which will be discussed later in the Chapter. On 13 March 1918 there were 13 Europeans including the Chief Commissioner and 12 Indians in the Council.

L cal B dies c nstituency

The distribution of Commissioners and members of the Local Bodies, electorates and seats for election of representatives are shown in the next table.[27]

Table 1.1

	No. of Local Bodies	No. of Commissioners/ Members	No. of Voters	No of Seats alloted
Municipalities				
Surma Valley	3	NA	9	1
Assam Valley	9	NA	18	1
	12	119	27	2
Local Boards				
Surma Valley	7	NA	11	1
Assam Valley	12	NA	16	1
	19	217	27	2
Total	31	336	54	4

Altogether 31 Local Boards and Municipalities with 336 Commissioners and Members had an electorate of 54 voters who elected four representatives. In other words, for each seat there were 14 voters. The number of votes and seats given to local bodies were based on annual income and as such every Commissioner or Member could not vote individually, hence the apparent anomaly between the number of electors and voters. The total numbers of Commissioners and Members are shown together as separate numbers could not be traced. However, in 1912, fourteen out of 19 Local Boards were numerically dominated by the Europeans. There were 82 elected planters on the Boards and 57 represented the rate payers. Details of 5 Local Boards and 78 members could not be traced.

The remaining seven elective seats representing the three other groups were filled up as follows.[28]

	Numbers of electors	Number of Seats
1. Muslim	1188	2
2. Landholders	192	2
3. Tea Planters	126	3
	1506	7

The figures would show that a total of 1842 electors with 1560 votes elected 11 members. The average voters per constituency numbered 142. Each Muslim representative was elected by 594 voters. Ninetysix landholders chose one representative and every 42 tea planters had one seat. Though the Muslims had the largest electorate they had the lowest share of seats in the Council.

The extent of people's representation during the Council's two terms from 2nd January 1913 to 31 May 1916 and from 31 May 1916 to 30 November 1920 was insignificant. The total population of the electoral areas was 433826 and the percentage of electorate of population was .042. The actual population of the plains district according to the Census of 1911 was 6083713 and the Hills had 629923 persons totalling to the provincial population of 6713636. The third election due in 1916 was not held. The Council's life was extended twice by executive orders upto the implementation of the Montagu-Chelmsford Reforms. A list of Indian Councilors is given in Appendix 2.

The Council 1912-1920 – A Review of its Functions[29]

How far was this Council endowed with parliamentary procedures, rights and responsibilities which could usher in Self-Government?

Full of deficiencies and drawbacks of the Morley-Minto Reforms already discussed, this Council fared no better than the Eastern Bengal and Assam Legislative Council. In the 25 member House, elected members constituted 44 per cent of the total strength. That was no doubt a numerical improvement over the earlier Council as therein Assam's share of elected seats was 27.8 per cent during its second term. We have referred to the so-called Assamese – Bengali and valley parity. According to an Assam historian,

> *Thus counterpoised in the Legislature the Bengali and the Assamese middle class elements often tended to act as rival groups. In the absence of a common political platform outside*

> *the Council, their narrow group interests, cleverly poised as their respective community interests, dominated the proceedings. Yet on such common questions as further democratization of the administration, non-official Indian members often forged a united stand although they did not necessarily think in terms of a stable opposition bloc.*[30]

With this mind-set, to the Indian members the Council became a sort of a debating society, a platform for discussion of matters of public interests, but of course subject to the Governor's pleasure and not as a matter of right. Therefore the legislature remained a predominantly Government machinery for dealing with the rulers' affairs. An attempt at liberalization was portrayed by partial peoples' representation through the extremely restricted and indirect franchise involving an infinitesimal section of the population. But the whole of its image was irreparably tarnished, as before, by the enforcement of separate electorate not only for the Muslims but also other sectarian or special interests. These pernicious divisions accepted and reaffirmed later by the Lucknow Pact were the precursors of political developments the country had to witness in less than four decades of British Indian politics. These in Assam not only dealt the severest blow to the idea of nationalism, as elsewhere, but also created a permanent wedge between the two Hindu communities, the Muslims and the two valleys. We shall not go into further details of disintegration. Suffice it to say that this has been the most persistent ailment in Assam till today. Since the Montagu-Chelmsford Reforms and more particularly the introduction of Provincial Autonomy in 1937, the Assamese have been at the helm of affairs. But no attempt has yet been made at reconstructing Assam on the basis of unity in diversity, which is essential not only for the development of a composite Assam, but also for democracy.

Now, how far were the members able to debate on matters of public interest, for instance, the Budget ?

This "opportunity was under the procedural rules of the Council Manual, more limited in practice than what was originally intended by the Morley -Minto Reforms." A five-day notice was a pre-requisite to a discussion on the Budget, but the Government never gave the Council that time for the purpose. Thus they not only could not author the Budget but were also deprived of the right to discuss it. Atleast upto 1917, "... not a single resolution was moved – and hence no specific discussion could follow – on the particular Budget items". A nominated member, Syed Mohammmad Saadulla, was constrained to remark in the Council on 6 April 1917 that "snatching away of such right from people's representatives put the councillors to shame". The same member observed on 25 April that year,

> *We consoled ourselves with the thought that we could not be authors of the Budget, yet we had the valuable right of discussing the Budget and try to persuade Government by moving resolutions to modify it according to popular view ... by an impractical procedure and on the strength of a rule in the Council Manual, this cherished right of real discussion ... is being snatched away and the right of the people to influence the main heads of the Budget turned into a sham.*

Another Councillor, Radha Benode Das gave vent to the general feelings on 6 April 1918 saying.

> *Sir, we have met today in this Council with the avowed object of talking and little besides. I fail to appreciate the usefulness of such talks, and I sincerely hope that the reforms scheme will sound the death knell of such solemn talks. We shall then be spared the necessity of participating in the discussion of the Budget without having the power to control it and of offering suggestions, which there is no obligation to carry out.*

The nature and functioning of the council was indicated by the Governor, John Henry Kerr who said on 16 August 1923, "The old council was in fact, a sort of advisory committee and had no pretensions to parliamentary status of any kind". The only notable achievement of that Council was the passing of the Assam Local Self-Government Act of 1915.

Thus, what at least some people of India had "acclaimed as a great and beneficial gift" and "Magna Carta," was "increasingly put under ridicule". So "uninteresting and useless" were the proceedings in the House that two eminent members, Tarun Ram Phukan and Radha Benode Das remained absent for long and ultimately, early in 1919 resigned from the Council. The same year while in course of the Budget discussion, Phani Dhar Chaliha, another prominent member, referred to the opium trade as "tainted money", Chief Commissioner and President of the Council, Nicholas Dodd Beatson Bell, derisively asked Chaliha to return the tainted money received by him as pay and allowances as well as pension. The member who had earlier praised the "Benign British Rule" was enraged at the derogatory remark from the Chair and tendered his resignation. Interestingly, the matter was repeatedly brought before the Secretary of State when the Assam delegation led by Nabin Chandra Bardalai met him at London in connection with the inclusion of the province in the forth-coming reforms. His reference to the shabby treatment meted out to Chaliha made the Secretary "Mum" and "perhaps the sullen silence at the time forecasted the downfall of Sir Beatson Bell". But this was a clear overestimation as Bell was appointed the first Governor of the province under the Montago-Chelmisford Reforms.[31] Despite the resignations, however, some loyalists continued in the Council.

One of those persons was Ghanashyam Barua who "breathed in the same loyalist-moderate tradition". He was elected to the Council from the Local Board Constituency and also represented Assam in the Imperial Legislative Council from 1913 to 1916. He extended full support to the Europeans. In Assam he almost emerged as the unofficial Opposition Leader in the second Reformed Council under the Morley-Minto Reforms. As a counter poise to the tide of nationalism after 1917, he was "increasingly favoured" by the authorities. They made him a Rai Bahadur and appointed him Vice-President of the Council in September 1919. "Indeed he was the first non-official Vice-President in the annals of Indian Legislative Councils". Baruah also became a member of the Council and a Minister during Dyarchy for two years till death in harness in 1929. His class mate, Abdul Majid, "the lone Assamese" non-official nominated as a Councillor also belonged to the loyalist group.[32]

How far were the members representative of the people?

During the working of the Council "almost all the loyalist or moderate members came from the educated top social stratum and owned big landed property, tea estates or had lucrative legal profession as their mainstay of political influence". Thirteen of the twenty Indian members including two officials had the same background. All these members were "already or in due course to be Government title holders". Thus they could hardly be called real people's representatives. It may be observed that much of the success claimed for Dyarchy was attributable to the co-operation of such loyalists.[33]

Section V
STRUGGLE FOR REFORMS – THE POLITICAL BACKGROUND

In absence of any well-organized, strong and effective political organisation, the constitutional reform movement in the Chief Commissioner's Province of Assam was not so forceful to begin with. It is, therefore, interesting and necessary to take a look into the political background which ultimately pushed Assam into the struggle for reforms along with the rest of the country.[34]

Till the Khilafat and Non-Co-operation Movement, there was neither Congress nor any other political organisation in the Brahmaputra Valley. In 1884, some educated Assamese like Jagannath Baruah founded the Jorhat Sarvajanik Sabha for expressing public opinion on topics of the day. It sometimes criticized the policy and action of Government and voiced public demands. However demise of Baruah in April 1907 and the subsequent disunity amongst the members practically terminated the Sabha "The need was already felt amongst the Assamese elite" of a broad-based provincial organization to represent to the Government the wishes and aspirations of the people. Such an organisation named Assam Association was formed in 1903 under the leadership of Raja Prabhat Chandra Baruah, Manik Chandra Baruah, Ghanshyam Barua and Faiznur Ali. Its headquarters were first located at Gouripur and then shifted to Gauhati. The first Session of the Association was held in April 1905 at Dibrugarh. It elected Prabhat Chandra Barua and Jagannath Barua President and Vice-President respectively Manik Chandra Baruah became the General Secretary. This was the first ever provincial orgaisation to interest and involve itself in political matters.

During the first two decades of the 20th century till the emergence of the Provincial Congress in the valley, the Assam Association served as its mouthpiece in respect of their "needs and grievances, hopes and aspirations". Of course till 1916, "Manik Chandra Baruah was the soul of the Association and kept its flag flying. During these years... The Assam Association was one man's show – that of its General Secretary". It was under the leadership of this organization that Assam entered the mainstream of Indian politics of constitutional agitation. However, it was more or less a Hindu outfit and never attracted much Muslim support. For example, the delegates who pleaded for Assam's case for reforms before Montagu, Chelmsford and British Parliamentary Committee were all Hindus. We shall know more about the Association later.

The earliest Muslim political organization in Assam was one of the 54 branches of the Central Mohammedan Association. The Branch existed at Shillong in 1888. But its activities were not traceable. Some other Muslim organizations of the late 19th and early 20th centuries were the Shillong Islam Mission, Shillong Muslim Institute, Anjuman Islamias of different districts, Mohammedan Defence Association, Surma Valley Muslim Federation, Assam Valley Mohammedan Association and others of valley denominations. In course of debate on the Montagu—Chelmsford reform proposals, the Assam Valley

Mohammedan Association appeared to be the most representative body of the community. In 1917 Syed Mohammed Saadulla represented their views with special reference to the reforms. However, till the emergence of the Muslim League as the sole representative of the Muslim masses, the Anjuman Islamias also looked after their interests. During those days, the Surma Valley Conference was the mouthpiece of Sylhet. Its most prominent leaders were Bipin Chandra Pal, Kamini Kumar Chanda, Kshirode Chandra Deb, and Sundari Mohan Das. Cachar had neither any separate organisation nor any voice of its own till the late twenties of the last century. The Conference was the precursor of the Congress in this part of the province . Through its successive Sessions it "stirred the depth of the Surma Valley and initiated the cult of nationalism". But it also did not attract any noticeable Muslim support and participation and none of its leading figures belonged to this community. As in the Brahmaputra Valley, the Anjuman Islamias also looked after the Muslim interests of Surma Valley although the Muslim League had appeared on the scence.

The demand for reforms in Assam was the same as elsewhere. It echoed the Congress approach though that organisation was yet to make its appearance in this province. This was indicated in the statement made by Ramani Mohan Das in the Assam Legislative Council on 25 April 1917. He said,

> *India of today, having rendered such valuable services both in men and money during this disastrous war in Europe, reasonably deserves recognition of all these and that in the shape of raised status in the British Empire like her sister colonies...*

We have referred to the Delhi Congress Session of December 1918, which demanded full responsible Government in the provinces. The English officers, traders and other diehards in Assam used to say that the country was not fit for Self – Government. The Montagu-Chelmsford proposals left it ambiguous whether or not Assam would be included in the reform scheme. Further, the Chief Commissioner, Nicholas Beatson Bell and the European community in a body "stood opposed" to the extension of the reforms to this province at par with others. Bell suggested that it should be treated separately on account of its peculiar geographical position and heterogeneous character of population which included a large number of European planters and mine owners. He advised treatment of Assam like Burma or North Western Frontier Province or postponement of the scheme in Assam pending testing elsewhere. However, he favoured the continuance of the existing Provincial Council supplemented by an Advisory Council. It should be constituted on a "liberal basis" and under the Chief Commissioner. The Surma Valley Branch of the Indian Tea Association opposed Assam's inclusion on the ridiculous plea that there was no "intelligentsia" in the province. Further, "...the number of people who could read a voting paper was so small that direct representation given to them would be a farce".

Sharing the same view, the European community pleaded that in case Assam was given the benefit of reforms, they should be adequately represented in both the provincial and central legislatures. It was, therefore, natural for the organisations like Surma Valley Mohammedan Association, Ahom Association, Assam Mohammedan Association and Mahishya Samiti of Sunamganj to make similar demands for representation on communal and valley considerations. A further hindrance was the demand of the Surma Valley People's

Association for reunion with Bengal. Side by side with this, Prabhat Chandra Barua who was the first President of the Assam Association also supported the Goalpara Zaminder Association's demand for transfer of their district to Bengal along with Sylhet. This was an embarassing situation for the Assam Association which claimed to represent the province as a whole. However it now came to the forefront and took positive moves for ensuring inclusion of Assam in the reform scheme through three important steps.

First, an Extra Ordinary General Meeting of it at Jorhat on 11 November 1917 decided to send a seven member delegation led by Nabin Chandra Bardalai to Minto who had come to Calcutta. The other members of the team were, Ghanashyam Barua, Chandradhar Barua, Prasanna Kumar Barua, Ganga Govinda Phukan, Tarun Ram Phukan and Padmanath Barua. In his oral and written evidence on 6 December 1917, Bardalai strongly refuted the arguments of the Chief Commissioner and other Europeans, communal groups and associations. He pointed out that during the Ahom rule "...the nobles and the nine councillors...elected the kings and that the Council of nobles backed by the people could and did depose tyranous rulers". He further asserted,

> *Even now every village containing several castes ... is nothing but a representative unit, the village namghar being the common meeting place ... The Great Satras of Assam are purely representative institutions. The election of the Barpetra Satra shows how keenly alive are even the commonest and the poorest man there, of their right to have a voice in the Government of their Satra.*

The second step was taken by the Association in its Goalpara Session of 27-29 December 1918 "in the teeth of opposition of a section of its members". The Conference was presided over by Tarun Ram Phukan. It "stoutly and successfully" opposed the "secessionists" and deprecated the Chief Commissioner and Europeans who wanted to keep Assam outside the purview of reforms. Ghanashyam Baruah, Secretary of the Association, in a lengthy Memorandum submitted to the Secretary of State strongly countered the contentions of the opponents to the reforms for Assam. Like the Congress, the Association also emphatically demanded Self-Government in the same Session. To disarm the opponents, Phukan argued that "one cannot learn swimming without plunging into water". Castigating the rulers, he observed,

> *The government is bad and bureaucratic ... the English officials and English traders and also a section of Indians do not advocate popular government, and Lord Sydenham and others say that India is not fit for self government ... If India is not fit for self-Government even after a century and a half of British rule, who is responsible for this ? It is the British rule which is to blame. The British officials who came from England to rule here knew neither the language nor manners and customs of the country and if they can manage to rule well why not educated Indians who know the country so well ? ... Indians today are much better fitted for self – government than the Canadians when self – government was given to Canada.*[35]

The third step was its decision to send a two-member delegation of Nabin Chandra Bardalai and Prasunna Kumar Baruah to London for presenting Assam's case before the Joint Parliamentary Select Committee referred to earlier. But due to crunch of financial resources, the Association could raise funds enough only to meet the expenses of one delegate. Baruah, a planter and member of the Association "volunteered to go on his own". William Reid, the Commissioner of Assam Valley Division, allegedly "endeavoured" to dissuade him from joining the delegation and allured him by offering him membership of the Assam Legislative Council then left vacant by the resignation of Phukan. Reid also said that the delegation would be fruitless since reforms were meant only for the advanced provinces. But Barua did not relent and decided to accompany Bardalai.[36]

A copy of the Memorandum mentioned above had been sent to the Select Committee in advance. But when the two leaders reached London and reported their arrival on 24 August 1919 to the Secretary of the Commission, they were "taken aback" being told that their evidence was scheduled for the same after noon. However, they "mustered courage" and prepared for the "ordeal". They appeared before the Commission at the appointed hour "like a pair of goats for sacrifice". Montagu then told them that their memorandum being "wrongly addressed" was misplaced. They were advised either to adduce oral evidence forthwith or wait till the resumption of the Parliament in October. "This was a bolt from the blue and our faces at once elongated, with heart throbs not knowing what to do as the memorial submitted by Assam Association was our sheet anchor...", wrote Prasanna Baruah.

However, the duo accepted the first course with "courage and confidence". They presented their case with "irrefutable" arguments in favour of Assam's case. Bardalai's presentation was "in a manner consistent with the Congress stand as noted by Congressmen like S.Satyamurti, Bepin Chandra Pal as well as an Assamese student Bidyananda Duara, then in London. The delegates also contacted the Indian political heavy weights there like Pal, Tilak,Tej Bahadur Sapru, Shankaran Nayar, Sarojini Naidu, British Conservative Party and Labour Party and secured their support. When the two met Montagu he told them that they had won their case but it must be supported by another representation. That was done on the resumption of the Parliament Session. A similar delegation from the Surma Valley "representing both Hindus and Muslims" was sent. It was led by Abdul Karim, a domicile in Bengal and a member of that Council. He pleaded with Montagu for constituonal reforms and of course the transfer of Sylhet to Bengal.

The Congress resolution mentioned above had in a general way demanded the inclusion of all provinces in the reform scheme but no record could be traced to show that Assam's case was emphasized from any other quarter in the face of strong opposition of the Local Government and the Europeans. Therefore, according to Assam historians, "Admittedly the personal endeavours made by the members of the delegation and the persistant efforts of the Assam Association had enabled Assam to occupy her rightful place as a major province in the new political set up". Ghanashyam Barua moved a resolution in the Assam Legislative Council on 13 March 1920 tendering "dutiful homage, loyal devotion and profound gratefulness for the Gracious Royal Proclamation on the reforms".[37]

Section VI
IMPLEMENTATION OF MONTAGU-CHELMSFORD REFORMS

We have given separately the provisions of the Government of India Act 1919 and a summary of the Report on Indian Constitutional Reforms. Now we study these vis-à-vis Assam, keeping in mind that the intention of the framers of the reforms was

...to provide a training school for politicians and to test the ability of Indian to profit by their training in the use of Parliamentary methods of Government rather than to confide the welare of the people in their hands.[38]

1. Assam was made a Governor's Province. The first Governor was the former Chief Commissioner Nicholas Dodd Beatson Bell. He was also the President of the Council. During its second term there came an elected President.
2. The twentyfive member Legislative Council was expanded to consist of 53 members.
3. The members were classified as elected, two Executive Councillors, ex-officio, appointed by the Governor and nominated officials and non-officials, not more then 20 per cent of them being officials. One of the Executive Councillors would be an Indian though these selections had nothing to do with popular support or otherwise.
4. Ministers were to be appointed from elected members who enjoyed the confidence of the House. However, they as well as the Executive Councillors could be removed at the Governor's discretion . He was empowered to hold meetings with them together or separately. A list of these constituents of the Government during Dyarchy is given in Appendix 3.
5. Three categories of constituencies were prescribed for representation through election. Those were territorial, communal and special interests.
6. The Council was empowered as in other provinces to make laws only on the Transferred Subjects, the Governor having overriding powers of passing or rejecting an enactment.

The following other provisions applicable to all provinces are noted below.[39] In this connection, the Government of India Notification dated 30th July 1923 for the second Council can be seen at Appendix 4.

1. Any Bill proposed on a Reserved Subject by Government and rejected by the Council could be passed by the Governor by certifying that "it was essential to the discharge of his responsibility" for the peace and tranquility of the province or any part thereof or for the discharge of his responsibility for the Reserved Subjects.
2. Any member could put questions and supplementaries not confined to the questions raised. Members were given full freedom of speech and voting thus introducing a healthy and democratic tradition.
3. A detailed Budget would be placed before the House giving it the right of detailed discussion, debate and approval or disapproval thus keeping an eye on the provincial finances.
4. Cut Motions could be moved on the proposed Budget provisions.
5. Adjourment Motions could be moved on matters of public interests.
6. A Public Accounts Committee was to be formed with the Members of the Coucil for keeping watch on the expenditure approved in the Budget.
7. The Council was allowed to adopt resolutions on any subject under the provincial list and jurisdiction.
8. Representation of local bodies as such was abolished.

The Legilative Council

The Council had a tenure of three years. Of the 53 members composing the House, 39 were elected and 14 nominated .Of the elective seats, thirty two were reserved for the two valleys and the two major communities, Hindus and Muslim and one seat for the

Shillong Urban constituency. Different aspects of distribution and allotment of the seats are shown in the Tables that follow. First we deal with the seats which were given on valley or territory, communal and population bases.[40]

Table 1.2 : Allotment of Seats

	Muslim population	Muslim seats	Population per seat	Hindu population	Hindu seat	Population per seat	Total ratio of population per seat
Assam Valley	565593	4	143898	3126949	12	260579	230784
Surma Valley	1604012	8	200501	1437813	8	179787	190114
Total	2169605	12	180800	4564762	20	228238	210448

Both the valleys were given 16 seats each.But Muslims of the Assam Valley were very much over-represented. While 143898 of them on an average elected one member, 260579 Hindus had one seat. The former's numerical strength in the valley was 18.08 per cent of the latter but they were given seats to the extent of 33.3 per cent. In the Surma Valley they were slightly under-represented. They numbered more than the Hindus but got the same number of seats. But in the province as a whole they accounted for less than half of the Hindus and yet got representation to the extent of sixty per cent of the latter. Again, the Surma Valley Hindus who numbered less than half of that of the other valley, were given more than their share, that is, 66.66 per cent of the other. Hill areas of the province, except the Mikir Hills, where elections were not held, have not been shown in the Table. The total population of Assam plains according to the Census of 1911 was 6083713 including the Sadiya and Balipara Frontier Tracts. The seats allocated on the bases of valley and community were classified as rural constituencies except Shillong which was an urban area. The details are shown in the next Table.

TABLE 1.3 : Distribution of valley and community-wise seats and electorates Surma Valley Muslim Rural Seats

Constituency	Seats	Electorate
1. Cachar District	1	
2. Sylhet-Sub-Divisions		
1. Habiganj North	1	
2. Habiganj South	1	
3. Karimganj	1	
4. South Sylhet	1	
5. Sunamganj	1	
6. Sylhet Sadar North	1	
7. Sylhet Sadar South	1	
Total Surma Valley	8	49104

Brahmaputra Valley Muslim Rural Seats		
1. Darrang, Kamrup and Nowgong Districts bunched together	1	
2. Dhubri Sub-Division	1	
3. Goalpara and South Salmara Sub-Division bunched together	1	
4. Lakhimpur and Sibsagar districts bunched together	1	
Total Brahmaputra Valley	4	24552
Total Assam Muslim Rural Seats	12	73656
Surma Valley Non-Muslim Rural Seats		
Cachar		
1. Hailakandi	1	
2. Silchar	1	
Sylhet		
3. Habiganj North	1	
4. Habiganj South	1	
5. Karimganj	1	
6. South Sylhet	1	
7. Sunamganj	1	
8. Sylhet Sadar	1	
Total Surma Valley	8	49104
Brahmaputra Valley Non-Muslim Rural Seats		
1. Barpeta	1	
2. Dhubri	1	
3. Dibrugarh	1	
4. Gauhati	1	
5. Goalpara	1	
6. Golaghat	1	
7. Jorhat	1	
8. Mangaldai	1	
9. North Lakhimpur	1	
10. Nowgong	1	
11. Sibasagar	1	
12. Tezpur	1	
Total Brahmaputra Valley	12	73656
Total Assam Non-Muslim Rural Seats	20	122760
Total Assam Muslim and Non-Muslim Rural Seats	32	196416

It can be seen that in the Surma Valley the district of Cachar as a whole was given one seat. But in the district of Sylhet each Sub-Division elected one member. In the Brahmaputra Valley bunching of districts was resorted to except in case of Dhubri Sub-Division. As a result six districts got four seats. But in both the valleys, every Sub-Division was allotted one non-Muslim Rural Seat. Further details were given in Government of India Notification No. F213-X dated the 30th July 1923. The figures given above would show that so far as the Muslim Rural Seats were concerned, 6138 voters elected one member. The average number of voters for each non-Muslim Rural Seat was the same. Interestingly, the Muslim population in the Surma Valley was almost three times that of other valley. The Hindus of the latter numbered more than twice that of the former. The total number of Hindus in the province exceeded that of Muslims by more than twice. The constituencies and electorates were wonderfully manoeuvred to maintain a balance between the two valleys. Surprisingly again, the 12 Muslim Seats of the province and 12 Hindu Seats of the Bahmaputra Valley had the same number of voters.

The remaining seven elective seats called Special Interest Seats were classified and distributed as follows:

Table 1.4 : Distribution of Special Interest Seats and Electorates

Constituency	*Surma Valley*	*Assam Valley*	*No.of Seats*	*Electorate*
1. Shillong Urban General	1	-	1	6138
2. Planting Community	2	3	5	126
3. Commerce and Industry				
Province as a whole	-	-	1	24
Total Assam	3	3	7	6288

Of the 126 Planting community voters only 14 were Indians and 112 Europeans. In Commerce and Industry, 4 votes went to the former and 20 to the latter. Of the 39 elective seats, each valley got 19 and one belonged to the province as a whole. Only 3.93 per cent of the population excluding the Hill districts and the Sadiya and Balipara Frontier Tracts formed the electorate. Valley and community considerations were the guiding factors in the distribution of seats. Taken together, the 39 seats had a total electorate of 202704 voters or on an average, 5198 of them elected one member.

We now summarise this entire discussion in the following manner.

Table 1.5 : Distribution of Elective Seats 1921

	Surma Valley	Assam Valley	Province as whole	Total
1. Non-Muslim Rural	8	12	-	20
2. Muslim Rural	8	4	-	12
3. Urban General Shillong	1	-	-	1
4. Planting	2	3	-	5
5. Commerce and Industry	-	-	1	1
Total	19	19	1	39

Valley and community-wise distribution of electorate is shown in the following Table.

Table 1.6 :

	Non-Muslim	Muslim	Province	Total
1. Surma Valley	55292	49104	-	104396
2. Assam Valley	73732	24552	-	98284
3. Province-wise	-	-	24	24
Total	129024	73656	24	202704

The proportions of electorates to population during Dyarchy are shown below. Only the enfranchised areas with the exclusion of Frontier tracts and Hills are considered.

Table 1.7

	Population of enfranchised area	Electorate	% of Electorate to population
First Council 1921-1923	5157789	202704	3.93
Second Council 1923-1926	6790537	224063	3.30
Third Council 1926-1929	6790537	250751	3.70
Fourth Council 1929-1937	6790537	288832	4.68

The actual populations of the British territories during the period were as follows according to the Census of India Paper 1 of 1962.

1911	1921	1931
6579281	7459657	8622791

During the sixteen years of the Council's life the electorate increased by 86128 or 42.5 per cent . However, only 5.6% of the population (Census 1921) were enfranchised.

The next Table gives us an idea of the proportions of elective Communal and Special Seats in the Council.

Table 1.8 :

	% of Communal seats	% of Spl. Interest seats	Total
A. Communal			
Muslim	30.77	-	30.77
Non-Muslim	51.28	-	51.28
	82.05	-	82.05
B. Special Interest			
1. Shillong Urban	-	2.56	2.56
2. Planting	-	12.83	12.83
3. Commerce and Industry	-	2.56	2.56
	82.05	17.95	100

The Muslim and non-Muslim Seats were distributed on community basis but others had income criterion.

We now study the enfranchisement ratios of population during the first, second and third elections to indicate the extent of people's representation in the Council.[41]

Table 1.9 : Enfranchisement Ratio of Urban and Rural Population between 1920 and 1926

Constituencies	Urban		Rural	
	1920	1926	1920	1926
1. Sylhet Sadar	8	11	2.1	3.3
2. Habiganj	10	13	3.1	3.9
3. South Sylhet	3.1	8	2.3	3.1
4. Sunamganj	5.8	6.6	2.6	3.1
5. Dibrugarh non-Muslim	5.6	14	3.1	2.5
6. Karimganj	7.6	7.7	3.1	3.6
7. North Lakhimpur	5.6	11	3.1	3.6
8. Tezpur non-Muslim	6.7	9.1	2.3	2.3
9. Tezpur Muslim	10.4	13.8	2.2	3.1
10. Mangaldai non-Muslim	5.26	8.6	3.9	3.4
11. Mangaldai Muslim	9.8	5.4	2.7	3.4
12. Silchar non-Muslim	5.9	7.7	2.2	2.5
13. Hailakandi	8.2	10.1	1.9	2.5
14. Cachar Muslim	5.3	6.3	3.9	4.5
15. Nowgong	8	15	3.7	4.9
16. Jorhat non-Muslim	8.3	12.6	4.5	5.2
17. Sibsagar non-Muslim	10.3	10.7	4.3	4.4
18. Golaghat non-Muslim	4.7	7.1	3.4	3.3
19. Sibasagar-cum Lakhimpur Muslim	10.8	12.4	3.3	4.4
20. Gauhati	2.2	3.2	2.2	2.1
21. Dhubri	3.3	8.9	4.3	4.2
22. Goalpara	5.3	7.7	5.3	5.6

Between 1911 and 1931, Assam's electoral population increased from 4333826 to 6165612 or by 42.27 per cent. The highest percentage of urban enfranchisement in 1920 was 10.8 at Sibsagar-cum Lakhimpur and the lowest, 2.2 at Gauhati. The corresponding figures for 1926 were 15 at Nowgong and 3.2 at Gauhati. The highest and lowest percentages for Rural constituencies in 1920 were 5.3 at Goalpara and 1.9 at Hailakandi respectively. The corresponding figures in 1926 were 5.6 at Goalpara and 2.1 at Gauhati.

Though there were 32 rural constituencies, the figures of some of these were shown together, hence the number of constituencies in the statement is shown as 22. The constituencies were named after Sub-Divisional towns.

The 39 elected members belonged to different professions as shown below.

1. Zaminders 7, 2. Pleaders12, 3. Merchants 1, 4. Tea Planters5, 5. Retired Government Servants2, 6. Editor 1, 7. School Teacher1, 8. Clerks in Local Bodies 1, 9. Christian Missionary 1, 10. Othere8.

On 25 September 1929 the following classes of members took oath in the Council:

Surma Valley Hindus –10, Brahmaputra Valley 13, Christianl, Europeans 10 and Muslims of both valleys 19.

A list of Transferred or provincial subjects was appended to the previous Chapter. To begin with Assam was allowed to deal with the following subjets:

1. Local Self-Government,
2. Education other than European and Anglo-Indian and University,
3. Public Health including Medical Education,
4. Agriculture,
5. Veterinery,
6. Industries,
7. Co-operative Society,
8. Religious and Charitable Endowments and
9. Registration.

Ministers were in charge of administration relating to those subjects.

The following Reserved Subjects were allotted to the Executive Councillors of the Governor who remained responsible directly to the Government of India alone.

1. Forest, 2.Finance, 3.Home, 4. Land Reveue and 5. Public Works.

The Executive Councillors had no responsibilities to the Council. There was a provision in the Act to increase devolution of subjects to the provinces. At the beginning twentynine of the subjects were transferred to various provinces.

Now we have an idea of the 14 Nominated components of the Council as per the Government of India Notification No.4883 published in Assam Gazette Part II dated 2.6.20.

1. Executive Councillors	2
2. Nominated Officials	5
3. Nominated non-officials	7
	14

The nominated officials belonged to unspecified but obviously the more impotant Departments of the Government. The non-official members represented interests such as landholders,lawyers, medical profession, Christain clergy, retired Assam Rifles officers, domiciled Bengalis, Ahoms and Hill Tribes. The nominated constituents accounted for 26.5 per cent of the total strength of the House.

Reaction to Reforms

There was hardly any agitation against the reforms. Despite the Congress boycott of the first Council, a fair trial was given to Dyarchy by the moderates and loyalists in the face of the Non-Co-Operation Movement. However even some of those members were critical . Some examples given below indicated the minds of the Assam Councillors.

Krishna Sundar Dam from the Surma Valley observed in the Council on 29 March 1921 that the "Reforms here has imposed upon us the burden of a recurring expenditure of over five lakhs of rupees".According to him the salaries of public servants had "almost eaten" half the revenues of Assam and that meant that "...the public service does not exist for the country but the country for the public service".

Nilmony Phukan from the other valley said on 15 March 1922,

> *...to my mind the Dyarchy which was the birth of undue labour, by unnecessarily duplicating the machinery raised the cost of administration not a little, and when all round retrenchment was expected in every department of Government due to financial crises, civil services led the way and others followed suit to entrench themselves behind the new machinery.*

A resolution was moved in the Central Legislative Assembly on 8 February 1924 demanding a full fledged Self-Governing Dominion for India. In keeping with that spirit, Faiznur Ali, Leader of the Natioalist Party from the same valley moved a resolution in the Assam legislative Council on 25 March 1924,

> *This Council recommends to the Government to request the Secretary of State for India and the Governor General-in-Council to take immediate steps as may be necessary in order to establish full responsible Government in Assam.*

In course of debate on the motion the Swarjists condemned Dyarchy as "almost unworkable and utterly unsatisfactory". Abdul Hamid of the same valley observed,

> *...the narrow communal differences that stood in the way of Indian Unity has almost vanished and the persons who were opposing the grant of responsible Government have come to agree that it is necessary that we should have full responsible Government.*

Basanta Kumar Das of Sylhet supported the motion. He defined full responsible Government "...as complete association of Indians in every branch of administration and complete development of self-governing institutions. Complete association means also complete control." In the face of "strong opposition" from the Treasury benches the resolution was adopted by 29 votes to 17. Nine officials, five Europeans and three nominated Indians, namely, Nilmoni Phukan, Sibaprasad Baruah and Fazil Ahmed voted against such an important resolution. Sadananda Dowerah's resolution of 27 September 1924 demanding immediate replacement of Dyarchy by full provincial autonomy was adopted by 26 votes nem.con. However, even after eight years of working of the reforms, the prominent Assamese leader Nabin Chandra Bardalai commented that the "Reforms that was granted to us was nothing. What is there in this Reformed system except that it is a sham; there is nothing substantial in it".

The Composition of Government

During the first term of the Council, one of the Executive Councillors was a Muslim and the other a European, the latter as provided in the Act. During the first five years except 1923, one of the ministers was also a Muslim. If the Executive Councillor was an Assam Valley Muslim, a ministership went to his coreligionist of the Surma Valley. The first Council members had no political affiliations and the Governor chose Ministers on the basis of territory and community. The Swarajists entered the Council in 1925 in good numbers but they refused to accept office as a matter of policy. Therefore, the Government could not appoint ministers on "constitutional model". As communal and territorial lines of cleavage prevailed in the Council, these considerations were the guiding factors in the selection of ministers. Between 1921 and 1934 there was no Hindu Executive Councillor though there was a Hindu Minister except in 1927. Between 1927 and 1929, an Indian Christian from Shillong represented the Surma Valley. Government policy in this regard was clear from the official evidence before the Joint Session of the Assam Provincial Committee the Co-operate with the Simon Commission, the Indian Central Committee and the Commission itself, except its Chairman, on 3 January 1929 at Shillong.

Chief Secretay to the Government of Assam, G.E.Soames, said that as there was no party organisation in the Council, selection of Ministers could not ensure collective responsibility. There was also no possibility of the appearance of any party in the near future. But he told the Session that Ministers would be nominated 'with due regard" to their commanding a possible majority in the Council. But how would that be possible in absence of political parties?, he was asked. Soames's reply was that Government could rely on private groups in the House and it would be possible for a Muslim more or less to rely on the votes of his community. When Hari Sing Gour, a member of the Indian Central Committee asked whether Muslims representing 29 per cent of the provincial population were not over-represented, the officer replied that it was the Governor's discretion. Gour also observed that Hindus were being kept out as Executive Councillors and Ministers as a "design". Soames replied that many of the Hindu members refused to accept office and so the Government's choice was dependent only on a few Hindus of the Surma Valley,

The Government's difficulties were also explained by the Governor in the Council on 24 March 1924. He said,

> *Lord Lytton recently compared the task of forming a Ministry in Bengal to a jigsaw puzzle. My difficulties have not been exactly of that character. I may venture to use a more homely simile; I would say that the Governor setting out to form a Ministry in Assam is in the position of a cook who is called upon to make a pudding out of a dozen excellent ingradients but is only allowed to use two of them.*[42]

The ingradients were obviously the Hindus and the Muslims and the two valleys. The Governor said that those considerations were to be given priority. Therefore, he maintained a proportion of two to one, between Muslims and Hindus in the total strength of the Executives. This pattern of Government formation prevailed till the Government of India Act of 1935 was implemented. A popular Cabinet enjoying the confidence of the legislature, a democratic norm, then came into operation.

Formation of Council, Electoral Politics and Functioning of Dyarchy

Dates of elections to the Council and First Sessions are shown below:

	Election	First Session
First Council	November 1920	22 February 1921
Second Council	November 1923	24 March 1924
Third Council	November 1926	27 February 1927
Fourth Council	May 1929	7 September 1929

The fourth Council lasted till February 1927, as it was extended twice in course of the deliberations on the forthcoming reforms. During the second tenure of the Council, the Swarajists appeared in it. They adopted a policy of continuous and sustained obstruction with a view to "wrecking" it from within. Further, the Hindu-Muslim co-operation generated by the Khilafat and Non-Co-operation Movemets dissipated with the failure of the Movements. These factors only further strengthened Anglo-Muslim collaboration, though the Muslims themselves were divided into splinter groups even on issues which concerned community interests. Hindus and Muslims remained apart, the latter being supported by the Europeans. It was on Jinnah's appeal in 1937 that the Muslims placed themselves under the discipline of the All India Muslim League and its provincial Branch. During the same period, community antagonism exhibited itselp in the form of communal riots and few Muslim Swarajists left the party in Assam. The Council debates from 1921 to 1926 were characterized by community divergences. On more than a hundred occasions the members were divided on communal lines even on matters of common public interests.

Entry of the Swarajists made the Councils' work more difficult but further strengthened the co-operation between the Government and the Muslim members. Though the Assam Swarajists were led by Faiznur Ali of Dibrugarh, most of his co-religionist members remained out of the party . Two factors, namely the Swarajists' withdrawal from the Council in 1926 as well as Hindu-Muslim rivalry influenced the elections of that year. The Swarajists themselves were in disarray and their decision to withdraw only disguised their situation. As communalism dominated the political scence, in the election the only Swarajist candidate was defeated as "where there were no separate electorates, the communal principle usually wins". Refering to the election results, the Governor urged the members to look after the interests of the vast majority of people who "had neither lot nor part" in the making of the Legislative Council as it stood then.[43]

The Government naturally took advantage of the situation. They pleaded that more attention to racial lines of cleavage was necessary due to communal representation, territorial arrangement of constituencies and the direct hand of ministers in the Government. They were of the view that the refusal of the most important party to enter Government must "make it impossible to determine whether a ministry obtaining a fare share of confidence from all groups and not merely fortuitious majority could be formed by mutual compact". The Swarajists could not achieve much and lost the two No-Confidence Motions moved by them.

The only other group, the Independent Party led by a Surma Valley Hindu, Rai Bahadur Promode Chandra Datta, was created in 1923 allegedly to counteract the

Swarajists. But it was united only upon political question and "died for lack of a common programme in other matters." Both the groups lacked compactness though these had created party hierarchies of President, Vice-President and Whip and so on.That was done to "satisfy different interests and ambitions rather than to ensure a smooth and rigidly disciplined party function". Even these posts represented communal and valley divergences. For example, the leader of the Swarajists was a Muslim from Dibrugarh while his deputy was a Hindu from Sylhet. According Government, the Council had "...only a collection of dissolving groups."

Such circumstances even made it difficult to form a definitely organised Government group in the Council. However, the Europeans and the nominated members always supported the Government even though officially free to vote according to their choice. Sayed Muhammad Sadhulla was the most prominent moderate loyalist who was a pillar of support to the Government and was knighted in 1928. The list of Executive Councillors and Minister would show how others, of both the communities also co-operated with the Government . But the absence of party organizations, based on any difference of opinion as to administration, with the refusal of the only cohesive group to undertake any responsibility, limited the power of the ministry to frame any constructive programme and a secular approach. The work inside the Council lacked the spirit of usefulness. Questions, on too many occasions were put " particularly for the satisfaction of communal demands". Personal favour of individuals was the "guiding spirit behind the working of the reforms". There was hardly any popular base behind it.[44]

Now we give statistical data showing the quality and nature of work done by the first two Councils except in cases of Bills and select Committee Reports for which the entire period from 1921 to 1936 is covered. [45] Further details are given in Appendix 5. We begin with working days and attendence of the first two Councils followed by other aspects.

1		No. of Sessions	No. of working days	No. of Members Attending	Average daily attendence
1st Council	1. 6–7	February'21	2	45	23
	2.14–29	March'21	11	400	36
	3. 7–13	September'22	6	261	43
			19	706	37
2nd Council					
only 1923	1. 3–10	March'23	7	265	38
	2. 5–12	April'23	7	262	38
	3.13–16	Aug.'23	4	178	44
			18	705	39

Between 6 February 1921 and 16 August 1923, the Council had 6 sittings and 37 working days. The average daily attendence of members was 38.

2. Now we take into acoount the Bills Passed.

	Bill in Introduced	Bills passed or Acts
1921	2	1
1922	9	4
1923	5	2
1924	8	2
1925	10	3
1926	16	6
1927	7	5
1928	5	2
1929	2	1
1930	6	2
1931	14	2
1932	18	10
1933	6	3
1934	9	5
1935	15	8
1936	26	10
	158	66

In Appendix 5 to this Chapter, a list of subjects on which enactments were made has been given. It would show that most of the enactments were amendmends to the existing Acts. The most important enactment was the removal of sex disquilification and enfranchisement of women. Another, the Municipal Act, extended separate electorate to the local bodies.

3. Cut Motions

	Moved	Carried	Lost
1922	11	3	8
1923	1	0	1
1924	12	4	8
1925	NA	NA	NA
1926	5	3	2
	29	10	19

The figures for 1925 were not available.

One cut Motion in 1922, one in 1923, six in 1924 and one in 1926, i.e. altogether nine were rejected by the casting vote of the President. Of the three Motions carried in 1922, two fully and one partially were restored by the Governor's certification.

4 Divisions

	Moved	Carried	Lost
1921	NA	NA	NA
1922	22	8	14
1923	18	6	12
1924	39	20	19
1925	NA	NA	NA
1926	22	11	11
	101	45	56

Obviously the opposition unity failed on majority of occasions.

5. No Confidence Motions

No such motions could be traced during the period from 1921 to 1926. The first ever No-Confidence Motion in the annals of the Council was moved on 28 February 1927 by an Independent Member, Bipin Chandra Ghosh from Goalpara. It was targetted against Syed Mohammad Saadulla and James Joy Mohan Nichols Roy, Ministers of Education and Local Self-Government respectively. The mover charged them with "anti-people stand on all vital issues" in the previous Council. Supporting Ghosh, Munawar Ali "directed his venom" particularly against Saadulla. He said that the Minister did not enjoy the confidence of the Muslims of Sylhet and Cachar. He devoted himself "exclusively, or almost exclusively to doing good to the handful of Mussalmans of the Valley from which he comes", complained Munawar Ali. The motion was defeated by 28 votes against 22 for. The second Motion was brought about by Basanta Kumar Das from Sylhet on 29 March 1928 against J.J.M.Nichols Roy "questioning his British Indian Citizenship" status. It was lost by 27 to 21 votes an 3 April. The third Motion was moved by Munawar Ali against J.J.M.Nichols Roy on 27 March 1929. The Swarajists supported him and the Motion was adopted by 17 votes to 14. The Governor first prorogued the House and then prematurely dissolved it in April without showing any reason to justify his arbitrary action.

6. Resolutions

	Notice given	Admitted	Moved	Withdrawn	Carried	Lost
1921–1923	186	164	164	83	42	39
1924	131	112	48	17	24	7
1925	167	100	36	10	18	8
1926	67	55	39	17	14	8
	551	431	287	127	98	62

Yearwise figures from 1921 to 1923 could not be traced.

7. Questions

	No. put	No. admitted.	No. answered.
1921	761	726	717
1922	442	418	400
1923	405	298	283
1924	643	565	553
1925	978	917	900
1926	341	332	302
	3570	3256	3155

More than 91 per cent of the questions put were admitted. Ninetyseven per cent of the questions were answered.

8. Reports of Select Committee Submitted

1921	-	1926	4	1931	2
1922	1	1927	2	1932	6
1923	-	1928	1	1933	-
1924	-	1929	-	1934	1
1925	1	1930	1	1935	6
				1936	9
				Total	34

Details of rejection, acceptance and modification of the Reports were not traceable. The Reports related to Assam Local Self-Government, women's franchise, Municipalities, temperance and tenancy etc. and amendments to various existing enactments and proposals therefor on various transferred subjects.

It could be seen that despite defects, deficiences and difficulties, the Council certainly did some work and it became a platform for training in parliamentary practices. Almost all members of the Council under Dyarchy became members of the first Legislative Assembly in 1937 and made a name for themselves in parliamentary politics. However, according to an Assam historian

> *Working within the constraints of a sham constitutional framework and lacking a popular base, first Council could not but play a colourless and subservient role. It even assumed an anti-National role when it passed unanimous resolutions welcoming the Prince of Wales to India and conveying a message of loyalty, homage and profound gratefulness to the King Emperor.*

Nilmoni Phukan said in the Budget Session on 15 March 1922,

> *What we want most at this moment is larger sympathy and recognition of people's aspiration for higher and freer life. I do not consider British connection a necessary evil, nor the sole outcome of 'merchant adventurers'. This connection has come to stay for the good of both Englishmen and Indians.*

We close this discussion by quoting the Governor of Assam, John Henry Kerr (10 October 1922 to 27 June 1927). In his farewell address to the Council on 30 September 1926, he praised the working of the Council and said,

> *Well, gentlemen, all that you have done in the way of questions and resolutions and legislation and control over finance represents a good deal of solid work for which I have no doubt that Assam will receive due credit from the Royal Commission. It is moreover work, which has been accomplished without any breakdown, and I think, I may say, without any undue friction or cracking of the administrative machine.*

Regarding the Swarajists' policy he observed that when a walk out had occurred, the Government had the "consolation" of knowing that it was not due to any trouble in the House but to the policy of the Congress to which they were attached. That, therefore, "caused no ill feeling" and when they came back, "we have been glad to welcome the party back again and to see them to take part in our deliberations". Lauding the conduct of the first elected President of the Council he said that both of them "stood on a delicate relation and if they collided there would be trouble but they did not collide".

Dyarchy works on

The Swarajists' plan of wrecking the Councils from within did not succeed. The Non-Co-operation Movement also failed to obstruct its functioning. The Swarajists also failed to ensure their majority on some vital issues. Further, their boycott of the Council had paved the way for its smooth functioning.

After the elections to the third Council the Congress returned with a good number but still far short of majority and in the first Session of 1927 the party had 14 members. However, they succeeded in carrying out a good number of Censure Motions and proved themselves effective members of the opposition. But the Government had a solid block of 22 to 24 members who included seven officials, eight Europeans, five nominated members and two Ministers who often joined hands with the Executive Councillors. Thus although the Council had an elected majority, for all practical purposes and on many occasions, the Government managed to have a working majority. According to the Indian Statutory Commission, "There was no legislature in which the official block was not a potential balancing factor".

The technique and strategy of its working was succinctly explained by the "Mouthpiece of British capital in India," *The Statesman*. Its editorial comment on 5 June 1929 read,

> *... In Assam's happy hills there is no doubt that Dyarchy has succeeded, for the delightful reason that it has never been tried. There, if nowhere else, the Government has been really one, not a co-location of two committees, in one row of chairs. Assam's Legislative Council has seen no distinction of Right and Left on the Government bench. Immediately on appointment Executive Members and Ministers forget their difference of origin; and with the Governor they form a Panchayat working the Government as a matter of mutual arrangement ...*

Amalendu Guha said, "If the dyarchy functioned like this in Assam till 1929, it was more so during the years 1930-36, with a Council without the Congress Swarajits".[46] However in the final assessment, the Council had a brighter side too and all said and done, one comment seems irresistible. As the members belonged to the cream of the society, the high standard of debate was characterized by facts and figures, most often dispassionate logic and reasoning. Unlike in free India of recent times where our legislators resort to hooliganism and physical violence, those Houses witnessed sober, useful and constructive debates on matters of public interests.

Section VII
ASSAM IN POLITICAL MAINSTREAM

Before we proceed further it is felt necessary to discuss a few political developments in Assam in the all India perspective. We have seen how this province, mainly under the leadership of the Assam Association had been able to become a Governor's province. The demand for further reforms became forceful in Assam under the leadership of the Indian National Congress and the Assam Provincial Congress Committee. It is necessary, therefore, to look back into this development.[47]

Birth of Assam Provincial Congress

In the Special Calcutta Session of the Indian National Congress on 4-9 September 1920, Assam was represented by the members of the Assam Association. They were Nabin Chandra Bordalai, Secretary of the Association, leader, Chandranath Sarma, Faiznur Ali, Dalim Chandra Bora, Hem Chandra Baruah and others. Three opinions are on record about the Assam delegation's role in the debate on the Non-Co-operation Resolution. Hem Chandra Baruah wrote, "It may seem like a paradox, but at the same time it is quite true that myself and the other gentlemen who went as delegates, opposed the Non-Co-operation resolution as put forth by Mahatma Gandhi". But according to an Assam historian, they were actually divided on the question. Chandradhar and Dalim remained neutral. Bardalai told Gandhi's advocates that he had no power to support the resolution without the mandate of his Association, which was, however, likely to accept it. According to one Assamese leader, H.N.Barua, Bardalai had supported Gandhi's resolution. A third opinion was that "In any case the Assam delegation absented from voting". The leaders, however, " apparently saw the writing on the wall" after returning to Gauhati. They now began to work for the Calcutta Resolution and sought the support of various sections of the people. Bardalai even demanded a Special Session of the Association to discuss the resolution. However, the matter was debated first at a district level meeting at Jorhat in the first week of October 1920.

Differences appeared again. Ghanashyam Baruah, Ganga Govinda Phukan, Chandradhar Baruah and Tara Prasad Chaliha "opposed the very idea of participating in mass politics". They preferred to maintain the Association's identity "solely to fight on local issues". Only the Jorhat District Committee endorsed the Calcutta Resolution. To resolve the controversy, the Association convened a Special meeting at Gauhati on 11 October 1920. It was attended by 25 delegates from the Brahmaputra Valley. There also the leaders disagreed on the issue. Ghanashyam Baruah refused to chair the Session and Faiznur Ali was elected President. The disagreement centred round election, Council Entry, renunciation of tittles, boycott of courts and educational institutions. However, in the meantime the Non-Co-operation campaign had been started by Nabin Chandra

Bardaloi, Tarun Ram Phukan and others.

The 17th Annual Planary Session of the Assam Association was held at Tezpur from 26 to 28 December 1920 under the presidentship of Prasanna Kumar Baruah. The moderates were conspicuous by their absence. The Conference, while endorsing the resolution on Non-Co-operation, declared its object to "work for the attainment of Swaraj by all legitimate means and to adopt such measures as to effectively educate the people to that end". With regard to the constructive programme of Non-Co-operation, the Association decided to follow the lead of the Indian National Congress. The Conference was a "Congress affair out and out", Gandhi's image dominating it. The Association virtually "ceased to exist" and function thereafter. The name of the Association was changed to Assam National Assembly.

We have referred to the new Congress Constitution adopted at Nagpur. Nabin Chandra Bardalai was elected a member of the A.I.C.C. from Bengal quota. The constitution also provided for the formation of Assam Pradesh Congress Committee (APCC) for the Brahmaputra Valley with Head Quarters at Gauhati. In January 1921, the Congress Working Committee allotted 5 AICC seats to the Provincial Congress to be set up, thus broadening its organizational base in the province.

The Assam Association or Assam National Assembly met at Sibsagar on 16 and 17 April 1921 to review the post-Nagpur political scenario. Another meeting, the last of the organization, was held at Jorhat on 18 April with Chhabilal Upadhyaya in the chair. Both meetings discussed the issue of Non-Co-operation and organizational matters. The former had formulated the following guidelines:

(a) Withdrawal of lawyers from courts to be advisory and voluntary and not mandatory.

(b) Students above sixteen years of age only would withdraw from educational institutions.

(c) Money for Tilak Memorial Swarajya fund should be collected from villagers. Thus it would be unambiguously clear that the Assam Association had started sailing on the Congress boat.

Simultaneously with the implementation of the Montagu-Chelmsford Reforms, the Non-Co-operation programme also gathered momentum. The demand for constitution of a Provincial Congress for the Brahmaputra Valley gained "popular support". Prominent non-co-operators of the valley who belonged to the Assam Association and represented Congress supporters now took the initiative in this direction. The idea "assumed a concrete shape" when some of them, at the invitation of Nabin Chandra Bordalai met at his Gauhati residence on 5 June 1921. As Bordalai was busy elsewhere, Krishna Kanta Bhattacherjee, Editor, Assam Bilasini, Presided over the meeting. The first Assam Provincial Congress Committee (excluding the Surma Valley which remained under the Bengal Provincial Congress Committee) was formed with Head Quarters at Gauhati. But according to one source the meeting was held on 5 May 1921. The first temporary office bearers of the A.P.C.C. were,

President	Kuladhar Chaliha
Vice-President	Badrinarayan Agarwala
General Secretary	Nabin Chandra Bardalai
Assistant Secretaries	Kali Prasad Baruah
	Muhibuddin Ahmed
Treasurer	Jogendranath Baruah
Auditor	Durganath Barua

From that day onward and especially from 1923, polical life of the Assamese, particularly the Hindus, was dominated by the Indian National Congress. This was also the beginning of electoral politics in the province, which we shall discuss later.

A controversy arose on the question of election of APCC President as the prospective candidate, Tarun Ram Phukan had not yet resigned from teaching in the Government Earle Law College. However, under pressure from some of his colleagues like Chandranath Sarma, he resigned from the post and was elected President. Kuladhar Chaliha consented to become the Vice-President. The reconstituted A.P.C.C. elected Phukan, Chaliha, Chandranath and Krishnanath as Assam's representatives in the A.I.C.C. in addition to Bardalai. It also decided to constitute Congress Committees at district, mauza and village levels, thus completing the process of Assam's entry into the mainstream of Indian politics under the leadership of the Indian National Congress.

Political Development after Chouri Choura

On 31 January 1922, the Congress Working Committee asked the people of Bardoli, a small Tehshil in the Surat district of Gujarat to launch a mass Civil Disobedience. This gave a fillip to the Non-Co-operation Movement and Gandhi announced that he would lead the campaign at Bardoli. We have referred to the Chouri Choura massacre and Gandhi's reaction as a set back to the Non-Co-operation Movement. On 12 February he started a five-day fast as a "penance for the crime of Chouri Choura". The same day the Congress Working Committee meeting at Bardoli passed a resolution suspending all law-breaking activities. But it advised Congressmen to carry out the party's constructive programme.

On 16 February 1922, Gandhi wrote in *'Young India"*,

> *God has been abundantly kind to me. He has warned me the third time that non-violent and truthful atmosphere which alone can justify mass civil disobedience which can be at all described as civil which means gentle, truthful, humble, knowing, wilful yet loving, never criminal and hateful...*
>
> *If we learn the full lesson of the tragedy we can turn the cause into a blessing. By becoming truthful and non-violent, both in spirit and deed, and by making Swadeshi, i.e., the Khadi programme complete, we can establish full Swaraj and redress the Khilafat and the Punjab wrongs without a single person having to offer civil disobedience.*

It may be observed that similar incidents had taken place at Bombay on 17 November 1921 and at Madras on 13 January 1922. The A.P.C.C. meeting of 24 and 25 February endorsed Gandhi's unilateral suspension of the Movement despite strong protests. This decision thoroughly dissatisfied a large number of committed Congressmen of Assam as elsewhere in the country. It created a situation in which the followers felt gloomy and pessimistic about the future of the movement. Since November 1921, Gandhi was developing a "religious Mania" and mixing up political issues with those of religious morality". The Calcutta and Nagpur resolutions of the party were not "loaded with any such moral and religious values" but defined its aim at attaining Swaraj by legitimate and peaceful means.

Reaction in Assam

Towards the end of 1921, the Government adopted a policy of repression through arrest, promulgation of Section 144 of the Criminal Procedure Code, Prevention of Seditious Meetings Act, police firing on peaceful processions and large scale arrest of leaders including Nabin Chandra Bordalai, Tarun Ram Phukan and Kuladhar Chaliha. The reaction of Assam was expressed by a prominent Assamese, Chandra Nath Sarma, the "real founder of the Congress movement in the Brahmaputra Valley". At the time a tuberculosis patient at Puri, he wrote to a friend, Durganath Barooah on 22 February 1922,

> *I am stunned after receiving the Congress Working Committee Resolutions of Bardoli.... The fact that the Congress is not a religious body is known pretty well by Mahatma Gandhi... If this Non-Co-Operation Movement is entirely a religious and spiritual movement, then why did he not say so at the very outset?. In fact, in order to purify Indian people and initiate them to the religion of non-violence, there was no need of non-cooperation with the British Government. Nor was there any need of fighting with the Government to achieve the sort of independence he now wants to give Indians.*[48]

All India

Leaders like Subhas Chandra Bose, Jawaharlal Nehru, Chitta Ranjan Das and Lala Lajpat Rai "all felt anguished and shared the popular resentment". The Bardoli resolution "killed political excitement that had brewed up" centreing the Movement. The Government "correctly gauged the situation" and "took full advantage of the unpopularity of Gandhi" in having him arrested on 10 March 1922 on charge of disaffection against Government. It was a step which the authorities had not "dared so long in the face of public outbreak". He was tried and sentenced on 18 March to imprisonment for six years.

After Gandhi's arrest, all "subversive" activities were suspended by the non-co-operators. Thus ended the first phase of the Movement. As the whole programme had centered round a single person, his decision gave a deathblow to it atleast for the time being. It "illustrated the precarious nature of a political movement whose success depends entirely upon a man, however great"[49]. But the Government failed to refrain from the policy of persecution and repression. This aroused a feeling that the civil disobedience should be resumed. On 7 June 1922 the A.I.C.C. met at Lucknow. It requested the President to nominate some eminent Congressmen to go round the country and review the prevailing situation and assess whether civil disobedience in some form or other measure of a similar character should be adopted. The Civil Disobedience Enquiry Committee was formed with the Acting President Hakim Ajmal Khan (C.R.Das was then in prison) in the Chair and Motilal Nehru, M.A.Ansari, Chakravorty Raja Gopalachariar and Kasturiranga Ayenger as members.

The Committee examined 44 witnesses in Bengal, which included the Surma Valley, then under that Provincial Congress Committee. All members except the Chairman reached Gauhati on 7 August 1922 and examined 14 witnesses in the Brahmaputra Valley. A majority of Assam leaders were then in jail and therefore could not be examined. The Committee's Report was submitted to the Congress President after his release at the end of

October. The Report showed that there was no consensus in favour of mass civil disobedience. There was also not much enthusiasm for the constructive programme of the Non-Co-operation activities. The witnesses in Assam pleaded for individual civil disobedience. Majority of them deprecated the idea of Council Entry, a contentious issue amongst Congressmen. The situation "undoubtedly gave a fillip to the views of council entry" but a majority of witnessess were opposed to it.

On a similar mission, seven members of the Central Khilafat Enquiry Committee, namely Tasadduque Ahmed Sherwani (Secretary), Moajjam Ali, Majid Bux, Jehar Ahmed, Ashfaque Ali, Nawab Ismail Khan and Abdul Majid Badauni visited the Surma Valley on 8 August 1922. They also found that the witnesses were opposed to mass Civil Disobedience. Their other finding was that the Bardoli decision "had cast a gloom over the non-co-operators and Khilafat workers". It was told that the "Government repression had succeeded in breaking the nationalist movement". Under the prevailing circumstances, therefore, the witnesses "decided in favour of offering co-operation-cum resistance to the authorities. The idea of Council Entry was not opposed". Very soon, however, the Khilafat issue died with the establishment of a State in Turkey by Mustafa Kamal Pasha in November 1922 under a modern constitution abolishing the Khilafat and separating religion and State. By that time the first Reformed Council in Assam had already worked for almost two years. In India, by the end of the year all was quiet.[50]

Birth of the Swarajya Party and Assam Politics

The developments narrated above undoubtedly brought the differences among Congressmen on the reforms and working thereof to the forefront. This divergence began to crystallise into a division in the party. A section under the leadership of Das, Pandit Matilal Nehru and V.J.Patel advocated the idea of Council Entry. But Gopalachariar who led the group of no-changers equally opposed it. The Das-Nehru group "devised a plan to make the best out of a bad situation" and decided to carry on with the national struggle within the legislatures functioning under the reforms and started a vigorous campaign for the purpose., The question came to a head at the Gaya Congress of 26-31 December 1922. In his presidential address Das vigorously advocated Council Entry. Motilal moved a resolution granting permission to Congressmen to contest the forth-coming elections. The resolution was defeated and Gapalachariar's motion supporting continuation of boycott of the Council was carried by 303 votes against 87. The Assam delegates under Tarun Ram Phukan's leadership supported the Council Entry resolution. Das resigned presidentship of the party on 1 January 1923 and along with Motilal and many others formed a new organization within the Congress on the same day and named it Congress Khilafat Swarajya Party or Swarajya Party. Das became the President and Nehru the Secretary. The Swarajists then launched a more vigrous propaganda of their views. In the Allahabad Session of March 1923, it drafted a Constitution and laid down the programme of action. [51]

The Assam Swarajya Party

The Assam Congress leaders' arrests had been in keeping with the policy of repression. The Government's approach was succinctly expressed by the Governor who said, "Non-

Co-operation is a kind of Malaria. One can be easily cured if a dose of quinine is administered". 'Assamiya', a vernacular magazine retorted on 19 November 1922,

> *When the Non-Co-operation Malaria was going on the military came like quinine and the malaria abated ... common people were terrorised and the excited people became quiet ... seeing all these we venture to say that the Military is really working like quinine against the Non-Co-operation disease.*

Phukan was released from jail on 25 November 1922 and Bardalai came out in June 1923. Both first decided to devote themselves to the constructive programme of Gandhi. Following release Phukan said at a meeting at Gauhati, "we could not complete our sadhana for swaraj and that is why we could not obtain it." Phukan soon established contact with C.R.Das and supported him on the Council Entry issue. At the Allahabad Conference, the Assam delegation led by him as the APCC President supported the Swarajists' resolution for Council Entry and "almost committed the whole organization to the Swarajists' cause". After the formation of the Swarajya Party as described earlier, "a process of rethinking had started also in Assam" in favour of that Party. A scathing attack was made on Phukan for his Swarajya politics by the non-co-operators led by Hariprasad Das. "Reprimanded severely" for his new stand in a Congress organisational meeting, he resigned from the A.P.C.C. Presidentship. A new Executive Committee was formed with the following office bearers: Kuladhar Chaliha – President, Nabin Chandra Bardalai – Ganeral Secretary and Hem Chandra Baruah – Assistant Secretary.[52] "To persue the plan and programme of the Swarajya Party in a more "systematic way," he formed its Assam Branch on 25 July 1923 with Head Quarters at Gauhati. The Provincial Committee consisted of the following members.[53]

President	Tarun Ram Phukan.
Secretary	Rohini Kumar Choudhury.
Asstt. Secretary	Gopinath Bardalai.
Member Bishnu	Ram Medhi.
	Kamakhyaram Baruah.
	Dhaniram Talukdar.
	Jadav Chandra Das.

In August 1923, Phukan along with many other lawyers resumed their practice. The Congress at the centre had adopted a "compromise" resolution at its Bombay session in May 1923. It included the party's directive that "no propaganda be carried out amongst the voters relating to the boycott of councils". The Swarajya Party issued its Election Manifesto from Allahabad on 14 October 1923, keeping in view the forthcoming elections to the second Reformed Councils.

In Assam the opponents to co-operation and entry into the legislature were led by Kuladhar Chaliha and Nabin Chandra Bardalai. They began to propagate their views. The Congress had not split either at the centre or at the provincial level and the Swarajists remained an " integral part" of the parent party though the non-co-operators stood firm on their commitment. However, following the emergence of a party within a party, the absence of many leaders due to imprisonment and the confusion that followed, "The whole Congress organization lapsed into inactivity and lethergy". But Phukan made "conciliatory efforts" to bring all Congressmen including Bardalai to a single platform though due to his own popularly, the Swarajya Party in Assam was growing in strength.

To discuss the prevailing political situation, a meeting was held on 18 August 1923 at Gauhati. It was attended by 28 delegates. Phukan made the following points before them.

1. All Congress workers to remain united.
2. Though the formation of a separate party in Assam with "serious limitations" particularly in respect of number of workers was "impracticable," he emphasized the necessity of allowing individual Congress workers sufficient liberty "to serve the country in his own way," thus hinting at the Swarajya Party's programme.
3. Persons having no faith in the programme "might keep aloof, but they should not obstruct or put obstacles in the way entering into useless controversy which only created disaffection among those who were themselves willing to work.
4. Referring to the Congress Resolution of May 1923, he appealed to all to abide by it and function in a harmonious way to attain the common objective.
5. Formation of a Swadeshi Board for the propagation of Khadi and
6. Collection of funds by the District Committee.

However, Phukan's opponents did not seem to react.

At the central level, leaders like Abul Kalam Azad made efforts to bring the divergent groups together. At the Delhi meeting of the party on 15 September 1923 another compromise resolution was adopted to that effect. It read,

> *While reaffirming its adherence to the principle of Non-Co-Operation, the Congress declares that such Congressmen as have not religious and other conscientious objections against entering the legislatures are at liberty to stand as candidates and to exercise the right of voting at the forthcoming elections and this Congress therefore suspends all propaganda against entering councils. The Congress at the same time calls upon all Congressmen to double their efforts to carry out the constructive programme of their great leader Mahatma Gandhi and by united endeavour to achieve Swaraj at the earliest possible moment.*

Thus the resolution paved the way for the Congress Swarajists and others in the party to participate in the elections. Gandhi finally said on 22 May 1924,

> *I would ... be no party putting any obstacle in their way or carrying out any prapaganda against the Swarajists' entry into the legislatures.*

The Assam Swarajya Party had issued its Election Manifesto in September 1923, i.e., simultaneously with the compromise formula of Congress and Phukan started his compaign outlining its objectives as follows;

1. prevention of pro-Government and anti-people elements from entering the Council.
2. protest against anti-Indian legislation.
3. refusal of office i.e., ministership.
4. wholesale obstruction of official measures considered unfavorable to the country.

The central body of the Swarajya party declared that as an "integral part" of the Congress, it would follow the principle of non-violent non-co-operation with the object of "uniform, continuous and consistent obstruction with a view to wrecking the Councils from within". Thus for the first time in Assam election was to be fought on the basis of a manifesto and the legislature was to witness electoral politics on party lines with the pragmatic Congress approach.

We take a look back to the elections of 1920 to the first Reformed Council under Dyarchy. Both the Assam Association and the Muslims had boycotted the elections in separate meetings of 11 October and 26 October 1920 respectively. However, they could not prevent elections. All prominent leaders of the two major communities of the two valleys in general supported the decisions. But a good number of persons whose loyalty was not questionable were available for election and formation of the Council as we saw earlier. As a result most of those councillors were strongly denounced by the public as not "True representatives of the people" and at least one of them, Kumudram Baruah of Mangaldai had to abstain from attending the Council. Under the changed circumstances, such a problem did not exist and the Congress Swarajists contested the elections in a big way in November 1923. They put up candidates for almost all the 29 contested seats but could capture only8.[54]

New Political Alignment in Assam

The Swarajists with a strength of eight members could not persue their policy of wrecking the Council without support from other sources like the Responsivists and the Independents. For this purpose, Phukan convened a meeting on 7 February 1924 with his party members and others of these two groups. He got support of 12 of them and these twenty elected members joined hands to form a coalition entitled Assam Nationalist Party, a similar combination at the Central level as mentioned in a preceding Chapter. Thus, interestingly, for the first time in Assam history an well organized nationalist party with more than one third of the total strength of the House and more than fifty per cent of the elected members appeared as the main opposition to the Treasurey Benches. The two groups pledged themselves to work for the Swarajists programme. Faiznur Ali, Brajendra Narayan Choudhury and Kamakhyaram Baruah were elected the Legislature Party's Leader, Deputy Leader and Secretary respectively. There were three Whips, namely, Tara Prasad Chaliha, Kshirode Chandra Deb and Abdul Hamid. Prominent leaders like Saadulla, Tara Prasad Chaliha and Brojendra Narayan Choudhury and many others were opposed to the obstructive programme of the party. Saadulla refused to pledge non-acceptance of office and in fact became a Minister. However, the coalition achieved a number of success on the floor of the House, such as electing the President and the Vice-President of the Council defeating the Government supporters and passing resolutions on devolution of more subjects to the province. Abdul Hamid was the first President elected to the 2nd council in 1925, that is, after the initial four year period during which under the provision of the Act of 1919, the President was nominated by the Governor.[55]

Section VIII
MUDDIMAN COMMISSION, SIMON COMMISSION, NEHRU CONSTITUTION AND DEMAND FOR REFORMS

Now we revert to our main concern, the reform of legislatures and Assam's voice in the process. The Muddiman Commission was practically ignored by the Congress.

According to the Government of Assam's memorandum to the Commission, the Ministers were unable to refute the charge that the reforms had "bestowed no benefit on the electors" . The general attitude of the Assam Legislative Council had a " widespread dislike of Dyarchy" and it favoured the introduction of a responsible Government. On 8 February 1924, the Central Legislative Assembly adopted a resolution recommending an early revision of the Government of India Act of 1919 for establishing a full-fledged Dominion status.

On 19 March 1925, Faiznur Ali moved an Adjournment Motion in the Assam Legislative Council for discussion of the Muddiman Report. During the deliberations which followed, he observed that "... the only privilege" enjoyed by the people was to be cajoled by the candidates and cast their votes every three years. No official members participated in the debate. The House condemned the majority report as "retrograde, disappointing and calculated to delay the attainment of full responsible Government". Accepting the Minority Report of the Commission described earlier, the Council recommended steps as would lead to the appointment of a Royal Commission or a Round Table Conference for framing a suitable constitution. Interestingly, the suggestion for a Round Table Conference also came from an Assam representative, K.K. Chanda in the Central Legislative Assembly.

The political bon homie between the Swarajists and Independents at the all-India level and its break down have been referred to. Though the former lost dominance in the Central Legislature, they continued to criticise Dyarchy and oppose the Government according to its own programme till the parent body decimated. The A.I.C.C. Session held at Delhi on 6 and 7 March 1926 directed the Swarajists to walk out of the legislatures. They also walked out of the Budget Session of the Assam Legislative Council. But they participated in the September Session the same year.The Assam Branch of the Swarajists also faced divergences like the central body. Though it was not split formally, a group of moderates held a meeting at Gauhati on 12 September 1926 and formed a new outfit named Assam Valley Responsive Co-operation Party. Its Executive Committee consisted of Radha Kamal Choudhury, Kaliram Barman, Hem Chandra Goswami, Jyotish Chandra Das and Siba Prasad Barua.

Unlike the Swarajya Party which had split with the resignation of Jayakar, Kelkar and some others as stated earlier, its Assam Branch with the divergent groups presented a united picture at the Gauhati Congress Session of 1926 "By and large, the proceedings of the Session were dominated by the Swarajists". Even Gandhi who attended the Session " remained somewhat aloof since he had entrusted all the political works to the Swarajya Party" as shown in his letter dated 19 July 1925 addressed to Motilal Nehru and the Congress resolution of the Patna Congress of 22 September mentioned earlier. He also "left the Swarajists free to persue their programme in the legislatures, unfettered by any obstruction from the no-changers." Tarun Ram Phukan, elected to the 15 member Congress Working Committee was the first ever Assamese Swarajist Congressman to enter the highest body of the organization. Not only that, he and Mohammed Tayabulla practically captured the Assam Congress.[56]

There was a gradual increase of the members of the Congress Swarajists bloc in the Assam Legislative Council. Beginning with 8 members in 1923, there came 16 of them in 1929, as shown in Appendix 6. Phukan was unanimously elected to the Indian Legislative Assembly during the second term of the Reformed Council. Thus the Congress in Assam meant the Swarajists who continued with their policy of opposition to the Government under Dyarchy and supported and advocated the demand for further reforms in keeping with the national Movement. Srinivas lyenger in his presidential address to the Gauhati Congress had observed,

> *On a question whether a particular course is wise, unwise, will succeed or fail, will accelerate Swaraj or retard it, to make one's opinion or judgement or feeling a matter of conscience is false philosophy – I fail to see how we may rely on our right to differ from one another and yet uphold the discipline necessary for an organisation fighting for Swaraj.*

But interestingly, however, though there were groups and subgroups in the party in Assam, the Pradesh Congress maintained an official and outward unity. They also joined hands with others to embarrass the Government.

The Simon Commission and Assam

We have referred to the all-white Simon Commission and Indian response in the form of Nehru Constitution framed for meeting the country's political aspirations. The efforts failed mainly due to Hindu-Muslim divergences. No special reaction in this regard could be traced in Assam. The Simon Commission came to India on 3 February 1928. Under leadership of the Congress and other Nationalists irrespective of their party affiliations, the occasion was observed as a day of national protest in the form of black flag demonstrations and slogan of "Simon go back." "The feeling of exasperation touched even Assam". As elsewhere, the anti-Commission sentiment prevailed all over the province except in a small section of Muslims who did not respond to the call. Therefore, "To counteract the pro-Commission attitude of a handful of Muslims, the local Khilafatists of Sylhet met on 3 June 1928 under the presidency of Abdul Matin Chaudhury", a recognized leader of the community. The meeting "urged them to preserve their identity as nationalists" and not to "sell themselves for a mass of pottage." It also decided to form a Provincial Council of the Muslim League with Faiznur Ali as President and Mohammed Tayyabulla as Secretary "in order to organise the Muslims along nationalist lines." The prapaganda against Simon Commission continued over the whole year.

The depletion of Swarajist-Nationalist combine as referred to earlier encouraged the Assam Government to move a resolution in the Legislative Council on 3 April 1928 to constitute a Committee of seven members to co-operate with the Commission on constitutional reforms. Nabin Chandra Bordalai, a leader of the Swarajists opposed the motion. Pointing to the futility of reforms, he said,

> ... *No member of this Council should be a party, should be member of this Committee and should agree to give evidence before it unless a better state of things prevails.*[57]

A section of the All India Muslim League led by Jinnah boycotted the Commission. But another section under Sir Mohammad Shafi favoured co-operation. In Assam this group was strong and supported the Commission. Rising to speak after Bardalai, Sayidur Rahman, an Assamese Muslim Planter told the Council,

> *It is the sincerest desire of our community at the present moment despite what Hon'ble members like Mr.Jinnah may say, that this separate electorate is absolutely vital to our existence. This separate electorate has been enforced in Kenya, Palestine, Cyprus, Austra – Hungary and other countries.*[58]

Echoing this voice, the Government of Assam also maintained that

> *Communal representation was essential especially in the light of communal tension and clash of sectional interests and that communal representation did not create tension but only recognized the existence of differences.*

Governments' proposal was adopted by 31 votes against 15.

The Committee was constituted by the Council on 9 April 1928 under the Chairmanship of W.D.Smiles, an Irish Tea Planter. Other members were,

1. Arjan Ali
2. Munawar Ali
3. Keramat Ali
4. Mukunda Narayan Baruah
5. Rai Bahadur Sadananda Dowerah and
6. Rai Bahadur Amarnath Roy

Dowerah and Boruah were Brahmaputra Valley Hindus, Roy was a Surma Valley Hindu, Arjan and Munawar belonged to the Surma Valley and Keramat Ali hailed from the former. Thus valley and community parity was maintained. Being dissatisfied with the Governments' action, the Swarajists moved a resolution. It recommended that "..the members of the Committee be directed not to submit or make any recommendation to the Commission without previously taking the approval of the Council." But the President disallowed the motion arguing that it was not the concern of the Local Government to issue such a directive. A second attempt was also nullified later. The Commisson came to Shillong on 2 January 1929. At that time, most of the Assamese leaders were attending the Calcutta Congress Session. Therefore "effective boycott demonstrations were not organised anywhere" and there was no "hostile demonstration". Rather a Mauzadar received the Commission with five hundred men and the Syiem of Mylliem erected a Welcome Arch in honour of the Commission. As many as 27 organisations, most of them representing communal and sectional interests, submitted Memoranda in addition to the Government of Assam. The Anjuman Islamias also decided to welcome the Commission. A list of these oirganisations is given at Appendix 7.

The Provincial Committee made the following recommendations:

1. Abolition of Dyarchy
2. Enlargement of the Legislative Council to consist of 100 members as follows:
   (a) Elected – Hindus 41, Muslims 31, 23 other interests
   (b) Nominated – not more than 5
3. No Official Bloc in the Council
4. Retention of separate electorate

5. Revision of Muslim quota of seats after every Census by the Governor. The Committee was particularly anxious that the minorities should not have any grievance in the new constitution and "... would rather they were slightly over represented than they should consider themselves under-represented."
6. Adult franchise at 25 years of age or universal household franchise.[59] Assam Government's Confidential Memorandum of July 1928 was leaked out to the Amrita Bazar Patrika. Publishing a synopsis on 5 October it commented," ... the constitution evolved by the Government of Assam is admirably united to keep the antagonism between the forces of nationalism and communalism".

The Government of Assam suggested a unicameral Legislative Assembly of 70 members, 60 elected and 10 nominated as follows:[60]

General Constituencies And Seats – Elective		Special Constituencies And Seats – Elective	
Muslims	15	Landholders	2
Hindus	20	Tea Planters	7
Europeans	1	Commerce	
Ahoms	1	and Industries	1
Marwaris	1		
Shillong Urban	1		10
Primitive Races and			
Backward Classes	8	Total elected	60
Labour	3	Nominated	10
	50	Total	70

Excluding the seats for Europeans, Marwaris and Commerce and Industries for which the electorate would be formed for both the valleys jointly, there would be 33 seats for the Assam Valley and 24 for the Surma Valley. " These proposals will maintain the balance between Muhammadans and Hindus and except in the case of the constituencies in which there were special considerations such the landholders and Marwaris as the seats will be fairly divided according to the strength of the communities". The nominated members would be, one Napali, one Indian Christian and eight non-officials. Officials would be altogether excluded from the Assembly. The Government also suggested the abolition of Dyarchy.

The Assam Muslims' case before the Simon Commission [61]

Two prominent Muslim leaders of the two valleys of the province submitted separate Memoranda to the Commission. Abdul Hamid of Sylhet who had been elected President of the Legislative Council and held office for two terms, apprehended the worsening of his community's position "... if they are thrown into the mercy of the high caste people..." He demanded continuation of separate electorate not only for the Muslims but also for other minorities in the province. In justification he asserted that in the Council, resolutions banning cow slaughter except for religious purposes would have been adopted if the chances of success had not been neutralised by the existence of nominated blocs and other interests. The attitude of different groups in communal matters in the reformed Council could not be a true index of the necessity of special interests, he observed. He also objected to the inclusion of ten lakhs of tea labourers in the Hindu community.

Hamid traced the genesis of the inter-communal feelings to the Census Reports showing greater increase in Muslim population than that of the Hindus. Further, the reforms had only pointed to the disadvantage of allowing that to proceed undisturbed. The leader, therefore, demanded that for alloting seats to his community, their actual increase during the preceding and probable addition during the succeeding ten years should be taken into consideration. Otherwise, the advantage in the following twenty years would be lost to them for the period of next constitutional advancement. He suggested,

1. Constitution of a legislature with 80 members classified below:

Hindus	29
Muslims	27
Tea Industry	12
Primitive People	7
Indian Christian	2
Commerce and Industry	3
	80

2. A second Chamber consisting of 30 members of whom 11 would be Hindus, 9 Muslims and 10 for other interests.
3. Abolition of the practice of nomination.
4. Lowering of franchise qualifications.

Syed Mohammad Saadulla, then a Minister from the other valley, complained that the Caste Hindus, better situated and organised educationally and economically "have monopolized at least in Assam all the seats reserved for non-Muslims." Further, bunching of Caste Hindus, non-Caste Hindus, Primitive Races, Christians and Tea garden Labourers in a polyglot electorate had left lakhs of labour population of the province actually un-represented. He, therefore, demanded representation and allocation of seats on the basis of average increase in the population of communities during the past three or four Censuses. He praised the working of Dyarchy perhaps because he was an Executive Councilor and a Minister. Interestingly, he was supported by a Surma Valley Hindu, Rai Bahadur Pramode Chandra Dattta. He of course pleaded for joint electorates with reservation of seats for minorities in proportion to their population.[62]

The Simon Commission left Assam on 11 January 1929. Elections to the fourth Reformed Council in Assam were held on 13-27 May as scheduled. The Swarajists boycotted the Council. However, the House highly appreciated and welcomed the statements of the British Prime Minister and the Governor General of India and the decision to hold a Round Table Conference as mentioned earlier. Kumar Gopika Raman Roy, a new member "who held allegiance to the All India Landholders' Association", considered the Round Table Conference as a gift "that we should welcome with gratefulness". We have referred to the Simon Commission Report of 7 June 1930. The Government of Assam's views on the Report were as follows: [63]

1. The Provincial Executive should be unitary and jointly responsible to the Council.
2. There should be no-distinction between administration of subjects. In other words; Dyarchy would cease to function.
3. Members of the Cabinet should be no less than four for ten years.
4. All Ministers should be chosen from the elected members of the Council. "An official Minister will be in an even worse position than that of an Executive Councilor under the present regime."
5. The Finance Member of the existing Council, however, " would propose that it should be open to the Governor to ... take a non-official of standing from outside the Council with whom the elected Ministers were willing to work".
6. Election of Ministers by the Council "...is under the present conditions impracticable and therefore a system of proportional representation in the Cabinet must be ruled out".
7. The Chief Minister –

   For similar reasons it is considered that the appointment of a Chief Minister would not ordinarily be possible ... and for the province of Assam would not under present condition be practicable. The Government of Assam note that the power proposed by the Commission is permissive and that no definite statutory provision for the appointment of a Chief Minister will be made in the constitution.

   ... To complete the picture it is anticipated that on defeat of the Ministry by a duly passed vote of censure in the legislature or in the event of acute and incurable differences arising in the Cabinet, it must be open to the Governor to reconstruct the Cabinet (of 4 Ministers-non-official) as an alternative to dissolution.
8. The Government of Assam "accept the conclusion of the Commission regarding the separate representation of Mahammadans" and naturally agreed to maintain it for the community. Further,

   If separate electorates are accorded to distinct classes now thrown into partnership with the Hindus they (Government of Assam) consider that the distribution of seats might throughout India be made on the basis of population. If however, the general non-Mohammedan electorates are to be maintained even with reservation of seats, they agree with the Commission that weightage should be given to Mohammedans on the present scale.
9. "It is thought almost desirable that the Landholders should always be represented in the Council and it had been indicated to the Commission that assured representation would go far to reconcile the Zaminders of Goalpara to retention of that district in Assam."
10. Provincial services

    So far as those services were concerned the Government recommended the system advocated by the Minister of Local Self-Government that appointments would be reserved for different communities provided that the candidates had reached a standard set in examinations held by the Central Commission rather than sharing of a Commission with other Provinces.

11. Responsible Government

    The Government of Assam was of the view that it should be established in various provinces before it was introduced at the Centre. They also held that the Commission's proposals " provide a constitution adapted to the needs of eight large different countries (provinces)".

The Lahore Congress Programme and Assam's approach to Legislature [64]

Eight Assam Congress leaders had attended the session. Five of them were A.I.C.C. members. According to them the boycott of councils was "meaningless and would not serve any constructive purpose". They rather emphasized that a strong nationalist presence in the legislatures was necessary "to stall the Government's repressive measures" especially within the context of the nation's "resolve to fight for complete independence". Phukan was then the President of the A.P.C.C. Thus the party was in doldrum because of dissension on the issue of Council Entry for a second time. The triumvirate who had led the Non-Cooperation Movement in the Assam Valley were "unwilling to give the lead once more". There were differences also on the question of Civil Disobedience Movement. Phukan had by then "turned a responsivist" and opposed the "militant Congress programme". Similarly, Nabin Chandra Bardalai and Kuladhar Chaliha also disfavoured any such action. After returning from Lahore, Gapinath Bordalai and Rohini Kumar Choudhury jointly and Phukan individually in separate statements to the Press opposed resignation from the Council and boycott thereof. However the A.P.C.C. appeared to maintain unity till the first Independence Day Celebrations on 26 January 1930. But in a joint meeting organised at Jorhat, Phukan, Bardalai and Chaliha decided to resign and they did so on the 27th. The first two along with Rohini Kumar Choudhury also resigned from the A.I.C.C. Fourteen Swarajists left the Council. A young leader, Bishnu Ram Medhi, became the A.P.C.C President and Tayyabulla remained the General Secretary.

The old leaders who had resigned now formed a new organisation named Assam Swaraj Party with Phukan as the leader and an eleven-member Executive Committee; but they would remain in the Congress. It would work on the ideal of C.R. Das and decided to contest the bye elections to both central and provincial legislatures. They believed that their members capturing the Council "could serve the Congress better ... both inside and outside" it. Phukan was reelected to the Legislative Assembly. Choudhury was returned to the provincial Council along with Sarveswar Barua. But Bardalai who contested from Mangaldai was defeated. The Congress members from Surma Valley who had resigned did not seek reelection. But for two seats, South Sylhet and Sunamganj, two illiterate cobblers, Chirtan Muchi and Kalicharan Muchi respectively were elected with substantial majority. They were sponsored by the Congress to "put Dyarchy in Assam to ridicule". Other "responsivists and stooges filled in other Council vacancies".

The Simon Commission Report was discussed in the Assam Legislative Council in its September Session of 1930. A.W. Botham, Judicial Member of the Executive Council, told the House that the Government's views had been sent to the Government of India and the proccedings of the current session would also be sent and so the Government members would not participate in the deliberations. The debates that followed were indicative of the type of the Assam legislature the Councillors were pleading for. To the loyalists, Dominion Status seemed to be the real solution of the Indian problem. By that time the British authorities at home decided to convene a Round Table Conference in London and those leaders were eager to accept the offer. A motion to that effect brought to the Council by a Sylhet Hindu, Pyari Mohan Das, was supported by Muslim leaders from Goalpara, Nowgong and his district. A similar motion was also tabled by Manawar Ali but it could not be moved due to his absence. However, Chandradhar Baruah, a poet, planter and Member of the Council of State was selelcted by the Government of India from Assam to attend the Conference.

Brindaban Chandra Goswami from the Assam Valley moved a resolution on 30 September 1930 and observed that the Commission's recommendations were far short of expectation. These according to him were not inspired by any genuine and liberal statesmanship to help usher in complete Self-Government within a time frame. Further, the clauses like Governor's extra-ordinary powers, appointment of non-elected persons as Ministers and retention of separate electorates were retrograde steps. Significant modifications thereof must precede the fulfillment of the "legitimate aspirations" of the people.

Munawar Ali now moved the following amendment to Goswami's resolution and observed,

> *... The Report of the Simon Commission is unacceptable and this Council is of the opinion that Dominion Status with autonomous provinces forming into a federation as well as of the Central Government to their respective legilatures be immediately established in India with adequate safeguards of the interests of the Muslims and other minority communities.*

Ali claimed that his draft motion had the support of many Hindu Members of the House. His objection to the Report was due to universal condemnation and inherent deficiencies of the Report like the total absence of even the commitment to Dominion Status for India. He quoted Sir Sankaran Nayar, Chairman of the Indian Central Committee as saying that he was not dissatisfied at the Report as he had expected nothing out of it. He then said, "Let me take this opportunity to note my personal disappointment and regret as a member of the Assam Provincial Committee. I wonder, Sir, if I could not have utilised my time and energy better".

Criticizing the Report which, according to him, proposed to make the ruler "A veritable autocrat," he commented, "What is given by the one hand is taken away by the other, all that in the name of safeguarding the interest of the minority community." As regards autonomy and fully responsible Government, he said,

> *I do not mean ideal autonomy. Ideal autonomy is untenable... By autonomy I feel the fullest measure of powers for Self-Government to the provinces in the management of their internal affairs compatible with the federation of the provinces under a Central Government.*

Further,

... Those who are familiar with federal constitutions must admit that the Sub-continent of India is only the fittest place for a federation of different provinces or a federal Government. Other forms will not suit her, and the Indian constitution makers, with the only exception of the draft proposed by Mr. Vijoyaraghavachariar have advocated a federal constitution of British India. A unitary form never to be within the range of practical politics...

Advocating a fully responsible Government, both at the centre and the provinces and Dominion Status, the member said,

We are convinced sir, that it is largely due to the absence of responsibility in the Governments that is greatly responsible for the present undesirable state of things in India ... Sir, Dominion Status and no less a federated British India, would be a misnomer without full responsibility of the Central Government and the provincial Governments to their legislatures ...Dominion status is the universal demand of British India.

He seemed to ignore the Lahore Resolution of the Congress.

As regards safeguards for minorities suggested by Simon, Munawar observed,

...I differ with them only in this that they recommend that safeguards are to rest with the rulers. What we Mussalnous want is that they must be embodied in every constitution. They must be organic and not superficial. It is but natural that under the status of a Dominion and a scheme of federation the Moslems and other minority communities should put forward their grievances for redress and press for certain legitimate safeguards.

He then practically repeated the 14 Points of Jinnah enume-rating the safeguards in India in general and Assam in particular. He quoted Chintamoni Panigrahi of the United Provinces as saying that this would lessen the cause of friction. But at the same time he hoped that "It is a question of time, it seems to me, a few years only, when the Muslims themselves will demand their abolition".[65]

Munawar Ali Constitution for Assam Legislative Council [66]

Interestingly, the Councillor suggested a "constitution in a nut-shell" for a unicameral legislature. Its composition was to be as shown here:

	Constituencies.	No. of Seats.
1.	Muslims	35
2.	Hindus	41
3.	Europeans	2
4.	Depressed Classes	2
5.	Backward Tracts	2
6.	Labour	2
7.	Commerce and Industry	2
8.	British part of Khasi and Jaintia Hills	1
9.	Tea Industry	
	European	11
	Indian	2
		100

He also demanded that the backward territories as well as the districts of Cachar, Goalpara and Sylhet should remain in the province and "Assam should not be dismembered". Last but not the least,

> *On the completion of the Census of the year 1931 and at the end of each subsequent decennial censuses, the Governor shall redistribute the one hundred seats in the legislature increasing or decreasing the Muslim quota on the basis of the proportion just suggested, i.e., on the basis of 33 per cent. The principle will be found in the report of the Assam Provincial Committee.*

Another Muslim Member, Keramat Ali, held a slightly different view of the Simon recommendations. To him those were not "wholly unacceptable" but the "Report may be made to meet the Indian aspiration by additions and alterations". He agreed with Goswami that the recommendations would have to be largely modified. He also observed, "... That Dyarchy is not a success there is no doubt and Dyarchy is inconsistent with provincial autonomy". Again, "provincial autonomy will be inconsistent with a Ministry not responsible to Government". Agreeing with the Muslim League and Munawar Ali he also pleaded for federal legislatures and Governments as "... it is in fact the only workable method by which the diverse interests of the British Indian provinces and the Indian States can be served." For the Federal legislature he wanted indirect election as it was in vogue then. But a Member of the provincial Council, once elected to that legislature should resign from the latter. He supported communal representation as sugested by the Provincial Committee. Munawar Ali, at the end of the debate, categorically assured that he would oppose secession from the British Empire. Goswami's resolution with Ali's amendment was unanimously adopted. Interestingly, the idea of federation was incorporated in the next set of reforms.[67]

Section IX
REACTION TO GANDHI-IRWIN PACT AND COMMUNAL AWARD

The Pact, already discussed, had a mixed reaction. To the younger generation it was of little value without a general amnesty for all political prisoners including the revolutionaries. But it was accepted by the older leaders as a move in the right direction and they were appreciative of it. Brindaban Chandra Goswami moved the following resolution in the Council on 29 April 1931.

> *This Council welcomes the declaration of British Policy regarding constitutional development in India outlined in the Prime Minister's speech at the end of the Round Table Conference in London and records its opinion that the principles enunciated should afford a satisfactory basis for further discussion and eventually provide India with a Constitution that will satisfy Indian aspirations.*

E.S.Roffey suggested the addition of the words "and be acceptable to all sections of the people". Goswami accepted the amendment.Munawar Ali moved a second resolution which read,

> *That this Council records its deep sense of appreciation of the steps taken by the Government of India and the National Congress Working Committee to create a favourable atmosphere*

for making a proper Constitution for India and fervently hopes that a Constitution satisfying Indian aspirations and acceptable to all sections of the community will ultimately be formed.And this Council further records its profound sense of gratefulness to Lord Irwin and Mahatma Gandhi for the untiring zeal and energy and farsighted statesmanship displayed by them in bringing about the aforesaid happy State of things.

Both the motions were adopted nem. con.[68]

Assam's reaction to Communal Award and Poona Pact

We have seen how the Gandhi-Irwin Pact and the second Round Table Conference had failed to solve the Hindu-Muslim and Hindu-Scheduled Caste problems. Macdonald's Communal Award and Ambedkar-Gandhi confrontation on the question of the Scheduled Caste representation brought about a serious crisis in the Indian political situation. The Gandhi-Ambedkar or Poona Pact, as discussed earlier brought a temporary truce in the struggle for reforms. Assam's reaction to the Award and the Pact can be studied under three heads, namely, the Government views, Hindu views and Muslim views.

Government views

The Government of Assam accepted the Communal Award. They submitted an Explanatory Memorandum to the Government of India with the following suggestions for reservation and allocation of seats in the provincial legislature.[69]

Constituencies and Seats

A. General	
1. Non-Muslim General	46
2. Muslims – Separate Electorate	34
3. Khasi and Jaintia Hills British Portion and Shillong Urban area	2
4. Garos	2
5. Mikirs	1
6. Backward Plain Tribes – Kacharis, Miris, Lalungs and others	4
7. Depressed Classes	
Surma Valley	3
Brahmaputra Valley	1
B. Special Constituencies	
8. European Planters	8
9. Indian Planters	2
10. Indian Commerce and Industry	1
11. Tea Garden Labourers	4
	108

The labour population other than tea gardens numbered 979000 but as they did not pay land revenue or Choukidari Tax, they were given no representation. The Memorandum did not suggest a Second Chamber for the province.

Hindu Views

This was best represented by Promode Chandra Datta, a former Minister and present Member of the Council. In a letter to the Chief Secretary, Assam, he said,

> *I have failed to discover any consistent principle in the distribution made in the Award. The Muhamamdans have been given seats in proportion to their number with a right to contest additional seats in special circumstances ... In their case not only has the population basis been maintained but a possible weightage has been conceded to them. In the case of the Hindus a very different principle seems to have been adopted. Not only have they not been allowed the seats to which on population basis they are entitled but their very majority has been virtually converted into a minority in utter disregard of the fundamental principle of responsible Government ... Nor does the Award take into consideration the fact that in wealth, education and political progress Hindus are far away in the front and their contributions to the provincial revenue far exceed those made by the Muslims. These considerations should have weighed in favour of the Hindus. Any differential treatment is always keenly resented.*[70]

Further, Datta pointed out that no party or group would have a majority in the legislature and ruled out the reconcilability of the two communities. Therefore, the European bloc would have a decisive voice in Ministry making. Thus the Award had created a "fundamentally unsound" situation. He therefore warned that any discrimination against either of the two major groups would antagonize the Hindus and "lead to a disturbance of those amicable relations which now subsists between them and the European tea planters who have come to work among the Indians will feel the force of that antagonism".

In an interview with C.S. Gunning, Inspector General of Police, Assam, Datta suggested the following composition of the legislature:

Hindus	56	seats
Europeans	6	"
Muslims	34	"
Others	9	"
Indian Christians	3	"
	108	

He claimed that on the basis of population, Hindus deserved 61 seats. But to provide for European representation, 5 seats were to be taken from them and I from others. The Member did not provide for any specific number of seats for the Depressed Classes and Hill Tribes but these were included in the category of 'others'. Gunning commented,

> *In short, he voiced the view which is being loudly expressed elsewhere by the Hindu community that they are being relegated to a position of inferiority on the new Council and that where extra seats are required in order to give weightage to other minor communities, they have been taken unfairly at the expense of the Hindus and not of the Mohammedan Community.*[71]

The offer of 34 seats to the Muslims made both by Datta and the Government was incorporated in the Government of India Act of 1935.

All-Party Convention

An All-Party Convention was held at Allahabad from 12 to 14 December 1932. It was attended by the representatives of the following organizations of Assam.

1. Assam Association	Kuladhar Chaliha.
2. Assam Muslim Association	Mohammad Tayyuabulla.
3. Jamiat-Ul-Ulema-E – Hind	S.Ambia.
4. Assam State Khilafat Committee	Abdul Karim.

The Convention suggested the composition of the legislature as shown here:

Contituencies.	Seats.
Hindus	61
Muslims	43
Indian Christians	2
Backward Classes	4
Agriculture, Trade and Commerce	6
	116

Interestingly, in the bigger House, they did not provide for representation of Labour and Europeans.

Muslim Views[72]

The most pominent Muslim leader of Assam was Sir Mohammad Saadulla (Knighted in 1928). He had an unbroken administrative experience during the period of Dyarchy as a Minister and as an Executive Councillor. The Governor of Assam wanted to know from him the peoples' views on the Communal Award. Then an Executive Member, he reacted with the following observations.

> *I am confident that 99 per cent of Assam Muslims if not cent per cent endorses my view that they were not satisfied with the Award. So far I have been informed that the Assam Muslim League, with headquarters at Sylhet, proposed to protest against the Award on 21st August but as the All India Muslim League is also sitting on that very date at Delhi to discuss the Award, the Sylhet League has not passed any formal protest. They are waiting to see the result of the All India League.*

He also claimed that every Muslim he had met and spoken with at Shillong was dissatisfied. To him the award was "disappointing" and unjustifiable" and "The Muslims of this province got a bitter pill to swallow in the shape of this award and they connot therefore, be satisfied with it." He demanded that, the Muslims should be given 38 seats on the basis of their population in the province and the population of the enfranchised area. The former numbered 8622251 and the latter 7869132. The Muslims had a numerical strength of 2744108. The figures collected by us from the Census Report of 1931 show small differences in the figures as shown later.

The Assam Muslim Conference,Sylhet, and the Anjuman Islamias were equally dissatisfied. The former's representative, Abdur Rashid, complained that weightage was not given to the Muslims as a result of misrepresentation of their position at the Round Table Conference as they were not allowed to send a delegate there. He said,

> *...Great injustice has been done to the Mussalmans as they have been permanently put in a disadvantageous position and along with them the Europeans and other non-Hindus as no combination of non-Hindus can check a selfish motion of the other Hindus in the coming Council. The injustice done is so glaring that it is awkward for a community to remain in a permanently disadvantageous position.*

He demanded forty seats for his community, 35 on the basis of population and 5 as weightage. He also demanded Muslim repsresentation in the Third Round Table Conference so that their interests might be safeguarded from any other "encroachment as they experienced in the past".[73]

Abdur Rahman representing the Anjuman said that unlike in other provinces which gave them "considerable weightage," "the blessed followers of the Prophet have not only been denied weightage but they have not been given their birth-right". He saw "an all pervading Hindu supremacy in the Award". According to him, all the seats allotted to the Depressed and Backward Classes, Labour and Commerce and Industry seats would go to the Hindus raising their strength to 65 as against 34 of his community. He demanded 38 seats. Secretary of the Assam Muslim Association, Tayyabulla also expressed dissatisfaction and said that the Award could satisfy none. Thus we can see that both the Hindus and the Muslims were unhappy with the proposed scheme of representation, though obviously for different reasons.

The Government of Assam gave the following correct assessment of the political atmosphere in the province vis-à-vis the strength of the forthcoming legislature and the proportion of representation. They said,

> *Muhammadans seem pleased with the communal decesion. Hindus, even "moderates" think the Award unfair to them but except for irreconcilables there is no strong feeling aroused or expressed. The objection is forensic on the untenable assumption that the Hindus deserve larger representation because of their advanced political demands.*[74]

Section X
THE LAST PHASE OF REFORMS AND WORKING (1937-1947)

We have discussed the White Paper, Joint Parliamentary Committee Report, the proceedings of the Round Table Conferences and the Government of India Bill. The White Paper came up for discussion in the Assam Legislative Council on 18 March 1933. Rohini Kumar Choudhury moved a resolution which read,

> *In view particularly of the fact that Assam was not at all represented in the third Round Table Conference, this Council is of the opinion that the Government of Assam should call the immediate attention of the Governor General and the Secretary of State for India to the imperative necessity for appointment of at least two representative persons from Assam among those Indians to be selected for consultation with the Joint Select*

Committee, to be appointed by parliament for the consideration of the constitution of India and provinces....[75]

Sir Saadulla, Leader of the House, left the discussion to the non-official Members. Rohini Kumar Choudhury moved an adjournment of discussion till April on the plea that the House of Commons would discuss the document. Others supported him arguing that it would be better not to castigate the proposed reforms before that debate. On 9 March 1935 again, Choudhury opposed the debate on the Report of the Committee and the Government of India Bill saying that no fruitful debate would be possible at that stage. "Some what surprised at this reluctance of a fellow Indian member to seize one more opportunity of launching wordy battle against the coming Act of 1935, the European members enthusiastically supported him in order to avoid the debate". The official Motion for discussion of the White Paper was lost when put to vote.

The final resuslt of all political movements, various reform schemes of Commissions and administrative exercises during a decade and a half following the Montagu – Chelmsford Reforms was the Government of India Act 1935 passed by the Brlitish Parliament. Article 321(a) of the Act laid down that nothing in it should affect the Preamble to the Government of India Act 1919. This showed that the authorities were sticking to their earlier intention of progressive realisation of responsible Government even though there was persistent demand for immediate constitutional reforms. By that time, the Lahore Resolution on complete Independence seemed not to be on the forefront of political discourse. Samuel Hore, Secretary of State, wrote to the Viceroy that it was impossible to have a Preamble with any mention of Dominion Status. Further not only the Conservatives but also many Liberals and Labour Leaders in England were against the mention of the words. A historian commented,

About the centre it would not be in-appropriate to say that the mighty Parliamentary Mountain heaved and delivered a mouse which, however, was stillborn. It ought to be admitted that responsible Government remained as distant a goal as ever while Dominion Status vanished in thin air.[76]

Political Rhetories

Now we have a glimpse into the reactions of the Muslim League and the Congress and then trace Assam's response.

Both the Muslim League and the Congress severely criticized that Act. The former felt that "A constitution is literally being forced on us by the British Parliament which nobody likes, no one approves of". After years of various exercises, "a monstrosity" was invented and was presented to India in the garb of a constitution which was "anti-democratic. It will strengthen all the most reactionary elements in the country". Further, instead of helping the country to develop. "... On a progressive line it will enchain and crush the forces working for democracy and freedom". The Muslim classes and masses "will suffer" from the new scheme as any other section of the Indian people. The party adopted a resolution in its Bombay Session of 11 and 12 April 1936 condemning "enforcement" of the Act. It declared the rights and responsibilities conferred on the provinces as worthless and ineffective and the scheme of Indian Federation as "mischievous and evil". [77]

Jawaharlal Nehru castigated the White Paper itself as guilty of converting the "whole country into a glorified Indian State," binding India to the city of London, creating an "impregnable defence of all vested interests..." There was provincial autonomy but the Governor who "...would be a benevolent and all powerful dictator keeping us in order. A high above all would sit the All-Highest, the Supreme Dictator, the Viceroy with complete power to do what he will and check when he desires". In April 1936, the party had pronounced that the proposals contained in the Act were "even worse" than the those of the White Paper and the Joint Parliamentary Committee Report. Further it "designed to facilitate and perpetrate the domination and exploitation" of the people of India. In order to prevent that the party decided to participate in the elections under the Act. The purpose of sending Congressmen to the legislatures was not to co-operate but "to combat it and seek to end it", clearly in the Swarajist way. Their activities were aimed at helping the party's work outside in the strengthening of the people and in the development of the "sanctions essential to freedom". Further, the Congress representatives would resist the British imperialists' designs. [78]

The A.I.C.C. Foreign Department Circular No.10 of 26 November 1936 asserted that "The Congress policy is more important than the winning of seats and capturing of a fictitious majority in the legislatures". Congress President Nehru said in December 1936,

> *We go to the legislatures not to cooperate with the apparatus of British Imperialism..., We are not going to the legislatures to pursue the path of constitutionalism or barren reformism.*

The federal part of the Act was also criticised by him not merely on theoretical grounds but because it was a "vital matter which affects our freedom struggle and our future destiny". With regard to acceptance of office, he said that the only logical consequence of the Congress policy was to have nothing to do with it as that would inevitably mean a kind of "partnership with British Imperialism...in the hateful task of repression of our advanced elements..." Therefore, "we must think in terms of deadlock and not in terms of carrying on with the office", he concluded. Among other parties, some wanted to work the scheme while others wanted to destroy it. However, the differences were "more verbal than substantial".[79] Now, in this perspective, what was Assam's response vis-à-vis the reforms ?

Assam's Reaction

We do not have much record of criticism of the Act as such either inside the Assam Legislature or outside it. The reforms came into force towards the end of the fourth extended Reformed Council under the Act of 1919. According to one author,

> *The fight against the coming Act of 1935 inside the fourth Reformed Council was not only weak, but also halting and sterile. Councillors were not only tantalized by the carrot of constitutional advance but also goaded by the stick.*

They were repeatedly reminded by the provincial Governors of their limited powers. Michael Keane for instance told them "bluntly" that their membership was "conditional to one's loyalty to the constitution" and "you may and you do aim at amending this constitution, but year presence here means first of all that". Further,

> *You are opposed to those who would overthrow the Government by revolution, whether violent or non-violent. Otherwise you are here on a false pretence. The corollary of this should be that you will not hesitate to carry out in your action your pledged opposition to revolution.*[80]

In absence of the Swarajists from the Council during the second phase of the Civil Disobedience Movement, there was a "tiny bloc" of opposition led by Rohini Kumar Choudhury and the Governor's advice did not fall flat on the Council. Choudhury's bloc "dared not or desired not" to exceed the limits though they were sympathetic to the revolutionaries.[81] Without going into further details we may say that as both the Indian National Congress and the All India Muslim League had no choice but to participate in the working of the Act of 1935, the Assam leaders could not but follow them when it come into operation. By the time of implementation of the Act, the Congress's declared policy of having nothing to do with office had been somewhat diluted. It now decided not to accept office in provinces where it could not obtain a majority.

In Assam, the Congress captured the largest number of seats but a majority was not achieved. Therefore, Sir Muhammad Saadulla formed a Coalition Cabinet and assumed office on 1 April 1937. Perhaps the last criticism of the Act in the provincial legislature was made on 10th August 1937 by a Congress Member, Dakshina Ranjan Gupta Choudhury who said in a humour,

> *...The white bureaucrats speak through their brown successors – the grip of imperialism – the chains of slavery tighten. It was well, Sir, that the new constitution was inaugurated on All Fools' Day – I mean the 1st of April and the country has been befooled.*

Despite the rhetorics and denunciation, it did not take long for the Assam Congress to capture power and form a Ministry on 19 September 1938. That was done by Gopinath Bardalai throwing to the winds all the so called Congress principles and in the face of severe criticism of leaders like Rajendra Prasad and Abul Kalam Azad.[82]

The New Assam Legislatures

Now we deal with the various provisions of the Act relating to Assam. The important provision was the creation of a bicameral legislature in the province. It consisted of the Legislative Assembly or Lower House and the Legislative Council or Upper House. The former completed the evolution of a wholly elected legislature, though still on restricted franchise. The last session of the Legislature Council under the Government of India Act of 1919 was held from 19 September to 3 October 1936. It was prorogued on the same day and terminated on 31 March 1937. The tenures of the New Houses were five years and three years respectively with effect from 1 April 1937. These reflected Assam politics till the first general elections of Free India held in 1952. Interestingly, the Government of India Notification No.725 Fr. of 18 June 1936 elaborating the constituencies and allotment of seats tallied with those suggested in the Assam Government's Exalanatory Memorandum referred to above. All relevant detailed Notifications can be seen at Appendix 8.

The Legislative Assembly

It consisted of 108 elected members categorised and distributed as shown below:

Category wise Distribution of constituencies and Seats.

	Constituency	Seats
1.	General – other then Scheduled Castes	40
	Scheduled Castes	7
2.	Muslim (Muhammadan)	34
3.	Women – Shillong	1
4.	European	1
5.	Indian Christian	1
6.	Backward Tribal – Plains	4
7.	Backward Areas – Hills	5
8.	Planting –	
	European	7
	Indian	2
9.	Commerce and Industries –	
	European	1
	Indian	1
10.	Labour - Tea Gardens	4
	Total	108

Source : The East India Constitutional Reforms : Return giving the Results of Elections in India 1937 (New Delhi 1937) at pp.100-5 shows the first five categories under Territorial Constituencies and the remaining five under Special Category. According to this the former numbered 84 and the latter 24.

Scheduled Castes

The seven Scheduled Caste seats were distributed as follows among geographical and administrative areas of Thanas and Sub-Divisions.[83]

Surma Valley	
Habiganj	1
Karimganj	1
Sunamganj	1
Silchar	1
	4
Assam Valley	
Kamrup Sadar South	1
Nowgong North East	1
Jorhat North	1
	3

The Surma Valley got 4 seats and 3 went to the other. A list of Scheduled Castes in both the valleys on the basis of the Poona Pact and this constitution (and later

Constitution Order 1950 is given in Apprendix 9.) Of the 20 Scheduled Castes shown in the list, Namasudras, Methors, Lalbegs and Bansphores were common in both the valleys. According to one author four untouchable castes of the Brahmaputra Valley and ten of the other were designated as Scheduled Castes.

1. Other General

The forty other seats under the general categories were alloted as follows also on geographical and administrative divisions like Mouzas, Thanas and Sub-Divisions of different districts.

Distribution of 40 General Seats.[84]

	District	Seats
1.	Cachar	2
2.	Darrang	4
3.	Goalpara	5
4.	Kamrup	7
5.	Lakhimpur	4
6.	Nowgong	3
7.	Sibsagar	6
8.	Sylhet	9
		40

2. Muslims

Next comes the distribution of Muslim seats. This was done on the basis of Thanas, Circles, Sub-Divisions and Districts as shown bellow:

	District	Seats
1.	Cachar	2
2.	Darrang	1
3.	Goalpara	5
4.	Kamrup	3
5.	Lakhimpur	1
6.	Nowgong	2
7.	Sibsagar	1
8.	Sylhet	19
	Total	34

Twenty-one seats were given to the Surma Valley and the other got13.

3. Women

This constituency consisted of the Shillong Cantonment and Municipal areas.

4. European

The European constituency covered the eight plain districts of both the valleys excluding the Lakhimpur Frontier Tracts, North Cachar Hills, Garo Hills and the British Territories of Khasi and Jaintia Hills.

5. Indian Christian

It consisted of all the plains districts of the province. But the areas of Mikir Hills except the Lumding Kheraj Block, Barapathar and Sarupather Mauzas, Lakhimpur Frontier Tract and North Cachar Hills were excluded.

6. Backward Tribal (Plains)

	Contituency	Seat.
1.	Goalpara	1
2.	Kamrup	1
3.	Lakhimpur and Majuli (Tribal)	1
4.	Nowgong (Tribal)	1
		4

7. Backward Tribal (Hills)

1.	Garo Hills North	1
2.	Garo Hills South	1
3.	Shillong	1
4.	Jowai Sub-Division	1
5.	Mikir Hills	1
		5

A list of Backward Tribes of the province as notified by the Government of India is given in Appendix 8.

8. Planting

	Constituency	Seat
1.	European District of Cachar excluding North Cachar Hills, Darrang, Goalpara, Kamrup, Lakhimpur Excluding Frontier Tract, Nowgong, Sibsagar and Sylhet	7
2.	Indian Brahmaputra Valley – six Districts excluding Lakhimpur Frontier Tract	1
	Surma Valley – District of Cachar excluding North Cachar Hills and Sylhet	1
		9

While the European planters got almost one seat for each district, the Indian counter part of each valley was bunched together.

9. Commerce and Industries

European	1
Indian	1
The two seats of this category were allotted for the province as a whole	

10. Labour – Tea gardens

Constituency	Seat
Brahmaputra Valley	
1. Darrang District	1
2. Lokhimpur Distrrict	1
3. Sibsagar District	1
Surma Valley	
Cachar and Sylhet District.	1
	4

Each district in the former had three groups of tea gardens based on radial distance. In the latter, there were three groups based on Police Station areas. Further details are shown in Government Notification dated 18 June 1936 in Appendix 9.

Distribution of Electorates of different categories and proportion to total electorates are given in the table below:

Constituencies	No. of seats	Electorates	% to total Electorate
1. Scheduled Castes	7	66370	8.14
Other than Scheduled Castes	40	379256	46.51
2. Muslims	34	277677	34.05
3. Women	1	2199	00.26
4. European	1	2357	00.28
5. Indian Christian	1	5743	00.70
6. Backward Tribal Plains	4	27588	03.38
7. Backward Area Hills	5	18338	02.24
8. Planting			
European	7	975	00.11
Indian	2	344	00.04
9. Commerce and Industries			
European	1	18	00.00
Indian	1	197	00.03
10. Labour – Tea Gardens	4	34279	04.20
Total	108	815341	100.00

Under the Act the Hill Tribes of Assam were placed under the following categories and geographical areas.

1. Excluded Area

North Cachar Hills Sub-Division, Lushai Hills and Naga Hills districts and Balipara and Sadiya Frontier Tracts. These areas had no representaiton in the Legislative Assembly. The Governor was responsible to the Governor General for administration of these parts of the province.

2. Partially Excluded areas

Garo Hills, Khasi-Jaintia and Mikir Hills came under this group. These people had franchise and elected their representatives. They were the Minister's responsibility though under seciton 52(e) of the Act, the Governor had special responsibility to ensure peace and good governance of the areas. He could override the Minister's advice in exercise of his "individual judgement". The backward tribes included the Garo, Kachari, Khasi, Lalung, Mikir and Miri communities.

To indicate the percentage of enfranchisement, the population figures under the Census of 1931, are given here.

	Hills	Planis	Sadiya & Balipara Frontier Tract	Total
Surma Valley	413174	3294873	-	3708047
Brahmaputra Valley	190911	4664540	59293	4914744
Total	604085	7959413	59293	8622791

Sadiya and Balipara Frontier Tracts were not brought under electoral area which had 0.69 per cent of the population. Seven mouzas of Garo Hills (North and South) were included. In the Khasi and Jaintia Hills the British territory of Shillong Sub-Division, Shillong Municipality area and the Cantonment areas were given the benefit. Part of Mikir Hills was also represented. Population figures and electorates for individual constituencies could not be found. The Second Round Table Conference had appointed the Lothian Committee to determine franchise and electorates. It came to India on 17 January 1932, visited all provinces except Assam and Central Provinces. The Lothian Committee, "In view of scarcity of population and difficult communications in Assam", recommended enfranchisement of 13 per cent of the population. The Assam Franchise Committee wanted to make and electorate of 25 per cent, by reducing payment of Land Revenue and Choukidari Tax. The provincial Government did not favour an electorate greater than 10 per cent. Taking the census figure of 1931, and the electorate on the eve of elections of 1937, the percentage of franchise was 10.24. However, according to an Assamese scholar, Kunja Medhi, the electorate consisted of 13.22 out of every 100 people. Muslims constituted 32.24 per cent of the total population as shown above. The figures were nearly the same on the calculations of Saadulla and Medhi. Under the Act, the community got 31.48 per cent of the seats in the Assembly though they accounted for 34.05 per cent of the electorate.

Muslims and people of Scheduled Castes and other than Scheduled Castes of the general constituencies together shared 88.90 per cent of the electorate and 75 per cent of the total seats. One third of the remaining seats went to the Europeans who belonged to the General, Planting and Commerce and Industry groups. In the House as a whole they had a strength of 8.33 per cent with an electorate of 3350 voters which formed 0.41 per cent of the electorate.

The proportions of electorate to population in respect of the General and Muslim constituencies were more or less maintained. As these seats in the House were all elective, the concept of majority could play its part in a democratic way. But the divisive policy still remained the trumpcard in the hands of the Government. The numerically small European Planters and other Europeans were economically the most powerful section of the people. They were given inexplicably high representation and weightage. On an average 372 of them elected one member of the Assembly. Again every 139 planters had one seat. The average electors for each of the 47 general seats numbered 9481. The Muslims got one seat for every 8167 voters. The average electorate for a Tea Garden Labourers' seat was 8570. Other labourers numbering about the same as tea labourers had no voting rights as stated earlier.

Next we show the category-wise percentage of seats to total strength of the Assembly.

Constituency	No. of Seats	% of seats to total strength of the House
1. General	47	43.51
2. Muslims	34	31.48
3. Women – Shillong Urban	1	00.92
4. European	1	00.92
5. Indian Christian	1	00.92
6. Backward Tribal Plains	4	03.70
7. Backward Areas Hills	5	04.63
8. Planters		
European	7	06.48
Indian	2	01.85
9. Commerce and Industries		
European	1	00.92
Indian	1	00.92
10. Labour – Tea Garden	4	03.70
Total	108	99.95

It would be seen that neither the general nor the communal group of members could form a Government without coalition and that was exactly what happened in case of the first Cabinet formed under the Act by Sir Muhammad Saadulla as well as the subsequent ones including that of 1946.

Numbers of voters in each and every seat could not be traced except for 2 general and 3 Muslim seats in the South Sylhet Sub-Division of the Sylhet District shown below :[85]

Constituency	Number of Voters		
General –	1 seat		14872
	1 seat		11609
		Total	26481
Muslim –	1 seat		8597
	1 seat		7133
	1 seat		6463
		Total	22193

Numbers of votes allotted to the Sub-Division for provincial seats were as follows:

Indian Christians	16	votes.
Europeans	159	"
European Planters	78	"
Indian Planters	27	"
European Commerce and Industry	-	
Indian Commerce and Industry	2	"
Total	282	"

Now we depict the valley and category-wise strength vis-à-vis the seats in the following table :

	General		Muslim	Women	European	Indian	Backward	Planters		Commerce	Tea Garden			Total
	S.C.	Others				Christian	Hills	Plains	Indian	European	& industry		Labour	
											Indian	European		
Surma Velley	4	11	21	1	–	–	4	–	1	–	–	–	1	43
Assam Valley	3	29	13	–	–	–	1	4	1	–	–	–	3	54
Province as a whole	–	–	–	–	1	1	–	–	–	7	1	1	–	11
Total	7	40	34	1	1	1	5	4	2	7	1	1	4	108

To sum up, the Assam Valley had 54 seats, the other had 43 and the rest went to the province as a whole.

Next comes the ethnic composition of the Assemby; only major communities are detailed.

Bengali Caste Hindu	13
Bengali Scheduled Caste	4
Assamese Caste Hindu	23
Assamese Scheculed Caste	4
Bengali Muslims	21
Assamese Muslims	13
Garo	2
Mikir	1
Khasi	3
European	9
	93

of these 93 seats, Bengalis got 38, Assamese 40 and the rest went to other ethnic groups. Of the remaining 15 seats, 4 went to a number of plain tribes who lived in mixed groups in the four districts of the Brahmaputra Valley. The tea garden labourers included Santhal, Bhim, Tamil, Telugu and other communities. Other seats were not reserved for any particular community. There might be slight variations in the figures of Assamese and Bengalis as the latter lived in the Brahmaputra Valley in considerable numbers.

We summarise the whole discussion on the Assam Legislative Assembly. One hundred one or 93.5 per cent of the seats were allotted in the names of communities, religions and valleys. Assamese got 37.03 per cent of the seats, Bengalis got 35.19 and Europeans had 8.33; Tribals of the hills were given 4.62 and those of the plains got 3.70 per cent of total strength of the House. Together they shared 8.3 per cent.

As per directions of the Government of India Notification No. 2564 El. Dated the 7th December 1936, elections were to be held on or before 18 February, 1937. The seats secured by the contesting political groups and parties are shown below:

Groups and Parties	seats won
1. Indian National Congress	32
2. Surma Valley United Muslims	17
3. Assam Valley Muslim Group	13
4. Europeans	13
5. Progressive	12
6. Assam Valley United Party	8
7. Independents	5
8. Muslim League	4
9. Constitutionalists	4
	108

Working of the Assembly 1937 – 1947

The newly elected and constituted Assembly functioned from 1 April 1937. It lasted till 1 October 1945 on which date it was dissolved in view of the general Elections scheduled for 21 January 1946 vide Government Notification No.GS/MIS/21/47/7 dated 24.09.1945. During its life of 9 years six months, there was a spell of Governor's rule from 25 December 1941 to 24 August 1942. The entire period of Provincial Autonomy was characterized by coalition politics for the reason already stated. There is no doubt that Assam was the pioneer in this respect of pre-Independence Indian politics. However, except for 14 months of Congress Coalition rule and 6 months of Governor's rule, the province was under the Muslim League Coalition of Saadulla. Interestingly, though the League and the Congress opposed each other tooth and nail, Gapinath Bardalai and Rohini Kumar Choudhury entered into a Tripartite Agreement with Saadulla on 23 March 1945, during his 5th stint as Premier. One of the terms of the Agreement prescribed the reconstitution of Saadulla Cabinet.

The climax of power politics was reached in respect of that term which is quoted verbatim as well as other details.

(a) "The present Cabinet will resign on 23rd March 1945 and will be reconstituted by Sir Muhammad Saadulla so that members of the new Cabinet may take their seats in the House on the 24th March before prorogation". (Scheduled for 25th March).

(b) The Cabinet shall be formed in the following manner:

1. "Five Muslims including the Premier to be selected by Muslim members of Sir Saadulla's party.
2. "Five non-Muslims by the opposition (Congress mainly) in the following manner. 1. "3 Caste Hindus, 2. 1 Plains Tribal, 1 Scheduled Caste.

   In selecting 2 opinion of the group shall prevail. The Scheduled Caste representative will be taken from the members of the community either by selection or election under the supervision of the opposition.

"We wish that the Hill Tribes and the Indian Christians are represented by a seat in the Cabinet to be selected by them if an eleventh seat is available"

Saadulla said,

> *...if the spirit in which negotiations had been carried on for an All Party Government could be kept up, it would usher in a new era in the history of Assam.*

Associating himself with Saadulla, Bardalai assured that the Congress "would stand by the Government". The enunciation of a new policy

> *would go a great way in removing discontent and ill feeling and promoting better relationship among all communities.*

Further elaborating his party's stand, he observed,

> *...We are all experimenting upon bringing a new era in Assam. It has become necessary not to insist on some of these principles on account of which we have been opposed hitherto. Particular problems in particular times demand particular view of things and it is with this end in view of things that we have decided to support this new Government.*[86]

This agreement remained operative till the dissolution of the Assembly as mentioned above. However, neither there was a new era in Assam politics nor the ill feelings arising out of the Hindu-Muslim, Congress-League and valley issues could be overcome. Rather, taking into consideration the perspective Indian political picture as a whole, this was only a pious wish similar to one expressed by Muhammad Ali Jinnah on 1 October 1936. He had said,

> *If out of 80 Million Muslims I can produce a patriotic and liberal minded nationalist bloc, who will be able to march hand in hand with the progressive elements in other communities, I will have rendered great service to my country.*[87]

Within the next two years the separation became complete in each and every aspect of politics. The dissolution of the Assembly was followed by the General Elections in Assam on 21 January 1946.

Next let us have a detailed picture of the political parties, combinations of groups of members and individual elements of the Assembly during the period from 1937 to 1947, as well as the findings of the Indian Statutory Commission.[88]

Groups, Parties and Individuals	38	39	40	41	42	43	44	45	46-47
1. Assam Valley United Party					21	14	11		
2. Assam Nationalist Party									
3 Assam Nationalist Coalition								11	
4. Assam Valley United People's Party	6								
5. Assam United Party		52	52	51	49	58	59	59	
6. Assam Valley Muslim Group									
7. Congress	32		-	-	32	30	30	30	
8. Congress Coalition/Muslim Independent		55	55	56					57
9. Constitutionalists	3								
10. European	10								9
11. Jamiat-Ul-Ullema-E-Hind									3
12. Independent	11				5	5	6	7	
13. Independents									7
14. Muslim League	25								31
15. Progressive									
16. Progressive Nationalist	11								
17. Surma Valley United Muslim.									
18. United Muslim	9								
Total	107	107	107	107	107	107	106	107	107

During the whole period, the Speaker belonged to the Congress.

In 1937, there were 10 groups of legislators. The Congress started with a strength of 32 and the Muslim League had 4. The 34 Muslim members were divided into 3 groups of which 17 members belonged to the Surma Valley United Muslim. In 1938, there was a regrouping raising the League's strength to 25. These members were earlier divided on valley alliances though they had been elected on separate communal electorates. The first serious attempt of the All India Muslim League to bring all their supporters under the control of one central organization was made on the eve of elections of 1937. At the party's Annual Session held at Lucknow from 15 to 18 December 1937, Jinnah as its Chairman appealed to all Muslims to work unitedly for their social, economic and political uplift by rallying round one common platform and the flag of the the party. The same Session declared its aim of full independence of India in the form of a Federation of democratic States. Jinnh's appeal had a significant effect on the community in Assam as elsewhere. Saadulla along with Fazlul Haque of Bengal and Sir Sikandar Hyat Khat of Punjab decided to join the All India Muslim League along with the Muslim legislators of their respective provinces.Interestingly enough, in the Muslim majority provinces of Bengal, Punjab, U.P., Sind and N.W.F.P., the community had allegiance to parties other than the Muslim League.

After the elections of 1946 Congress strength with the Jamiat's support rose to 61. The grouping of members changed as follows:

Congress	58
Muslim League	31
Jamiat-Ul-Ulema-E-Hind	3
Independent	7
Eropean	9
Total	108

The Sind Provincial Muslim League Conference of October 1938 for the first time officially asserted that the Hindus and the Muslims were two distinct nations. It appointed a Sub-Committee to consider the question of a future constitution on that basic idea.

The Committee recommended the creation of a separate Muslim State as the only effective safeguard against the community being submerged by the Hindus. In December the same year the League Session authorized Jinnah to take necessary action on the issue raised in the Sind Conference. The Working Committee met at Meerat on 16 March 1939 and appointed a Sub-Committee under his Chairmanship with 9 members including Abdul Matin Choudhury of Assam for examining a number of draft schemes that had already been there and those which might follow. The net result of all these exercises was the famous Lahore Resolution of 25 March 1940. [89] By that time the unification of Muslim members in the Assam Legislative Assembly as in other places had been completed. In the elections of 1946, the Muslim League captured 31 out of 34 reserved seats, 3 only going to the Jamiat-Ul-Ulema-E-Hind. Since then the community's representatives steadfastly worked for the League's scheme of separate independent State. The Congress strength in the Assembly remained 32 from 1937 to 1942 and 30 from 1943 to 1945.

Other members of the House were fluid in their political allegiance and took advantage of the situation whichever favoured them. Their undefined allegiance on a number of occasions made or marred Governments and also played money games on some occasions. The "Aya Rams and Gaya Rams" helped both the Muslim League and the Congress in the struggle for powers. In 1942, the Saddulla group's strength slightly deteriorated but it was regained next year to an absolute majority which remained almost constant till the elections of 1946 after which the Congress alliance emerged with an absolute majority in the legislature. While the League at first had its base in the Surma Valley, the Congress had supporters from both the valleys. The Congress had an earlier ancestry in Sylhet but the ledership of its Legislalture Party went to Gopinath Bardalai of Kamrup. Similarly the League politics originated in Sylhet but its provicial leader was Saadulla of Kamrup who ultimately controlled all but three Jamiat members.

In this connection, an assessment was made by the Indian Statutory Commission, which is quoted here at length. This applied to both Dyarchy and Provincial Autonomy periods.

> *Except for the Congress or Swaraj Party which entered the Council in 1921 and maintained a common political programme until communal differences resulted in 1926 in the break away of Muhammadan members and the failure of the only Muhammadan candidate who stood as a Swarajist at the election, the only party was the Independent Party and formed to counteract the Swarajists. This was united only upon political questions. It died for lack of common programme in other matters during the life time of the second Council. Party organisation within the Council has been of a very loose character though nominally a Leader, Deputy Leader and Whips have been appointed by the Independents. There is no party in the Council but only a collection of dissolving groups.*

Further,

> *There is no definite organization of a Government Party, nominated members voting in accordance with their personal predilections. The planting members formed a small compact group, similarly not subservient to the Government's desire and frequently voting against Government where interests of the tea industry were not affected directly or indirectly.*
>
> *The absence of party organization based on any difference of opinion as to administration, with the refusal of the only cohesive group to undertake any responsibility, limited the power of the ministry to frame constructive policy.*

No further comment is called forth.

Now, the chart that follows gives us a detailed statistical picture of working of the first Legislative Assembly.[90]

STATISTICS ON THE WORKING OF ASSAM LEGISLATIVE ASSEMBLY 1937-1945

Parameters	37	38	39	40	41	42	43	44	45	Total	Average per Session
1. Number of Sessions	3	2	1	2	2	1	2	2	1	16	-
2. Average attendance	106	103	102	101	74	46	57	63	73	725	46
3. Questions admitted	4395	3220	782	1535	1183	290	650	1016	636	13707	857
4. Questions replied to	3222	2340	632	1105	727	196	434	643	467	9766	610
5. Supplementary asked	570	465	247	338	202	70	156	209	170	2427	152
6. Cut-Motions notified	459	456	286	354	234	118	191	365	467	2930	183
7. Cut-Motions discussed	71	63	59	70	65	36	58	60	91	573	36
8. Divisions on Cut-Motions	29	10	27	10	-	4	15	16	9	120	8
9. For Government	14	9	27	7	-	4	13	12	7	93	6
10. Against Government	12	1	0	1	0	0	0	1	1	16	1
11. No-Confidence against Government	0	0	0	0	1	0	0	0	0	1	-
12. For Government	0	1	1	0	0	0	0	0	1	3	-
13. Bills with amendments intorduced	18	12	5	8	16	4	14	12	7	96	6
14 Enactments	10	3	10	5	11	7	14	10	0	70	5

The figures are indicative enough of the work done by the Assembly and no comments are perhaps called for in this regard. Under the Act, subjects to be dealt with and legislation enacted were divided into three groups, namely, Federal, Provincial and Concurrent. All Bills mentioned in the chart related to the second group only. However, all legislations were subject to the Governor's consent. He could disallow discussion or a Bill at any stage and issue Ordinances. The Assembly's power in financial matter was very restricted, as 50 per cent of the Budget allotment was non-votable.[90]

We have discussed the scenario vis-à-vis representation and composition of the Assembly during the first term of its tenure. The second and last elections under the Government of India Act of 1935 were held in Assam on 21 January 1946. Composition of the Assembly remained the same as in 1937. The most notable change was the increase in electorate from 815341 voters to 1465686 i.e., by 79.76 per cent. This was due to the rise in population and a nominal extension of franchise. The population of British territories, which included the 8 plains and 2 Hill districts, was 9795676. The electorate covered only 14.96 of the population of the enfranchised area. Distribution of electorate is shown next.[91]

Sl. No.	Constituencies	No. of Seats	No. of voters	% of total electorate
1.	Scheduled Castes	7	59195	4.03
	Other than Scheduled Castes	40	751505	51.27
2.	Muslims	34	519627	35.45
3.	Europeans	1	2837	0.19
4.	Indian Christian	1	13977	0.95
5.	Women.	1	5087	0.35
6.	Backward			
	Plains	4	46220	3.15
	Hills	5	26142	1.78
7.	Planting	9	2006	0.14
8.	Commerce and Industry	2	646	0.04
9.	Labour – Tea Gardens	4	38444	2.62
	Total	108	1465686	99.97

The Congress contested all the 47 General and 15 other seats. They won all the former and nine of the latter. After the elections two unattached members joined the party. It was also supported by 3 members belonging to the Jamiat-ul-ulema-e-Hind thus raising the Congress strength to 61 and ensuring it more than an absolute majority in the Assembly.

Depletion of the Assembly

The referendum held in the district of Sylhet on the eve of Partition resulted in the transfer of almost the whole territory to Eastern Pakistan. Strength of the Assembly diminished by 37 seats. Of them 10 were Hindus and 16 Muslims and eleven others. Of the 71 remaining members, thirty-four were Hindus including 3 Harijans, 18 Muslims and 19 others. Only one of the three Jamiat members remained in Assam. Thus the separation of the district except 2 General and 1 Muslim seat areas, very much affected the strength of both the Congress and the League. Of the remaining 71 members, 34 were Hindus, 18 Muslims and 19 others.

Assam Legislative Council Background

Under the Government of India Act 1935 six out of eleven provinces were provided with a bicameral legislature. So far as Assam was concerned, the idea was advocated by Abdul Hamid, twice President of the Assam Legislative Council under the Montagu-Chelmsford Reforms. But the Assam Provincial Muslim League in its memorandum to the Simon Commission " was unequivocally opposed" to the idea. The Provincial Committee to Cooperate with the Simon Commission did not recommend a second Chamber. But the European Planters and Indian " propertied section", the Assam Railway and Trading Company, the Assam Oil Company as well as the commercial interest groups, both Indian and European, were interested in it. So the Assam Franchise Committee by 9 votes against 5 recommended a second Chamber in its Report of March 1932.

On 17 September 1932, Brindaban Chandra Goswami moved a resolution in the Council to that effect. Interestingly 16 members supported the proposal and an equal number voted against it. But it was rejected by the casting vote of the President. This "adverse public opinion and financial constraints" prompted the White Paper and the Joint Parliamentary Committee not to make any such recommendation. The Lothian Committee also did not do so. Even the original draft of the India Bill was not in favour of it. But "A lot of wire pulling by the Assam Planters in India and London meanwhile" unsettled the settled fact. The House of Commons now took an opposite stand. W.D.Smiles was told on 22 March 1935 that Assam could get a second chamber if a substantial section of the people wanted it. The Government of Assam now made a volte face. It informed the Secretary of State that such a demand was prevailing in the province. This was done with a view to satisfy the European and commercial interests.

On 31 May 1935, Abdul Rashid Choudhury moved an Adjournment Motion in the Council for discussion of the issue. He claimed that the Government had no right to make such a recommendation without taking the House in confidence. Supporting the mover, Rohini Kumar Choudhury observed,

> *There is no doubt that an astute body like the British Parliament was misled into the belief that the opinion of the province has changed. Labouring under this misapprehension, they have upset a lot of things. They have disregarded, practically speaking the opinion or decision of this provincial Committee which co-operated with the Simon Commission, they have disregarded the opinion expressed in this House, that a second Chamber was not necessary for this province.*

Another member, J.J.M.Nichols Roy also opposed the Government's action. However, the motion was rejected by 26 votes against 13 for it. Thus "almost at the last stage of the making of the Act of 1935 in London, Assam was saddled with a bicameral legislature" without asking for it and for "safeguarding the European and commercial interests".

Composition of the Legislative Council

It consisted of 22 members of whom 18 were elected and 4 nominated. Its tenure was three years. But it was not subject to dissolution like the other House. One third of the elected members would retire every third year. The Governor had to nominate a minimum of 3 and maximum of 4 members. Elaborate details of composition of the House were laid down in Government of India notification No.673 Fr. Dated 8 June 1936. A copy of the same has been given in Appendix 8 to this Chapter. The territorial and communal distributions of the seats are depicted below.[92]

CONSTITUENCIES AND SEATS

	General	Muslim	European	Hills	Total
Surma Valley Districts					
1. Cachar	1	-	-	-	1
2. Sylhet East	1	-	-	-	1
3. Sylhet West	1	-	-		1
	3				3
Assam Valley Districts					
1. Darrang	1	-	-	-	1
2. Goalpara	1	-	-	-	1
3. Kamrup	1	-	-	-	1
4. Lakhimpur	1	-	-	-	1
5. Nowgong	1	-	-	-	1
6. Sibsagar	1	-	-	-	1
	6				6
Total Province	9				9
Surma Valley					
Central		1	-	-	1
North East		1	-		1
North West		1	-		1
South West		1			1
		4			4
Assam Valley					
Lower	1	-	-	1	
Upper	1	-	-	1	
		2			2
Total Province		6			6
Surma Valley			1	-	1
Assam Valley			1	-	1
			2		2
Province as a whole				1	1
Total	9	6	2	1	18

There were 9 general, 6 Muslim, 2 European and one Hill Tribe members. The first three were distributed on communal and territorial basis. The last represented the province as a whole. Surma Valley had 3 general, 4 Muslim and 1 European seat. Assam Valley was given 6 general, 2 Muslim and one European seat. The Hill Tribe had one seat for the whole province. The Surma Valley as a whole had a Muslim majority, Cachar district having a greater number of non-Muslims. The total electorate for the Council was a mere 2789 voters of lwhom 553 were Muslims and 2236 belonged to the General, European and Hill area constituencies. On an average, 155 voters elected one member to the House. Each Muslim seat was filled by 92 voters on an average. Detailed distribution of electors in the different constituencies could not be traced. However, the number varied from 57 to 375. Figures of voters of some electoral areas are shown.

CONSTITUENCY

	General	Muslim	European	Total
South Sylhet East	30			30
South Sylhet West	38			38
Surma Valley Central		21		21
Surma Valley South- West		18		18
Surma Valley as a whole			128	128
Total	68	39	128	235

These were parts of two General, three Muslim and one European constituencies. It may be observed that while the Assembly had ten categories of members, the Council had only three. So far as the nomination of 4 members was concerned, the Governor was authorised to remove inequity of representation. He was officially directed to nominate at least a lady and a Scheduled Caste member and he did so. It can be clearly seen that distribution of seats in the Council was done on the same basis of check and balance as in the case of the Lower House. Referring to the divergences prevailing in the province, an Assamese member, Sarveswar Baruah, had said way back in July 1924 that the two valleys were forced to run a "three-legged race in which no progress whatsoever is possible". Again another Assamese member had observed in 1936 that "... the line of division in Assam politics is primarily not between Hindu and Muhammadan or on caste lines, but between the inhabitants of the Assam Valley and those of the Surma Valley". However, the problem was a little bit simplified. The division had by that time actually extended to the spheres of community, language, and employment and, in fact, every aspect of life in the province. The divergences were noticeable in the debates on almost every issue of public interests in both the Houses.[93] The Council started functioning simultaneously with the Assembly. It was abolished in 1948 under the provision of the Indian Independence Act of 1947.

Presiding and Deputy Presiding Officers of Legislatures

During the period of Dyarchy, they were designated President and Vice- President. The first two Presidents were nominated by the Governor. From the third term of the Council the position became elective. The Vice-President was elected by the members of the Council from the very beginning. The first nominated President was J.C.Arbuthnott. He retired before the end of his tenure and was succeeded by Nalini Kanta Roy Dastidar for the remaining period. The second nominated President left office in March 1925. Now both the posts became elective. Abdul Hamid of the Surma Valley was elected President on 2 March 1925. He was re-elected in 1927 and continued in office till September 1929. Keramat Ali and Faizhur Ali, both from the Brahmaputra Valley contested. The later was elected by 27 votes against 21 and remained in office till 1937. The first Vice-President elected was Khan Bahadur Mohiuddin who was succeeded after death by Mohammad Bakht Majumder. The next Vice-President was Gopendralal Das Choudhury who was elected by defeating three candidates by securing 27 votes out of 47, 20 going to his rivals K.N.Saikia and Sayidur Rahman. Das Choudhury held office, being later elected uncontested, till 10 March 1930. He was succeeded by Hirendra Chandra Chakravorty of Hailakandi.

With the implementation of the Government of India Act of 1935, the Presiding Officers of the Assembly were designated as Speaker and Deputy Speaker. In the other House, they were President and Vice-President. The first election of Speaker was held on 7 April 1937. Out of 8 candidates who initially submitted nomination papers, 6 withdrew from contest. Basanta Kumar Das of Surma Valley defeated Keramat Ali of the other valley by 56 votes to 51. For the post of Deputy Speaker, Kumer Ajit Narayan Deb from Goalpara and Muhammad Amir Uddin from Nowgong contested, the latter winning by 62 votes against 38, thus balancing the valley and community. Deb's name was proposed by Purandar Sharma and seconded by Santosh Kumar Barua. Amir Uddin's proposer was Fakhruddin Ali Ahmed and the proposal was supported by Mubarak Ali of Sylhet. In the political situation described earlier, Das resigned and was succeeded on 12 March 1946 by Debeswar Sarma of the other valley who was elected unanimously and remained in position till 10 October 1947. He was replaced by Laksheswar Barua who was elected uncontested and held office from 5 November 1947 till 5 March 1952 on which date he was succeeded by Kuladhar Chaliha, also uncontested. He was speaker till 7 June 1952.

The Deputy Speaker's term and ended on 14 March 1946 on which date, Bonnily Khongman, a Khasi lady of Shillong, was elected uncontested and continued to hold office till 6 March 1952. On that day Rajendra Nath Barua was elected by defeating Ajira Singh Khongpai by 84 votes to 19.

Legislative Council (Upper House)

The first President of the Assam Legislative Council under the Government of India Act 1935 was Mono Mohan Lahiri. He was elected by defeating Heramba Prasad Barua by 11 votes against 9. For the post of Deputy President there was no contest. Begum Zubaida Ataur Rahman, a nominated member from Kamrup, was elected unanimously. Thus two ladies had the pride of such exalted positions in the Assam Legislatures. Following the death of Lahiri on 17 February 1938, election was held on 29 August 1938 for Presidentship of the Council and Heramba Prasad Barua was elected by defeating his rival by 12 votes against 6 . Barua completed his term on 28 June 1943 land was succeeded by Begum Rahman, the first Lady President of the Council who defeated Satyendra Mohan Lahiri by 10 votes to 9. The Deputy President whose name could not be ascertained, was elected uncontested when another candidate withdrew from election, that name was also not a available.

We can see that since the Speaker hailed from the Surma Valley, the Deputy speaker came from the other. Again as the former was a Hindu, the latter was a Muslim in keeping with the same old policy of check and balance inherited from the days of Dyarchy.[94] Appendix 10 gives a list of the names of Members and Councils of Ministers of the province during the two terms of the Assam Legislative Assambly from 1937 to 1947.

Depletion of the Council

As in the case of the Assembly, after Partition, strength of the Council depleted by five seats. The remaining 13 were as follows:

CONSTITUENCIES

	General	Muslim	European	Hills	Total
Surma Valley					
Cachar	1	-	1	-	2
Surma Valley East	-	1	-	-	1
	1	1	1		3
Assam Valley Plains – one seat for each district	6	2	-	1	9
Province as a whole	-	-	1	-	1
Total	7	3	2	1	13

To sum up, the Surma Valley had three seats and Assam Valley nine and one seat was provided for the province as a whole. Due to Referendum the Surma Valley's (Sylhet) representation was a reduced by two General and three Muslim seats.

Section XI
ASSAM'S REPRESENTATION IN THE CENTRAL LEGISLATURES

As in the case at home, Assam's representation in the Central Legislatures also evolved through different phases. The Indian Councils Act of 1861 had set up the Governor General's Council. But it did not have any elected representative of the people though nomination of members representing some interests was introduced. Official supremacy was maintained. The Council "assembled for the purpose of making laws and Regulations" and came to be known as the Supreme or Imperial Legislative Council. It consisted of 5 ordinary and two extra-ordinary members. For the purpose of legislation the Governor General expanded it by nomination of not less than six and not more than twelve members of whom only half would be non-officials but not necessarily Indians. People's representation was not in sight though the Council was further expanded by making additional members not less than ten and not more than sixteen. In that Council the only representative from the Chief Commissioner's Province of Assam was an Englishman named James Buckingham "who was concerned" with the interests of the European Planters.[95]

The political atmosphere in the country changed as Indian nationalism became more assertive taking even violent turn especially after the Partition of Bengal. Governor General Lord Minto had felt that a substantial concession would have to be offered to the nationalists. On 4 November 1906 he wrote to John Morley,

> *Our friendly recognition of a moderate Congress, I might believe, would do much good. If the extremists like Tilak and Bepin Chandra Pal gain ascendancy, it would be impossible to deal with them and the Congress itself will split up.*[96]

The two met half way and the outcome was the Morley-Minto Reforms. In terms of section 6 of the Act, the Governor General-in-Council issued Regulations for constitution and composition of both the central and the provinced legislatures.

During the period from 1909 to 1919, the Unicameral Imperial Legislative Council, as approved by the Secretary of State-in-Council, had the following composition.[97]

A. Nominated Members

1.	Ex – Officio	7
2.	Officials representing Provinces	8
3.	Not more than 20 to be officials while 3 must represent respectively the landlords of Punjab, Muslims thereof and Indian Commerce	27

B. Elected Members

1.	Provincial Councils and Central Provinces	12
2.	Landholders of Bengal, Bombay, Assam, Central Provinces, Madras and United Provinces – one each	6
3.	Muslims of Bengal, Bombay, Eastern Bengal and Assam, Madras and United Provinces	5
4.	Chambers of Commerce of Calcutta and Bombay, one each	2
		67

or including the Governor General, 68. The total electorate for the 25 elected seats had 4818 voters; Assam's share was 301.

In the first Imperial Legislative Council, Eastern Bengal and Assam was allotted 3 seats, one each for Muslims, landholders and non-officials. The Muslim member elected was Abdul Majid of Surma Valley, the other remaining unrepresented. This was natural as the vast majority of Muslim electors of Assam part belonged to that valley and in case of any election, the Assam Valley Muslim candidate was sure to be defeated. Similarly, the lanholders and other members would also come from the Eastern Bengal part unless any specific provision was made for the Assam part.

Assam's reconstitution into a Chief Commissioner's province with a Legislative Council of its own gave its non-official members the first ever opportunity to elect a representative to the Imperial Legislative Council. The Council, so formed, had its first sitting on 2nd January 1913. Ghanashyam Barooah, an Assamese Caste Hindu from Upper Assam was unanimously elected on 6 January 1913. Another seat reserved for an official of the Assam Government was filled by the Chief Commissioner's nominee of Sir Arbuthnott, the seniormost Divisional Commissioner. After Barooah's term was over, Kamini Kumar Chanda, a Bengali Caste Hindu from Silchar was elected to the Council on 20 January 1916. Thus, both the valleys were represented alternately, though on provincial basis.

The Government of India act 1919 had created a Bicameral Central Legislature as stated earlier. It was formally inaugurated on 9 February 1921 by the Duke of Cannaught in Delhi. The Lower House or Legislative Assembly consisted of 145 members of whom 41 were nominated and 104 elected. Of the former, 25 were officials and 16 non-officials. The elected members were classified into 6 groups.[98]

Muslims	30
Non-Muslims	52
Sikhs	2
Europeans	9
Landholders	7
Commerce	4
	104

Assam, now a Governor's Province was alloted four seats.[99]

	General	Muslim	European	Total
Surma Valley	1	-	-	1
Assam Valley	1	-	-	1
Province as a whole	-	1	1	2
Total	2	1	1	4

The total electorate for the 104 seats consisted of 909874 voters of whom Assam's share was 19503.[100] The total population of the province (Plains only) was 6080712 and thus a mere 0.32 per cent thereof was enfranchised and represented, and that also through indirect election. There was one seat for every 1520178 persons. The non-Muslims of both the valleys together constituted 69 per cent of the electorate and the Muslims and the Europeans together had 31 per cent. Assam electorate in 1920 consisted of three groups as shown here.

	Non-Muslim	Muslim and European	Total
Surma Valley	4079	-	4079
Assam Valley	9387	-	9387
Province as a whole	-	6037	6037
Total	13466	6037	19503

Separate numbers of Muslim and European electors could not be traced. But even in 1931, the latter had 1531 voters. Obviously the lion's share in 1919 belonged to the former group.

The Council of State or Upper House

Next we study the compsition of the House which consisted of 60 members of whom 33 were elected and 27 nominated. The elective seats were distributed amongst the following groups.[101]

Non-Muslim	16	Seats
Muslim	11	
Sikh	1	
European Commerce	3	
Non-Communal	2	
	33	

We have another detailed version of the distribution of seats. According to this, there were 18 non-Muslim and General seats including one for the Central Provinces and one for Burma. Three seats were allotted to Muslims and non-Muslims by rotation. European Commerce had two seats, one for Bengal and one for Burma. The seats in the Council were distributed on communal basis in each of the eleven provinces as shown here.[102]

Assam – by rotation	1
Bengal	6
Bombay	6
Bihar, East Punjab and West Punjab by rotation	2
Burma	2
Central Provinces	1
Madras	5
Orissa	3
Punjab	2
United Province	5
	33

Assam was given only one seat in the Council alternating between the two communities, the non-Muslims getting the first right of election. In the elections of 1921, a European tea planter, Malcom Megregor was elected by polling 92 votes against 78 of his two rivals. Thus for a second time Assam was represented by a non-Indian. In the elections of 1925, a Muslim was elected uncontested. As the majority of Muslim voters hailed from the Surma Valley, that community in the other valley could not expect to win and remained unrepresented.

In 1926, the Jorhat Muslims petitioned the Government of India for a seat for the community in their part of the province. The Government of Assam also suggested the addition of one Muslim member to the Council and one to the Assembly. Before the elections of 1930, one seat was provided for the Muslims separately but for the province as a whole. We now have an idea of the electorate of the province at that time.

Legislative Assembly

Constituency	Seats	Total Electorate
1. Non – Muslim		
(a) Surma Valley and Shillong	1	7324
(b) Assam Valley	1	18447
2. European – Province as a whole	1	1531
3. Muslim – Province as a whole	1	9891
	4	37193

That year the total electorate for the whole of India was 1142948 voters, i.e., Assam's share was 3.25 per cent.[103]

Council of States

1. Assam non -Muslim	1	594
2. Assam Muslim	1	270
	2	864

The total electorate for the Council in 1926 had 16571 voters. Assam had 864 that is, 5.1 per cent of the electorate.

The Assam Valley had almost half the electorate of the province and yet it got only one non-Muslim seat. Surma Valley's share of votes was less than half of the other valley but it had also one seat. The Assam Valley Muslims had, as before, no specific reservation for themselves. But the most glaring anomaly was that a mere 1531 voters of the Planter Raj had equal representation with the Muslims and non-Muslims though their total electorate was more than twenty three times of the former. The members elected were Devi Charan Barooah of the Assam Valley, Girish Chandra Nag and Amjad Ali of the Surma Valley and a European, Doughlas Harbert.

Under the Government of India Act of 1935, the Indian Legislative Assembly or Federal

Assembly consisted of 375 members; 250 represented British India and 125 came from the Indian Native States. The Council of State had 260 members, 156 representing the provinces of Brlitish India and 104, the States. Details of distribution of the elective seats in both the Houses can be found in Appendix B to Chapter 2. Assam was given ten seats in the Assembly and five in the Council. The former were distributed as follows.[104]

	General including SC	Muslim	European	Indian Christian	Labour	Total
SurmaValley.	2	2	-	-	-	4
AssamValley.	2	1	-	-	-	3
Province as a whole	-	-	1	1	1	3
Total	4	3	1	1	1	10

The four General seats included one for the Scheduled Castes. The seats in the Council were distributed as usual on the policy of check and balance between the two valleys and two communities. The last elections of Assam's representatives to the Central Legislatures were held on 21 January 1946. Assam's electorate had 33447 voters for the General and 12691 for the Muslim constituency.

The Central Legislatures were replaced by a Constituent Assembly. It came into being in July 1946 in terms of the declaration of the British Prime Minister. The Constituent Assembly had its first sitting on 9 December 1946. A Constitution Drafting Committee of 7 members headed by B.R.Ambedkar and including Sir Syed Muhammad Saadulla of Assam, was formed on 29 August 1947. A nominee of the Scheduled Caste Federation, Ambedkar was elected from Bengal. The new Constitution was adopted by the Constituent Assembly on 26 November 1949. Its composition is shown below.

Composition of the Constituent Assembly : Provincewise distribution of Seats[105]

Governor's Province.	General	Muslims	Sikhs	Total
1. Assam	7	3	-	10
2. Bengal	27	33	-	60
3. Bihar	31	5	-	36
4. Bombay	19	2	-	21
5. Central Pronvinces	16	1	-	17
6. Madras	45	4	-	49
7. North Western Frontier Province	-	3	-	3
8. Orissa	9	-	-	9
9. Punjab	8	16	4	28
10. United Provinces	47	8	-	55
11. Sind	1	3	-	4
Total	210	78	4	292

Other Member Representing				
1. Delhi in the Central Legislative Assembly				1
2. Ajmeer and Marwar				1
3. Coorg Legislative Council				1
4. British Baluchistan				1
Total	210	78	4	296

Two hundred ninetytwo members were elected indirectly on the principle of proportional representation by single transferable votes. Members from the last four territories were nominated by the Governor General. On an average, one million of population of the country was represented by one member. Party positions in the House are depicted below:

Partywise Representatives Elected

	General	Muslim	Sikhs	Total
1. Congress	198	3	1	202
2. Communist Party	1	-	-	1
3. Muslim League	-	73	-	73
4. Unionist Party	2	1	-	3
5. Krishak Praja Party	-	1	-	1
6. Akali Party			3	3
7. Sechuduled Caste Federation	2	-	-	2
8. Independents	7	-	-	7
Total	210	78	4	292

The Congress had its own strength of 202 seats. It also had alliance partners such as the Union Party with one and Akali Party with 3 seats. Of the others "no less than 6 members were, likely to follow the Congress". The Muslim League's strength rose to 79 with A.K.Fazlul Haque of the Krishak Praja Party of Bangal joining it after some time.

Assam's Representation in the Constituent Assembly 1946

The seats allotted to Assam were distributed as follows:[106]

	Caste Hindu	Scheduled Caste	Scheduled Tribes Hills	Muslims Plains	Total
Brahmaputra Valley	3	-		1	1 5
Surma Valley	1	1	1	-	2 5
Total	4	1	1	1	3 10

Election of these Members was held on 16 July 1946. The members were as follows:

A. Caste Hindus :

Brahmaputra Valley

1. Gopinath Bardalai
2. Rohini Kumar Choudhury
3. Omeo Kumar Das

Surma Valley

1. Basanta Kumar Das.

B. Scheduled Caste

Surma Valley

1. Akshoy Kumar Das

C. Muslims

Brahmaputra Valley

1. Sir Syed Muhammad Saadulla

Surma Valley

1. Abdul Hamid
2. Abdul Matin Choudhury

D. Scheduled Tribes

Surma Valley Hills –

1. J.J.M.Nichols Roy

Brahmaputra Valley Plains –

1. Dharani Kumar Basumatari

All the seven non – Muslim candidates were sponsored by the Congress though Rohini Kumar Choudhury did not belong to the party. The three Muslim members belonged to the Muslim League. Sir Saadulla was the only Muslim member of the Constitution Drafting Committee. After the Sylhet Referendum held on 6 and 7 July 1947 and inclusion of almost the entire district in East Pakistan, the Governor General alloted 6 General and 2 Muslim seats to the province. They now represented the Brahmaputra Valley and the truncated Surma Valley of which only the district of Cachar and the Karimganj Sub-Division of Sylhet remained in Assam.

Section XII
FRANCHISE AND ELECTORATE

We know that Assam's acquaintance with the elective principle had begun with local bodies elections of the late nineteenth century though in an extremely restricted manner of indirect election. The creation of the Province of Eastern Bengal and Assam slightly elaborated the process through the same mode of representation. But this was also only indirect election of members who represented only 0.36 per cent of the population of the province. We also know that those elections were only recommendatory, the Chief Commissioner or the Lt. Governor being the final authority and he could accept or reject any such recommendation. In 1907 there was a discussion of the matter in the official circle. Two broad viewpoints emerged. Both the Provincial and Central Governments favoured representation of class interests only. The Secretary of State suggested proportional representation by single transferable votes of Electoral Colleges. But the

Government rejected his proposal on the plea of protection of Muslim interests. After a lengthy discussion, both the Government of India and the provincial Governments decided to split the electorate into Muslim, Non-Muslim, classes and interest groups as under the Morley -Minto Reforms.

The question of franchise was debated again in 1912. Now the constituencies were divided into Muslim, Local Bodies, Landholders and Planters. Even with this reorganization of electorates, the authorities opposed the idea of further expansion of franchise. The Chief Commissioner of Assam preferred straight property qualifications and payment of land revenue of Rs.20. Though he favoured direct election and extension of franchise, he wanted to limit the number of voters to only one per cent of the population. He suggested one seat for every 300000 persons and 3000 to 6000 voters in a constituency. His other suggestion was that in Cachar the amount of revenue of Rs.20 might be reduced if the limit did not produce the requisite number of voters. In Sylhet, Chowkidary Tax was also considered a franchise qualification. In case land revenue was paid by a joint family, the oldest member would have the right to vote. The Franchise Committee suggested enfranchisement of pensioned officers of the Armed Forces but it did not favour extension of the right to women. Finally the following qualifications were prescribed:

1. Males above the age of 21 years
2. Residence within the constituency
3. Payment of Municipal or Cantonment tax
4. Military Officers on retirement
5. Officers of Assam Rifles within the constituencies
6. Superintendents or Managers of Tea Estates to exercise the franchise for votes alloted to the tea gardens
7. Ownership of houses with rental value of Rs.36 per annum
8. Payment of Income Tax
9. Payment of Agricultural Tax
10. Payment of land revenue not less than Rs.15 per annum
11. Payment of Chowkidari Tax no less than Rs.1
12. Investment of Rs.25000 in commerce

Non- Muslims were not allowed to vote in a Muslim Constituency and vice versa in respect of reserved seats. The broadening of franchise qualifications, however, did not entitle more than 15 per cent of Urban and 5.6 per cent of the rural populations and that also not on average but in two particular constituencies and in 1923-1926.

Women's Franchise

Till 1923 women were totally deprived of franchise. Only that year, in terms of the Government of India Act of 1919, the Assam Legislative Council through its Local Self-Government Act extended the franchise right to them but they had to wait to get the right to contest elections. Under the provision of the Government of India Act 1935, separate forms were prescribed for enrolment of women voters even in 1941.

She had to possess the following additional qualifications for enrolment.

1. Age above 21 years.
2. If she was the pensioned widow or a pensioned mother of a person who was an officer, non-commissioned officer or soldier in the army or Assam Rifles.
3. If she was the pensioned widow or pensioned mother of an officer or man in the Indian Police Force.
4. If she was literate.
5. If her husband possessed the following qualifications:

A retired pensioned or discharged officer, non-commissioned officer or a soldier of His Majesty's regular military forces or the Assam Rifles. Caste would be mentioned only if she belonged to any of 13 specified castes.

Now we give some statistics in this regard beginning with the Chief Commissionership and ending with the Provincial Autonomy.

The Assam Legislative Council under Chief Commissionerate (1912 to 1920).

Total electorate – Males only 1842 voters

The Assam Legislative Council under Dyarchy 1921 – 1936

	Total electorate.	Women Electorate.
1921-23	202704	-
1923-26	224063	-
1926-36	228832	-
1937-45	815341	2199
1946-47	1465686	5087

After the abolition of sex disqualification, the Khasi women were the first among the class to be enfranchised. But women were allowed to contest elections only under the provision of the Act of 1935 and that also in the British part of Shillong where one seat was reserved for them. They constituted 0.27 per cent of the electorate. Ms. Mavis Dunn of Shillong was the first lady Member of the Assam Legislative Assembly. She defeated her only rival Ms. Berlina Diengdoh by a margin of 290 votes, securing 938 or 76.4% of the 1228 valid votes cast. In 1946, the women voters of Shillong constituted .35 per cent of the total electorate. In the elections of that year, for the first time, an Assamese lady, Ms. Padmakumari Gohain also contested. But that year also the woman member elected was Ms. Bonnily Khongmen. The total electorate in Assam increased from 1937 to 1946 by 80 per cent and population by 4 per cent.[107]

References

1. Report on Indian Constitutional Reforms 1918, p. 29, para 42 and Guha, Amalendu, *Planter Raj to Swaraj*, p.29.
2. *Ibid*, p.70.
3. Government of India (GI) File. *Home Public Proceedings* A, Feb. 1904 quoted in Sarkar, Sumit, *The*

Swadeshi Movement in Bengal 1903-1908, n.1, pp.17-18, quoted in Guha, p.71.

4. *Parliamentary Paper (PPHC)* Vol.81, 1906 quoted in Barpujari, H.K., (Gen. Ed.), *Political History of Assam*, Volume 1, 1826 – 191, p.180, pp.257 – 259.
5. Chand, Tara, *History of the Freedom Struggle in India*, Volume 3, p.313.
6. Guha, p.71 and Barpujari, p.179.
7. Majumdar, R.C., *History of Freedom Movement in India*, Vol.III, p.5.
8. Bhattacharyya, K.K., *North-East India - A Study*, pp.115 – 116, and Chapter-5 for full details, *Assam Bani*, 10 July 1905 onward cited in Guha, p.73.
9. *Eastern Bengal and Assam Legislative Council Proceedings* 1909, pp.57-62.
10. Dutt, K.N., *Landmarks of the Freedom Struggle in Assam*, p.45, Assam Prakasan Parishad(Pub), Jibani Sangraha, p.320, Sastri Biswanarayan and Promode Chandra Bhattachrjee, *This is Assam*, p.16, Guha, p 80.
11. *Abstract Intelligence*, Eastern Bengal and Assam, *Assam Memorial*, quoted in Barpujari, p.200.
12. Nevinson, H.W., *The New Spirit in India*, p.192, cited in Chand, Tara, Volume 3, p. 326.
13. *Minto Papers*, Morley to Minto, 23 April 1906 and Chand, p.343.
14. Regulations, Majumdar, Bimanbehari, *Indian Political Associations and Reform of Legislature (1818 – 1917)*, pp.404-417, pp.422-424, pp.431d-432, pp.435-436 and pp.441-442 for all details that follow. (Appendix-II).
15. *Ibid*, p.422.
16. Barpujari, 203.
17. Majumdar, Bimanbehari, p.431 – 432.
18. Ibid, p.432.
19. Chand, Tara, Volume 4, p.236, p.223, p.87.
20. Guha, p.78.
21. Banerjee, Surendra Nath, *A Nation in Making*, p.283 and Chand, Tara, p.433.
22. *Hardinge Papers*, Crew to Hardinge, 27 January 1911.
23. *Ibid*, quoted in Chand, Tara, Volume 3, Majumdar, R.C.(Gen. Ed.), *History and Culture of the Indian People*, Vol.XI, pp.162-163.
24. Hardinge, Lord, *My Indian Years*, 1910-1916, pp.36-40.
25. Majumdar, R.C., p.166 and Guha, p.81.
26. Majumdar, , p.166, p.169.
27. Rao, V.Venkata and Niru Hazarika, *A Century of Government and Politics in North East India,* Volume-I, Assam, pp.114-115.
28. Guha, p.82.
29. *Assam Legislative Council Proceedings (ALCP)* 1912-1917.
30. Guha, pp.82-83.
31. Barpujari, p.209, p.220.
32. ALCP 1923, Vol.3, pp.694-697.
33. Guha, pp.84-85.
34. Kar, M., *Muslims in Assam Politics* (1990), pp.268-270.
35. *Report of the Franchise Committee* (1918-1919), Chief Commissioner's statement, History of Freedom Movement Records in National Archives, New Delhi, Memorandum of W.D.Cooper, Secretary, Surma

Valley Tea Association to the Committee on Franchise and constituencies quoted in Barpujari, pp. 216- 218 and Guha, p.115.

36. *Ibid*, Abstract of Intelligence, *Assam Police* Vol.VIII 1918, Barua, P.K., *The Assam Association*, foreword, p.7, and Barpujari, pp.216-220.
37. Barpujari, p.221 and Guha, p.116.
38. Gl – Notification No.489 F dated 5 May 1920, published in Assam Gazette of 2 June 1920, p.894, Indian Statutory Commission Report (ISCR), Vol.I p.19, p.108, ALCP No.1, 13 March 1920, pp.51-54 quoted in Guha, p.155 Chand, Tara, Volume 3, pp.465-468 and Majumdar, R.C., *History of Freedom Movement in India*, Vol.3, pp.47-49.
39. Schedule-I of Government of India Act 1919 and Government of India Notification No.F 213X dated 30 July 1923.
40. ISCR, Vol. XIV, Statement 7, pp.14-19.
41. *Ibid.*
42. *Ibid*, Vol.1, p.258, Vol.XIV, pp.197-199, Vol.XV, pp.321-326.
43. *Ibid*, Vol.XIV, p.24, p.217 and Kar, pp.203-206.
44. *Ibid*, pp.206-207, ISCR, Vol-I, pp.257-258, Vol.XIV, p.24, p.207, p.236, Lumby, E.W.R., The Transfer of Power in India 1945-1947, pp.22.
45. *Index of Assam Gazette*, Part-IV, ALCP of respective years, Guha, Chapter-4, Bhuyan, Arun Chandra and Sibopada De (Editors), *Political History of Assam*, Volume 2 1920-1939, Chapter-2, own calculations and Borgohain, Munindra Nath, *The Assam Legislative Assembly 1937-1962*, pp.51-65.
46. Guha, p.150.
47. Bhuya and Sibopada De, Chapter-I and Guha, pp.118-148, Barua, Hem Chandra, *Kongressor Buranji* (in Assamese), p.58.
48. Kalita, Dandinath, Karmabir Chandranath (Assemese), p. 92, Guha, pp.145-146.
49. Majumdar (Ed), Vol.XI, p.351.
50. Bhuyan and Sibopada De, pp.81-83.
51. Majumder, Vol.III, pp.178 onward and Vol. XI, p.390.
52. Guha, p.146 and 154, and Bhuyan and Sibopada De, p.96.
53. *Ibid*, p.94.
54. *Ibid*, p.98.
55. *Ibid*, p.99 and ALCP 1925, 1926.
56. Prasad, Rajendra, An Autobigraphy, p.261 and Bhuyan and Sibopada De, p.113.
57. ALCP Vol.8 1928, p.260 and Bhuyan and Sibopada De, p.123.
58. Majumdar, Vol.XI, p.349. Gupta, D.C., I*ndian National Movement and Constitutional Development*, p.105.
59. Report of the Committee, *Indian Quarterly Register*, July – december 1929, p.53, Franchise Committee Report, ISCR Vol.XIV. pp.596-597.
60. *Ibid*, pp.47-54 for further details.
61. *Ibid*, p.9, p.15, pp.27-32.
62. *Ibid.*
63. Letter No.8/8801 AP dated 18 August 1930, views of Local Government on the Recommendations of the ISCR Vol. XIV, pp.385-387.

64. Guha, pp.170-171 and Bhuyan and Sibopada De, Chapter 2 for further details.
65. ALCP, 1930, pp.1051 – 1068.
66. *Ibid*, p.109.
67. *Ibid*, pp.1070 – 1071.
68. *Ibid* 1931, pp.259-271 and Guha, p.191.
69. Assam Secretariat File (ASF) Confdl B. File No.230 C of 1932 quoted in Bhuyan and Sibopada De, p.317.
70. P.C.Dutta to Chief Secretary, Assam, Conf. A File No.234 C of 1932 poll.
71. Bhuyan and Sibopada De, p.323.
72. ASF (PollP). Conf A File No.234C of 1932, No.28-51 cited in Bhuyan and Sibopada De, p.318.
73. *Ibid*, pp.320-321.
74. G.D.Walker to Scott, dated 5.9.32 in ASF(Poll) Conf. A. No.234C of 1932.
75. Bhuyan and Sibopada De, p.325 and Guha, pp.191-192, ALCP, 1933, pp.815 onward.
76. Chand, Tara, Volume 4, pp.206-207.
77. Ibid.
78. Nehru, Jawaharlal, *An Autobiography*, p.386 and Chand, Tara, pp.213-216.
79. Ibid, p.217.
80. ALCP 1934, Vol.4, p.3 and Guha, p.193.
81. Ibid. 82.
82. Kar, Chapter 10 for full details and references to sources.
83. Government of India Notification No.725 Fr dated the 18th June 1936, pp.7-8 and Guha, p.220 quoting Elections. Return Showing the Results of Election in India 1937 (New Delhi), pp.100-105.
84. Government of India Notification dated the 18th June 1936 and No.2564 – El, dated the 7th December 1936, pp.1-3 for all details that follow.
85. Hand written notes attached to the Government of India Notifications on the Act of 1935 found in an unnumbered pesonal file of the Late Pratap Chandra Nag of Sylhet who was an Officer in the Deputy Commisioner's establishment in Darrang and Khasi Jaintia Hills districts during the period of Provincial Autonomy; obtained from his daughter Prof. Sukla Nandi and son-in-law Prof.(Dr.) S.D.Nandi who are my sister and brother-in-law respectively.
86. *Indian Annual Register* (IAR) 1945, Vol.1, p.213, Tayyabulla, M., Karagaror Chithi (in Assamese), Assam Pradesh Congress Committee Record, Packet No.26(A) (Tayyabulla claimed that all relevant records were preservered in the Congress Archive at Gauhati but those could not be traced), and Kar (1990), pp.249-251.
87. Chand, Tara, p.225.
88. *Report on the Working of the Assam Legislative Assembly 1937-1947*, National Archives of India, New Delhi, File No.F.106/8 – 45R, IAR, January – June 1937, Vol.I, p.168 and Bureau of Public Information, Government of India – Provincial Autonomy, Ministries and parties in Assam (1937 -1945) and ISCR, Vol. XIV, p.264.
89. Lumby, p.121, Hardy, P., *The Muslims of British India*, p.223, Syed Khalid, B., *Pakistan the Formative Phase (1857-1948)*, p.106 and Kar, pp.296-297.
90. Report on the Working of the Assam Legslative Assembly 1937-1947.
91. Guha, p.255.
92. Government of India Notification No 673 Fr. Dated the 8th June 1936, pp.4-5. And ALCP, 31 May 1935, pp.894-899 and pp.903-922.

93. *Ibid*. Private paper of the Late Pratap Chandra Nag and proceedings of the legislatures of the period.
94. ALCP of the period.
95. Barpujari, p.202.
96. Sen, S.N., *History of Modern India 1765-1950*, second Edition 1986, p.114.
97. Majumdar, Bimanbehari, pp.411 – 412.
98. Jones, Morris, *Parliament in India*, p.71 and Rao and Hazarika, p.128.
99. *Ibid*, Rao and Niru Hazarika, p.128 and Guha, p.122.
100. Mahajan, V.D., *Modern Indian History*, Reprint 1997, p.303 and Guha, p.122. According to Rao and Hazarika the number was 17799. However in neither case the split up of European and Muslim votes was given.
101. Jones, p.71.
102. Anand, C.L., *Constitutional Law and History of India*, (Sixth Edition), p.251.
103. Jones, p.71 and Proceedings of Government of Assam, quarter ending December 1930, Record No.122, File No. A. December 1930.
104. Anand, pp.786 – 788.
105. Banerjee, A.C. *The Constituent Assembly of India*, p.46. For all details including party positions in the House.
106. *Assam Legislative Assembly Proceedings*,16 July 1946.
107. Rao and Niru Hazarika, pp.171 – 173, Medhi, Kunja, *State Politics in India (A study of the Assam Legislative Assembly)* p. 20, and Census Reports 1931, 1941.

APPENDIX 1

REGULATIONS FOR ELECTION OF MEMBERS FOR THE IMPERIAL LEGISLATIVE COUNCIL 1909—THE CONSTITUTION OF THE INDIAN LEGISLATURES

The Regulations

In exercise of the powers conferred by section 6 of the Indian Councils Act, 1909 (9th Edw. VII. Ch.4.) the Governor General in Council has, with the approval of the Secretary of State in Council, made regulation for the nomination and election of Additional Members of Legislative Council of the Governor-General of India and of the Provincial Legislative Councils.

The following are the regulations relating to the Imperial Legislative Council :-

I. The Additional Members of the Legislative Council of the Governor-General shall ordinarily be 60 in number and shall consist of –

A. – Members elected by the classes specified in Regulation II, who shall not be less than 25 in number; and

B. – Members nominated by the Governor-General, who shall not exceed 35 in number, and of whom-

a) not more than 28 may be officials, and

b) three shall be non-official persons to be selected-

(i) one from the Indian commercial community ;

(ii) one from the Muhammadan community in the Punjab ; and

(iii) one from the landholders in the Punjab;

Provided that it shall not be lawful for the Governor General to nominate so many non-official persons under these regulations that the majority of all the members of the Council shall be non-officials.

II. The 25 elected members specified in Regulation I shall be elected as follows, namely :

(i) By the non-off Additional Members of the Council of Fort St. George ... 2

(ii) By the non-official additional Members of the Council

(xi) By Landholders in Bengal... 1

(xii) By Landholders in the United Provinces of Agra and Oudh.. 1

(xiii) By Landholders in Eastern Bengal and Assam... 1

of Bombay ... 2

(iii) By the non-official Members of the Council of Bengal ... 2

(iv) By the non-official Members of the Council of the United Provinces of Agra and Oudh... 2

(v) By the non-official members of the Council of the Punjab 1

(vi) By the non-official Members of the Council of Eastern Bengal and Assam... 1

(vii) By the non-official Members of the Council of Burma... 1

(viii) By the District Councils and Municipal Committees in the Central Provinces... 1

(ix) By Landholders in Madras... 1

(x) By Landholders in Bombay... 1

(xiv) By Landholders in the Central Provinces ... 1

(xv) By the Muhammadan community in Madras ... 1

(xvi) By the Muhammadan community in Bombay... 1

(xvii) By the Muhammadan community in Bengal... 1

(xviii) By the Muhammadan community in the United Provinces of Agra and Oudh... 1

(xix) By the Muhammadan community in Eastern Bengal and Assam... 1

(xx) By the Bengal Chamber of Commerce... 1

(xxi) By the Bombay Chamber of Commerce... 1

Provided that in the case of the second, fourth and succeeding alternate elections by the classes specified in sub-heads (xii) and (xiii), a second member shall be elected by the Muhammadan members of each of the said classes.

Explanation.-The expression "alternate elections" shall not be deemed to include elections to fill casual vacancies.

III. The election of the members specified in Regulation II shall be effected by the electorates and in accordance with the procedures respectively prescribed in the schedules to these regulations.

IV. No person shall be eligible for election as a member of the Council if such person-

(a) is not a British subject, or

(b) is a female, or

(c) has been adjudged by a competent civil court to be of unsound mind, or

(d) is under 25 years of age, or

(e) is an uncertificated bankrupt or an undischarged insolvent, or

(f) has been dismissed from the Government service, or

(g) has been sentenced by a criminal court to imprisonment for an offence punishable with imprisonment for a term exceeding six months, or to transportation, or has been ordered to find security for good behaviour under the Code of Criminal Procedure, such sentence or order not having subsequently been reversed or remitted, or the offender pardoned, or

(h) has been debarred from practising as a legal practitioner by order of any competent authority, or

(i) has been declared by the Governor General-in-Council to be of such reputation and antecedent that his election would, in the opinion of the Governor General-in-Council, be contrary to the public interest :

Provided that in cases (f), (g), (h) and (i) the disqualification may be removed by an order of the Governor General-in-Council in this behalf.

V. No person shall be eligible for election under any sub-head or Regulation II unless he possesses the qualifications prescribed for candidates in the schedule regulating elections under that sub-head.

VI. No person shall be qualified to vote at any election held under these regulations if such person-

(a) is a female, or

(b) is a minor, or

(c) has been adjudged by a competent civil court to be of unsound mind.

VII. Every person, who is elected or nominated under these regulations to be a Member of Council, shall, before taking his seat, make, at a meeting of the Council, an oath in the following form, namely :-

I, A.B., having been elected/nominated an Additional Member of the Legislative Council of the Governor-General do solemnly swear (or affirm) that I will be faithful and bear true allegiance to His Majesty the King-Emperor of India, his heirs and successors, and that I will faithfully discharge the duty of the office upon which I am about to enter.

VIII. (1) If any person,-

(a) not being eligible for election, is elected under these regulations, or,

(b) having been elected or nominated, subsequently becomes subject to any of the disabilities stated in clause (c), (e), (f), (g) or (h) of Regulation IV, or fails to make the oath of affirmation prescribed by Regulation VII within such time as the Governor-General in Council considers reasonable,

the Governor-General shall, by notification in the Gazette of India, declare his election or nomination to be void or his seat to be vacant.

(2) When any such declaration is made, the Governor-General shall, by notification as aforesaid, call upon the electorate concerned to elect another person within such time as may be prescribed by such notification, or shall nominate another person, as the case may be.

(3) If any person elected at such fresh election is not eligible for election, the Governor-General may nominate any person who is eligible for election by the electorate concerned.

IX. (1) If any person is elected by more than one electorate, he shall, by notice in writing signed by him and delivered to the Secretary to the Government of India in the Legislative Department, within seven days from the date of the publication of the result of such elections in the Gazette of India, choose, or in his default the Governor-General shall declare for which of these electorates he shall serve, and the choice or declaration shall be conclusive.

(2) When any such choice or declaration has been made, the votes recorded for such person in any electorate for which he is not to serve shall be deemed not to have been given, and the candidate, if any, who, except for the said votes, would have been declared elected for such electorate, shall be deemed to have been duly elected for the same.

X. (1) Save as provided in clause (2) and subject to the provisions of Regulation XVIII, the term of an Additional Member shall be three years from the date of his election or nomination, as the case may be :

Provided that official members and members nominated as being persons who have expert knowledge of subjects connected with proposed or pending legislation shall hold office for three years or such shorter period as the Governor-General may at the time of nomination determine.

(3) A member elected or nominated to fill a casual vacancy occurring by reason of absence from India, inability to attend to duty, death, acceptance of office or resignation duly accepted, or otherwise, or a member nominated on failure of an electorate to elect an eligible person, shall hold office so long as the member whose place he fills would have been entitled to hold office if the vacancy had not occurred.

XI. (1) When a vacancy occurs in the case of a member who represents any interest specified in Regulation II. or at ay time within three months of the date when such a vacancy will occur in the ordinary course of events, the Governor-General shall, by notification as aforesaid, call upon the electorate concerned to elect a person for the purpose of filling the vacancy within such time as may be prescribed by such notification.

(2) When a vacancy occurs in the case of a nominated member, the Governor-General may nominate any person to the vacancy :

Provided that when a casual vacancy occurs-

(a) in the case of an elected member, the election shall always be made by the same electorate as that which elected the member whose place is to be filled and shall be subject to the same conditions in respect of eligibility of candidates for nomination as those which governed the election of such member, and

(b) in the case of a member nominated as representing any class specified in Regulation I, sub-head B, clause (b) the person nominated shall be selected from the same class.

XII. If within the time prescribed by a notification issued under Regulation VIII, clause (2), or Regulation XI, clause (1), the electorate concerned fails to elect, the Governor-General may nominate at his discretion any person who is eligible for election by such electorate.

XIII. The power of making laws and regulations or of transacting other business vested in the Legislative Council of the Governor-General shall be exercised only at meetings at which-

(a) the Governor-General, or

(b) the President nominated by the Governor General-in- Council under section 6 of the Indian Councils Act, 1861, or

(c) the Vice-President appointed by the Governor-General under section 4 of the Indian Councils Act, 1909, or

(d) in the case of the discussions referred to in section 5 of the Indian Councils Act, 1909, a rule made under that section, and 15 or more members of the Council, of whom 8 at least shall be Additional Members, are present.

XIV. (1) No election shall be valid if any corrupt practice is committed in connection therewith by the candidate elected.

(2) A person shall be deemed to commit a corrupt practice within the meaning of these regulations-

(i) who, with a view to inducing any voter to give or to refrain from giving a vote in favour of any candidate, offers or gives any money or valuable consideration, or holds out any promise of individual profit, or holds out any threat of injury to any person, or

(ii) who gives, procures, or abets the giving of a vote in the name of a voter who is not the person giving such vote.

And a corrupt practice shall be deemed to be committed by candidate, if it is committed with his knowledge and consent, or by a person who is acting under the general or special authority of such candidate with reference to the election.

Explanation.- A "promise of individual profit" includes a promise for the benefit of the person himself, or of any one in whom he is interested.

XV. No election shall be invalid by reason of a non-compliance with the rules contained in the schedules to these regulations or any mistake in the use of forms annexed thereto, if it appears that the election was conducted in accordance with the principles laid down in such rules and that such non-compliance or mistake did not affect the result of the election.

XVI. (1) If the validity of any election is brought in question by any person qualified either to be elected or to vote at such election on the ground of the improper rejection or reception of a nomination or of a vote or of any corrupt practice in connection with such election, or for any other cause, such person may, at any time within 15 days from the date of the publication of the result of such election in the Gazette of India, apply to the Governor General-in-Council to set aside such election.

(2) The Governor General-in-Council shall, after such inquiry (if any) as he may consider necessary, declare, by notification as aforesaid, whether the candidate whose election is questioned or any or what other person was duly elected, or whether the election was void.

(3) If the election is declared void, the Governor General shall, by notification as aforesaid, call upon the electorate concerned to elect another person within such time as may be prescribed by prescribed by such notification.

(4) If within the time so prescribed the electorate fails to elect, the Governor General may nominate any person who is eligible for election by such electorate.

XVII. The decision of the Governor General-in-Council on any question that may arise as to the intention, construction or application of these regulations shall be final.

XVIII. (1) As soon as conveniently as may be after these regulations come into force, a Council shall be constituted in accordance with these provisions.

(2) For this purpose the Governor General shall, by notification as aforesaid, call upon the electorates referred to in Regulation III to proceed to elect members in accordance with these regulations within such time as may be prescribed by such notification.

(3) If within the time so prescribed any such class fails to elect, the Governor General may nominate at his discretion for a period not exceeding six months any person who is eligible for election by such class.

The Provincial Councils

The regulations framed by the Governor General-in-Council for nomination and election of Additional Members for the Provincial Legislatures are similar. Regulations I and II prescribe the strength of the Councils and the proportion of elected to nominated members. The proviso to Regulation I does provide for a non-official majority in the Councils in the following terms : "Provided that it shall not be lawful for the Governor or Lieutenant-Governor, as the case may be, to nominate so many officials under these regulations that the majority of all the members of the Council shall be officials."

As in the case of the Imperial Legislative Council, it is provided by Regulations II and III in each of the Provincial Regulations that the elected members specified in Regulation I shall be elected by the electorates specified in accordance with the procedures respectively prescribed in the schedules to the regulations. The schedules and the electorates for the election of members to all the Councils, Imperial and Provincial, are summarized in full in the next section. The rest of the Regulations IV-XII, XIV-XVIII, are identical in terms with those made for the Imperial Legislature, reproduced above, with the substitution of the words, 'Governor' or 'Lieut.-Governor' for the words 'Governor General' and of 'Governor-in-Council' for Governor General-in-Council as the case may be.

In the case of nominations to the Provincial Legislatures, it is provided in the regulations that members to the Provincial Legislative Council of Bengal, the United Provinces of Agra and Oudh, Eastern Bengal and Assam and Burma should be nominated by the respective Lieutenant Governors with the sanction of the Governor General. No sanction is required in the case of nominations made to their Legislative Councils by the Governors of Madras and Bombay.

In the regulation corresponding to Regulation XIII of those relating to the Imperial Council fixing the quorum for legislative meetings, in the regulations of each province, the quorum has been fixed as follows :-

Excluding the President, 10 or more members in the Legislative Councils of Madras, Bombay, Bengal, United Provinces of Agra and Oudh and Eastern Bengal and Assam and 8 or more members in that of the Punjab and 6 in that of Burma.

(ii) The Imperial Legislative Council

The following is the constitution of the Imperial Legislative Council as approved by the Secretary of State for India-in-Council:-

A.-	Ex-officio members	7
B.-	Officials representing provinces	8
C.-	Nominated members not more than 20 to be officials, while 3 must represent respectively the landholders of the Punjab, the Muhammadans of the Punjab and Indian Commerce	27
D.-	Elected members (25) –	
(1)	by the Provincial Legislative Councils and the Central Provinces	12
(2)	by the landholders of Madras, Bombay, Bengal Eastern Bengal and Assam, the United Provinces and the Central Provinces	6

(3) by the Muhammadans of Madras, Bombay, Bengal, Eastern Bengal and Assam and the United Provinces 5

(4) by the Chambers of Commerce, Calcutta and Bombay 2

or, including His Excellency the Viceroy 68

The 25 elected members of the Imperial Legislative Council are elected as follows:-

1. Territorial Electorates (12):

ii. In the Punjab, Eastern Bengal and Assam and Burma, the non-official members of the Provincial Legislative Councils elect one member each to the Viceroy's Council.

Any person not eligible for election under the regulations and having a place of residence within the province concerned and such practical connection with that province as qualifies him to represent may be nominated for election in the above two cases.

II. Landholders (6):

(v) In Eastern Bengal and Assam landholders who vote must

(a) hold in their own right as proprietors within the province or more estates or shares of estates in respect of which land revenue amounting to not less than five thousand rupees or cess amounting to not less than twelve hundred and fifty rupees is payable per annum; or

(b) hold titles conferred or recognised by the Government not lower in rank than that of Raja or Nawab.

III. The Muhammadan Community (5):

(v) The Muhammadans who vote for a Member in Eastern Bengal and Assam must be those who

(a) hold a title recognised or conferred by the Governmet of India or are Members of the Order of the Star of India, or of the Order of the Indian Empire, or are holders of the Kaisar-I-Hind Medal;or

(b) are Ordinary Honorary Fellows of the University of Calcutta; or

(c) hold in their own right as proprietors or permanent tenure holders, one or more estates or shares of estates or one or more tenures held direct from the zemindars or shares of such tenures in respect of which land revenue amounting to not less than seven hundred and fifty rupees or cess amounting to not less than one hundred and eighty seven rupees and eight annas is payable annually ; or

(d) have during the financial year immediately preceding the commencement of the election individually paid income-tax in respect of an annual income of not less than six thousand rupees; or

(e) are in receipt of pensions for service as Gazetted or Commissioned Officers of Government.

It is provided that no elector shall have more than one vote though he may possess more than one of the qualifications described above.

IV. The Chambers of Commerce(2):

One Member is elected by the Members of each of the Chambers of Commerce of Bengal and Bombay in such manner as a Commissioner for the Port of Calcutta or Trustee for the Port of Bombay is for the time being elected by the Members of the respective Chambers.

Any person not ineligible for election under the regulations and whose name is on the electoral roll or who is a Member of the Chamber as the case may be, is eligible for nomination or election as the case may be in the cases of II,III and IV.

III. The Provincial Legislative Councils
Eastern Bengal and Assam Council

The following is the constitution of the Legislative Council of the Lieutenant Governor of Eastern Bengal and Assam :-

A-	Nominated Members, not more than 17 to be officials, and one to be a representative of the Indian Commerce	22
B.	-Nominated experts, either officials or non-officials,	2
C.	-Elected Members (18):	
	(i) By the Municipal Commissioners	3
	(ii) „ the District and Local Boards	5
	(iii) „ the Landholders	2
	(iv) „ the Muhammadan community	4
	(v) „ the Tea Interest	2
	(vi) „ the Jute Interest	1
	(vii) „ the Commissioners of the Port of Chittagong	1
	or, including the Lieutenant Governor	43

I. It is provided that, for the purpose of electing three Members by the Municipal Commissioners, the Municipalities possessing an annual income of not less than Rs.5,000 shall be formed in the following four groups :-

Group (1).-The Municipalities in the Dacca Division.

Group (2).-The Municipalities in the Rajshahi Division.

Group (3).- The Municipalities in the Chittagong and Surma Valley Divisions.

Group (4).- The Municipalities in the Assam Valley Division.

The Commissioners in groups (1) and (2) are to elect one Member each. The Commissioners in groups (3) and (4) are to elect the third Member alternately.

II. The five Members to be elected by the District and Local Boards, are to be elected one each by the District Boards of each division of the Province. (The term 'District Board' includes a Local Board in the districts of the Surma Valley and Assam Valley Divisions.)

III. The two Members to be elected by the landholders are to be elected, one by the landholders of the Dacca and the Rajshahi Divisions alternately, and the other by the landholders of the Chittagong and the Surma Valley and Hill Districts (excluding the

Hill Districts) Divisions alternately.

But the landholders of the Dacca and Chittagong Divisions, respectively, are to have the first right of election. The district of Goalpara is deemed to be included in the Surma Valley and Hill Districts Division.

IV. Of the four Members to be elected for the Muhammadan community, it is provided that one Member shall be elected for each of the following divisions :-

(1) the Dacca Division;

(2) the Chittagong Division (excluding the Chittagong Hill Tracts); and

(3) the Rajshahi Division;

and one Member shall be alternately elected for

(4) the Surma Valley and Hill Districts Division (excluding the Hill Tracts);

(5) the Assam Valley Division (excluding the Garo Hills District).

It is also provided that the Surma Valley and Hill Districts Division shall have the first right of election.

V. The two Members of the Tea Interest are to be elected by the Assam Branch of the Indian Tea Association, the Surma Valley Branch of the Indian Tea Association and the Duars Planters' Association .

The first branch has four votes, the second four and the Duars Planters' Association two, and no Association can give to one candidate more than half the number of votes allotted to it.

Any person not ineligible for election under the regulations may be nominated as a candidate.

Each Association nominates one member.

Nominations are made and votes given by each Association in the manner laid down in the rules of the Association.

If there is an equality in the number of votes, it is provided that votes shall be taken again under the same procedure to determine which of the candidates shall be declared to be elected.

VI. The Member for the Jute Interest is to be elected by the Members of the Naraingunj Chamber of Commerce.

Eastern Bengal and Assam

(i) Municipal Commissioners

Electoral groups and qualifications of electors-For the purpose of the election of three Members, the Municipalities possessing an annual local income of not less than five thousand rupees are formed in the following four groups:-

Group (1)- The Municipalities in the Dacca Division.

Group (2)- The Municipalities in the Rajshahi Division.

Group (3)- The Municipalities in the Chittagong and Surma Valley Divisions.

Group (4)- The Municipalities in the Assam Valley Division.

The Commissioners other than the Chairman, if an official, and the members appointed ex-officio, of the Municipalities in groups (1) and (2) elect each one member.

The Commissioners, other than the Chairman, if an official, and the members appointed ex-officio, of the Municipalities in groups(3) and (4) having the first right of election.

The number of votes which the Commissioners of each Municipality are entitled to give is regulated by the local income possessed by it according to the following scale:-

Municipalities		Votes
With an annual local income of		
	Rs. 5,000 and less than Rs.10,000	1
Do	Rs.10,000 and less thanRs.20,000	2
Do	Rs.20,000 and less than Rs.50,000	3
Do	Rs. 50,000 and less than Rs.80,000	4
and for every additional Rs. 30,000 or part thereof		
in excess of Rs. 80,000		1

(ii) District and Local Boards

Electoral groups.- The five Members are elected, one each by the District Boards of each division of the province.

Qualification of electors- The election is made by the votes of the Members of the District Boards in the division other than (a) the Chairman, if an official, and (b) the Members appointed ex-officio.

The number of votes which the Members of each District Board are entitled to give is regulated by the ordinary (which is taken to be the total income of the Board, excluding the opening balance, and entries under the account head, "Debt") possessed by it as follows :-

One vote, if the ordinary income of the Board does not exceed Rs.1,00,000 and one additional vote for every additional Rs.1,00,000 or portion thereof.

Qualifications of candidates-Any person who has a place of residence within the division and such practical connection with it as qualifies him to represent it, may be nominated as a candidate for election, if he-

(a) is a member of any District Board in that division; or

(b) has served as a member of a District Board within that division for a period of not less than three years; or

(c) is entered in the electoral roll of landholders entitled to elect a Member or Members for the Legislative Council of the Lieutenant Governor of Eastern Bengal and Assam.

IV. The Electorates of Landed Classes

Eastern Bengal and Assam

Electoral groups-Two Members are elected, one by the landholders of the Dacca and the Rajshahi Divisions alternately, and the other by the landholders of the Chittagong and Surma Valley and Hill Districts (excluding the Hill Districts) Division alternately, the first division of the two groups having the first right of election.

Qualifications of electors-The election is made by landholders qualified to vote and having a place of residence within the division concerned, who-

(a) hold in their own right as proprietors or as permanent tenure holders within the division one or more estates or shares of estates, or one or more tenures held direct from the Zamindar or shares of such tenures, and pay in respect thereof land revenue or cess as follows, namely :-

i. in the case of the Surma Valley and the Hill Districts Divisions, land revenue amounting to not less than five hundred rupees or cess amounting to not less than one hundred and twentyfive rupees per annum; and

ii. in the case of the other divisions, land revenue amounting to not less than three thousand rupees or cess amounting to not less than seven hundred and fifty rupees per annum; or

(b) hold titles conferred or recognised by the Government not lower in rank than that of Raja or Nawab:

Provided that no elector shall have more than one vote though he may possess more than one of the qualifications above described.

V. The Muhammadan Electorates

Eastern Bengal and Assam

Electoral groups-The four Members are elected, one by the qualified electors in each of the (1) Dacca, (2) Chittagong (excluding the Chittagong Hill Tracts) and (3) Rajshahi Divisions and one alternately by the qualified electors in (4)the Surma Valley and Hill Districts Division (excluding the Hill Districts), and (5) the Assam Valley Division (excluding the Garo Hills District), the electors of the Surma Valley and Hill Districts Division having the first right or election.

Qualifications of electors-The election is made by the votes of delegates to be selected by Muhammadans qualified to vote and having a place of residence in the electoral area concerned, who

(a) hold titles conferred or recognized by the Government; or
(b) hold the Kaisar-i-Hind Medal;or
(c) are Members of the Order of the Star of India or of the Order of the Indian Empire; or
(d) are Ordinary or Honorary Fellows of the University of Calcutta; or
(e) are Graduates of any University in the United Kingdom or British India; or
(f) are Honorary Magistrates; or
(g) being holders of certificates of having passed the final examination of a recognized Madrassa, are teachers in any High School recognised by the Calcutta University, or any College affiliated thereto, or any Madrassa recognized by the Government, or are Registrars authorised to act under the Bengal Muhammadan Marriages and Divorces Registration Act, 1876; or
(h) are holders in their own right as proprietors or permanent tenure holders within the division of one or more estates or shares of estates, or of one or more permanent tenures held direct from Zamindars, or shares of such tenures, and pay in respect thereof land revenue or cess as follows, namely:-

(i) in the case of Assam Valley Division, land revenue amounting to not less than fifty rupees per annum; and

(ii) in the other divisions, land revenue amounting to not less than fifty rupees per annum; or

(i) are jotedars in the district of Goalpara paying rent amounting to not less than two hundred rupees per annum; or

(j) pay income-tax on their own account on an income of not less than one thousand rupees per annum; or

(k) are in receipt of pensions from the Government of not less than fifty rupees per mensem:

Provided that no elector shall have more than one vote though he may possess more than one of the qualifications above described.

The electors of the districts or sub-divisions are to elect the following number of delegates:-

District	Delegates
Dacca Division	
Dacca	7
Mymensingh	12
Faridpore	5
Bakarganj	7
Total	31
Chittagong Division	
Chittagong	4
Tipperah	6
Noakhali	4
Total	14
Rajshahi Division	
Rajshahi	5
Dinajpur	4
Jalpaiguri	1
Rangpur	6
Bogra	3
Pabna	5
Malda	2
Total	26
Assam Valley Division	
Goalpara	1
Kamrup	1
Darrang	1
Nowgong	1
Sibsagar	1
Lakhimpur	1
Total	6
Surma Valley and Hill Districts Division	
Cachar	1
Sylhet	5
Total	6
Total delegates	83

Qualification of candidates-Any person whose name is on the electoral roll of the division concerned may be nominated as a candidate for election.

VI. The Planting Interest

Eastern Bengal and Assam

Two Members are elected by the Assam Branch of the Indian Tea Association, the Surma Valley Branch of the Indian Tea Association, and the Duars Planters' Association, as described already.

One Member is elected by the Members of the Naraingunj Chamber of Commerce and any person not ineligible under the Regulations, may be elected.

VII. Commerce-European and Indian

The Commissioners of the Port of Chittagong elect one member to the Legislative Council of Eastern Bengal and Assam.

APPENDIX 2

LEGISLATIVE COUNCILLORS OF ASSAM (INDIANS ONLY) 1912-1920

	Term	Mode of Representation	Period of Service
Officials:			
1. Abdul Majid	I – II		for most of the period
2. Col. H.L. Banatvala	"		"
Non-Officials:			
	A. Brahmaputra Valley:		
1. Rai Sahib Padmanath Gohain Baruah	I	Nominated	
2. Raja Prabhat Chandra Barua Zamindar, Goalpara	I	"	
3. Rajendranarayan Chaudhury	II	"	
4. Syed Muhammad Saadulla, M.A. B.L.(Knigted in 1928)	I – II	Muslim	
5. Tarun Ram Phukan Bar-at Law, Landholder	I – II		Resigned in 1919
6. Rai Bahadur Ghanashyam Baruah, Planter	I – II	Local Board	Elected to Imperial Legislative Council in
	1913		
7. Manik Chandra Baruah, Planter	I	Municipality	Died in July 1915
8. Rai Bahadur Phanidhar Chalia, Retd. Govt. employee	I – II	"	1915-1919 (resigned)
9. Rai Bahadur Krishna Kumar Barua, Planter	II	Landholder	From September 1919
10. Chandradhar Barua, Planter	II	Municipality	"
	B. Surma Valley		
1. Rai Bahadur Dulaal Chandra Deb to early 1913	I	Nominated	For a short stint 1912
2. Rai Bahadur Sitamohan Das	I	"	After Deb

3. Radha Binod Das, Lawyer	II		Resigned in 1919
4. Kahn Bahadur Muhammad Bakht Majumdar, Zamindar	II	"	
5. Khan Bahadur Saiyid Abdul Majid, Planter	I – II		
6. Munshi Riaz Baksh	II	Muslim	
7. Rai Bahadur Nalini Kanta Ray Dastidar	I – II	Landholder	
8. Ramani Mohan Das, Zamindar-Planter-Merchant-Banker	I – II	Local Board	
9. Kamini Kumar Chanda, Lawyer Legislative Councl	I – II	Municipality	Elected to Imperial 1916
10. Nagendranath Chaudhury	II	Nominated	from September 1919

Note: First term of the Council 1913-1916, Second term, 1916-1919, extended till the formation of the new Council under the Montagu-Chelsford Reforms.

Manik Chandra Baruah was the first non-official and Indian Chairman of the Gauhati Municipality (26 March 1913 to 24 July 1915.)

Sources : Proceedings of the Assam Legislative Council published in the Assam Gazatte of the relevant years, Guha, pp. 346-347.

APPENDIX 3

LIST OF EXECUTIVE COUNCILLORS AND MINISTERS 1921-1936

First Council 1921-1936

1. W.J. Reid
2. Abdul Majid
3. Ghanashyam Baruah
4. Syed Abdul Majid
5. Promod Chandra Dutta (after the death of Majid)

Second Council 1924- 1926

1. W. J. Reid replaced by A.W.Botham in 1925
2. Kutubuddin Ahmed
3. Promode Chandra Datta
4. Syed Muhammad Saadulla

Third Council 1927-1929

1. A.W. Botham
2. Kutubuddin Ahmed
3. Syed Muhammad Saadulla (Knignted in 1928).
4. J.J.M. Nichols Roy

Fourth Council 1929-1936

(a). 1. A.W. Botham
2. Syed Muhammad Saadulla
3. Abdul Hamid
4. Kanaklal Baruah

(b). 1. Syed Muhammad Saadulla
2. A.J. Laine
3. Abdul Hamid

4. Kanaklal Baruah

(c) 1. A. J. Laine
2. Promode Chandra Datta
3. Abdul Hamid
4. Kanaklal Baruah

(a) covers the period from 1929-1932,

(b) covers the period from 1932-1934,

(c) covers the period from 1934-1936, till the implementation of Provincial Autonomy. The fourth Council was extended twice. During the tenure of the first Council, Ghanashyam Baruah died in harness and Abdul Majid was appointed in his place. The first two persons in the list during each tenure of the Council were Executive Councilors and the third and the fourth were Ministers. While one of the Executive Councilors was an Indian, both the Ministers were natives.

LIST OF CHIEF COMMISSIONERS, LT. GOVERNORS AND GOVERNORS 1874-1946

CHIEF COMMISSIONERS

1. R.H. Keatinge	7 Feb. 1874 - 21 June 1878
2. S.C. Bayley	22 June 1878 - 4 March 1881
3. C.A. Elliot	25 March 1881 - 7 July 1883
4. W.E. Ward (Offg.)	8 July 1883 - 7 Oct. 1883
5. C.A. Elliot	8 Oct. 1883 - 25 Feb 1885
6. W.E. Ward	27 Feb. 1885 - 30 Oct. 1887
7. D. Fitzpatrick	31 Oct. 1887 - 15 July 1889
8. J. Westland	16 July 1889 - 21 Oct. 1889
9. J.W. Quinton	21 Oct 1889 - 24 March 1891 (murdered in Manipur on 24 Mar. 1891)
10. H.Collet	25 March 1891 - 26 May 1891
11. W.E. Ward	27 May 1891 - 3 July 1894
12. C. J. Layall	4 July 1894 - 3 Oct. 1894
13. W.E. Ward	4 Oct. 1894 - 27 Nov. 1896
14. H. J. S. Cotton	28 Nov. 1896 - 30 April 1900
15. J.B. Fuller	1 May 1900 - 31 July 1900
16. H.J.S. Cotton	1 Aug. 1900 - 28 April 1902
17. A. Earle	1 April 1912 - 12 May 1914
18. P.R.T. Gordon	13 May 1914 - 8 Sept. 1914
19. A. Earle	9 Sept. 1914 - 8 Sept. 1914
20. N.D. B. Bell	1 April 1918 - 2 Jan. 1921

L.T. GOVERNORS

1. J.B. Fuller	16 Oct. 1905 - 19 Aug. 1906

2. L. Hare	20 Aug. 1906 - 18 May 1908
3. C.S. Bayley	19 May 1908 - 13 Nov. 1908
4. L. Hare	14 Nov. 1908 - 22 Aug. 1911
5. C.S. Bayley	23 Aug. 1911 - 31 March 1912

GOVERNORS

1. N.D.B. Bell	3 Jan. 1921 - 2 March 1921
2. W. Sinclair	3 March 1921 - 10 Oct. 1922
3. J.H. Kerr	11 Oct.1922 - 10 April 1925
4. W.J. Reid (Offg.)	11 April. 1925 - 5 Aug. 1925
5. J.H. Kerr	5 Aug. 1925 - 11 Aug. 1925
6. W.J. Reid	12 Aug. 1925 - 8 Dec. 1925
7. J.H. Kerr	9 Dec. 1925 - 27 June 1927
8. E.L.L. Hammond	28 June 19270 - 10 May 1932
9. M.Keane	11 May 1932 - 2 June 1935
10. A.J. Laine	3 June 1935 - 11 Oct. 1935
11. M. Keane	11 Oct. 1935 - 3 March 1937
12. R.N. Reid	4 March 1937 - 24 June 1938
13. G.P. Hogg	25 June. 1938 - 24 Oct. 1938
14. R.N. Reid	25 Oct. 1938 - 24 Feb. 1939
15. H.J. Twynam	24 Feb. 1939 - 5 Oct. 1939
16. R.N. Reid	5 Oct. 1939 - till elections of 21 January 1946.

Sources: Assam Secretariat Files, Proceedings of the Assam Legislative Councils and the Assam Legislative Assembly, Report of the Indian Statutory Commission (Simon Commission), Vol. 1, Part II, p. 134, p. 137, Bhuyan and Sibopada Dey (Eds.), Political History of Assam Volume two 1920- 1939, Appendix A and B, Kar, M., Muslims in Assam Politics, (1990), Chapters 9 and 10.

APPENDIX 4

GOVERNMENT OF INDIA HOME DEPARTMENT PUBLIC NOTIFICATION

Simla, the 30th July 1923

No. F. 213 X.- In exercise of the powers conferred by sections 72 A and 129 A of the Government of India Act, and in supersession of the notification of the Government of India in the Reforms Office No. 767-F, dated the 27th July, 1920, and of all notifications amending the rules issued therewith, the Governor-General in Council, with the sanction of the Secretary of State in Council, is pleased to make the following rules for the nomination and election of members of the Legislative Council of the Governor of Assam:-

Preliminary

1. (1) These rules may be called the Assam Electoral Rules.
   (2) They shall come into force at once.

2. In these rules, unless there is anything repugnant in the subject or context, –
   (a) "the Act" means the Government of India Act;
   (b) "Commissioners" means Commissioners appointed for the purpose of holding an election inquiry under these rules;
   (c) "currupt practice" means any act deemed to be a corrupt practice under the provisions of Schedule V;
   (d) "election agent" means the person appointed under these rules by a candidate as this agent for an election;
   (e) "Gazette" means the Assam Gazette; and
   (f) "Schedule" means a Schedule to these rules.

PART I
COMPOSITION OF COUNCIL AND CONSTITUENCIES

3. The Legislative Council of the Governor of Assam shall consist of-
   (1) the members of the Executive Council ex-officio;
   (2) thirty nine elected members; and
   (3) such number of members nominated by the Governor; as with the addition of the mem-

bers of the Executive Council shall amount to fourteen; of the members so nominated-

(a) not more than seven may be officials, and

(b) two shall be non-official persons nominated to represent respectively the following classes, namely :-

(i) the labouring classes; and

(ii) the inhabitants of backward tracts.

For the purpose of selecting persons to be nominated under sub-clause (b) of clause (3) of this rule the Governor may at his discretion make regulations providing for their selection by the communities concerned.

4. These elected members shall be elected by the constituencies specified in Schedule I, and the number of members to be elected by each constituency shall be as stated therein against that constituency:

Provided that the local Government may by regulation divide into two or more constituencies any of the plural-member constituencies and may distribute among the new constituencies so created the seats entered in Schedule I against the constituency which has been so divided.

PART II
QUALIFICATIONS OF ELECTED MEMEBRS

5.(1) A person shall not be eligible for election as a member of the Council if such person –

(a) is not a British subject ; or

(b) is a female ; or

(c) has already made the oath or affirmation as a member of the Council or of any other legislative body constituted under the Act ; or

(d) having been a legal practitioner has been dismissed or is under suspension from practicing as such by order of any competent court; or

(e) has been adjudged by a competent court to be of unsound mind; or

(f) is under 25 years of age; or

(g) is an undischarged insolvent; or

(h) being a discharged insolvent has not obtained from the court a certificate that his insolvency was caused by misfortune without any misconduct on his part :

Provided that the local Government may direct that, subject to such conditions as it may presecribe, a Ruler of any State in India or the Rulers of any such States or a subject of any such State or any class of such subjects shall not be ineligible for election by reason only of not being a British subject or British subjects :

Provided, further, that the disqualification mentioned in clause (d) may be removed by an order of the local Government in this behalf.

(2) A person against whom a conviction by a criminal court involving a sentence of transportation or imprisonment for a period of more than six months is subsisting shall, unless the offence of which he was convicted has been pardoned, not be eligible for election for five years from the date of the expiration of the sentence.

(3) If any person is convicted of an offence under Chapter IX-A of the Indian Penal Code punishable with imprisonment for a term exceeding six months or is, after an inquiry by Commissioners appointed under any rules for the time being in force regarding elections to a legislative body constituted under the Act, reported as guilty of a corrupt practice as specified in Part I, or in paragraph 1, 2 or 3 of Part II, of Schedule V, such person shall not be eligible for election for five years from the date or such conviction or of the finding of the Commissioners, as the case may be ; and a person reported by any such Commissioners to be guilty of any other corrupt practice shall be similarly disqualified for three years from such date.

(4) If in respect of an election to any legislative body constituted under the Act a return of the election expenses of any person who has been nominated as a candidate at that election is not lodged within the time and in the manner prescribed by or under the rules made in that behalf, or if any such return is lodged which is found, either by Commissioners holding an inquiry into the election or by a Magistrate in a judicial proceeding, to be false in any material particular, neither the candidate nor his election agent shall be eligible for election for five years from the date of such election :

Provided that nay disqualification mentioned in sub-rule (3) or sub-rule (4) of this rule may be removed by an order of the Local Government in that behalf.

6. A person shall not be eligible for election as a member of the Council to represent –

(a) the Shillong constituency or a non-Muhammadan rural constituency (which constituencies are hereinafter in these rules referred to as general constituencies) unless his name is registered on the electoral roll of the constituency or of another constituency in the province ; or

(b) a Planting, or Commerce and Industry constituency (which constituencies are hereinafter in these rules referred to as special constituencies) unless his name is registered on the electoral roll of the constituency.

PART III
THE ELECTORAL ROLL

7. (1) Every person shall be entitled to have his name registered on the electoral roll of a constituency who has the qualifications prescribed for an elector of the constituency and who is not subject to any of the disqualification hereinafter set namely :-

(a) is not a British subject; or

(b) is a female; or

(c) has been adjudged by a competent court to be of unsound mind; or

(d) is under 21 years of age.

Provided that the local Government may direct that, subject to such condition as it may prescribe, a Ruler of any State in India or the Rulers of any such States or a subject of any such State or any class of such subjects shall not be disqualified for registration by reason only of not being a British subject or British subjects :

Provided, further, that, if a resolution is passed by the Council after not less than one month's notice has been given of an intention to move such a resolution, recommending that the sex disqualification for registration should be removed either in respect of women generally or any class of women, the local Government shall make regulations providing that women or a class of women, as the case may be, shall not be disqualified for registration by reason only of their sex :

Provided, further, that no person shall be entitled to have his name registered on the electoral roll of more than one general constituency.

(2) If any person is convicted of an offence under Chapter IX-A of the Indian Penal Code punishable with imprisonment for a term exceeding six months or is, after an inquiry by Commissioners appointed under any rules for the time being in force regarding elections to a legislative body constituted under the Act, reported as guilty of a corrupt practice as specified in Part I or in paragraph, 1, 2, or 3 of Part II, of Schedule V, his name, if on an electroral roll, shall be removed therefrom and shall not be registered thereon for a period of five years from the date of the conviction or the report as the case may be or if not on the electroral roll shall not be so registered for a like period; and if any person is reported by any such Commissioners as guilty of any other corrupt practice, his name, if on the electoral roll, shall be removed there-from and shall not be registered thereon for a period of three years from the date of the report or, if not on the electoral roll, shall not be so registered for a like period :

Provided that the local Government may direct that the name of any person to whom this sub-rule applied shall be registered on the electoral roll.

8. (1) The qualifications of an elector for a general constituency shall be such qualifications based on –

(i) residence, and

(ii) save in the case of the Shillong constituency, community, and

(iii) (a) assessment to municipal or cantonment rates or taxes, or

(b) assessment to tax in a union under Chapter III of the Bengal Municipal Act, 1876, or

(c) assessment to chaukidari tax under the Village-Chaukidari Act, 1870, or

(d) assessment to income-tax or

(e) military service, or

(f) the holding of land, as are specified in Schedule II in the case of that constitu ency.

(2) The qualifications of an elector for a special constituency shall be the qualifications specified in Schedule II in the case of that constituency.

9. (1) An electoral roll shall be prepared for every constituency, on which shall be entered the names of all persons appearing to be entitled to be registered as electors for that constituency. It shall be published in the constituency together with a notice specifying the mode in which and the time within which any person whose name is not entered in the roll and who claims to have it inserted therein, or any person whose name is on the roll and who objects to the inclusion of his own name or of the name of any other person on the roll, may prefer a claim or objection to the Revising Authority.

(2) Subject to the provisions of these rules, the local Government shall make regulations providing for –

(1) the authority by whom the electoral roll shall be prepared and particulars to be

contained in the roll ;

(2) the time at which the roll shall be prepared;

(3) the publication of the roll in such manner and in such language as to give it wide publicity in the constituency to which it relates;

(4) the mode in which and the time within which claims and objections may be preferred;

(5) the constitution and appointment of Revising Authorities to dispose of claims and objections;

(6) the manner in which notices of claims or objections shall be published; and

(7) the place, date and time at which and the manner in which claims or objections shall be heard; and may make such regulations to provide for other matters incidental or ancillary to the preparation and revision of the roll as it may consider desirable. Such regulations may be made as to rolls generally or any class of rolls or any particular roll.

(3) The orders made by the Revising Authority shall be final, and the electoral roll shall be amended in accordance therewith and shall, as so amended, be republished in such manner as the local Government may prescribe.

(4) The electoral roll shall come into force from the date of such republication and shall continue in force for a period of three years after the expiration of which period a fresh roll shall be prepared in accordance with these rules:

Provided that the local Government may, by notification in the Gazette, direct the preparation in accordance with these rules of a fresh roll at any time before the expiration of the said period.

(5) If a constituency is called upon to elect a member or members after an electoral roll has ceased to have force and before the completion of the new electoral roll, the old electoral roll shall, for the purposes of that election, continue to operate as the electoral roll for the constituency.

(6) Notwithstanding anything hereinbefore contained, any person may apply to such authority as may be appointed in this behalf by the local Government for the amendment of any electoral roll for the time being in force, and the local Government may, at any time after any such application has been made in respect of an electoral roll, by notification in the Gazette direct the preparation of list of amendments thereto, and all the provisions of this rule shall apply in the case of every such list in like manner as they apply in the case of electoral rolls :

Provided that, where any such application is made for the correction of an existing entry in the electoral roll and the said authority is satisfied after such inquiry as the local Government may by regulation prescribe that the entry relates to the applicant and is erroneous or defective in any particular, it may amend the roll or cause it to be amended accordingly.

(7) When any list of amendments has been republished under sub-rule (6), the electoral roll to which it relates shall be deemed to have been amended accordingly.

10. (1) Every person registered on the electoral roll for the time being in force for any constitu-

ency shall, while so registered, be entitled to vote at an election of a member or members for that constituency.

Provided that-

a) no person shall vote at any general election in more than one general constituency, and

b) no person shall vote at any election if he is subject to any disability stated in rule 7.

(2) If any person is in the course of the hearing of an election petition under these rules proved to have voted at the election in contravention of the proviso to sub-rule (1) his vote shall be void.

PART IV
ELECTIONS

11. (I) Any person may be nominated as a candidate for election in any constituency for which he is eligible for election under these rules.

(2) The local Government shall appoint for each constituency–

(a) a date, not later than the fourteenth day after the date of the notification calling upon the constituency to elect a member, for the nomination of candidates;

(b) a further date, not later than the seventh day after the first-mentioned date, for the scrutiny of nominations; and

(c) a further date or dates on which a poll shall, if necessary, be taken; and the dates so appointed shall be notified in the constituency in such manner as the local Government thinks fit.

(3) On or before the date so appointed for the nomination of candidates each candidate shall either in person or by his proposer and seconder together, between the hours of eleven o'clock in the forenoon and three o'clock in the afternoon deliver to the Returning Officer or to such other person as may be authorised in this behalf by regulation a nomination paper completed in the form prescribed in Schedule III and subscribed by the candidate himself as assenting to the nomination and by two persons as proposer and seconder whose names are registered on the electoral roll of the constituency.

(4) Any person whose name is registered on the electoral roll of the constituency; and who is not subject to any disability stated in rule 7, may subscribe, as proposer or seconder, as many nomination papers as there are vacancies to be filled but no more.

(5) Every nomination paper delivered under sub-rule (3) shall be accompanied by declaration in writing subscribed by the candidate that the candidate has appointed or does thereby appoint as his election agent for the election either himself or some one other person who is not disqualified under these rules for the appointment and who shall be named in the declaration; and no candidate shall be deemed to be duly nominated unless such declaration is delivered along with the nomination paper.

(6) Any nomination paper which is not received before three o'clock in the afternoon

on the date appointed by the local Government for the nomination of candidates shall be rejected.

(7) The Returning Officer or other person authorized shall, on receiving a nomination paper under sub-rule (3) inform the person or persons delivering the same of the date, hour and place appointed for the scrutiny of nominations, and shall enter in the nomination paper its serial number and shall sign thereon a certificate stating the date on which and the hour at which the nomination paper has been delivered to him; and shall, as soon as may be thereafter, cause to be affixed in some conspicuous place in his office a notice of the nomination containing descriptions, similar to those contained in the nomination paper, both of the candidate and of the persons who have subscribed the nomination paper as proposer and seconder.

(8) Any candidate may withdraw his candidature by notice in writing subscribed by him and delivered to the Returning Officer or other person authorized on or before three o'clock in the afternoon on the date succeeding that appointed by the local Government for the scrutiny of nominations. A candidate who has withdrawn his candidature shall not be allowed to cancel the withdrawal or to be re-nominated as a candidate for the same election.

(9) The Returning Officer or other person authorized shall, on receiving a notice of withdrawal under sub-rule (8), as soon as may be, cause a notice of the withdrawal to be affixed in some conspicuous place in his office.

12. (1) On or before the date appointed for the nomination of candidates, each candidate shall deposit or cause to be deposited with the Returning Officer the sum of two hundred and fifty rupees in cash or in Government Promissory Notes of equal value at the market rate of the day; and no candidate shall be deemed to be duly nominated unless such deposit has been made.

(2) If a candidate by whom or on whose behalf the deposit referred to in sub-rule (1) has been made withdraws his candidature in the manner and within the time specified in sub-rule (8) of Rule 11, or if the nomination of any such candidate is refused, the deposit shall be returned to the person by whom it was made; and, if any candidate dies before the commencement of the poll, any such deposit, if made by him, shall be returned to his legal representative or, if not made by the candidate, shall be returned to the persons by whom it was made.

(3) If a candidate by whom or on whose behalf the deposit referred to in sub-rule (1) has been made is not elected and the number of votes polled by him does not exceed one-eighth of the total number of votes polled the deposit shall be forfeited to the Government.

(4) For the purpose of sub-rule (3), the number of votes polled shall be deemed to be the number of ballot papers, other than spoilt ballot papers, counted; and where the election is held according to the system of proportional representation by means of the single transferable vote, the number of votes polled by a candidate shall be the number of votes polled by him as first preferences.

(5) If a candidate by whom or on whose behalf the deposit referred to in sub-rule (1) has been made is elected and thereafter his seat is declared vacant under these

rules owing to his failure to make the oath or affirmation hereinafter prescribed, the deposit shall be forfeited to the Government.

(6) The deposit made in respect of a candidate who is not elected shall, if it is not forfeited under sub-rule (3) be returned to the candidate or to the person who has made the deposit on his behalf, as the case may be, as soon as may be after the publication of the result of the election in the Gazette; and the deposit made in respect of a candidate who is elected shall, if it is not forfeited under sub-rule (5), be so returned as soon as may be after the candidate has made the oath or affirmation hereinafter prescribed:

Provided that, if a candidate is duly nominated at a general election in more than one constituency, not more than one of the deposits made by him or on his behalf shall be returned, and the remainder shall be forfeited to the Government.

13. If a candidate who has been duly nominated dies after the date appointed for the scrutiny of nominations and before the date appointed for the taking of a poll, the Returning Officer or other authorized person referred to in sub-rule (3) of rule 11 shall, upon being satisfied of the fact of the death of the candidate, countermand the poll and report the fact to the local Government and all proceedings with reference to the election shall be commenced anew in all respects as if for a new election:

Provided that no fresh nomination shall be necessary in the case of a candidate who stood nominated at the time of the countermanding of the poll.

14. (1) if the number of candidates who are duly nominated and who have not withdrawn their candidature in the manner and within the time specified in sub-rule (8) of rule 11 exceeds that of the vacancies, a poll shall be taken.

(2) If the number of such candidates is equal to the number of vacancies, all such candidates shall be declared to be duly elected.

(3) If the number of such candidates is less than the number of vacancies, all such candidates, if any, shall be declared to be elected, and the Governor shall, by a notification in the Gazette, call upon the constituency to elect a person or persons as the case may be, within such time as may be prescribed by the notification :

Provided that where the constituency, having already been called upon under this sub-rule, has failed to elect a person or the requisite number of persons, as the case may be, to fill the vacancy or vacancies, the Governor shall not be bound to call again upon the constituency to elect a person or persons until such time if any, as he thinks fit.

(4) Vote shall be given by ballot, and in general constituencies in person :

Provided that the local Government may-

(a) in the case of any specified general constituency or of any specified part of any general constituency, or

(b) in respect of any person attending at a polling station in any constituency under the orders of, or under authority from, the Returning Officer of such constituency,

by regulation direct that votes may be given otherwise than in person :

Provided, further, that no votes shall be received by proxy.

(5) In plural-member constituencies every elector shall have as many votes as there

are members to be elected : but no elector shall give more than one vote to any one candidate.

(6) Votes shall be counted by, or under the supervision of, the Returning Officer, and each candidate, the election agent of each candidate, and one representative of each candidate authorized in writing by the candidate shall have a right to be present at the time of counting.

(7) When the counting of the votes has been completed, the Returning Officer shall forthwith declare the candidate or candidates, as the case may be, to whom the largest number of votes has been given to be elected.

(8) Where an equality of votes is found to exist between any candidates and the addition of one vote will entitle any of the candidates to be declared elected, the determination of the person or persons to whom such one additional vote shall be deemed to have been given shall be made by ballot to be drawn in the presence of the Returning Officer and in such manner as he may determine.

(9) The Returning Officer shall without delay report the result of the election to the Secretary to the Council, and the name or names of the candidate or candidates elected shall be published in the Gazette.

15. (1) Subject to the provisions of these rules, the local Government shall make regulations providing –

(1) for the scrutiny of nominations and, in particular, for the manner in which such scrutiny shall be conducted and for the conditions and circumstances in which any person may be present or may enter objections thereat;

(2) for the appointment in each constituency of Returning Officer and for his powers and duties, and for the performance by other persons of any power or duty of the Returning Officer;

(3) in the case of general constituencies, for the division of the constituencies into polling areas in such manner as to give all electors such reasonable facilities for voting as are practicable in the circumstances and for the appointment of polling stations for these areas;

(4) for the appointment of officers to preside at polling stations, and for the duties of such officers;

(5) for the checking of voters by reference to the electoral roll;

(6) for the manner in which votes are to be given, and in particular for the case of illiterate voters or voters under physical or other disability;

(7) for the procedure to be followed in respect of tender of votes by persons representing themselves to be electors after other persons have voted as such electors;

(8) for the scrutiny of votes;

(9) for the safe custody of ballot papers and other election papers, for the period for which such papers shall be preserved, and for the inspection and production of such papers; and

may make such other regulations regarding the conduct of elections as it thinks it.

(2) Notwithstanding anything in these rules, if a resolution in favour of the introduction

of proportional representation is passed by the Council after not less than one month's notice has been given of an intention to move such a resolution the local Government may, for any plural-member constituencies, introduce the method of election by means of the single transferable vote, and may make all necessary regulations for that purpose and to that end may group together single-member constituencies so as to make new plural-member constituencies.

(3) In the exercise of the powers conferred by this rule regulations may be made as to elections generally or any class of elections or in regard to constituencies generally or any class of constituency or any particular constituency.

16. (1) If any person is elected by a constituency of the Council and by a constituency of either chamber of the Indian legislature, the election of such person to the Council shall be void and the Governor shall call upon the constituency concerned to elect another person.

(2) If any person is elected either by more than one constituency of the Council or by a constituency of the Council and a constituency of the Legislative Council of another province, he shall, by notice in writing signed by him and delivered to the Secretary to the Council or the Secretaries to both Councils, as the case may be, within seven days from the date of the publication of the result of such election in the local official Gazette, choose for which of these constituencies he shall serve, and the choice shall be conclusive.

(3) When any such choice has been made, the Governor shall call upon the constituency or constituencies for which such person has not chosen to serve to elect another person or persons.

(4) If the candidate does not make the choice referred to in sub-rule (2) of this rule, the elections of such persons shall be void and the Governor shall call upon the constituency or constituencies concerned to elect another person or persons.

Election Agent and Return of Expenses

17. No person shall be appointed an election agent who is himself ineligible for election as being subject to any disqualification mentioned in sub-rule (3) or sub-rule (4) of rule 5.

18. (1) The appointment of an election agent, whether the election agent appointed be the candidate himself or not, may only be revoked in writing signed by the candidate and lodged with the officer receiving nominations and shall operate from the date on which it is so lodged.

(2) In the event of such a revocation or of the death of any election agent, whether such event occurs before, during or after the election, then the candidate shall appoint forthwith another election agent and declare his name in writing to the said officer.

19. (1) Within thirty-five days from the date of the publication of the result of an election under sub-rule (9) cf rule 14, there shall be lodged with the Returning Officer in respect of each person who has been nominated as a candidate for the

election a return in such form as the local Government may by regulation prescribe of the election expenses of such person containing the particulars specified in Schedule IV and signed both by the candidate and by his election agent.

(2) Every such return shall contain a statement of all payments made by the candidate or by his election agent or by any persons on behalf of the candidate or in his interest for expenses incurred on account of, or in respect of, the conduct and management of the election, and further a statement of all unpaid claims in respect of such expenses of which he or his election agent is aware.

(3) The return shall be accompanied by declarations by the candidate and his election agent which shall be in the form contained in Schedule IV and shall be made on oath or affirmation before a Magistrate.

(4) Notwithstanding anything hereinbefore contained, where a candidate is owing to absence from India unable to sign the return of election expenses and to make the declaration within the period prescribed in this rule, the return shall be signed and lodged by the election agent only and shall be accompanied by a declaration by the election agent under sub-rule (3), and within fourteen days after the return of the candidate to India he shall cause to be lodged with the Returning Officer a declaration made on oath or affirmation before a Magistrate in the special form for the purpose contained in the said Schedule.

(5) When any return and the declarations made in respect thereof have been lodged with the Returning Officer, the Returning Officer shall, as soon as may be, cause a notice of the date cn which the return and declarations in question have been lodged and of the time and place at which they can be inspected, to be fixed in some conspicuous place in his office and to be published in the Gazette, and any person shall, on payment of a fee of one rupee, be entitled to inspect any such return or declaration and, on payment of such fee as the local Government may by regulation prescribe, to obtain a copy or copies thereof or of any part thereof.

(6) The local Government shall cause to be prepared in such manner, and maintained for such time, as it may direct, a record showing the names of all candidates at every election under these rules and the name of the election agent of each such candidate and the date on which the return of election expenses of each candidate has been lodged with the Returning Officer.

20. (1) The Governor General-in-Council may by notification in the Gazette –

(a) fix maximum scales of election expenses which shall be applicable to any election held after the first elections under these rules; and

(b) prescribe the numbers and descriptions of persons who may be employed for payment in connection with any election held under these rules.

(2) Any notification issued under this rule may make different provisions for different constituencies.

21. Every election agent shall for each election for which he is appointed an election agent keep separate and regular books of account in which the particulars of all expenditure of the nature referred to in rule 19 shall be entered, whether such

expenditure is incurred by the candidate or by the election agent or by any person under the direction of the candidate or the election agent.

PART V
NOMINATED MEMBERS

22. (1) No person shall be nominated to the Council who-
(a) is not a British subject; or
(b) is a female; or
(c) has already made the oath or affirmation as a member of the Council or of any other legislative body constituted under the Act; or
(d) having been a legal practitioner has been dismissed or is under suspension from practising as such by order of any competent court; or
(e) has been adjudged by a competent court to be of unsound mind; or
(f) is under 25 years of age; or
(g) is an undischarged insolvent; or
(h) being a discharged insolvent has not obtained from the court a certificate that his insolvency was caused by misfortune without any misconduct on his part

Provided that the local Government may direct that, subject to such conditions as it may prescribe, a Ruler of any State in India or the Rulers of any such States or a subject of any such State or any class of such subjects shall not be disqualified for nomination by reason only of not being a British subject or British subjects:

Provided, further, that the disqualification mentioned in clause (d) may be removed by an order of the local Government in this behalf.

(2) A person against whom a conviction by a criminal court involving a sentence of transportation or imprisonment for a period of more than six months is subsisting shall, unless the offence of which he was convicted has been pardoned, not be eligible for nomination for five years from the date of the expiration of the sentence.

(3) If any person is convicted of an offence under Chapter IX-A of the Indian Penal Code punishable with imprisonment for a term exceeding six months or is, after an inquiry by Commissioners appointed under any rules for the time being in force regarding elections to a legislative body constituted under the Act, reported as guilty of a corrupt practice as specified in Part I, or in paragraph 1,2 or 3 of Part II, of Schedule V, such person shall not be eligible for nomination for five years from the date of such conviction or the finding of the Commissioners, as the case may be; and a person reported by any such Commissioners to be guilty of any other corrupt practice shall be similarly disqualified for three years from such date.

(4) if in respect of an election to any legislative body constituted under this Act a return of the election expenses of any person who has been nominated as a candidate at the election is not lodged within the time and in the manner prescribed by or under the rules made in that behalf, or if any such return is lodged which is found either by Commissioners holding an inquiry into the election or by a

Magistrate in a judicial proceding to be false in any material particular, neither the candidate nor his election agent shall be eligible for nomination for five years from the date of the election:

Provided that any disqualification mentioned in sub-rule(3) or sub-rule (4) of this rule may be removed by an order of the local Government in that behalf.

23. (1) A nominated non-official member shall hold office for the duration of the Council to which he is nominated.

(2) Official members shall hold office for the duration of the Council to which they are nominated or for such shorter period as the Governor may, at the time of nomination, determine.

PART VI
GENERAL PROVISIONS

Obligation to take Oath

24. Every person who is elected or nominated to be a member of the Council shall, before taking his seat, make at a meeting of the Council, an oath or affirmation of his allegiance to Crown in the following form, namely:-

I, A. B, having been elected/ nominated a member of this Council do solemnly swear (or affirm) that I will be faithful and bear true allegiance to His Majesty the King, Emperor of India, His heirs and successors, and that I will faithfully discharge the duty upon which I am about to enter.

Vacation of Seat

25. If any person having been elected or nominated subsequently becomes subject to any of the disabilities stated in clauses (a), (c), (d), (e), (g) and (h) of sub-rule (1) or in sub-rules (2), (3) and (4) of rule 5 or rule 22, as the case may be, or fails to make the oath or affirmation prescribed by rule 24 within such time as the Governor considers reasonable, the Governor shall, if the disqualification has not been removed under these rules, by notification in the Gazette, declare his seat to be vacant.

26. (1) When a vacancy occurs in the case of an elected member by reason of his election being declared void, or his seat being declared vacant or by reason of absence from India, inability to attend to duty, death, acceptance of office or resignation duly accepted, the Governor shall, by notification in the Gazette, call upon the constituency concerned to elect a person for the purpose of filling the vacancy within such time as may be prescribed by such notification.

(2) If a vacancy occurs in the case of a nominated member, the Governor shall nominate to the vacancy a person having the necessary qualification under these rules.

General Elections

27. (1)On the expiration of the duration of a Council or on its dissolution a general election shall be held in order that a new Council shall be constituted.

(2) On such expiration or dissolution the Governor shall, by notification in the Gazette, call upon the constituencies referred to in rule 4 to elect members in accordance with these rules within such time after the date of expiration or dissolution as may be prescribed by such notification:

Provided that, if the Governor thinks fit, such notification may be issued at any time not being more than three months prior to the date on which duration of the Council would expire in the ordinary course of events.

(3) Before the date fixed for the first meeting of the Council, the Governor shall make such nominations as may be necessary to complete the Council.

28. As soon as may be after the expiration of the time fixed for the election of members at any general election, the names of the members elected for the various constituencies at such election shall be notified in the Gazette.

29. If any difficulty arises as to the preparation or publication of any electoral roll or of any list of amendments to any such roll or as to the holding of any election under these rules the local Government may by order do anything not inconsistent with these rules which appears to it to be necessary for the proper preparation or publication of the roll or for the proper holding of the election.

PART VII
FINAL DECISION OF DOUBTS AND DISPUTES AS TO THE VALIDITY OF AN ELECTION

30. In this Part and in Schedule V, unless there is anything repugnant in the subject or context,-

(a) "agent" includes an election agent and any person who is held by Commissioners to have acted as an agent in connection with an election with the knowledge or consent of the candidate;

(b) "candidate" means a person who has been nominated as a candidate at any election or who claims that he has been so nominated or that his nomination has been improperly refused, and includes a person who, when an election is in contemplation, holds himself out as a prospective candidate at such election, provided that he is subsequently nominated as a candidate at such election;

(c) "electoral right" means the right of a person to stand or not to stand as, or to withdraw from being, a candidate, or to vote or refrain from voting at an election; and

(d) "returned candidate" means a candidate whose name has been published under these rules as duly elected.

31. No election shall be called in question except by an election petition presented in accordance with the provisions of this Part.

32. (1) An election petition against any returned candidate may be presented to the Governor –

(a) by any candidate or elector within fourteen days from the date on which the return of the election expenses of the returned candidate and the declarations, referred to in rule 19, are received by the Returning Officer; or

(b) within thirty days from that date by an officer empowered by the local

Government in this behalf on the ground that the election has not been a free election by reason of the large number of cases in which undue influence or bribery has been exercised or committed; or

(c) on the ground that the returned candidate or his election agent or any other person acting with the connivance of the candidate or of his election agent has been guilty of the offence of bribery, undue influence or personation as defined in Chapter IX-A of the Indian Penal Code in respect of the election, by any candidate or elector within fourteen days from the date on which such returned candidate, election agent or other person is convicted of such offence.

(2) An election petition shall be deemed to have been presented to the Governor when it is delivered to the Governor or to any officer appointed by him in this behalf –

(a) by the person making the petition ; or

by a person authorized in writing in this behalf by the person making the petition; or

(b) by registered post.

(3) When the last day of the period for the presentation of an election petition under this rule is a public holiday within the meaning of section 25 of the Negotiable Instruments Act, 1881, or has been notified by the local Government as a day to be observed as a holiday in Government offices, the petition shall be considered as having been received in due time if it is presented on the next succeeding day which is neither such a public holiday nor a day so notified.

(4) For the purposes of clause (a) of sub-rule (1), the date on which the return of the election expenses and the declarations referred to in rule 19 are received by the Returning Officer shall, in the case of a candidate who has made such return and declaration in the manner provided in sub-rule (4) of that rule, be deemed to be the date on which the declaration of the candidate under that sub-rule is received.

33. (1) The petition shall contain a statement in concise form of the material facts on which the petitioner relies and shall, where necessary, be divided into paragraphs numbered consecutively. It shall be signed by the petitioner and verified in the manner prescribed for the verification of pleadings in the Code of Civil Procedure, 1908.

(2) The petition shall be accompanied by a list signed and verified in like manner setting forth full particulars of any corrupt practice which the petitioner alleges, including as full a statement as possible as to the names of the parties alleged to have committed any corrupt practice and the date and place of the commission of each such practice.

(3) The Commissioners may upon such terms as to costs and otherwise as they may direct at any time allow the particulars included in the said list to be amended or order such further and better particulars in regard to any matter referred to therein to be furnished as may in their opinion be necessary for the purpose of ensuring a fair and effectual trial of the petition.

34. The petitioner may, if he so desires, in addition to calling in question the election of the returned candidate, claim a declaration that he himself or any other candidate

has been duly elected; in which case he shall join as respondents to his petition all other candidates who were nominated at the election.

35. At the time of presentation of the petition, the petitioner shall, except where the petition is presented under clause (b) of sub-rule (1) of rule 32, deposit with it the sum of one thousand rupees in cash or in Government Promissory Notes of equal value at the market rate of the day as security for the costs of the same.

36. (1)If the provisions of rule 32, rule 33 or rule 35 are not complied with, the Governor shall dismiss the petition.

(2) If the petition is not dismissed under sub-rule (1) –

(a) the Governor shall appoint as Commissioners for the trial of the petition three persons who are or have been, or are eligible to be appointed, Judges of a High Court within the meaning of section 101 (3) of the Act, and shall appoint one of them to be the President, and thereafter all applications and proceedings in connection therewith shall be dealt with and held by such Commissioners;

(b) the President of the Commission shall, as soon as may be, cause a copy of the petition to be served on each respondent and to be published in the Gazette, and may call on the petitioner to execute a bond in such amount and with such sureties as he may require for the payment of any further costs. At any time within fourteen days after such publication, any other candidate shall be entitled to be joined as respondent on giving security in a like amount and procuring the execution of a like bond:

Provided that the execution of such a bond by the petitioner shall not be required in any case where the petition has been presented under clause (b) of sub-rule (1) of rule 32.

(3) When in respect of an election in a constituency more petitions than one are presented, the Governor shall refer all such petitions to the same Commissioners, who may at their discretion inquire into the petitions either in one or in more proceedings as they shall think fit.

(4) If the services of any Commissioner are not available for the purposes of the inquiry, or if, during the course of the inquiry any Commissioner is unable to continue to attend the same, the Governor shall appoint another Commissioner and the inquiry shall recommence before the Commission as so reconstituted :

Provided that the Commissioners may direct that any evidence already recorded may remain upon the record, in which case it shall not be necessary to re-examine those witnesses who have already been examined and discharged.

(5) Nothing in this rule shall be deemed to prevent the appointment of the President of a Commission before the other Commissioners are appointed and , if the President is not appointed, all references to the Commissioners in these rules shall, in respect of any matter which may be or is to be done before the commencement of the inquiry, be deemed to be references to the President.

37. Subject to the other provisions of these rules, every election petition shall be inquired into by the Commissioners, as nearly as may be, in accordance with the procedure applicable under the Code of Civil Procedure, 1908, to the trial of suits:

Provided that it shall only be necessary for the Commissioners to make a memorandum of the substance of the evidence of any witness examined by them.

38. The inquiry shall be held at such place as the Governor may appoint :
Provided that the Commissioners may in their discretion sit at any other place in the province for any part of the inquiry, and may depute any one of their number to take evidence at any place in the Province.

39. (1) An election petition may be withdrawn only by leave of the Commissioners or, if an application for withdrawal is made before any Commissioner has been appointed, of the Governor.
(2) If there are more petitioners than one, no application to withdraw a petition shall be made except with the consent of all the petitioners.
(3) When an application for withdrawal is made to the Commissioners notice thereof fixing a date for the hearing of the application shall be given to all other parties to the petition and shall be published in the Gazette.
(4) No application for withdrawal shall be granted if, in the opinion of the Governor or of the Commissioners, as the case may be, such application has been induced by any bargain or consideration which ought not to be allowed.
(5) If the application is granted –
(a) the petitioner shall, where the application has been made to the Commissioners, be ordered to pay the costs of the respondent therefor incurred or such portion thereof as the Commissioners may think fit;
(b) notice of the withdrawal shall be published in the Gazette by the Governor or by the Commissioners, as the case may be; and
(c) any person who might himself have been a petitioner may, within fourteen days of such publication, apply to be substituted as petitioner in place of the party withdrawing, and, upon compliance with the conditions of rule 35 as to security, shall be entitled to be so substituted and to continue the proceedings upon such terms as the Commissioners may think fit.

40. (I) An election petition shall abate only on the death of a sole petitioner or of the survivor of several petitioners, provided that, where such sole petitioner was an officer empowered under clause (b) of sub-rule (1) of rule 32, the proceedings may be continued by any other officer empowered in this behalf by the local Government.
(2) Notice of the abatement of an election petition shall be published in the Gazette by the Commissioners or, if the petition abates before any Commissioner has been appointed, by the Governor.
(3) Any person who might himself have been a petitioner may, within fourteen days of such publication, apply to be substituted as petitioner, and, upon compliance with the conditions of rule 35 as to security, shall be entitled to be so substituted and to continue the proceedings upon such terms as the Commissioners may think fit.

41. If before the conclusion of the trial of an election petition the respondent dies or gives notice that he does not intend to oppose the petition, the Commissioners shall cause notice of such event to be published in the Gazette, and thereupon any person who might have been a petitioner may, within fourteen days of such publication, apply

to be substituted for such respondent to oppose the petition, and shall be entitled to continue the proceedings upon such terms as the Commissioners may think fit.

42. (1)Where at an inquiry into an election petition any candidate, other than the returned candidate, claims the seat for himself, the returned candidate or any other party may give evidence to prove that the election of such candidate would have been void if he had been the returned candidate and a petition had been presented complaining of his election :

Provided that the returned candidate or such other party as aforesaid shall not be entitled to give such evidence unless he has, within fourteen days from the date of the publication of the election petition under clause (b) of sub-rule (2) of rule 36, given notice of his intention to the Commissioners and made the deposit and procured the execution of the bond referred to in rules 35 and 36, respectively.

(2) Every notice referred to in sub-rule (1) shall be accompanied by the statement and list of particulars required by rule 33 in the case of an election petition and shall be signed and verified in like manner.

43. When at any inquiry into an election petition the Commissioners so order, such officer as the Local Government may from time to time appoint in this behalf shall attend and take such part therein as they may direct.

44. (1) Save as hereinafter provided in this rule, if in the opinion of the Commissioners–

(a) the election of a returned candidate has been procured or induced, or the result of the election has been materially affected, by a corrupt practice, or

(b) any corrupt practice specified in Part I of Schedule V has been committed, or

(c) the result of the election has been materially affected by the improper acceptance or refusal of any nomination or by the improper reception or refusal of a vote, or the reception of any vote which is void, or by any non-compliance with the provisions of the Act or the rules or regulations made thereunder, or by any mistake in the use of any form annexed thereto, or

(d) the election has not been a free election by reason of the large number of cases in which undue influence or bribery, within the meaning either of Part I or of Part II of Schedule V has been exercised or committed, the election of the returned candidate shall be void.

(2) If the Commissioners report that a returned candidate has been guilty by an agent (other than his election agent) of any corrupt practice specified in Part I of Schedule V which does not amount to any form of bribery other than treating as hereinafter explained or to the procuring or abetment of personation and if the Commissioners further report that the candidate has satisfied them that –

(a) no corrupt practice was committed at such election by the candidate or his election agent, and the corrupt practices mentioned in the report were committed contrary to the orders and without the sanction or connivance of such candidate or his election agent, and

(b) such candidate and his election agent took all reasonable means for preventing the commission of corrupt practices at such election, and

(c) the corrupt practices mentioned in the said report were of a trivial, unimportant and limited character, and

(d) in all other respects the election was free from any corrupt practice on the part of such candidate or any of his agents,

then the Commissioners may find that the election of such candidate is not void.

Explanation – For the purposes of this sub-rule "treating" means the incurring in whole or in part by any person of the expense of giving or providing any food, drink, entertainment or provision to any person with the object, directly or indirectly, of inducing him or any other person to vote or refrain from voting or as a reward for having voted or refrained from voting.

45. (1) At the conclusion of the inquiry, the Commissioners shall report whether the returned candidate, or any other party to the petition who has under the provisions of these rules claimed the seat, has been duly elected, and in so reporting shall have regard to the provisions of rule 44.

(2) The report shall further include a recommendation by the Commissioners as to the total amount of costs which are payable and the persons by and to whom such costs should be paid. Such recommendation may include a recommendation for the payment of costs to the officer attending in pursuance of an order made under rule 43.

(3) The report shall be in writing and shall be signed by all the Commissioners. The Commissioners shall forthwith forward their report to the Governor who, on receipt thereof, shall issue orders in accordance with the report and publish the report in the Gazette, and the orders of the Governor shall be final.

46. If either in their report or upon any other matter there is a difference of opinion among the Commissioners, the opinion of the majority shall prevail, and their report shall be expressed in the terms of the views of the majority.

47. Where any charge is made in an election petition of any corrupt practice, the Commissioners shall record in their report –

(a) a finding whether a corrupt practice has or has not been proved to have been committed by any candidate or his agent, or with the connivance of any candidate or his agent, and the nature of such corrupt practice, and

(b) the names of all persons (if any) who have been proved at the inquiry to have been guilty of any corrupt practice and the nature of such corrupt practice with any such recommendations as they may desire to make for the exemption of any such person from any disqualifications they may have incurred in this connection under these rules:

Provided that no person shall be so named in the report unless he has been given a reasonable opportunity of showing cause why his name should not be so recorded.

PART VIII
SPECIAL PROVISIONS

48. If any question arises as to the interpretation of these rules otherwise than in connection with an election inquiry held thereunder, the question shall be referred for the decision of the Governor, and his decision shall be final.

SCHEDULE I (See rule 4.)
LIST OF CONSTITUENCIES

Name of Constituency	Class of Constituency	Extent of Constituency	Number of members
Shillong	General Urban	The municipality and cantonment of Shillong	1
Silchar	Non-Muhammadan Rural	The Silchar sub-division of the Cachar District	1
Hailakandi	Ditto	The Hailakandi sub-division of the Cachar District	1
Sylhet Sadr	Ditto	The Sadr sub-division of the Sylhet District	1
Sunamganj	Ditto	The Sunamganj sub-division of the Sylhet District	1
Habiganj (North)	Ditto	The Habiganj (North) sub –division of the Sylhet District	1
Habiganj (South)	Ditto	The Habiganj (South) sub-division of the Sylhet District	1
South Sylhet	Ditto	The South Sylhet sub-division of the Sylhet District	1
Karimganj	Ditto	The Karimganj sub-division of the Sylhet District	1
Dhubri	Ditto	The Dhubri sub-division of the Goalpara District	1
Goalpara	Ditto	The Goalpara sub-division of the Goalpara District	1
Gauhati	Ditto	The Gauhati sub-division of the Kamrup District	1
Barpeta	Ditto	The Barpeta sub-division of the Kamrup District	1
Tezpur	Ditto	The Tezpur sub-division of the Darrang District	1
Mangaldai	Ditto	The Mangaldai sub-division of the Darrang District	1
Nowgong	Ditto	The Nowgong District	1
Sibsagar	Ditto	The Sibsagar sub-division of the Sibsagar District	1
Jorhat	Ditto	The Jorhat sub-division of the Sibsagar District	1
Goalghat	Ditto	The Golaghat sub-division of the Sibsagar District	1
Dibrugarh	Ditto	The Dibrugarh sub-division of the Lakhimpur District	1
North Lakhimpur	Ditto	The North Lakhimpur sub-division of the Lakhimpur district	1

contd.

Cachar	Muhammadan Rural	The Cachar District	1
Sylhet Sadr (North) (Muhammadan)	Ditto	The Sadr (North) sub-division of the Sylhet District	1
Sylhet Sadr (South) (Muhammadan)	Ditto	The Sadr (South) sub-division of the Sylhet District	1
Sunamganj (Muhammadan)	Ditto	The Sunamganj sub-division of the Sylhet District	1
Habiganj(North) (Muhammadan)	Ditto	The Habiganj (North) sub-division of the Sylhet District	1
Habiganj (South) (Muhammdan)	Ditto	The Habiganj (South) sub-division of the Sylhet District	1
South Sylhet (Muhammadan)	Ditto	The South Sylhet sub-division the Sylhet District	1
Karimganj (Muhammadan)	Ditto	The Karimganj sub-division of the Sylhet District	1
Dhubri (Muhammadan)	Ditto	The Dhubri sub-division of the Goalpara District, excluding South Salmara Thana	1
Goalpara and South Salmara	Ditto	The Goalpara sub-division of the Goalpara District with the South Salmara thana	1
Kamrup and Darrang cum Nowgong	Muhammadan Rural	The Districts of Kamrup, Darrang and Nowgong	1
Sibsagar cum Lakhimpur	Ditto	The Districts of Sibsagar and Lakhimpur	1
Assam Valley Planting	Planting	Assam Valley	3
Surma Valley Planting	Ditto	Surma Valley	2
Commerce and Industry	Commerce and Industry	(Non-territorial)	1

SCHEDULE II (See rule 8)
QUALIFICATIONS OF ELECTORS

1. For the purposes of this Schedule –
   (a) "company" means a company incorporated in accordance with law in any part of His Majesty's dominions;
   (b) "estate" means an estate as defined in section 2 of the Assam Labour and Emigration Act, 1901;

(c) "manager" in relation to a tea estate includes an assistant manager in separate charge thereof;

(d) "previous year" means the financial year preceding that in which the electoral roll or the list of amendments thereto, as the case may be, for the time being under preparation is first published under these rules.

General Constituencies

2. A person shall be qualified as an elector for the Shillong constituency who has during the previous year resided within the constituency and who–

(a) was in the previous year assessed in respect of municipal or cantonment rates or taxes to an aggregate amount of not less than Rs.3; or

(b) was in the previous year assessed to income-tax; or

(c) is a retired, pensioned or discharged officer, non-commissioned officer or soldier of His Majesty's regular forces or of the Assam Rifles.

3. A person shall be qualified as an elector for a rural constituency who has during the previous year resided within the constituency and who-

(a) was in the previous year assessed in respect of municipal or cantonment rates or taxes to an aggregate amount of not less than Rs. 3 or, in the case of an assessment in the Nowgong Municipality, of not less than Rs.2, or, in the case of an assessment in the Sylhet Municipality, of not less than Rs. 1-8-0; or

(b) was in the previous year assessed to a tax of not less than Re.1 in a union under Chapter III of the Bengal Municipal Act, 1876; or

(c) in the case of constituencies in the Sylhet, Cachar and Goalpara Districts, was in the previous year assessed to a Choukidari Tax of not less than Re.1 under the Village-Choukidari Act, 1873; or

(d) in the case of any constituency other than those referred to in clause (c):

(i) owned land the land revenue upon which has been assessed or is assessable at not less than Rs.15 per annum, or

(ii) is liable to pay a local rate of not less than Re. 1 per annum, or

(e) was in the previous year assessed to income-tax; or

(f) is a retired, pensioned or discharged officer, non-commissioned officer or soldier of His Majesty's regular forces or of the Assam Rifles :

Provided that–

(i) no person other than a Muhammadan shall be qualified as an elector for a Muhammadan constituency, and

(ii) no Muhammadan shall be qualified as an elector for a non- Muhammadan constituency.

4. Where property is held or payments are made jointly by the members of a joint family, the family shall be adopted as the unit for deciding whether under this Schedule the requisite qualification exists; and, if it does exist, the person qualified shall be, in the case of a Hindu joint family, the manager thereof and in other cases the member authorized in that behalf by the family concerned :

Provided that any other member of such family shall also be qualified if the proportion of the joint property which corresponds with his share therein would be sufficient so to qualify him if held separately.

Special Constituencies

5. A person shall be qualified as an elector for the Assam Valley Planting constituency who is the superintendent or manager of, or an engineer or medical officer employed on, a tea estate in the Assam Valley, and a person shall be qualified as an elector in the Surma Valley Planting constituency who is the superintendent or manager of, or an engineer or medical officer employed on a tea estate in the Surma Valley.
6. A person shall be qualified as an elector for the Commerce and Industry constituency who –
   (a) is the owner of a factory, other than a tea factory, situated in Assam and which is subject to the provisions of the Indian Factories Act, 1911, or is a person appointed by the owner of such a factory for the purpose or voting on his behalf; or
   (b) has been appointed for the purpose of voting by any company, other than a company principally engaged in the tea industry, having a place of business in Assam and having a paid-up capital of not less than Rs. 25,000.

SCHEDULE III (See rule 11)
Form of Nomination Paper
NOMINATION PAPER

Name of the Constituency for which the candidate is nominated ... ...
Name of candidate ... ...
Father's name ... ...
Age ... ...
Address ... ...
Denomination (state whether non-Muhammadan or Muhammadan) ....
Constituency on the electoral roll of which the Candidate is registered as an elector ... ...
*No. of the candidate in the electoral roll of the constituency in which he is registered as an elector ... ...
Name of proposer ... ...
*No. of the proposer in the electoral roll of the Constituency ... ...
Signature of the proposer ... ...
Name of the seconder ... ...
*No. of the seconder in the electoral roll of the ... .
constituency ... ...
Signature of the seconder ....

Declaration by Candidate

I hereby declare that I agree to this nomination.

Date...................... Signature of Candidate..

* Where the electoral roll is sub-divided and separate serial numbers are assigned to the electors entered in each sub-division, a description of the sub-division in which the name of the person concerned is entered must also be given here.

\+ Not to be entered in case of special constituency.

(To be filled in by the Returning Officer or other authorized person)

Certificate of Delivery

This nomination paper was delivered to me at my office at (date and hour..............)

....

Returning Officer or other
authorized person.

Certificate of Scrutiny

I have scrutinized the eligibility of the candidate, the proposer and seconder, and find that they are respectively qualified to stand for election, to propose and to second the nomination.

....

Returning Officer or other
authorized person

(N.B. – This nomination paper will not be valid unless it is delivered to the Returning Officer, or other person authorized to receive it, at his office before 3-0 P.M. on ....192)

SCHEDULE IV (See rule 19)
RETURN OF ELECTION EXPENSES

1. Under the head of receipts there shall be shown the name and description of every person (including the candidate), club, society or association from whom any money, security or equivalent of money was received in respect of expenses incurred on account of, or in connection with, or incidental to, the election, and the amount received from each person, club, society or association separately.
2. Under the head of expenditure there shall be shown–
   (a) the personal expenditure of the candidate incurred or paid by him or his election agent, including travelling and all other personal expenses incurred in connection with his candidature;
   (b) the name, and the rate and total amount of the pay, of each person employed as an agent (including the election agent), clerk or messenger;
   (c) the travelling expenses and any other expenses incurred by the candidate or his election agent on account of agents (including the election agent), clerks or messengers;
   (d) the travelling expenses of persons, whether in receipt of salary or not, incurred in connection with the candidature, and whether paid or incurred by the candidate, his election agent or the person so travelling;
   (e) the cost whether paid or incurred of–

(i) printing.
(ii)advertising
(iii)stationery
(iv)postage
(v) telegrams and
(vi)rooms hired either for public meetings or as committee rooms;
(vii) any other miscellaneous expenses whether paid or incurred.

NOTE –(1)All expenses incurred in connection with the candidature whether paid by the candidate, his election agent, or any other person, or remaining unpaid on the date of the return are to be set out.

(2)For all items of Rs. 5 and over, unless from the nature of the case (e.g., travel by rail or postage) a receipt is not obtainable, vouchers are to be attached.

(3)All sums paid but for which no receipt is attached are to be set out in detail with dates of payment.

(4)All sums unpaid are to be set out in a separate list

3. The form of the declarations referred to in rule 19 shall be as follows :-

Form of Declaration by Election Agent

I,........................., being the appointed election agent for a candidate for election in the .... constituency do hereby solemnly affirm that the above return of election expenses is true to the best of my knowledge and belief and that, except the expenses herein set forth, no expenses of any nature whatsoever have to my knowledge or belief been incurred in, or for the purposes of..................'s candidature

Election Agent

Solemnly affirmed before me

(Magistrate)

Form of Declaration by Candidate

I, , being a candidate for election in the constituency do hereby solemnly affirm that the above return of election expenses is true to the best of my knowledge and belief, and that, except the expenses herein set forth, no expenses of any nature whatsoever have to my knowledge or belief been incurred in, or for the purposes of, my candidature.

(Candidate)

Solemnly affirmed before me

(Magistrate)

Special Form of Declaration by a Candidate under rule 19, sub-rule (4)

I, , being a candidate for election in the constituency do hereby solemnly affirm that the return of election expenses signed by my election agent is (with the exceptions noted below) true to the best of my knowledge and belief, and that (with the exceptions noted below) no expenses of any nature whatsoever other than the expenses therein set forth have to my knowledge or belief been incurred in or for the purposes of my candidate.

Particulars of Exceptions..

(Sd.)

(Candidate)

Solemnly affirmed before me

(Sd.)

(Magistrate)

SCHEDULE V (See rules 5, 7, 22, 33, 44 and 47)

The following shall be deemed to be corrupt practices for the purposes of these rules :-

PART I

1. A gift, offer or promise by a candidate or his agent, or by any other person with the connivance of a candidate or his agent, of any gratifications to any person whomsoever, with the object, directly or indirectly, of inducing–
   (a) a person to stand or not to stand as, or to withdraw from being, a candidate, or
   (b) an elector to vote or refrain from voting at an election, or as a reward to-
   (a) a person for having so stood or not stood or for having withdrawn his candidature, or
   (b) an elector for having voted or refrained from voting.

   Explanation – For the purpose of this clause the term "gratification" is not restricted to pecuniary gratifications or gratifications estimable in money, and includes all forms of entertainment and all forms of employment for reward; but it does not include the payment of any expenses bona fide incurred at or for the purposes of any election and duly entered in the return of election expenses prescribed by these rules.

2. Any direct or indirect interference or attempt to interfere on the part of a candidate or his agent or of any other person with the connivance of the candidate or his agent with the free exercise of any electoral right.

   Explanation – (1) Without prejudice to the generality of the provisions of this clause, any such person as is referred to herein who-
   (a) threatens any candidate or voter or any person in whom a candidate or voter is interested, with injury of any kind ; or
   (b) induces or attempts to induce a candidate or voter to believe that he or any person in whom he is interested will become or will be rendered an object of divine displeasure or spiritual censure,

   shall be deemed to interfere with the free exercise of the electoral right of such candidate or voter within the meaning of this clause.

   (2) A declaration of public policy or a promise of public action or the mere exercise of a legal right without intent to interfere with an electoral right shall not be deemed to be interference within the meaning of this clause.

   (3) The procuring or abetting or attempting to procure by a candidate or his agent, or by any other person with the connivance of a candidate or his agent, the application by a person for a voting paper in the name of any other person, whether living or dead or in a fictitious name, or by a person who has voted once at an election for a voting

paper in his own name at the same election.

(4) The publication by a candidate or his agent, or by any other person with the connivance of the candidate or his agent, of any statement of fact which is false and which he either believes to be false or does not believe to be true in relation to the personal character or conduct of any candidate or in relation to the candidature or withdrawal of any candidate, which statement is reasonably calculated to prejudice the prospects of such candidate's election.

(5) The incurring or authorizing by a candidate or his agent of expenditure or the employment of any person by a candidate or his agent in contravention of the provisions of any notification of the Governor General in Council issued under rule 20 of these rules.

PART II

1. Any act specified in Part I. when done by a person who is not a candidate or his agent or a person acting with the connivance of a candidate or his agent.
2. The application by a person at an election for a voting paper in the name of any other person, whether living or dead, or in a fictitious name, or for a voting paper in his own name after he has already voted at such election.
3. The receipt of, or agreement to receive, any gratification, whether as a motive or a reward, –
   (a) by a person to stand or not to stand as, or to withdraw from being, a candidate, or
   (b) by any person whomsoever for himself or any other person for voting or refraining from voting, or for inducing or attempting to induce any elector to vote or refrain from voting or any candidate to withdraw his candidature.
4. Any payment or promise of payment to any person whomsoever on account of the conveyance of any elector to or from any place for the purpose of recording his vote.
5. The hiring, employment, borrowing or using for the purposes of the election of any boat, vehicle or animal usually kept for letting on hire or for the conveyance of passengers by hire.
   Provided that any elector may hire any boat, vehicle or animal, or use any boat, vehicle or animal which is his own property, to convey himself to or from the place where the vote is recorded.
6. The incurring or authorization of expenses by any person other than a candidate or his election agent on account of holding any public meeting or upon any advertisement, circular or publication or in any other way whatsoever for the purpose of promoting or procuring the election of such candidate, unless he is authorized in writing so to do by the candidate.
7. The hiring, using or letting, as a committee-room or for the purposes of any meeting to which electors are admitted, of any building, room or other place where intoxicating liquor is sold to the public.
8. The issuing of any circular, placard or poster having reference to the election which does not bear on its face the name and address of the printer and publisher thereof.

C.W. GWYNNE,

Joint Secretary to the Government of India

APPENDIX 5

LIST OF BILLS ENACTED BY THE ASSAM LEGISLATIVE COUNCIL 1921-1936 (ACTS)

1921

1. Salary for Deputy President of Legislative Council

1922

1. Court Fees
2. Indian Stamp (Amendment)
3. General Clauses (Amendment)
4. Court Fees (Amendment)

1923

1. Municipal
2. Students and Juvenile

1924

1. Deputy President's Salary (Amendment)
2. President's Salary

1925

1. Court Fee (Amendment)
2. Municipal (Amendment)
3. Stamp (Amendment)

1926

1. Increase in President's Salary
2. Municipal
3. Eradication of Water Hyacinth
4. Local Rates and Local Self Government (Amendment)
5. Primary Education
6. Temperance

1927

1. Local-Self Government (Amendment)
2. Introduction and Development of Rural Self-Government
3. Excise (Amendment)

4. Opium Smoking

1928
1. Local Self-Government (Amendment)
2. Highways

1929
1. Goalpara Tenancy

1930
1. Goalpara Tenancy (Amendment)
2. Better Provision for Audit and Safeguarding of Local Funds

1931
1. Forest Regulation (Amendment)
2. Regulation of Succession in the Bijni Raj

1932
1. Municipal (Amendment)
2. Forest Regulation
3. Indian Tolls
4. Indian Tolls
5. Court Fees
6. Prevention of Adulteration of Food in Assam
7. Local Rates Regulation (Amendment)
8. Opium Smoking (Amendment)
9. Municipal (Amendment)
10. Standing Orders of Assam Legislative Council

1933
1. Opium (Amendment)
2. Bengal and Assam Excise (Amendment)
3. Land and Revenue (Amendment)

1934
1. Criminal Law (Amendment)
2. Opium Smoking
3. More effective Control of Money Lending
4. Assam Rifles
5. Rural Self-Government (Amendment)

1935
Eight Amending Acts relating to Municipalities, Criminal Laws and Landlord–Tenant Relation in Temporary Districts etc.

1936
1. Voluntary Registration of Muslim Marriages

2. Criminal Law (Amendment)
3. Cattle Trespassers (Amendment)
4. Land and Revenue
5. Disorderly Houses
6. Local Boards (Emergency Provisions)
7. Stamp (Amendment)
8. Births and deaths Registration
9. Land Revenue and Reassessment
10. Goalpara Tenancy

Total 65 Acts.

APPENDIX 6

SWARAJYA PARTY MEMBERS ELECTED TO THE ASSAM LEGISLATIVE COUNCIL UNDER THE MONTAGU-CHELMS-FORD REFORMS

1923

1.	Basanta Kumar Das	North Sylhet
2.	Faiznur Ali	Dibrugarh
3.	Jegesh Chandra Gohain	Dibrugarh
4.	Jonaram Borah	Nowgong
5.	Kamala Kanta Das	Barpeta
6.	Kamakhyaram Baruah	Gauhati
7.	Rohini Kanta Hatibaruah	Jorhat
8.	Sarveswar Baruah	North Lakhimpur

1926

1.	Basanta Kumar Das	Sylhet Sadar
2.	Brajendranarayan Choudhury	Sunamganj
3.	Gopendra Lal Das Choudhury	South Habiganj
4.	Jatindranarayan Deblaskar	Silchar
5.	Kameswar Das	Barpeta
6.	Kuladhar Chaliha	Golaghat
7.	Laksheswar Baruah	Dibrugarh
8.	Mahadev Sarma	Tezpur
9.	Nabin Chandra Bardalai	Mangaldai
10.	Rashiklal Nandi Majumdar	North Habiganj
11.	Rohini Kanta Hati Baruah	Jorhat
12.	Rohini Kumar Choudhury	Gauhati
13.	Sarveswar Baruah	North Lakhimpur
14.	Pareshlal Shom	South Sylhet
15.	Taraprasad Chaliha	Sibsagar

1929

1. Basanta Kumar Das
2. Brajendra Narayan Choudhury
3. Faiznur Ali – Sibsagar, Lakhimpur

4. Gopendra Lal Das Choudhury – North Habiganj
5. Jogendra Kishore Chakravarty – South Habiganj
6. Kameshwar Das
7. Kamini Kumar Sen – Karimganj
8. Kuladhar Chaliha
9. Lakheswar Borua
10. Lakshmi Kanta Barua
11. Mahadev Sarma
12. Nabin Chandra Bardaloi
13. Praneshlal Shom Choudhury
14. Rohini Kumar Choudhury
15. Sarat Kumar Das
16. Sarveswar Baruah

Source :

1. Proceedings of the Assam Legislative Councils of the relevant years.
2. East India Constitutional Reforms, p.5, and 'Assamiya', 18 November 1923, cited in Bhuyan and Sibopada De, Volume two, 1920-1939, p.98 and p.116.
3. 'Bangabani, Calcutta, 19 and 23 May 1929 and 'Assamiya' 7 and 17 May 1929 cited in Bhuyan and Sibopada De, p.127.

APPENDIX 7

LIST OF MEMORANDUM SUBMITTED TO THE INDIAN STATUTORY COMMISSION BY ASSAM ORGANISATIONS

1. Assam and Surma Valley Branches, Indian Tea Association
2. Assam Provincial Committee, European Association
3. Assam Civil Service Association
4. Assam Junior Civil Service Association
5. Assam Provincial Muslim League
6. Goalpara Zamindars' Association
7. Surma Valley Yogi Sammilani
8. Bodo Community of Goalpara District
9. Assam Kachari Yubok Sammilani
10. Anjuman-I-Islamia, Jaintia Parganas
11. Mahishya Samiti, Sunamganj, Sylhet
12. Pragjyotishpur Brahman Samaj
13. Assam Subodinate Educational Services Union
14. Non-Muhammadan Voters of Nowgong District
15. Bodos and Rabhas of Goalpara District
16. Nagas of Mokakchung Sub-Division
17. Naga Club of Kohima
18. Non-Assamese Indian Domiciled Settlers, Assam Valley Districts
19. Non-Assamese Indian Settlers
20. Pro-Assam League, Sylhet
21. Bengal and Assam Fishermen's Association
22. Goalpara District Association
23. Sanatan Dharma Sabha, Gauhati
24. Goalpara Prantik Kshatriya Samiti
25. Khasi National Darbar
26. Depressed People of Assam Valley
27. Representatives of Khasi and Jaintia Hills

Source : The Statesman, 5,6 and 8 January 1929.

APPENDIX - 8

GOVERNMENT NOTIFICATIONS 1936

The 7th December 1936.

NO 2564- EL.- In pursuance of the second provision to sub-rule (2) of rule 4 of Part IX of the Assam Legislative Assembly Electoral (Governor's) Rules, the Governor in Council is pleased to call upon the constituencies of the Assam Legislative Assembly specified in the appended schedule to elect members in accordance with the said rules on or before the 18 th February, 1937.

SCHEDULE
LIST OF CONSTITUENCIES
I. GENERAL CONSTITUENCIES

Name of Constituency	Extent of Constituency	Number of members
Dhubri (Central)	Bilasipara and Gossaingaon thanas	1
Dhubri (South)	Dhubri, Golakganj, South Salmara and Mankachar thanas plus the following three plains mauzas in the Garo Hills districts, viz., Mahendraganj, Rangapani and Fulbari	1
Dhubri (North)	Bijni and Kokrajhar thanas	1
Goalpara (North-West)	Lakhipur and North Salmara thanas	1
Goalpara (South-East)	Goalpara and Dudnai thanas	1
Barpeta (South)	Barpeta and Tarabari thanas	1
Barpeta (North)	Sorbhog and Patacharkuchi thanas	1
Nalbari	Nalbari thana	1
Kamrup Sadr (North)	Rangia and Barama thanas	1
Kamrup Sadr (Central)	Kamalpur and Hajo thanas	1
Kamrup Sadr (South)	Gauhati, Palasbari, Chhaygaon and Boko thanas	1 3

		of whom one is reserved for the members of the Scheduled Castes
Mangaldai (South)	Mangaldai and Dalgaon thanas	1
Mangaldoi (North)	Kalaigaon, Paneri, Udalguri and Majbat thanas	1
Tezpur (West)	Tezpur and Dhekiaijuli thanas	1
Tezpur (East)	Sootea, Behali and Gohpur thanas	1
Nowgong (West)	Lohorighat, Dhing and Marigaon thanas (excluding all areas in the Mikir Hills) plus Juria mauza from Rupahi Hat thana	1
Nowgong (South-East)	Raha and Jamunamukh thanas (excluding all areas in the Mikir Hills) plus the Lumding Kheraj Block	1
Nowgong (North-East)	Nowgong, Kaliabor and Samaguri thanas (excluding all areas in the Mikir Hills) plus Rupahi Hat thana less Juria mauza	2 of whom one is reserved for the members of the Scheduled Castes.
Golaghat (North)	Dergaon and Bokakhat thanas (excludIng all areas in the Mikir Hills) plus Mahura and Khumtai mauzas from Golaghat thana	1
Golaghat (South)	Golaghat thana (excluding all areas in the Mikir Hills except Barpathar and Sarupathar mauzas) less Mahura and Khumtai mauzas	1
Jorhat (South)	Titabar and Teok thanas	1
Jorhat (North)	Jorhat and Majuli thanas	2 of whom one is reserved for the members of the Scheduled Castes.
Sibsagar (West)	Sibsagar and Amguri thanas excluding the portion of Dopdar Mauza in Amguri thana	1
Sibsagar (East)	Nazira and Sonari thanas plus the portion Of Dopdar Mauza in Amguri thana	1
Dibrugarh (Central)	Tinsukia, Bardubi and Jaipur thanas	1
Dibrugarh (West)	Dibrugarh, Moran and Dhemaji thanas	1
Dibrugarh (East)	Doom Dooma, Digboi and Marghertita thanas (excluding the Lakhimpur Frontier Tract)	1

North Lakhimpur	The whole of north Lakhimpur sub-division	1
Sunamganj	The whole of Sunamganj sub-division	1
Habiganj (North)	Lakhai, Nabiganj, Baniyachung and Ajmiriganj thanas	2 of whom one is reserved for the members of the Scheduled Castes
Habiganj (South)	Habiganj, Madhupur, Chunarighat and Bahubal Thana	1
South Sylhet (west)	Maulvi Bazar, Srimangal and Kamalganj thanas	1
South Sylhet(East)	Kulaura and Rajnagar thanas	1
Sylhet Sadr (South)	Fenchuganj, Golabganj, Balaganj, and Biswanath thanas	1
Sylhet Sadr (North)	Sylhet, Gowainghat, Kanarighat and Jaintiapur thanas	1
Karimganj (West)	Jaldhup and Patharkandi thanas	1
Karimganj (East)	Karimganj, Badarpur and Ratabari thanas	2 of whom one is reserved for the Members of the Scheduled Castes.
Hailankandi	The whole of Hailakandi sub-division.	1
Silchar	The whole of Silchar sub-division.	2 of whom one is reserved for the members of the Scheduled Castes.

II. MUHAMMANDAN CONSTITUENCIES

Dhubri (West)	Dhubri and Golakganj thanas	1
Dhubri (South)	South Salmara and Mankachar thanas Plus the following three plains mauzas of the Garo Hills district, viz., Mahendraganj, Rangapani and Fulbari	1
Dhubri (North)	Bilasipara, Kokrajhar, Gossaingaon and Bijni Thanas	1
Goalpara (West)	Lakhipur thana	1
Goalpara (East)	Goalpara, Dudnai and North Salamara thanas	1

Barpeta	Barpeta and Tarabari thanas	1
Kamrup (South)	Gauhati,Palasbari, Chhayagaon, Boko, Kamlapur and Hajo thanas	1
Kamrup (North)	Nalbari, Rangia and Barama thanas of the Kamrup Sadr sub-division and Sorbhog and Patacharkuchi thanas of the Barpeta sub-division	1
Nowgong (West)	Dhing, Lahorighat, Raha, Marigaon and Jamunamukh thanas (excluiding all areas in the Mikir Hills) plus the Lumding Kheraj Block	1
Nowgong (East)	Nowgong, Samaguri, Rupahi Hat and Kaliabor Thanas (excluding all areas within the Mikir Hills)	1
Darrang	The whole of Darrang district	1
Sibsagar	The whole of Sibsagar district (excluding all areas in the Mikir Hills except Barpathar and Sarupathar mauzas)	1
Lakhimpur	The whole of Darrang district	1
Sunamganj (West)	Tahirpur, Dharampasha and Sulla thanas	1
Sunamganj (Central)	Sunamganj thana	1
Sunamganj (East)	Chhatak thana	1
Sunamganj (South)	Derai and Jagannathpur thanas	1
Habiganj (North-West)	Baniyachung and Amiriganj thanas	1
Habiganj (North-East)	Habiganj and Nabiganj thanas	1
Habiganj (South-West)	Lakhai and Madhabpur thanas	1
Habiganj (South- East)	Chunarighat and Bahubal thanas	1
South Sylhet (West)	Maulvi Bazar and Srimangal thanas	1
South Sythet (Central)	Rajnagar and Karimganj thanas	1
South Sythet (East)	Kulaura thana	1
Sylhel Sadr (Central)	Part of Sylhet Sadr thana containing Chaukidari Circles Nos. 1– 41 and 51 – 55 (inclusive) including the Municipal area.	1
Sylhet Sadr (North)	Gowainghat and Jaintiapur thanas plus the North Eastern half of Kanairghat	1

	thana containing Chaukidari Circles Nos. 1 – 12, 15 – 20 and 32 – 34 (inclusive)	
Sylhet Sadr (West)	Part of Sylhet Sadr thana containing Chaukidari Circles Nos. 42 – 50 and 56 – 67 (inclusive) and Biswanath thana	1
Sylhet Sadr (East)	Golabganj thana plus the South Western half of Kanairghat thana containing Chaukidari Circles Nos. 13, 14 and 21 – 31 (inclusive).	1
Sylhet Sadr (South)	Balaganj and Fenchuganj thanas	1
Karimganj (West)	Jaldhup thana	1
Karimganj (Central)	Karimganj thana less Chaukidari Circles Nos. 22 – 28 (inclusive), 61, 62 and 64 – 68 (inclusive)	1
Karimganj (South)	Badarpur, Ratabari and Pathakandi thanas plus the following Chaukidari Circles of Karimganj thana :- Nos. 22 – 28 (inclusive), 61, 62 and 64 – 68 (inclusive)	1
Hailakandi	The whole of Hailakandi sub-division	1
Silchar	The whole of Silchar sub-division	1

III. WOMEN'S CONTITUENCY

Name of Constituency	Extent of Constituency	Number of members
Women's (Shiliong)	Shillong Municipality and Cantonment	1

IV. EUROPEAN CONSTITUENCY

Name of Constituency	Extent of Constituency	Number of members
European	The districts of Goalpara, Kamrup, Nowgong, Darrang, Sibsagar, Lakhimpur (excluding the Lakhimpur Frontier Tract), Sylhet, Cachar (excluding the North Cachar Hills), the Garo Hills and the British Territory of the Khasi and Jaintia Hills.	1

V. INDIAN CHRISTIAN CONSTITUENCY

Name of Constituency	Extent of Constituency	Number of members
Indian Christian	The districts of Goalpara, Kamrup, Nowgong (excluding all areas in the Mikir Hills except the Lumding Kheraj Block), Darrang,	1

Sibsagar, (excluding) all areas in the Mikir Hills except Barpathar and Saruparthar mauzas), Lakhimpur (excluding the Lakhimpur Frontier Tract), Sylhet and Cachar (excluding the North Cachar Hills).

VI. BACKWARD TRIBAL (PLAINS) CONSTITUENCIES

Name of Constituency	Extent of Constituency	Number of members
Goalpara (Tribal)	Kokrajhar and Bijni thanas of Goalpara district	1
Kamrup (Tribal)	Nalbari, Barama, Rangia, Patacharkuchi and Sorbhog thanas of Kamrup district.	1
Lakhimpur and Majuli (tribal)	North Lakhimpur sub-division of the Lakhimpur district Plus the Majuli thana of the Jorhat sub-division of the Sibsagar district plus the Dhemaji thana of the Dibrugarh Sub-division of the Lakhimpur district.	1
Nowgong (Tribal)	Raha, Marigaon and Jamunamukh thanas excluding all areas in the Mikir Hills	1

VII. BACKWARD AREAS (HILLS) CONSTITUENCIES

Name of Constituency	Extent of Constituency	Number of members
Garo Hills (North)	Mauzas III, IV and V	1
Garo Hills (South)	Mauzas I, II, IX and X (Tura Town)	1
Shillong	The British territory of the Shilllong sub-division plus the non–British areas in which the Municipality and Cantonment exercise jurisdiction	1
Jowai	The whole of Jowai sub-division	1
Mikir Hills	The Mikir Hills (in Nowgong and Sibsagar districts) less Barpathar and Sarupathar mauzas in Golaghat sub-division and less the Lumding Kheraj Block in Nowgong district.	1

VIII. PLANTING CONSTITUENCIES

Name of Constituency	Extent of Constituency	Number of members
European Planting	The districts of Goalpara, Kamrup, Darrang, Nowgong, Sibsagar, Lakhimpur (excluding the Lakhimpur Frontier Tract), Sylhet and Cachar (excluding the North Cachar Hills).	1
Indian Planting	The districts of Goalpara, Kamrup,	1

(Assam Valley)	Darrang, Nowgong Sibsagar and Lakhimpur (excluding the Lakhimpur Frontier Tract)	
Indian Planting (Surma Valley)	The districts of Sylhet and Cachar (excluding the North Cachar Hills)	1

IX. COMMERRCE AND INDUSTRY CONSTITUENCIES

Name of Constituency	Extent of Constituency	Number of members
European Commerce and Industry	The Province	1
Indian Commerce and Industry	Ditto	1

X. LABOUR CONSTITUENCIES (TEA GARDENS)

Name of Constituency	Extent of Constituency	Number of members
	I. – IN LAKHIMPUR DISTRICT	
Doom Dooma (District Lakhumpur)	All gardens within a radius of three and a half miles from Doom Dooma police station	1
	II. – IN SIBSAGAR DISTRICT	
Jorhat (Sibsagar District)	All gardens in Jorhat thana within the area included in the following boundaries :– North – Assam Trunk Road West – Jorhat Provincial Railway Titabor Branch East – Thana boundary South – Thana boundary	1
	III. –IN DARRANG DISTRICT	
Thakurbari (Darrang District)	All gardens within a radius of three and half miles from Thakurbari railaway station	1
	IV. – IN SURMA VALLEY	
Silchar (District Cachar)	All gardens in the Silchar thana which lie south of the Barak river	

J.A. DAWSON
Chief Secretary to the Government of Assam

The 7th December 1936

No. 2565-El. – Whereas by Notification No. 2564-El., dated the 7th December, 1936, the Governor in Council has called upon the constituencies of the Assam Legislative Assembly to elect members in accordance with the Assam Legislative Assembly Electoral (Governor's) rules, 1936, the Governor in Council is pleased, under the provisions of clause (a) of sub-rule 2 part IV of the said Assam Legislative Assembly Electoral (Governor's) Rules, 1936, to appoint Monday, the 21st December, 1936, as the date for the nomination of candidates and for the scrutiny of nominations.

J. A. DAWSON,
Chief Secretary to the Government of Assam

THE GOVERNMENT OF INDIA (PROVINCIAL ELECTIONS) (CORRUPT PRACTICES AND ELECTION PETITIONS) ORDER, 1936.
AT THE COURT AT BUCKINGHAM PALACE,
The 3rd Day of July 1936.
Present,
THE KING'S MOST EXCELLENT MAJESTY IN COUNCIL

WHEREAS by section two hundred and ninety one of the Government of India Act, 1935 (hereafter in this order referred to as 'the Act") His Majesty in Council is empowered to make provision with respect to certain matters connected with elections under the Act:

AND WHEREAS by subsection (1) of section sixty-nine of the Act His Majesty in Council is empowered to declare certain offences and practices to be offences and practices involving disqualification for membership of Provincial Legislatures and to fix the periods for which the disqualifications are to operate:

AND WHEREASa draft of this Order has been before Parliament in accordance with the provisions of subsection (1) of section three hundred and nine of the Act and an Address has been presented to his Majesty by both Houses of Parliament praying that an order may be made in terms of this Order:

NOW, THEREFORE, His Majesty, in the exercise of the powers conferred on him as aforesaid and of all other powers enabling him in that behalf, is pleased by and with the advice of his Privy Council to order, and it is hereby ordered, as follows:–

PART I
INTRODUCTORY

1. THIS order may be cited as "The Government of India (Provincial Elections) (Corrupt practices and Election petitions) Order, 1936."
2. The Interpretation Act, 1889, applies for the interpretation of this Order as it applies for the interpretation of an Act of Parliament.
3. (1) In this Order, except where it is otherwise expressly provided or the context otherwise requires—
"election" means an election to fill a seat or seats in either Chamber of a Provincial Legislature;

"prescribed" means prescribed by Act of the Provincial Legislature or by Rules;
"Rules" means rules made under paragraph twenty of the Fifth Schedule to the Act;
"sign" in relation to a person who is unable to write his name means authenticate in such manner as may be prescribed;
"oath" includes affirmation.

(2) The provisions of parts II and III of this Order shall, in relation to constituencies in which seats are reserved for candidates of any particular class, or in which the final voting is by members of an electoral college previously constituted for that purpose, have effect with such exceptions and subject to such adaptations and modifications as may be prescribed , but subject as aforesaid, any primary election for the purpose of electing candidates for reserved seats, or of constituting any such electoral college, shall be deemed to be part of the election of persons to fill the seats to be filled in the constituency.

(3) Where under any of the provisions of this order anything is to be prescribed, different provision may be made for different cases or classes of cases.

(4) Any reference in this Order to any of the provisions of any Indian Act shall be construed as a reference to those provisions as amended by or under any other Act or, if those provisions are repealed and re-enacted with or without modification, to the provisions so re-enacted.

(5) Anything which under the provisions of the Act or of this Order is required or authorized to be done by, to or before the Governor of a Province in connection with any matters to which this Order relates (whether or not the Governor is to act in his discretion or to exercise his individual judgement) shall before the commencement of part III of the Act be done by, to or before the Governnor in Council, or in the case of Sind or Orissa, the Governor.

PART II
ELECTION AGENTS AND EXPENSES

1. Every person nominated as a candidate at an election shall at the prescribed time and in the prescribed manner appoint either himself or some one other person to be his election agent.
2. No person shall be appointed an election agent who is disqualified from being an election agent under the subsequent provisions of this Order.
3. (1) Any revocation of the appointment of an election agent who is disqualified from being an election agent, whether he be the candidate himself or not, shall be signed by the candidate, and shall operate from the date on which it is lodged with the returning officer.

   (2) In the event of such a revocation or of the death of an election agent, whether that event occurs before or during the election, or after the election but before a return of the candidate's election expenses has been lodged in accordance with the provisions of the next but one succeeding paragraph, the candidate shall appoint forthwith either himself or some other person to be his election agent, and shall give notice in writing of the appointment to the returning officer.

4. Every election agent shall, for each election for which he is appointed election agent, keep separate and regular books of account, and shall enter therein such particulars of expenditure in connection with the election as may be prescribed.
5. (1) Within the prescribed time after every election there shall be lodged with the returning officer in respect of each person who has been nominated as a candidate a return of the election expenses of that person signed both by him and his election agent.
   (2) Every such return shall be in such from and shall contain such particulars as may be prescribed, and shall be accompanied by declarations in the prescribed from by the candidate and his election agent on oath before a magistrate.
   (3) Notwithstanding anything in this paragraph, where a candidate is owing to absence from India unable to sign the return of election expenses and to make the required declaration, the return shall be signed and lodged by the election agent only and shall be accompanied by a declaration by the election agent only, and the candidate shall within fourteen days after his return to India cause to be lodged with the returning officer a declaration made on oath before a magistrate in such form as may be prescribed.
6. In each Province provision shall be made, by an Act of the Provincial Legislature or by Rules, fixing the maximum scales of election expenses at elections and the numbers and descriptions of persons who may be employed for payment in connection with elections:

   Provided that no provision need be so made in any province with respect to any election held before the expiration of two years from the commencement of Part III of the Act.
7. Except so far as may be prescribed this Part of this Order does not apply to an election by the members of a Provincial Legislative Assembly to fill seats in the Provincial Legislative Council.

PART III

DECISION OF DOUBTS AND DISPUTES AS TO THE VALIDITY OF AN ELECTION AND DISQUALIFICATIONS FOR CORRUPT PRACTICES.

1. In this part of this Order and in the First Schedule to this Order, except where it is otherwise expressly provided or the context otherwise requires–

   "agent" includes an election agent and any person who, on the trial of an election petition, is held by the Commissioners to have acted as an agent in connection with the election with the knowledge or consent of the candidate;

   "Candidate" means a person who has been or claims to have been duly nominated as a candidate at any election, and a candidate who, with the election in prospect, has held himself out as a prospective candidate, shall be deemed to have been a candidate as from the time when he began so to hold himself out;

   "electoral right" means the right of a person to stand as, or to withdraw from being, a candidate, or to vote or refrain from voting at an election;

"returned candidate" means a candidate whose name has been published in the prescribed manner as duly elected;

"Corrupt practice", in relation to an election by the members of a Provincial Legislative Assembly to fill seats in the Provincial Legislative Council, means one of the practices specified in Part I and II of the First Schedule to this Order, and in relation to any other election, means one of the practices specified in Parts I and II of that Schedule.

2. No election shall be called in question except by an election petition presented in accordance with the provisions of this Part of this Order.

3. (1) An election petition against any returned candidate may be presented to the Governor—

(a) by any candidate or elector on any ground ;

(b) by an officer empowered in that behalf by the Governor, exercising his individual judgment, on the ground that the election has not been a free election by reason of the large number of cases in which undue influence or bribery has been excised or committed. In this paragraph, "elector", in relation to a commerce and industry, mining or planting constituency, includes all the persons included in the electoral roll as the nominees of any body, notwithstanding that only one of them is entitled to vote.

(2) A petitioner may, if he so desires, in addition to calling in question the election of the returned candidate, claim a declaration that he himself has been duly elected, but such a declaration shall only be claimed on one or other of the following grounds—

(a) that in fact the petitioner received a majority of the valid votes; or

(b) that but for votes obtained for the returned candidate by corrupt practices, the petitioner would have obtained a majority of the valid votes.

4. (1) Unless the Governor, exercising his individual judgment, dismisses a petition for non-compliance with the prescribed requirements, he shall, exercising his individual judgment appoint as Commissioners for the trial of the petition three persons who are or have been, or are eligible to be appointed, judges of a High Court, and shall appoint one of them to be the President:

Provided that nothing in this sub-paragraph shall be deemed to prevent the appointment of the President of a Commission before the other Commissioners are appointed.

(2) Subject to the provisions of this paragraph, all applications and proceedings in connection with the petition shall be dealt with by, and carried on by or before, the Commissioners.

(3) Where in respect of an election in a constituency more petitions than one are presented, the Governor shall refer all those petitions to the same Commissioners, who may at their discretion inquire into the petitions either separately or in one or more groups, as they think fit.

(4) If the services of any Commissioner are not available for the purpose of the inquiry or if during the course of the inquiry any Commissioner is unable to continue to attend thereat, the Governor, exercising his individual judgment,

shall appoint another Commissioner and the inquiry shall recommence before the Commission as so reconstituted:

Provided that the Commissioners may direct that any evidence already recorded shall remain upon record, and in that case it shall not be necessary to re-examine those witnesses who have already been examined and discharged.

(5) References to the Commissioners in this part of this Order, shall, as respects any matter to be done before the commencement of the inquiry, be deemed to be references to the President.

5. When at an inquiry into an election petition the Commissioners so order, the Advocate General of the Province, or some person acting under his instructions, shall attend and shall take such part therein as the Commissioners may direct.

6. Subject to the provisions of this Part of this Order, Acts of the Provincial Legislature and Rules may regulate the form of election petitions, the time and manner in which they are to be presented, the persons who are to be made parties thereto, the procedure to be adopted in connection therewith and the circumstances in which petitions are to abate, or may be withdrawn, and in which new petitioners may be substituted, may require security to be given for costs and may authorize the Governor, exercising his individual judgment, to dismiss petitions for non-compliance with the prescribed requirements.

7. (1) Subject to the provisions of this paragraph, if in the opinion of the Commissioners—

(a) the election of a returned candidate has been procured or induced, or the result of the election has been materially affected, by any corrupt practice; or

(b) any corrupt practice specified in Part I of the First Schedule to this Order has been committed in the interests of a returned candidate ; or

(c) the result of the election has been materially affected by the improper acceptance or rejection of any nomination, or by reason of the fact that any person nominated was not qualified or was disqualified for election or by the improper reception or refusal of a vote, or by the reception of any vote which is void, or by any non-compliance with the provisions of the Act or of this Order, or of any Act of the Provincial Legislature or Rules relating to the election, or by any mistake in the use of any prescribed form; or

(d) the election has not been a free election by reason of the large number of cases in which bribery or undue influence has been exercised or committed, the election of the returned candidate shall be void.

(2) If the Commissioners report that a returned candidate has been guily by an agent, other than his election agent, of any corrupt practice specified in Part I of the First Schedule to this Order, but further report that the candidate has satisfied them that–

(a) no corrupt practice was committed at the election by the candidate or his election agent, and the corrupt practices mentioned in the report were committed contrary to the orders, and without the sanction or connivance, of the candidate or his election agent;

(b) the candidate and his election agent took all reasonable means for preventing the commission of corrupt practices at the election;

(c) the corrupt practices mentioned in the report were of a trivial and limited character or took the form of customary hospitality which did not affect the result of the election; and

(d) in all other respects the election was free from any corrupt practice on the part of the candidate or any of his agents, then the Commissioners may find that the election of the candidate is not void.

(3) If a person (not being entitled so to do) votes more than once at the same election, all his votes shall be deemed for the purpose of this paragraph to be void.

8. (1) At the conclusion of the inquiry the Commissioners shall report whether the returned candidate, or any person who has lodged a petition and claimed a seat, has been duly elected and in so reporting shall have regard to the provisions of the last preceding paragraph.

(2) The report shall further include a recommendation by the Commissioners as to the total amount of costs, which are payable and the persons by and to whom the cost should be paid, and any such recommendation may include a recommendation for the payment of costs to the Advocate General of the Province or a person acting under his instructions attending the trial in pursuance of an order of the Commissioners.

(3) The report shall be signed by all the Commissioners and the Commissioners shall forthwith forward their report to the Governor, who on receipt thereof shall issue orders in accordance with the report and publish the report in the Government Gazette of the Province, and the orders of the Governor shall be final.

9. If either in their report or upon any other matter there is a difference of opinion among the Commissioners, the opinion of the majority shall prevail and their report shall be expressed in terms of the views of the majority.

10. Where any charge is made in an election petition of any corrupt practice, the Commissioners shall record in their report—

(a) a finding whether a corrupt practice has or has not been proved to have been committed by any candidate or his agent, and the nature of that corrupt practice ; and

(b) the names of all persons, if any, who have been proved at the inquiry to have been guilty of any corrupt practice and the nature of that practice with any such recommendations as the Commissioners may think proper to make for the exemption of any persons from any disqualifications which they may have incurred in this connection under paragraph two to five of Part IV of this Order:

Provided that no person shall be so named in the report unless he has been given a reasonable opportunity of showing cause why his name should not be so recorded.

PART IV
DISQUALIFICATIONS

1. The offences and practices specified, in relation to certain elections, in the Second Schedule to this Order shall, for the periods respectively specified in relation to those offences and practices in that Schedule, entail disqualification for membership of any Provincial Legislature.
2. If any person—
   (a) is in connection with an election to a Provincial Legislature, the Coorg Legislative Council or a local body in British India, convicted of an offence under Chapter IX A of the Indian Penal Code punishable with imprisonment for a term exceeding six months ; or
   (b) is after an inquiry under part III of this Order reported as guilty of any such corrupt practice as is specified in Part I or Part II of the First schedule to this Order, he shall, for a period of six years from the date of the conviction or report, be disqualified for voting at any election.
3. If, in relation to any election (other than an election by the members of a Provincial Legislative Assembly to fill seats in the Provincial Legislative Council), any person is after such an inquiry as aforesaid reported as guilty of any such corrupt practice as is specified in Part III of the said Schedule he shall be disqualified for voting at any election for a period of four years from the date of the report.
4. Where under either of the two last preceding paragraphs a person is, in connection with an election in a commerce and industry, mining or planting constituency, disqualified for voting for any period, then, if that person was at the date of the election either–
   (a) included in the electoral roll for the constituency as the nominee of a firm, Hindu joint family or corporation entitled to nominate persons for inclusion therein ; or
   (b) a member of any such firm or Hindu joint family, or a director ,managing agent or manager of any such corporation, or a person authorized to sign the name of any such firm, Hindu, joint family or corporation in the ordinary course its business, the firm, family or corporation shall, for the like period, be disqualified from nominating persons for inclusion in the electoral roll of any commerce and industry, mining or planting constituency.
5. If default is made in making the return of the election expenses of any person who has been nominated as a candidate at an election to which Part II of this Order applies, or if such a return is found, either by Commissioners holding an inquiry into the election or by any court in a judicial proceeding, to be false in any court in a judicial, proceeding, to be false in any material particular , the candidate and his election agent shall be disqualified for voting at any election for a period of five years from the date by which a return was required to be lodged.
6. Every person shall be disqualified for voting at any election who is for the time being disqualified for voting at elections to the Federal Legislature by reason of misconduct in connection with an election to that legislature, or by reason of a default in making, or of the falsity of, any return of election expenses at any election to that Legislature.

   References in this paragraph to the Federal Legislature shall until the establishment of the Federation be construed as references to the Indian Legislature.

7. Any person who is for the time being disqualified under the foregoing provisions of this part of this Order for being a member of a Provincial Legislature, or for voting at elections, shall, so long as the disqualification exists, also be disqualified for being an election agent at any election.
8. Any disqualification under paragraphs two to five of this Part of this Order arising in connection with an election to the Legislature of, or to a local body in, a province may be removed by the Governor of that Province in his discretion, and any other disqualification under the said paragraph two may be removed, before the establishment of the Federation, by the Governor General-in-Council, and, after the establishment of the Federation, by the Governor General in his discretion.
9. In paragraph one of this Part of this Order, "elections" includes all the elections referred to in the Second Schedule to this Order, but save as aforesaid, the references in this Part of this Order to elections, other than express references to elections of any other kind, shall be construed as references to elections of any other kind, shall be construed as references to elections as defined in paragraph three of Part I of this Order.

M. P. A. HANKEY

FIRST SCHEDULE
CORRUPT PRACTICES

PART I

1. Bribery, that is to say, any gift, offer or promise by a candidate or his agent, or by any other person with the connivance of a candidate or his agent, of any gratification to any person whomsoever, with the object, directly or indirectly, of inducing–
   (a) a person to stand or not to stand as, or to withdraw from being, a candidate at an election; or
   (b) an elector to vote or refrain from voting at an election, or as a reward to–
   (i) a person for having so stood or not stood, or having withdraw his candidature; or
   (ii) an elector for having voted or refrained from voting. For the purposes of this paragraph the term "gratification" is not restricted to pecuniary gratifications or gratifications estimable in money, and it includes all forms of entertainment and all forms of employment for reward; but it does not include the payment of any expenses bona fide incurred at, or for the purpose of any election and duly entered in the return of election expenses prescribed by this Order.
2. undue influence, that is to say, any direct or indirect interference or attempt to interfere on the part of a candidate or his agent, or of any other person with the connivance of the candidate or his agent, with the free exercise of any electoral right: Provided that–
   (a) without prejudice to the generality of the provisions of this paragraph, any such persons as its referred to therein who—
   (i) threatens any candidate or elector, or any person in whom a candidate or

elector is interested, with any injury of any kind; or

(ii) induces or attempts to induce a candidate or elector to believe that he, or any person in whom he is interested, will become or will be rendered an object of divine displeasure or spiritual censure, shall be deemed to interfere with the free exercise of the electoral right of that candidate or elector within the meaning of this paragraph;

(b) a declaration of public policy, or a promise of public action, or the mere exercise of a legal right without intent to interfere with an electoral right, shall not be deemed to be interference within the meaning of this paragraph.

3. The procuring or abetting or attempting to procure by a candidate or his agent, or by any other person with the connivance of a candidate or his agent, the application by a person for a voting paper in the name of any other person, whether living or dead, or in a fictitious name, or by a person for a voting paper in his own name when, by reason of the fact that he has already voted in the same or some other constituency, he is not entitled to vote.
4. The removal of a voting paper from the polling station during polling hours by any person with the connivance of a candidate or his agent.
5. The publication by a candidate or his agent, or by a any other person with the connivance of the candidate or his agent, of any statement of fact which is false, and which he either believes to be false or does not believe to be true, in relation to the personal character or conduct of any candidate, or in relation to the candidature or withdrawal of any candidate, being a statement reasonably calculated to prejudice the prospects of that candidate's election.
6. The incurring or authorizing by a candidate or his agent of expenditure, or the employment of any person by a candidate or his agent, in contravention of this Order or of any Act of the Provincial Legislature or Rules.

PART II

1. Any act specified in Part I of this Schedule, when done by a person who is not a candidate or a person acting with the connivance of a candidate or his agent.
2. The application by a person at an election for a voting paper in the name of any other person, whether living or dead, or in a fictitious name, or for a voting paper in his own name when, by reason of the fact that he has already voted in the same or some other constituency, he is not entitled to vote.
3. The receipt of, or agreement to receive, any gratification whether as a motive or a reward—

(a) by a person for standing or not standing as, or for withdrawing from being, a candidate; or

(b) by any person whomsoever for himself or any other person for voting or refraining from voting, or for inducing or attempting to induce any elector to vote or refrain from voting, or any candidate to withdraw his candidature.

For the purposes of this paragraph the term "gratification" has the same meaning as it has for the purposes of paragraph one of Part I of this Schedule.

4. The making of any return of election expenses, which is false in any material

particular, or the making of a declaration verifying any such return.

PART III

1. The incurring or authorization by any person other than a candidate or his agent of expenses on account of holding any public meeting, or upon any advertisement, circular or publication, or in any other way whatsoever, for the purpose of promoting or procuring the election of the candidate, unless he is authorized in writing so to do by the candidate.
2. The hiring, using or letting, as a committee room or for the purpose of any meeting to which electors are admitted, of any building, room or other place where intoxicating liquor is sold to the public.
3. The issuing of any circular, placard or poster having a reference to the election which does not bear on its face the name and address of the printer and publisher thereof.

SECOND SCHEDULE.

DISQUALIFICATIONS FOR MEMBERSHIP OF PROVINCIAL LEGISLATURES

Elections	Offence or Corrupt Practice	Period of Disqualification
Elections to which Chapter IXA of the Indian Penal Code applies.	Offences under Chapter IXA of the Indian Penal Code punishable with imprisonment for a term exceeding six months.	Six years from the date of conviction.
Elections as defined in Paragraph three of Part I of this Order.	Corrupt practices specified in Parts I and II of the First Schedule to this Order.	Six years from the date of the the report of the tribunal holding the inquiry.
Elections as defined in Paragraph three of Part I of this Order, other than elections by the members of a Provincial Legislative Assembly to fill seats in the Provincial Legislative Council.	Corrupt practices specified in Part III of the First Schedule to this Order.	Four years from the date of the report of the tribunal holding the inquiry.
Elections to Federal Legislature	Corrupt practices as defined in any Order under the Act relating to such elections. membership of Federal Legislature.	The period for which the corrupt practice entails disqualification for
Elections under the Government of India Act	Any corrupt practice within the meaning of the Electoral Rules Under the Government of India Act relating to the election in question	Such period, commencing on the date of the report of the Commissioners under the Electoral Rules relating to the election in question, as is the maximum period of disqualification specified in those Rules for inclusion in electoral rolls thereunder.

The 18th June 1936

No. 725Fr. – As the portion of the Government of India (Provincial Legislative Assemblies) Order, 1936, concerning Assam, which was published in the Assam Gazette of the 10 th June 1936, under Notification No. 672Fr., dated the 8 th June 1936, contained various printing mistakes it is again published for general information.

THE GOVERNMENT OF INDIA (PROVINCIAL LEGISLATIVE ASSEMBLIES) ORDER, 1936 AT THE COURT AT BUCKINGHUM PALACE,

The 30th Day of April, 1936.

Present,

THE KING'S MOST EXCELLENT MAJESTY IN COUNCIL

WHEREAS by section two hundred and ninety-one of, and the Fith and Sixth Schedules to the Government of India Act, 1935 (hereafter in this Order referred to as "the Act"), his Majesty in Council is empowered to make provision with respect to certain matters connected with Provincial Legislative Assemblies:

AND WHEREAS by sub-section (4) of section three hundred and eight of the Act His Majesty in Council is empowered to make amendments of the provisions of the Act relating to the qualifications of members of Provincial Legislative Assemblies and the qualifications entitling persons to be registered as voters for the purpose of elections to those Assemblies:

AND WHEREAS a draft of this Order has been laid before Parliament in accordance with the Provisions of sub-section (1) of section three hundred and nine of the Act, and an Address has been presented to His Majesty by both Houses of Parliament praying that an Order may be made in the terms of this Order:

NOW, THEREFORE, His Majesty, in the exercise of the powers conferred on Him as aforesaid and of all other powers enabling Him in that behalf, is pleased by and with the advice of His Privy Council to order, and, it is hereby ordered, as follows:—

PART I

Introductory and General Introductory

1. This Order may be cited as the Government of India (Provincial Legislative Assemblies) Order, 1936.
2. (1) In this Order, except where the context otherwise requires—

   "territorial constituency" means one of the territorial constituencies mentioned in paragraphs five and eight of the Fifth Schedule to the Act;

   "special constituency" means a constituency not being a territorial constituency;

   "seat", "election", and "constituency" in relation to any Province mean respectively a seat in the Legislative Assembly of that Province and an election or a constituency for the purpose of filling such a seat, and "election" includes a primary election:

"prescribed", except in the phrase "the prescribed date", has the same meaning as in the Fifth Schedule to the Act;
"rules" means rules made under paragraph twenty of the Fifth Schedule to the Act;
"commerce" includes banking, insurance and transport;
"mining" includes the getting of oil ;
"factory" means a factory within the meaning of the Factories Act, 1934, and " perennial factory" means a factory which is not a seasonal factory for the purposes of that Act;
"mine" means a mine which is subject to the provisions of the Indian Mines Act, 1923;
"Gazette" means the Government Gazette of the Province in question;
"preparation" in relation to an electoral roll includes the revision thereof, and "prepare" shall be construed accordingly;
"member" in relation to a constituent body for a commerce and industry, mining or planting constituency does not include an associate member;
and, subject as aforesaid and to any other provisions of this Order, expressions to which a meaning is assigned by the Sixth Schedule to the Act, either generally or in relation to any particular Province, have, except where the context otherwise requires, the same meanings for the purposes of this Order, either generally or in relation to that Province, as the case may be.

(2) The fact that one of two territorial constituencies is an urban and the other a rural constituency, or that in one of them the seat or one of the seats is a woman's seat or a reserved seat, shall not prevent them being deemed to be constituencies of the same communal description or constituencies of a similar class if they are both general constituencies or constituencies assigned to a specified community, and the expression "seat of the same communal description" and "seat of a similar class" shall for the purposes of the Schedules to the Act and of this Order be construed accordingly .

(3) Any reference in this Order to a paid up capital of not less than a specified amount shall be construed as including a reference to a paid up capital of not les than the equivalent of that amount in sterling.

(4) Any reference in this Order to all or any of the provisions of any Indian Act shall be construed as a reference to those provisions as amended by or under any other Act or, if those provisions are repealed and re-enacted with or without modification, to the provisions so re-enacted.

(5) The Interpretation Act, 1889, applies for the interpretation of this order as it applies for the interpretation of an Act of Parliament.

Special Constituencies

3. There shall be an electoral roll for every special constituency and no person who is not, and, except as expressly provided by the Fifth Schedule to the Act and this Order, every person who is, for the time being included in the electoral roll for any

such constituency shall be entitled to vote in that constituency.

4. The electoral rolls for the special constituencies shall be made up, and from time to time in whole or in part revised, by reference to such date, in this Order referred to as " the prescribed date", as may be directed in each case by the Governor exercising his individual judgment.

5. Subject to any express provisions of this Order, no person shall be included in the electoral roll for any special constituency unless he has attained the age of twenty-one years and is either:-

(a) a British subject ; or

(b) the Ruler or a subject of a Federated State ; or

(c) if and so far as it is so prescribed with respect to any Province, and subject to any prescribed conditions, the Ruler or a subject of any other Indian State.

6. No person shall be included in the electoral roll for, or vote at any election in, a special constituency if he is of unsound mind and stands so declared by a competent court.

7. No person shall be included in the electoral roll for, or vote at any election in, a special constituency if he is for the time being disqualified from voting under the provisions of any such Order in Council, Act of the Provincial Legislature or rules as may be made or passed under the Act with respect to corrupt practices and other offences in connection with elections, and the name of any person who becomes so disqualified shall forthwith be struck off all the electoral rolls for special constituencies in which it may be included.

8. No person shall vote at an election in a special constituency if he is for the time being undergoing a sentence of transportation, penal servitude or imprisonment.

9. For the purpose of the provisions of this Order relating to the qualifications for inclusion in electoral rolls for special constituencies, any property owned, held or occupied or payment made by, or assessment made on, a person as a trustee, guardian administrator or receiver, or in any other fiduciary capacity, shall, subject as hereinafter provided, be left out of account:

Provided that, except in the United Provinces, a person shall be qualified to be included in the electoral roll for a landholders' constituency if he——.

(a) is on the prescribed date the guardian of a minor who under this Order would have been entitled to be included in that roll if he were of full age and satisfied the relevant requirements of this Order as to residence ; and

(b) would himself have been entitled to be included in that roll, if the property of the minor were his own property.

10. For the purposes of the said provisions, where property is owned, held or occupied or payments are made jointly by, or assessments are made jointly on, the members of a joint family, the family shall be adopted as the unit for deciding whether any qualification exists, and if it does exist, the person qualified shall be, in the case of a Hindu joint family, the manager thereof, and, in the case of any other joint family, the member thereof authorized in that behalf by the family:

Provided that in the case of Bengal this paragraph shall not apply where members of a joint family have separate accommodation and separate messing, and in the case of the Punjab it shall not apply where the respective shares of the members of a joint family are specified in land records or municipal or cantonment records or a decree of a civil court.

11. Subject to the provisions of the last preceding paragraph, where any property is owned, held or occupied, or payments are made, jointly by, or assessments are made jointly on, more than one person, any reference in the provisions of this Order relating to special constituencies to any property, payment or assessment shall be construed as a reference to each person's share of that property, payment or assessment.

12. Where under the provisions of this Order any qualification for being included in an electoral roll for a special constituency depends upon the owning or holding of land in a specified area, or the being assessed or the making of payments in respect of land in a specified area, two or more parcels of land in that area owned or held by a person, and assessments made on or payments made by a person in respect of two or more parcels of land in the area, may be aggregated for the purpose of determining whether the qualification exists, but without prejudice, and subject, to any express provision in this Order with respect to such aggregation.

13. A person shall not be qualified to be included in the electoral roll for any labour constituency if he is subject to Indian military law.

General

14. (1) For the avoidance of doubt, it is hereby declared that a primary election held for the purpose of electing candidates for a seat reserved for members of the Scheduled Castes may be proceeded with notwithstanding that less than four candidates stand at that primary election, and that the remainder of the election may be proceeded with notwithstanding, that by reason of a deficiency of candidates at the primary election or by reason of the withdrawal or death of candidates elected thereat, there are or remain less than four duly elected Scheduled Caste candidates for the seat.

(2) At a poll at any such primary election no voter shall have more than one vote.

(3) Save as expressly provided in this Order with respect to Bengal, a member of the Scheduled Castes shall not be disqualified to hold a seat not reserved for members of the Scheduled Castes by reason that he has not been elected at a primary election as a candidate for a seat so reserved.

15. Subject to any express provisions of this Order to the contrary, where at an election a poll is taken for the purpose of filling more than one seat, a voter shall have as many votes as there are seats to be filled on the poll and may give all those votes to one candidate, or may distribute them between such candidates and in such manner as he thinks fit.

16. (1) The provisions of this paragraph shall apply in relation to any election in a constituency where the seats to be filled include a seat or seats reserved for members of the Scheduled Castes or a seat reserved for a Maratha, a representative

of backward tribes or areas, or in the case of the Bengal Anglo- Indian constituency, a woman.

(2) If the number of candidates qualified to be chosen to fill a seat or seats so reserved is equal to the number of seats so reserved all those candidates shall be declared to be elected to fill the reserved seat or seats and a poll shall only be taken, if necessary, for filling any seat or seats not filled under this sub-paragraph.

(3) If the number of candidates qualified to be chosen to fill a seat or seats so reserved is greater than the number of seats so reserved, then, when the counting of the votes has been completed, the Returning Officer shall first declare that one, or those, of the qualified candidates to whom the largest number of votes has been given to be elected to fill the reserved seat or the reserved seats.

(4) If the number of candidates qualified to be chosen to fill a seat or seats so reserved is less than the number of seats so reserved, all those candidates, if any, shall be declared to be elected to fill seats so reserved, and the Governor, exercising his individual judgment, shall by notification in Gazette call on the constituency to elect a person or persons, as the case may be, within such time as may be specified in the notification:

Provided that where a constituency having been already so called upon has failed to elect a person, or the requisite number of persons, as the case may be, to fill a vacancy or vacancies, the Governor shall not be bound again to call upon the constituency to elect a person or persons to fill the vacancy or vacancies until such time as, exercising his individual judgment, he may think fit.

17. If, when a poll has been taken at an election, an equality of votes is found to exist between any candidates, and the addition of one vote will entitle any of the candidates to be declared elected, one additional vote shall be given by the Returning Officer to the candidate, or, as the case may be, the candidates, selected by lot drawn in the presence of the Returning Officer in such manner as he may determine.

18. (1) The fact that a person or body has, in relation to any constituency, more than one qualification to be included, or to nominate persons to be included, in the electoral roll therefor, shall not increase his or its rights as respects inclusion, or, as the case may be, the nomination of persons for inclusion, in that roll.

(2) No person shall be entitled to be included twice in the electoral roll for any particular constituency, and the fact that a person is included twice in the electoral roll for a constituency shall not increase his rights as respects voting therein.

19. If a person is elected to more than one seat in the Legislative Assembly of a Province then, unless within the prescribed time he resigns all but one of the seats, all the seats shall become vacant.

20. (1) The dates on which nominations are to be made and scrutinized, polls held and other Acts done in connection with elections to a Provincial Legislative Assembly shall be fixed by the Governor in his discretion.

(2) Nothing in this paragraph shall be construed as preventing Acts of the Provincial Legislature or rules from making general provision with respect to the intervals which are to elapse between the successive stages of an election.

21. (1) In all constituencies the electoral rolls shall be prepared by such authority as the Governor exercising his individual judgement shall appoint :
Provided that in the preparation of such rolls the authority so appointed may, subject to any prescribed restrictions, employ such persons a he thinks fit.
(2) In all constituencies and at all elections the Returning Officer shall be a person in the service of the Crown in India.
22. (1) If the boundaries of any district or other administrative area mentioned in this Order or in the Sixth Schedule to the Act are altered, any reference in this Order or in the said Schedule to that district or area shall, as from such date or dates as may be fixed by the Governor, exercising his individual judgement, either for all purposes or for any particular purposes of this Order or of the said Schedule, be taken as a reference to the district or area as altered.
(2) Sub-paragraph (7) of paragraph thirteen of Part I of the Sixth Schedule to the Act (which relates to alterations in the boundaries of districts) shall cease to have effect.
23. The Provisions of the Fifth and Sixth Schedule to the Act shall have effect subject to the minor amendments specified in the First Schedule to this Order.
24. The Governor of the province may at any time by order vary the name of any territorial constituency if he deems it expedient so to do.
25. Notwithstanding anything in the Indian Income Tax Act, 1922, it shall be the duty of the appropriate income tax officers to give to any person charged by law with the duty of inquiring into the qualifications of electors such information as is necessary for the purpose of enabling him to discharge that duty.
26. Anything which under the provisions of the Act, or of this Order, is required or authorized to be done by, to or before the Governor of a Province in connection with the preparation of electoral rolls or the holding of elections, or otherwise for the purpose of constituting the Legislative Assembly of the Province in due time (whether or not the Governor is to Act in his discretion or to exercise his individual judgement) shall, before the commencement of Part III of the Act, be done by, to or before the Governor-in-Council or, in the case of Sind or Orissa the Governor.

PART IX

ASSAM

The Territorial Constituencies

1.- (1) The Territorial constituencies for the Province shall be those specified in the first column of the tables in Parts I to V of the Ninth Schedule to this Order, the extent thereof shall be as specified in the second column of those tables and the total number of seats to be filled in each of them shall be as specified in the third column of those tables.
(2) The Woman's (Shillong) constituency mentioned in Part III of the said Schedule is a constituency specially formed under sub –paragraph (b) of paragraph eight of the Fifth Schedule to the Act.

(3) In the case of the general constituencies, of the total number of seats to be filled in each constituency the number of the seats, if any, specified in the fourth column of the table shall be reserved for members of the Scheduled Castes.

The Women's Seat

2. A woman shall not be qualified to be chosen to fill the seat reserved for women unless she is entitled to vote in the choice of a member to fill some seat.

The European Seat

3. A person shall not be qualified to be chosen to fill the European seat unless he is a European entitled to vote in the choice of a member to fill that seat or some other seat.

The Indian Christian Seat

4. A person shall not be qualified to be chosen to fill the Indian Christian seat unless he is an Indian Christian entitled to vote in the choice of a member to fill that seat or some other seat.

Minor Amendment of Part IX of Sixth Schedule

5. Sub-paragraph (b) of paragraph 9 of Part IX of the Sixth Schedule to the Act shall cease to have effect and at the end of that paragraph there shall be inserted the following paragraph.

Special Provisions as to Shillong

9A. In the case of any territorial constituency comprising any part of Shillong, any reference in this Part of this Schedule to "the constituency" shall be construed as including a reference to so much of the areas under the jurisdiction of the Shillong Municipal Board and the Shillong Cantonment Authority as is not part of British India, and any reference to municipal or cantonment rates or taxes shall be construed as including a reference to any such rates or taxes assessed by or paid to that Board or that Authority in the exercise of any jurisdiction exercised by them in relation to areas outside British India.

Backward Areas and Tribes Seats

6.- (1) The seats to be filled by representatives of backward tribes shall be filled by elections in the special constituencies specified in the first column of the tables in Parts VI and VII of the Ninth Schedule to this Order and the extent of those constituencies shall be as specified in the second column of those tables.

(2) One seat shall be filled in each of those constituencies.

7. (1) a person shall not be qualified to the included in the electoral roll for any of the Backward Tribal (Plains) Constituencies unless he is a member of a backward

tribe, but, subject as aforesaid and subject to the provisions of this Order, the qualifications for inclusion in the said electoral rolls shall be those which are by Part IX of the Sixth Schedule to the Act specified as the qualifications for inclusion in the electoral rolls for general constituencies.

(2) A person shall not be qualified to be chosen to fill a seat in any constituency mentioned in this paragraph unless he is a member of a backward tribe who is entitled to vote in the choice of a member to fill that seat or some other seat.

(3) In this paragraph "backward tribes" means one of the tribes or communities specified in Part V of the Thirteenth Schedule to this Order.

8.- (1) Subject to the provisions of this Order, a person shall be qualified to be included in the electoral roll for the Garo Hills (North) constituency or the Garo Hills (South) constituency if he is a nokma in the constituency who is recognized as such by the Government.

(2) A person shall not be qualified to be chosen to fill a seat in either of the said constituencies unless he has a place of residence in one or other of them.

9.- (1) A person shall not be qualified to be included in the electoral roll for the Shillong constituency or the Jowai constituency if he is entitled to be included in the electoral roll for any territorial constituency other than the women's constituency.

(2) Subject to the provisions of this Order, a person shall be qualified to be included in the electoral roll for either of the said constituencies if he has a place of residence in the constituency and either—

(a) he has in the previous financial year been assessed to income tax or to house tax, or to an aggregate amount of not less than two rupees in respect of municipal or cantonment rates or taxes in the constituency, or would have been so assessed to house tax had he not been exempt therefrom by an order of a competent authority, or

(b) he has passed the Middle School Leaving Certificate Examination, or any examination prescribed as equivalent thereto; or

(c) he is a retired, pensioned or discharged officer, non-commissioned officer, soldier or man of His Majesty's regular military forces, of the Assam Rifles or of a British Indian Police Force, not being an officer, non-commissioned officer, soldier or man who was discharged or dismissed for disciplinary reasons ; or

(d) in the case of a widow, she is the pensioned window or pensioned mother of a person who was a non-commissioned officer, solider or man of His Majesty's regular military forces, of the Assam Rifles or of a British Indian Police Force.

(3) Subject as aforesaid a person shall also be qualified to be included in the electoral roll for the Shillong constituency if he is the owner of land in any British village of the Shillong sub-division outside the Shillong Municipality and cantonment the land revenue on which has been assessed, or is assessable, at not less than two rupees eight annas per annum.

(4) A Khasi or Synteng (Pnar) woman who is qualified to be included in the electoral roll for either of the said constituencies may, if she thinks fit, nominate one man to be included in the electoral roll for that constituency in her stead, and any man

so nominated shall be included accordingly.

Except within the Shillong municipality and cantonment and the area in which the Shillong Municipal Board and the Shillong Cantonment Authority exercise jurisdiction the same man may be nominated by more than one woman and notwithstanding anything in Part I of this Order may, in respect of each nomination, be separately entered in the roll and exercise a separate right to vote.

(5) A person shall not be qualified to be chosen to fill a seat in either of the said constituencies unless he is entitled to vote in the choice of a member to fill one or the other of those seats.

(6) Paragraph 9A of Part IX of the Sixth Schedule to the Act shall apply in relation to the Shillong constituency as it applies in relation to territorial constituencies.

10. (1) Subject to the provisions of this Order, a person shall be qualified to be included in the electoral roll for the Mikir Hills constituency if he is a village headman of a villagc in the constituency who is recognised as such by the Government.

(2) A person shall not be qualified to be chosen to fill a seat in the said constituency unless he has a place of residence in the constituency.

Commerce and Industry and Planting Seats

11. (1) Of the seats to be filled by representatives of the interests of Commerce and Industry and Planting–

(a) seven shall be filled by representatives of European planting;

(b) two shall be filled by a representatives of Indian planting;

(c) one shall be filled by a representative of European Commerce and Industry ;

(d) one shall be filled by a representative of Indian Commerce and Industry.

(2) The said seats shall be filled by elections in the constituencies mentioned in the first column of the tables in Parts VIII and IX of the Ninth Schedule to this Order, and the extent of those constituencies, and the number of seats to be filled in them respectively, shall be as specified in the second and third columns of those tables.

12. (1) Subject to the provisions of this Order, a person shall be qualified to be included in the electoral roll–

(a) for the European Planting Constituency, if he is the superintendent or manager of, or an engineer or medical officer employed on, any tea estate in the constituency which is under European control ;

(b) for either of the Indian Planting Constituencies, if he is the superintendent or manager of, or an engineer or medical officer employed on, any tea estate in the constituency in question which is not under European control.

(2) Notwithstanding anything in the last foregoing sub-paragraph but subject to the other provisions of this Order, where a tea estate is owned otherwise than by a corporation, the proprietors, a co-proprietor nominated in that behalf by co-proprietors owning more than half the proprietary interests in the estate, shall be entitled, on making application within the prescribed time and in the prescribed

manner, to be included in the electoral roll for the appropriate planting constituency in lieu of the superintendent or manager of the estate :

Provided that no proprietor or co-proprietor shall be so included in an electoral roll, unless the has a place of residence in the Province.

(3) Tea estates with less than seventy-five acres of tea under actual cultivation shall be left out of account for the purpose of this paragraph, and references therein to tea estates shall be construed accordingly.

13. (1) Subject to the provisions of this Order, a person shall be qualified to be included in the electoral roll for the European commerce and industry constituency if either—

(a) he is a European and carries on business in the constituency on his own account and not in partnership with any other person and was in any one of the five financial years preceding that in which the prescribed date falls assessed to income tax on an income derived from commerce or industry of not less than ten thousand rupees; or

(b) he is nominated in that behalf by a firm under European control carrying on business in the constituency which in any one of the said years was so assessed to income tax; or

(c) he is the nominee in that behalf of a qualified company.

(2) In this paragraph "qualified company" means a company incorporated by or under the law of any part of His Majesty's Dominions which—

(a) is under European control;

(b) is not principally engaged in the tea industry;

(c) has a place of business in the constituency;

(d) has a paid-up capital of not less them one lakh of rupees; and

(e) has in the constituency capital assets, other than money, to the value of at least twenty five thousand rupees.

14. (1) Subject to the provisions of this Order, a person shall be qualified to be included in the electoral roll for the Indian Commerce and Industry constituency if either—

(a) he carries on business in the constituency on his own account and not in partnership with any other person and was in any one of the five years preceding that in which the prescribed date falls assessed to income tax on an income derived from commerce or industry of not less than ten thousand rupees ;

(b) he is nominated in that behalf by a firm not under European control or a Hindu joint family being a firm or family carrying on business in the constituency which was in any of the said years so assessed to income tax;

(c) he is, or is nominated in that behalf by, the owner of a factory not under European control which is situate in the constituency and is subject to the provisions of the Indian Factories Act, 1934, not being a tea factory ; or

(d) he is nominated in that behalf by a qualified company.

(2) In this paragraph "qualified company" means a company incorporated under the Indian Companies Act, 1913, which is not under European control and is not principally engaged in the tea industry and either—

(a) has a paid-up capital of not less than fifty thousand rupees, has its registered office in Assam and is duly registered in the office of the Registrar of Companies at Shillong ; or

(b) has a paid-up capital of not less than one lakh of rupees and has in the constituency capital assets, not including money, to the value of not less than twenty-five thousand rupees.

15. (1) A firm, company or Hindu joint family shall be entitled to nominate not more than three persons for the purposes of the two last preceding paragraphs, and the names of the persons so nominated shall be inserted in the electoral roll as being the nominees of the firm, company or family in questions, but not more then one of those persons shall be entitled to vote at any election.

(2) No person shall be nominated as aforesaid by a firm or Hindu joint family unless he is a member thereof or a person who is and has for at least six months been authorised to sign documents in its name in the ordinary course of its business.

(3) No person shall be nominated as aforesaid by a company unless he is a director, managing agent or manager thereof or the secretary thereof, or a person who is and has for at least six months been authorised to sign documents in its name in the ordinary course of its business.

16. (1) A person shall not be qualified to be included in the electoral roll for more than one planting constituency, and any person who would, but for the provisions of this paragraph, be qualified to be included in more than one such roll shall be entitled to elect in which of the rolls he shall be included.

(2) If at a general election a person votes in more than one such constituency, his votes in all those constituencies shall be void.

17. A person shall not be qualified to be chosen to fill a planting seat, or a commerce and industry seat, unless he is included in the electoral roll for the constituency.

18. Acts of the Provincial Legislature or rules may contain provisions for defining the estates, companies and firms which are to be treated as being under European control or not under European control for the purpose of this Part of this Order.

Labour Seats

19. (1) The seats to be filled by representatives of labour shall be filled by elections in the constituencies specified in the first column of the tables in Part X of the Ninth Schedule to this Order.

(2) In the second column of the said tables are specified, in relation to each constituency, the tea gardens (hereafter referred to as "qualifying tea gardens") on employment in which the electoral roll for the constituency is, in the manner hereafter provided, to be based.

(3) References in those tables to gardens within a specified radius from any point or within a specified area include gardens the greater part of which is within that radius from that point or within that area.

20. (1) At the first and every third subsequent general election, one of the said seats shall be filled in each of the following constituencies, that is to say, the Doom

Dooma constituency, the Jorhat constituency, the Thakurbari constituency and the Silchar constituency.

(2) At the second and every third subsequent general election, one of the said seats shall be filled in each of the following constituencies, that is to say, the Tinsukhia constituency, the Nazira constituency, the Biswanath constituency and the Srimangal constituency.

(3) At the third and every third subsequent general election, one of the said seats shall be filled in each of the remaining labour constituencies.

(4) Casual vacancies in any of the said seats shall be filled in the constituency in which the seat was filled at the last preceding general election.

21. (1) Subject to the provisions of this Order, a person shall be qualified to be included in the electoral roll for any of the said constituencies, if he has, during the years ending on the prescribed date, worked as a permanent employee in one or more qualifying tea gardens on not less than one hundred and eighty days : Provided that a person who in the said year has not worked as aforesaid in one tea garden on sufficient days to qualify him for inclusion in the electoral roll shall not be included in the roll unless any prescribed requirements are complied with as to the making of an application for his enrolment and as to the production of evidence of his qualification.

(2) A person shall not be deemed to be working as a permanent employee in a tea garden on any day unless he is living either within the boundary of the garden or on land provided for that purpose by the owners thereof.

22. (1) A person shall not be qualified to be chosen to fill any of the said seats, unless either—

(a) he is a member of a qualifying tribe or caste and is entitled to vote in the choice of a member to fill some seat in the Province; or

(b) he is a member of one of the qualifying tribes or castes comprised in the Group I and is entitled to vote in the choice of a member to fill some seat in the Legislative Assembly of Bengal;

(c) he is a member of one of the qualifying tribes or castes comprised in Group II and is entitled to vote in the choice of a member to fill some seat in the Legislative Assembly of Bihar ; or

(d) he is a member of one of the qualifying tribes or castes comprised in Group III and is entitled to vote in the choice of a member to fill some seat in the Legislative Assembly of Orissa.

(2) In this paragraph "qualifying tribal caste" means a tribal caste belonging to any of the following groups, that is to say: -

Group I. – Bauri, Bhuyia, Bhutiya, Ghasi, Lepcha, Nepali, Paharia, Santal, Sikkimese:

Group II. – Ahir, Asor, Bauri, Bhogta, Bhuiya, Ghasi, Gond, Ho, Kharia, Kherwar, Lohar, Mahali, Munda, Malpaharia, Santal, Sauria, Turi :

Group III. – Barhi, Bhuyia, Ganda, Golla, Gonda, Kewat, Khond, Lohar, Munda, Oraon, Santal, Pan, Savara.

General

23. For the purpose of this Part of this Order, a person shall be deemed to have a place of residence in an area, if he ordinarily lives therein or has his family dwelling place therein and occasionally occupies it.

THE SCHEDULES
FIRST SCHEDULE
Minor Amendments of the Fifth and Sixth Schedules to the Act

1. In paragraph twelve of the Fifth Schedule to the Act (which relates to the qualifications to be possessed by members of a Provincial Legislative Assembly) for the words "shall not be qualified to hold a seat" there shall be substituted the words "shall not be qualified to be chosen to fill a seat".
2. In paragraph six of Part I of the Sixth Schedule to the Act (which relates to the preparation of electoral rolls) the words "or voted at any election to fill a general seat therein" shall be repealed.
3. At the end of paragraph seven of Part I of the Sixth Schedule to the Act, there shall be added the following provision :—
   "If a person votes in more than one constituency in contravention of this paragraph, his votes in each of the constituencies shall be void."
4. For the purpose of any provision of the Sixth Schedule to the Act which requires that in certain cases a person shall not be included in an electoral roll unless an application is made by or on behalf of that person for that purpose, an application made before the date of this Order with a view to facilitating the provisional preparation of electoral rolls may be treated as a sufficient application.

NINTH SCHEDULE
ASSAM CONSTITUENCIES
I. General Constituencies.

Name of Constituency	Extent of Constituency	No of Seats	Scheduled Castes seats
Dhubri (Central)	Bilasipara and Gossaingaon thanas	1	-
Dhubri (South)	Dhubri, Golakganj, South Salmara and Mankachar thanas plus the following three plain mauzas in the Garo Hills district, viz., Mahendraganj, Rangapani and Fulbari	1	-
Dhubri (North)	Bijni and Kokrajhar thanas	1	-
Goalpara (North-West)	Lakhimpur and North Salmara thanas	1	-
Goalpara (South-East)	Goalpara and Dudnai thanas	1	-
Barpeta (South)	Barpeta and Tarabari thanas	1	-
Barpeta (North)	Sorbhog and Patacharkuchi thanas	1	-
Nalbari	Nalbari thana	1	-

Kamrup Sadr (North)	Rangia and Barama thanas	1	-
Kamrup Sadr (Central)	Kamalapur and Hajo thanas	1	-
Kamrup Sadar (South)	Gauhati, Palasbari, Chhaygaon and Boko thanas	3	1
Mangaldai (South)	Mangaldai and Dalgaon thanas	1	-
Mangaldai (North)	Kalaigaon, Paneri, Udalguri and Majbat thanas	1	-
Tezpur (West)	Tezpur and Dhekiajuli thanas	1	-
Tezpur (East)	Sootea, Behalia and Gohpur thanas	1	-
Nowgong (West)	Lahorighat, Dhing and Morigaon thanas (excluding all areas in the Mikir Hills) plus Juria mauza from Rupahi Hat thana	1	-
Nowgong (South-east)	Raha and Jamunamukh thanas (excluding all areas in the Mikir Hills) plus the Lumding Kheraj Block	1	-
Nowgong (North-East)	Nowgong, Kaliabor and Samaguri thanas (execluding all areas in the Mikir Hills) plus Rupahi Hat thana less Juria mauza	2	1
Golaghat (North)	Dergaon and Bokakhat thanas (excluding all areas in the Mikir Hills) plus Mahura and Khumtai mauza from Golaghat thana	1	-
Golaghat (South)	Golaghat thana (excluding all areas in the Mikir Hills except Barpathar and Sarupathar mauzas) less Mahura and Khumatai mauzas	1	-
Jorhat (South)	Titabar and Teok thanas	1	-
Jorhat (North)	Jorhat and Majuli thanas	2	1
Sibsagar (West)	Sibsagar and Amguri thanas excluding the portion of Dopdar Mauza in Amguri thana	1	-
Sibsagar (East)	Nazira and Sonari thanas plus the portion of Dopdar Mauza in Amguri thana	1	-
Dibrugarh (Central)	Tinsukia, Bardubi and Jaipur thanas	1	
Dibrugarh (West)	Dibrugarh, Moran and Dhemaji thanas	1	
Dibrugarh (East)	Doom Dooma, Digboi and Margherita thanas (excluding the Lakuimpur Frontier Tract)	1	-
North Lakhimpur	The whole of North Lakhimpur sub-division	1	-
Sunamganj	The whole of Sunamganj sub-division	2	1
Habiganj (North)	Lakhai, Nabiganj, Baniyachung and Ajmiriganj thanas	2	1
Habiganj (South)	Habiganj, Madhupur, Chunarighat and Bahubal thanas	1	-
South Sylhet (West)	Bazar, Srimangal and Kamalganj thanas	1	-
South Sylhet (East)	Kulaura and Rajnagar thanas	1	-
Sylhet Sadr (South)	Fenchuganj, Golabganj, Balaganj and Biswanath thanas	1	-
Sylhet Sadr (North)	Sylhet, Gowainghat, Kanairghat and Jaintiapur thanas	1	-
Karimganj (West)	Jaldhup and Patharkandi thanas	1	-
Karimganj (East)	Karimganj, Badarpur and Ratabari thanas	2	1

Hailakandi	The whole of Hailakandi sub-dibision	1	-
Silchar	The whole of Silchar sub-divison	2	1

II. MUHAMMADAN CONSTITUENCIES.

Name of Constituency	Extent of Constituency	No. of Seats
Dhubri (West)	Dhubri and Golakganj thanas	1
Dhubri (South)	South Salamara and Mankachar thanas plus the following three plains mauzas of the Garo Hills districts, viz., Mahendraganj, Rangapani and Fulbari	1
Dhubri (North)	Bilasipara, Kokrajhar, Gossaingaon and Bijni thanas	1
Goalpara (West)	Lakhimpur thana	1
Golapara (East)	Golapara, Dudnai and North Salmara thanas	1
Barpeta	Barpeta and Tarabari thanas	1
Kamrup (South)	Gauhati, Palasbari, Chhaygaon, Boko, Kamalpur and Hajo thanas	1
Kamrup (North)	Nalbari, Rangia and Barama thanas of the Kamrup Sadar sub-division and Sorbhog and Patacharkuchi thanas of the Barpeta sub-division	1
Nowgong (West)	Dhing, Lahorighat, Raha, Marigaon and Jumunamukh thanas (excluding all area in the Mikir Hills) plus the Lumding Kheraj Block	1
Nowgong (East)	Nowgong, Samaguri, Rupahi Hat and Kaliabor thanas (excluding all areas within the Mikir Hills)	1
Darrang	The whole of Darrang district	1
Sibsagar	The whole of Sibsagar district (excluding all areas in the Mikir Hills except Barpathar and Sarupathar mauzas)	1
Lakhimpur	The whole of Lakhimpur district (excluding the Lakhimpur Frontier Tract)	1
Sunamganj (west)	Tahirpur, Dharampasha and Sulla thanas	1
Sunamganj (Central)	Sunamganj thana	1
Sunamganj (East)	Chhatak Thana	1
Sunamganj (South)	Derai and Jagannathpur thanas	1
Habjganj (North-West)	Baniyachung and Ajmiriganj thanas	1
Habiganj (North-East)	Habiganj and Nabiganj thanas	1
Habiganj (South-West)	Lakhai and Madhabpur thanas	1
Habiganj (South-East)	Chunarighat and Bahubal thanas	1
South Sylhet (West)	Maulvi Bazaar and Srimangal thanas	1
South Sylhet (Central)	Rajnagar and Kamalganj thanas	1
South Sylhet (East)	Kulaura thana	1
Sylhet Sadr (Central)	Part of Sylhet Sadr thana containing Chaukidari Circles Nos. 1 – 41 and 51 – 55 (inclusive) including the Municipal area	1
Sylhet Sadr (North)	Gowainghat and Jaintiapur thanas	

	plus the North Eastern half of Kanarighat thana containing Chaukidari Circles Nos. 1 – 12 , 15 – 20 and 32 – 34 (inclusive)	1
Sylhet Sadr (West)	Part of Sylhet thanas conataing Chaukidari Circles Nos. 42 – 50 and 56 – 67 (inclusive) and Biswanath thana	1
Sylhet Sadr (East)	Golabganj thana plus the South Western half of Kanairghat thana conataining Chaukidari Circles Nos. 13, 14 and 21 – 31 (inclusive)	1
Sylhet Sadr (South)	Balaganj and Fenchuganj thanas	1
Karimganj (West)	Jaldhup thana	1
Karimganj (Central)	Karimganj thana less Chaukidari Circles Nos. 22 – 28 (inclusive), 61, 62 and 64 – 68 (inclusive)	1
Karimganj (South)	Badarpur, Ratabari and Patharkandi thanas plus the following Choukidari circles of Karimganj thana Nos. 22 – 28 (inclusive), 61, 62 and 64 – 68 (inclusive)	1
Hailakandi	The whole of Hailakandi sub-dibvision	1
Silchar	The whole of Silchar sub-division	1

III. WOMEN'S CONSTITUENCY

Name of Constituency	Extent of Constituency	No. of Seats
Women's (Shillong)	Shillong Municipality and Cantonment.	1

IV. EUROPEAN CONSTITUENCY

Name of Constituency	Extent of Constituency	No. of Seats
European	The districts of Goalpara, Kamrup, Nowgong, Darrang, Sibsagar, Lakhimpur (excluding the Lakhimpur Frontier Tract), Sylhet, Cachar (excluding North Cachar Hills), Garo Hills and the British Territory of the Khasi and Jaintia Hills	1

V. INDIAN CHRISTIAN CONSTITUENCY

Name of Constituency	Extent of Constituency	No. of Seats
Indan Christian	The districts of Goalpara, Kamrup Nowgong. (excluding all areas in the Mikir Hills except Barpathar and Saru--pathar mauzas), Lakhimpur (excluding the Lakhimpur Frontier Tract), Sylhet and Cachar (excluding the North Cachar Hills)	1

VI. BACKWARD TRIBAL (PLAINS) CONSTITUENCIES

Name of Constituency	Extent of Constituency	No. of Seats
Goalpara (Tribal)	Kokrajhar and Bijni thanas of Goalpara district	1
Kamrup (Tribal)	Nalbari, Barama, Rangia, Patacharkuchi and Sorbhog thanas of Kamrup district	1
Lakhimpur and Majuli (Tribal)	North Lakhimpur sub-division of the Lakhimpur District plus the Majuli	1

	thana of the Jorhat sub-division of the Sibsagar district plus the Dhemaji Thana of the Dibrugarh sub-division of the Lakhimpur District	
Nowgong (Tribal)	Raha, Marigaon and Jamunamukh thanas excluding all areas in the Mikir Hills	1

VII. BACKWARD AREAS (HILLS) CONSTITUENCIES

Name of Constituency	Extent of Constituency	No. of Seats
Garo Hills (North)	Mauzas III, IV and V	1
Garo Hills (South)	Mauzas I, II, IX and X (Tura Town)	1
Shillong	The British territory of the Shillong sub-division plus the non-British areas in which the Municipalty and Cantonment exercise jurisdiction	1
Jowai	The whole of Jowai sub-division	1
Mikir Hills	The Mikir Hills (in Nowgong and Sibsagar districts) less barpathar and Sarupathar mauzas in Golaghat sub-division and less the Lumding Kheraj Block in Nowgong district	1

VIII. PLANTING CONSTITUENCIES

Name of Constituency	Extent of Constituency	No. of Seats
European Planting	The districts of Goalpara, Kamrup, Darrang, Nowgong, Sibsagar, Lakhimpur (excluding the Lakhimpur Frontier Tract), Sylhet and Cachar (excluding the North Cachar Hills)	7
Indian Planting (Assam Valley)	The districts of Goalpara, Kamrup, Darrang, Nowgong, Sibsagar and Lakhimpur (excluding the Lakhimpur Frontier Tract)	1
Indian Planting (Surma Valley)	The districts of Sylhet and Cachar (excluding The North Cachar Hills)	1

IX. COMMERCE AND INDUSTRY CONSTITUENCIES

Name of Constituency	Extent of Constituency	No. of Seats
European Commerce and Industry	The Province	1
Indian Commerce and Industry	Ditto	1

X. LABOUR CONSTITUENCIES (TEA GARDENS)

I.- IN LAKHIMPUR DISTRICT

First election

Name of Constituency	Extent of Constituency	No of seats
Doom Dooma (District Lakhimpur)	All gardens within a radius of three and a half miles from Doom Dooma police station	

	Second election	
Tinsukia (District Lakhimpur)	All gardens within a radius of five miles from Tinsukia police station	1
	Third election	
Dibrugarh (District Lakhimpur)	All gardens within a radius of six miles from Dibrugarh police station	

II.– IN SIBSAGAR DISTRICT

	First election	
Jorhat (District Sibsagar)	All gardens in Jorhat thana within the area included in the following boundaries North – Assam Trunk Road' West – Jorhat Provincial Railway Titabor Branch East – Thana boundary	
South – Thana boundary		
	Second election	
Nazira (Sibsagar District)	All gardens within Nazira thana which are within a radius of seven miles from Simalguri railway station	1
	Third election	
Golaghat East (Sibsagar District)	All gardens within the mauzas of Dergaon, Gurjogonia Kakodonga, Dakhinhengra, Kacharihat, Athgaon and Ghiladhari	

III.- IN DARRANG DISTRICT

	First election	
Thakurbari (District Darrang)	All gardens within a radius of three and a half miles from Thakurbari railway station	
	Second election	
Biswanath (Darrang District)	All gardens within a radius of six miles from Pabhoi inspection bungalow	1
	Third election	
Paneri (Darrang District)	All gardens within a radius of seven miles from Paneri club house	

IV. – IN SURMA VALLEY

	First election	
Silchar (District Cachar)	All gardens in the Silchar Thana which lie south of the Barak river	
	Second election	
Srimangal (District Sylhet)	All gardens within the jurisdiction of the Srimangal police station	1
	Third election	
Longai Valley (District Sylhet)	All gardens in the Longai Valley within the jurisdiction of the Pathakandi police station.	

THIRTEENTH SCHEDULE
BACKWARD TRIBES
PART V.
ASSAM

The following tribes and communities:–

1. Kachari
2. Boro or Boro-Kachari
3. Rabha
4. Miri
5. Lalung
6. Mikir
7. Garo
8. Hajong
9. Deori
10. Abor
11. Mishmi
12. Dafla
13. Singpho
14. Khampti
15. Any Naga or Kuki tribe
16. Any other tribe or community for the time being designated by the Governor in his discretion.

C. S. MULLAN,
Reforms Officer and Additional Secretary
to the Government of Assam.

GOVERNMENT OF ASSAM THE GOVERNOR-IN-COUNCIL

APPOINTMENT AND POLITICAL DEPARTMENT
REFORMS BRANCH
Letter No. 242 – 49Fr.

From

C.S.MULLAN, Esq., I.C.S.,
Reforms Officer and Additional Secretary to the
Government of Assam,

To

ALL DEPUTY COMMISSIONERS OF PLAINS DISTRICTS

Dated Shillong, the 24th March 1936

Sir,

In my Confidential letter No. 4026-33Fr., dated the 7th December 1935, instructions were issued for the preparation of provisional electoral rolls for the "territorial" and "backward tribal" constituencies in the Assam Legislative Assembly (Lower House) and since then separate instructions have issued to the Deputy Commissioner, Sibsagar, and the Deputy Commissioner, Nowgong, regarding the preparation of an electoral roll for the Mikir Hills "backward area" constituency. It remains, therefore, to address you as regards the preparation of provisional rolls for the following constituencies in the Assam Legislative Assembly, viz.:-

(i) European Planting,

(ii) Indian Planting,

(iii)European Commerce and Industry,

(iv)Indian Commerce and Industry,

(v) Tea Garden Labour.

2. As regards the European Planting constituency you may assume that this constituency (which will be a single constituency containing 7 seats) will cover the following districts, viz., Goalpara, Kamrup, Darrang, Nowgong, Sibsagar, Lakhimpur (excluding the Lakhimpur Frontier Tract), Cachar (excluding the North Cachar Hills) and Sylhet and that the franchise qualifications will be as follows:-

(a) A person shall be qualified to be included in the electoral roll for the European Planting constituency if he is the Superintendent or Manager of, or an Engineer or Medical Officer employed on, any tea estate which is under European control.

Tea estates with less than 75 acres of tea under actual cultivation shall be left out of account.

(b) Where a tea estate is owned otherwise than by a corporation the proprietor of the estate, or where there are several co-proprietors, a co-proprietor nominated on that behalf by co-proprietors owning more than half the proprietary interests in the estate shall be entitled, on application, to be included in the electoral roll in lieu of the Superintendent or Manager of the estate, provided that no proprietor or co-proprietor shall be so included in the roll unless he has a place of residence in Assam.

"European Control" will probably be defined as depending on whether the majority of the Board of Directors or other controlling authority consists of Europeans and you may assume this accordingly.

3. The Indian Tea Planting constituencies will be as follows:–

(i) Indian Planting (Assam Valley):– This will consist of one seat and will comprise the districts of Goalpara, Kamrup, Darrang, Nowgong, Sibsagar and Lakhimpur (excluding the Lakhimpur Frontier Tract).

(ii) Indian Planting (Surma Valley):– This will also consist of one seat and will comprise the districts of Sylhet and Cachar (excluding the North Cachar Hills).

You may assume that the qualifications for the Indian Planting constituencies will be same as for the European Planting constituency except that instead of the words "under European control" the words "not under European control" will be used.

You should now take steps to prepare a provisional electoral roll for so much of the European and Indian Planting constituencies as falls within your district.

The roll should be prepared in the following form:–

ASSAM LEGISLATIVE ASSEMBLY

European Planting Constituency
Indian Planting (Assam Valley) Constituency
(Surma Valley)

.... District
Sub-division

Serial No.	Name	Address	Age	Qualification	Remarks

4. The European Commerce and Industry constituency (1 seat) will cover the province of Assam (excluding the Sadiya, Balipara and Lakhimpur Frontier Tracts, the Naga Hills district, the Lushai Hills district and the North Cachar Hills) and you may assume that the following will be the franchise qualifications:-
   (i) being a European who carries on business in the constituency on his own account and not in partnership and who was in any one of the five financial years preceding that on which the prescribed date falls assessed to income-tax on an income derived from Commerce and Industry of not less than Rs.10,000; or
   (ii) being a person who is nominated in that behalf by a firm under European control which in any one of the said years was so assessed; or
   (iii)being the nominee in that behalf of a "qualified company".

   A "qualified company" means a company incorporated by or under the law in any part of His Majesty's Dominions which-
   (a) is under European control,
   (b) is not principally engaged in Tea Industry,
   (c) has a place of business in the constituency,
   (d) has a paid-up capital of not less than one lakh of rupees or the equivalent in sterling,
   (e) has in the constituency capital assets, other than money, to the value of at least Rs.25,000.
5. The Indian Commerce and Industry constituency (one seat) will cover the same area as the European Commerce and Industry seat and the franchise qualifications may

be assumed to be as follows:-

(i) not being a European who carries on business in the constituency on his own account and not in partnership and who was in any one of the five financial years preceding that on which the prescribed date falls assessed to income tax on an income derived from Commerce and Industry of not less than Rs. 10,000; or

(ii) being a person nominated in that behalf by a firm not under European control or by a Hindu joint family carrying on business in the constituency which was in any one of the said years so assessed to income tax; or

(iii)being the owner or the nominee in that behalf of the owner of a factory not under European control which is situate in the constituency and is subject to the provisions of the Indian Factories Act, 1934, not being a tea Factory; or

(iv)being the nominee in that behalf of a "qualified company".

"Qualified company" in the case of the Indian Commerce and Industry constituency means a company incorporated under the Indian Companies Act, 1913, having a place of business in the constituency, which is not under European control and is not principally engaged in the Tea Industry and either–

(a) has a paid-up capital of not less than Rs. 50,000, has its registered office in Assam, and is duly registered in the office of the Registrar of Companies at Shillong; or

(b) has a paid-up capital of not less than 1 Lakh of rupees and has in the constituency capital assets, not including money, to the value of not less than Rs. 25,000.

As regards both the European and Indian Commerce and Industry constituencies it may be assumed that there will be a special provision under which a qualified firm, company or Hindu joint family will be entitled to nominate not more than 3 persons for the purpose of voting and that the names of the persons so nominated shall be entered in the roll as being the nominees of the firm, company or Hindu joint family in question but not more than one of these persons shall be entitled to vote. Furthermore no person shall be so nominated by a firm or a Hindu joint family unless he is a member thereof or a person who is and has been for at least 6 months authorised to sign documents in its name in the ordinary course of its business and no person can be nominated by a company to vote in its behalf unless he is a Director, Managing Agent, or Manager thereof, or a person who is and has been for at least 6 months authorised to sign documents in its name in the ordinary course of business.

6. You should now take steps to prepare a provisional roll for so much of the European Commerce and Industry and the Indian Commerce and Industry constituencies as falls within your district.

The roll should be prepared in the following form:–

ASSAM LEGISLATIVE ASSEMBLY

(a) European Commerce and Industry Constituency

.... District

.... Sub-division

Serial No.	Name and address of qualified Company, Firm or individual	Qualification	In case of qualified Companies and Firms name or names of person or persons nominated to vote on their behalf	Remarks

(b) Indian Commerce and Industry Constituency

.... District

.... Sub-division

Serial No.	Name and address of qualified Company, Factory, Firm, Hindu joint family or individual	Qualification	In case of qualified Companies, Firms and Hindu joint families the name or names of person or persons nominated to vote on their behalf	In the case of Factories the name of owner or of person nominated by owner to vote on his behalf	Remarks

7.Both in the case of the Planting and Commerce and Industry constituencies no person can be entered in the roll unless he is over 21 years of age and is either–

(a) a British subject; or

(b) the Ruler or Agent of a Federated State; or

(c) if it is so prescribed, the ruler or subject of any other Indian State.

As there will not be any subjects of "Federated States" on the inception of Provincial Autonomy you may assume that the following classes of non-British subjects (if otherwise qualified) will be prescribed as eligible to be entered in the rolls of the Planting and Commerce and Industry constituencies.

(1) The Ruler or subject of Manipur State.

(2) The Ruler or subject of any Khasi State.

(3) The community known as "Marwari".

8. Separate instructions will issue in due course to the Deputy Commissioners concerned (Lakhimpur, Sibsagar, Darrang and Cachar) as regards the preparation of a provincial roll for the Tea Garden Labour constituencies.

Your obedient servant,

C. S. MULLAN,

Reforms Officer and Additional Secretary

to the Government of Assam.

Memo. No. 250 Fr.

Dated Shillong, the 24th March 1936.

Copy forwarded to the Deputy Commissioner, Khasi and Jaintia Hills, for information.

Special instruction will issue in due course to the Deputy Commissioner, Khasi and Jaintia Hills, as regards the preparation of rolls for the constituencies of the Assam Legislative Assembly which fall in that district. The orders contained in paragraphs 4 and 5 of this letter apply, however, to the Khasi and Jaintia Hills (British portion) and the Deputy Commissioner should now take steps to prepare a provisional roll for the European and Indian Commerce and Industry constituencies so far as the British portion of his district is concerned.

By order of the Government of Assam,
C.S.MULLAN,
Reforms Officer and Additional Secretary
to the Government of Assam.

Memo. No. 251 Fr.

Dated Shillong, the 24th March 1936.

Copy forwarded to the Deputy Commissioner, Garo Hills, for information.

The orders contained in paragraphs 4 and 5 of this letter apply to the Garo Hills and the Deputy Commissioner should now take steps to prepare a provisional roll for the European and Indian Commerce and Industry constituencies so far as his district is concerned.

By order of the Government of Assam,
C.S.MULLAN,
Reforms Officer and Additional Secretary
to the Government of Assam.

Memo. No. 252-53 Fr.

Dated Shillong, the 24th of March 1936.

Copy forwarded to the Commissioners of Divisions, for information.

By order of the Government of Assam,
C.S.MULLAN,
Reforms Officer and Additional Secretary
to the Government of Assam.

CORRECTION SLIP TO THE ASSAM LEGISLATIVE ASSEMBLY ELECTORAL (GOVERNOR'S) RULES.

No. 3

1. *Page 22:-* Insert the following as sub-rules (3) and (4) of rule 2 of Part V:–
"(3) A polling officer may, if so directed by the presiding officer, perform all or any of the duties assigned to a presiding officer under these rules."

"(4) If the presiding officer, owing to illness or other unavoidable cause is obliged to absent himself from the polling station, his duties shall be performed by such polling officer as has been previously authorized by the Returning Officer to perform such duties during any such absence."

2. *Page 26 - 27 :–* (i) Insert the words "other than the Women's Constituency" after the word "constituency" in line 2 of question (3), and
(ii) insert the following as new question 5 in rule 13 of PartV:-
"(5) (And, at a general election in the Women's Constituency), have you already voted at this general election in more than one other territorial constituency?"
and (iii) also insert the words "or fifth" after the word "fourth" in the last line of this rule 13 of Part V."

NOTICE TO WOMEN VOTERS TO SUBMIT APPLICATIONS TO BE ENROLLED

Notice is hereby given that the Deputy Commissioner Sylhet is preparing a list of women voters for the Assam Legislative Assembly relating to the North Sylhet Sub-division of the Sylhet district. Under the Government of India Act the following special additional qualifications have been laid for women but in order to obtain registration on the Electoral Roll in respect of such qualifications women must themselves apply for registration. In the case of a married woman such application can be made by the husband of the woman on her behalf. The following are the special additional qualifications which will qualify a woman over 21 years of age to be entered as a voter in the roll.

Qualifications

(i) if she is the pensioned widow or pensioned mother of a person who was an officer, non commissioned officer or a soldier in the Army or the Assam Rifles or the pensioned widow or pensioned mother of a person who was an officer or man of an Indian Police Force, or

(ii) if she is literate

Note– An application of a woman to be included in the electoral roll on the ground of being literate shall be accompanied by the certificate signed by a Government officer or by a Mauzadar or Sarpanch or by some respectable gentleman of the locality to the following effect:-

"Certified that .... of Village .... thana .... daughter/wife of .... is over 21 years of age and is able to read and write in the .... Language.

Date

Signature

Designation.

(iii) If her husband possesses the following qualification:–

(a) is a retired pensioned or discharged officer, non-commissioned officer or soldier of His Majesty's regular military forces or the Assam Rifles or is a retired, pensioned or discharged officer or man of an Indian Police Force.

Women who possess any of the qualifications mentioned above and who wish to be entered in the roll should therefore apply on or before 15-6-41 either by letter or in person to the Deputy Commissioner, Sylhet giving their names and addresses with full particulars of the qualifications (noted below) in respect of which they claim to be included in the Electoral roll.

The applications should contain the following particulars

(1) Name
(2) Father's / Husband's Name
(3) Address (Chaukidari circle, thana, or Municipal ward, or tea garden)
(4) Age
(5) Qualification
(6) Caste

Note:- Caste is required only in case of general constituency rolls to ascertain whether the applicant is a member of the Scheduled Caste viz (1) Mali or Bhuimali (2) Dhupi or Dhobi (3) Dugla or Dholi (4) Jhalo and Malo (5) Mahara (6) Sutradhar (7) Muchi (8) Patni (9) Namasudra (10) Kaiborta or Jalia (11) Lalbegi (12) Mehtor or Bhangi (13) Bansphor.

Sd/- G.P. Stewart.
Deputy Commissioner, Sylhet.
25-5-41.

APPENDIX 9

LIST OF SCHEDULED CASTES ON THE BASIS OF POONA PACT AND CONSTITUTION ORDERS 1950 (A), PART II

ASSAM

SURMA VALLEY

1. Bansphor
2. Bhuimali or Mail
3. Dholi
4. Dhubi
5. Jalia
6. Jhalo or Malo
7. Lalbegi
8. Mahara
9. Methor
10. Muchi
11. Namasudra
12. Patni
13. Sutradhar

BRAHMAPUTRA VALLEY

1. Bania
2. Bansphor
3. Hira
4. Koibarta
5. Lalbegi
6. Methor
7. Namasudra

APPENDIX 10

LIST OF MEMBERS OF THE ASSAM LEGISLATIVE ASSEMBLY 1937-1946 GENERAL, INDIAN PLANTING AND INDIAN COMMERCE AND INDUSTRY

1. Kumar Ajit Narayan Dev, M.A,, B.L., Dhubri (North)
2. Akshay Kumar Das, B.L., Sunamganj (Reserved seat).
3. Arun Kumar Chanda, Barrister –at –law, Silchar.
4. Baidyanath Mookerjee, B.A., Indian Plainting (Surma Valley)
5. Balaram Sircar, Karimganj (East) (Reserved seat).
6. Basanta Kumar Das, B.L., Sylhet Sadr (South)
7. Beliram Das, B.L., Kamrup Sadr (South) (Reserved seat).
8. Bepin Chandra Medhi, B.L. Mangaldai (North)
9. Bhuban Chandra Gogoi, Sibsagar (West)
10. Bipin Behari Das, Habiganj (North) (Reserved seat).
11. Bishnu Ram Medhi, M.SC., B.L., Kamrup Sadr (Central)
12. Dakshinaranjan Gupta Chaudhuri, M.A., B.L., South Sylhet (West)
13. Debeswar Sarmah, B.L., Jorhat (North)
14. Ghanashyam Das, B.A., Barpeta (South)
15. Gauri Kanta Talukdar, B.L., Nalbari
16. Gopinath Bordoloi, M.A., B.L., Kamrup Sadr (North)
17. Haladhar Bhuyan, Nowgong (West)
18. Harendra Narayan Chaudhuri B.A., Sylhet Sadar (North)
19. Hirendra Chandra Chakravarty, B.A., Hailakandi
20. Jadav Prasad Chaliha, B.Sc., Sibsagar (East)
21. Jogendra Chandra Nath, B. A., Goalpara (South-East)
22. Jogendra Narayan Mandal, B.L., Dhubri (Central)
23. Jagesh Chandra Gohain, B.L., Dibrugarh (West)
24. Kalachand Roy, Silchar (Reserved seat)
25. Kameswar Das, M.Sc., B.L., Barpeta (North)
26. Kamini Kumar Sen, B.L., (Karimganj (East)
27. Karuna Sindhu Roy, Sunamganj
28. Kedarmal Brahmin, B.L., Indian Commerce and industry

29. Krishna Nath Sarmah, B.Sc., B.L., Jorhat (South)
30. Lakshesvar Borooah, B.L., Dibrugarh (Central)
31. Lalit Mohan Kar, South Sylhet (East)
32. Mahadev Sarma, Tezpur (East)
33. Dr. Mahendra Nath Saikia, L.M.P., Nowgong (North-East)
34. Mahi Chandra Bora, B.L., Nowgong (South-East)
35. Naba Kumar Dutta, Indian Plainting (Assam Valley)
36. Omeo Kumar Das, B.A., Tezpur (West)
37. Paramananda Das, Goalpara (North-West)
38. Rai Bahaduar Promode Chandra Dutt, B.L., C.I.E., Habiganj (South)
39. Purandar Sarma, M.A., B.L., Mangaldai (South)
40. Purna Chandra Sarma, B.L., Nowgong (North-East)
41. Rabindra Nath Aditya, M.A., B.L., Karimganj (West)
42. Rajani Kanta Barooah, Dibrugarh (East)
43. Rajendra Nath Barua, B.L., Golaghat (North)
44. Ramnath Das, B.L., (Reserved seat), Jorhat (North)
45. Rohini Kumar Chaudhuri, B.L., Kamrup Sadr (South)
46. Sankar Chandra Baruah, Golaghat (South)
47. Santosh Kumar Barua, B.A., Dhubri (South)
48. Sarveswar Barua, B.L., North Lakhimpur
49. Shibendra Chandra Biswas, Habiganj (North)
50. Siddhi Nath Sarma, B.L. Kamrup Sadar (North)

MUHAMMADAN

51. Abdul Aziz, B.L., South Sylhet (Central)
52. Abdul Bari Chaudhury, M.A. B.L., Sunamganj (South)
53. Abdul Hamid Khan, Dhubri (South)
54. Khan Bahadur Hazi Abdul Majid Chaudhury, Karimganj (Central)
55. Abdul Matin Chaudhuri, B.L., Sylhet Sadr (East).
56. Abdur Rahman, Habiganj (South-East)
57. Syed Abdur Rouf, B.L., Barpeta.
58. Md. Abdus Salam, B.A., Sylhet Sadr (East)
59. Dewan Muhammad Ahbab Chaudhury Vidyabinode, B.A., Sunamganj (East)
60. Md. Ali Haidar Khan, South Sylhet (East)
61. Dewan Ali Raja, Habiganj (North-East)
62. Mahammad Amiruddin, Nowgong (East)
63. Muhammad Amiruddin, Nowgong (East)
64. Ashrafuddin Md. Chaudhury, B.A. , LL.B., Advocate, Habiganj (South –East)
65. Badaruddin Ahmed, B.L., Darrang.
66. Khan Bahadur Dewan Eklimur Roza Chaudhury, Sylhet Sadr (West)
67. Fakhruddin Ali Ahmed, Barister at – Law, Kamrup (North).
68. Ghyasuddin Ahmed, B.L., Dhubri (West)
69. Jahanuddin Ahmed, B.L., Dhubri (North)

70. Khan Bahaduar Keramat Ali, Sibsagar
71. Muhammad Maqbul Hussian Chaudhury, Sunamganj (West)
72. Khan Bahadur Mahumud Ali, Karimganj (South)
73. Matior Rahman Mia, Goalpara (West)
74. Mabarak Ali, B.L., Karimganj (West)
75. Khan Sahib Mudabbir Hussain Chaudhuri, B.L., Habiganj (North-East)
76. Khan Bahadur Mufizur Rahman, B.A., Sylhet Sadr (South)
77. The Hon'ble Munawwar Ali, B.A., LL.B., Sunamganj (Central)
78. Muzarrof Ali Laskar, Hailakandi.
79. Namwar Ali Barbhuya, B.L., Silchar.
80. Nazirruddin Ahmed, South Sylhet (West)
81. Shekh Osman Ali Sadagar, Nawgong (West)
82. Syed Muhammad Saadulla, M.A., B.L., Kamrup (South)
83. Kahn Bahadur Sayidur Rahman, M.A., B.L., Lakhimpur.
84. Shams-ul-Ulema Abu Nasr Muhammad Waheed, M.A., Sylhet Sadr (Central)

EUROPEAN, EUROPEAN PLANTING AND EUROPEAN COMMERCE AND INDUSTRY

85. Colonel A.B. Beddow, C.I.E., V.D., European Planting
86. A. F. Bendall, European Planting
87. J. R. Clayton, European Planting
88. W. R. Faull, European Commerce and Industry
89. H. F. Clark, European
90. F. W. Blennerhasset, European Planting
91. F. W. Hockenhull, European Planting
92. D. B. Moore, European Planting
93. R. A. Palmer, European Planting

WOMEN

94. Miss Mavis Dunn, B.T., B.L., Women's (Shillong)

INDIAN CHRISTIAN, BACKWARD TRIBAL (PLAINS), BACKWARD AREAS (HILLS) AND LABOUR

95. Benjamin Ch. Momin, Garo Hills (North)
96. Bhairab Chandra Das, Labour, Jorhat (Sibsagar district)
97. Bideshi Pan Tanti, Labour, Doom Dooma (Lakhimpur District)
98. Binode Kumar J. Sarwan, Lobour, Thakurbari (Darrang District)
99. Dhirsingh Deuri, Nowgong (Tribal)
100. Rev. L. Gatpoh, B.A., Jowai
101. C. Goldsmith, B.A., B.T., Indian Christian
102. Jobang D. Marak. Garo Hills (South)
103. Rev. J.J. M. Nichols-Roy, B.A, Shillong
104. Karka Dalay Miri, Lakhimpur and Majuli (Tribal)
105. Khorsing Terang, Mauzadar, Mikir Hills

106. P. Parida, Labour, Silchar (Cachar District)
107. Rabi Chandra Kachari, Kamrup (Tribal)
108. Rupnath Brahma, B.L., Goalpara (Tribal)

Assam Cabinets under the Government of India Act 1935 – All Coalitions From 1 April 1937 to 15 August 1947

1937

1. Syed Muhammad Saadulla	Kamrup	Premier
2. Shamsul Ulema M.A.N.M. Waheed	Sylhet	
3. Muhammad Ali Hyder Khan	Sylhet	
4. Rohini Kumar Choudhury	Kamrup	
5. J. J. Nichols Roy	Khasi and Jaintia Hills	

1938

Reconstituted on 5 February

1. Syed Muhammad Saadulla	Premier
2. Munawar Ali	Sylhet
3. Akshay Kumar Das	Sylhet
4. Abdul Matin Choudhury	Sylhet
5. Rohini Kumar Choudhury	
6. J. J. M. Nichols Roy	

Saadulla resigned 19 September 1938 to 16 November 1939

1. Gopinath Bardalai	Kamrup	Premier
2. Kamini Kumar Sen	Sylhet	
3. Akshay Kumar Das	Sylhet	
4. Muhammad Ali Haider Khan	Sylhet	
5. Khan Bahadur Mahmud Ali	Sylhet	
6. Fakhruddin Ali Ahemed	Kamrup	
7. Ramnath Das	Sibsagar	
8. Rupnath Brahma	Goalpara	

Bordoloi resigned on 16 November 17 November 1939 to 24 December 1941

1. Syed Muhammed Saadulla		Premier
2. Munawar Ali		
3. Mudabbir Hussain Choudhury	Sylhet	
4. Abdul Matin Choudhury	Sylhet	
5. Hirendra Chakravarty	Sylhet	
6. Khan Bahaduar Syidur Rahman	Lakhimpur	

7. Dr. Mahendra Nath Saikia — Darrang
8. Miss Mavis Dunn — Khasi and Jaintia Hills
9. Rupnath Brahma
10. Rohini Kumar Choudhury

Choudhury resigned on 9th December after an agreement with Bardalai. Saadulla resigned having lost majority. The province was placed under Governor's rule after hectic activities of Governor, Bardalai and others failed to enable the formation of a Cabinet. Assam remained under Governor's rule till 24 August1942. The Quit India Movement had started after the Congress Resolution of 8 August at Bombay.

25 August 1942 to 31 March 1946

1. Syed Muhammad Saadulla — Premier
2. Munawar Ali
3. Mudabbir Hussain Choudhury
4. Abdul Matlib Choudhury
5. Hirendra Chakravarty
6. Miss Mavis Dunn
7. Dr. Mahendra Nath Saikia
8. Khan Bahadur Sayidur Rahman
9. Rupnath Brahma
10. Naba Kumar Dutta — Lakhimpur

Reconstituted on 25 March 1945 after Saadulla – Bardalai–Choudhury or Tripartite Agreement

1. Syed Muhammad Saadulla — Premier
2. Munawar Ali
3. Mudabbir Hussain Choudhury
4. Abdul Matin Choudhury
5. Baidyanath Mukherjee — Sylhet
6. Akshay Kumar Das
7. Rohini Kumar Choudhury
8. Rupnath Brahma
9. Khan Bahadur Sayidur Rahman
10. Surendranath Buragohain — Lakhimpur

1 April 1946 to 15 August 1947

1. Gopinath Bardalai — Premier
2. Basanta Kumar Das — Sylhet
3. Baidyanath Mukherjee
4. Abdul Matlib Majumdar
5. Bishnu Ram Medhi

6. J.J.M. Nichols Roy
7. Ramnath Das

15 August 1947 to 6 August 1950

1. Gopinath Bardaloi		Premier or
2. Bishnu Ram Medhi		Chief Minister
3. Omeo Kumar Das	Nowgong	
4. Bhimbar Deuri	Lakhimpur	

Deuri was later replaced by Muhammad Tayyabulla of Kamrup who resigned in 1949

5. Ramnath Das	
6. Rupnath Brahma	
7. Abdul Matlib Majumdar.	
8. J. J. M. Nichols Roy	
9. Moti Ram Bora	Kamrup

Bardalai passed away on 6 August 1950 and Medhi became the Chief Minister.

BIBLIOGRAPHY

A

Acharyya, N. N. — *The History of Medieval Assam*, Guwahati, 1966.

" — *Assam and Neighbouring States, Historical Documents*, New Delhi, 1983.

" — *North East as viewed by Foreigners*, Gauhati, New Delhi, 1985.

" — *A Brief History of Assam (from earliest times to 1983)*, Gauhati, New Delhi, 1987.

Aditya, R. N. — *Fight for Freedom in Sylhet,* Karimganj, 1970.

Aditya, Rabindranath — *From the Corridors of Memory,* Karimganj, 1970.

Agarwala, R.N. — *National Movement and Constitutional Development in India,* Seventh Revised Edition, Delhi, 1969.

Ahmed, Aziz — *Islamic Modernism in India and Pakistan, 1857–1964,* Second Impression, Oxford University Press, 1970.

Ahmed, Aziz and Gustov Edmund Von Gunebaum — *Muslim Self-Statement in India and Pakistan*, London, 1970.

Ahmed Jamil Uddin (Ed) — *Some Recent Speeches and Writings of Mr. Jinnah*, Lahore, 1942.

Ahmed, Jamil Uddin — *Through Pakistan to Freedom,* Lahore, 1945.

" — *Final Phase of Struggle for Pakistan*, Second Edition, Lahore, 1968.

" — *Middle Phase of Muslim Political Movement*, Lahore, 1969.

Ahmed, Nafis — *The Basis of Pakistan*, Calcutta, 1947.

Aiyar, R. P. and L. S. Bhandare — *The Congress Caravan, 1885 – 1945,* Bombay, 1945.

Alberuni, A. B. — *Makers of Pakistan and Modern Muslim India*, Lahore, 1950.

Alexander, A. B. — 'Outline of the existing System for the Government of India 1832', the *'Journal of the Asiatic Society*, Vol. VIII, 1832', Calcutta.

Alexander, Horace — *India Since Cripps,* London, 1944.

" — *Gandhi through Western Eyes,* Philadelphia, 1984.

Ali, Choudhury Rahmat — *Now or Never*, Cambridge, 1933.

” *The Millat and the Mission*, Cambridge, 1942.

” *The Millat and Her Minorities*, Cambridge, 1943.

Ali, Mahmud *Resurgent Assam*, Dacca, 1967.

Allana, G. *Pakistan Movement*, Historic Documents, Karachi.

Allen, B.C., E.A. Gait, C.G.H. Allen and H. F. Howard *Gazetteer of Bengal and North East India*, Reprint, New Delhi, 1979.

Ambedkar, B. R. *Pakistan or the Partition of India,* Reprint, Bombay, 1946.

Amery, L. S. *The Nature of British Parliamentary Government,* London, 1952.

Anand, C. L. *Constitutional Law and History of India,* Sixth Edition, Allahabad, 1990.

Anderson, G. and M. Subedar *The Development of an Indian Policy,* Bombay, Allahabad, Calcutta, 1921.

” *Expansion of British India, 1818-1858,* London, 1921.

Andrews, C.F. *The Indian Problem*, Second Edition, Madras, 1923.

Andrews, C.F. and Girija Mukherjee *The Rise and Growth of the Congress in India*, London, 1938.

A Punjabi (pseudo) *Confederacy of India*, Lahore, 1939.

Appadorai *Dyarchy in Practice*, London, 1937.

Argov, Daniel *Moderates and Extremists in the Indian Nationalist Movement (1883 – 1920)*, London, 1967.

Austin, Lt. Col. H. H. Godwin *The Geography and Population of Assam,* 1928.

Ayyar, R.V. Krishna (Ed) *All India Election Guide*, Madras, 1956.

Azad, Maulana Abul Kalam *India Wins Freedom* (the complete version) Reprint, Delhi, 1989.

Aziz, A *Discovery of Pakistan*, London, 1963.

Aziz, K *The Making of Pakistan*, London, 1963.

Aziz, K.K. *Britain and Muslim India*, London, 1963.

” *History of Partition of India, Origin and Development of the Idea of Pakistan*, Vols. I – IV, New Delhi, 1988.

B

Bahadur, Lal *The Muslim League – Its History, Activities and Achievements,* Agra, Ajmeer, Allahabad etc., 1954.

Baig, M.R.A. 'The Partition of Bengal and its Aftermath', in *'The Indian Journal of Political Science'*, Vol. XXX, April – June 1969, No. 2.

Bakshi, S. R. *Gandhi and Hindu-Muslim Unity,* New Delhi, 1987.

Banerjee, A.C. *The Eastern Frontier of British India,* Calcutta, 1946.

” *The Constituent Assembly of India*, Calcutta, 1947.

” *The Indian Constitutional Documents*, 4 Vols., Calcutta 1964.

Banerjee, A.C. and D. R. Bose *The Cabinet Mission in India*, Calcutta, 1947.

Banerjee A. C. and A. N. Bose *The Making of Indian Constitution 1939–1947*, Calcutta, 1948.

Banerjee Anil Chandra *The Constitutional History of India,* Calcutta, 1977.

Banerjee, D. N. — *East Pakistan, a case Study in Muslim Politics*, New Delhi, 1969.

Banerjee, Nripendra Chandra — *At the Cross Roads (1885–1946)*, Calcutta, 1950.

Banerjee, Surendra Nath — *A Nation in Making,* Reprint, Calcutta, 1963.

Banerjee, Tarashankar — *Various Bengal*, Calcutta, 1987.

Barkataki, S. — *Tribes of Assam*, New Delhi, 1984.

Barpujari, H.K. — *Assam in the Days of the Company*, Gauhati, 1963.

Barpujari, H.K. (Gen. Ed) — *Political History of Assam*, Volume One, 1826 – 1919, Gauhati, 1977.

Barpujari, H.K. — *The Comprehensive History of Assam*, Vol. IV and Vol. V., Guwahati, 1992 and 1993 respectively.

" — *North East India, Problems, Policies and Prospects*, New Delhi, 1998.

Barua, Apurba Kumar — *Social Tensions in Assam Middle Class Politics*, Guwahati, 1992.

Barua, Birinchi Kumar — *A Cultural History of Assam*, Gauhati, 1969.

Barua, K.L. — *Early History of Kamarupa*, Gauhati, 1966.

Barua, Khandindra Chandra — *Critical Days of Assam*, Gauhati, 1972.

Barua, Lalit (Ed) — *Whither Assam*, Nowgong.

Barua, Upendra Nath — *A Glimpse of Assam*, Second Edition, Jorhat, 1946.

Basu, D.D. — *Government of India Acts (1800 – 1935)* with Indian Independence Act 1947, Calcutta, 1977.

Basu, Durga Das — *Introduction to the Constitution of India,* 19th Edition, Delhi, 2001.

Basu, Nirmal Kumar — *Assam in the Ahom Age,* First Edition, Calcutta, 1962.

Basu, T. K. — *Bengal Peasant from time to time*, Calcutta, 1962.

Bhagwan, Vishnu — *Constitutional History of India and National Movement*, Delhi, Chandigarh and Lucknow, 1974.

Bhat, Sudhakar — *The Challenge of the North East*, Bombay, 1975.

Bhattacharjee, Ajit — *Countdown to Partition*, New Delhi, 1977.

Bhattacharjee, J. B. — *Cachar under British Rule in North East India*, Calcutta 1977.

Bhattacharjee, J.B. (Ed) — *Social Tension in North East India,* Calcutta, 1982.

" — *Sequences of Development in North East India*, Delhi, 1989.

Bhattacharjee, J. B. (Ed. and Pub) — *Proceedings of the North East India History Association (NEIHA),* Shillong, 1980 – 1993.

Bhattacharjee, K. K. — *North East India, A Study,* Delhi, 1983.

Bhuyan, Arun (Ed) — *Nationalist Upsurge in Assam*, Guwahati, 2000.

Bhuyan Arun Chandra — *The Quit India Movement,* New Delhi, 1975.

Bhuyan Arund Chandra and Sibopada De (Eds) — *Political History of Assam,* Volume Two 1920 – 1939, Gauhati, 1978.

" — *Political History of Assam*, Volume 3, 2nd Edition, Guwahati, 1999.

Bhuyan, B.C. *Political Development of the North East*, Delhi, 1989.

Bhuyan, S. K. *Anglo-Assamese Relations*, Gauhati, 1949.

" *Studies in the History of Assam*, Gauhati, 1947.

Bhuyan, S. K. *Twenty Articles and Notes* – Literary and Historical, Gauhati.

" An Assamese Miscellany – *A Collection of Articles* written between 1918 and 1961, Gauhati.

Bolitho, H. *Jinnah, Creator of Pakistan,* London, 1954.

Bora, Mahendra *1857 in Assam*, Gauhati, 1947.

Borgohain, Munindra Nath *The Assam Legislative Assembly, 1937 – 1947,* Sibsagar, 1994.

Borua, H. N. *Reflections on Assam-cum Pakistan*, Calcutta, 1944.

Bose, M. L. *Historical and Constitutional Documents of North East India*, Delhi, 1979.

Bose, P. N. *Swaraj, Cultural and Political*, Calcutta, 1929.

Bose, Subhas Chandra *The Indian Struggle, 1920 – 1942*, Bombay, 1964.

Broomfield, J. H. *Elite Conflict in Plural Society: Twentieth Century Bengal*, Cambridge, 1968.

" *Political Leadership in India,* Delhi, 1969.

Buchanon, Hamilton Francis *An Account of Assam 1807 – 14*, Reprint of London Edition, 1820, Gauhati, 1940.

C

Campbell-Johnson, Allan *Mission with Mountbatten*, London, 1951.

Cantwell, Smith Wilfred *The Muslim League*, Lahore, 1945.

Chakravarty, Atulananda *Not by Politics Alone*, Calcutta, 1944.

Chakravarty, B. P. *Annexation of Cachar (1832)*, Proceedings of Indian Historical Records Committee, 1942.

Chand, Tara *History of the Freedom Movement in India*, Vols. Three and Four, Reprint, New Delhi, 1992.

Chander, Jog Parvesh *India Steps Forward*, Lahore, 1941.

Chandra, Kailash *The Tragedy of Jinnah*, Lahore, 1941.

Chatterjee, Nandalal *India's Freedom Struggle*, Allahabad, 1958.

Chatterjee, Suniti Kumar *The Place of Assam in the History and Civilisation of India*, Gauhati, University, 1955.

Chaube, Shibani Kinkar *Constituent Assembly of India: Springboard of Revolution*, New Delhi, 1973.

Chintamony, C. Y. *Indian Policy since the Mutiny*, London, 1940.

Chirol, Valentine *Indian Unrest*, London, 1910.

Chopra, P. N. (Ed) *The Gazetteer of India*, Indian Union, Vol. Two and Vol. Four, Delhi, 1972 and 1978 respectively.

Chopra, P. N. (Chief Ed) *Towards Freedom*, Vol. 1, Experiment with Provincial Autonomy, New Delhi, 1985.

Chopra, P.N. *Quit India Movement*, Delhi, 1992.

Choudhury, Benoyendra — *Muslim Politics in India*, Calcutta, 1946.

Choudhury P. C. — *The History of Civilisation of the People of Assam*, Gauhati, 1959.

Choudhury, S. B. (Ed) — *The National Diary*, Calcutta, 1964 –1965.

Clifford, Manshardt — *The Hindu-Muslim Problem in India*, London, 1936.

Coupland, Reginald — *The Cripps Mission*, Bombay, 1942.

" — *The Constitutional Problem in India*, Oxford, 1945.

D

Dalwai Hamid — *Muslim Politics in India*, Bombay, 1969.

Das, Bhakta — *A Glimpse of the Scheduled Castes and their Socio-Economic Development in Assam*, Delhi, 1983.

Das, Durga — *India From Curzon to Nehru and After*, London, 1969.

" — (Ed.) Sardar Patel's Correspondence (1945-1950), Vols. 1-10, Ahmedabad, 1971-1974.

Das, M. N. — *India under Morley and Minto – Politics Behind Repression and Reforms,* London, 1964.

Datt, D. — *Cachar District Records*, Silchar, 1969.

Datt, V. N. and B. E. Cleghorn (Ed) — *Nationalist Muslims and Indian Politics,* Delhi, 1974.

Datta, K. K. — *India's March to Freedom*, Calcutta, 1949.

" — *A Survey of Recent Studies on Modern Indian History*, Calcutta, 1963.

Datta, Prabhat — *Regionalisation of Indian Politics*, Sterling Publishers Private Limited.

Dey, Analendu — *Roots of Separatism in Nineteenth Century Bengal*, Calcutta, 1974.

Dey, Analendu — *Islam in Modern India*, Calcutta, 1982.

Dorothy, Norman — *Nehru, the first sixty years,* Vol. II, New Delhi, 1965.

Dube, S. M. — *North East India, A Sociological Study*, Delhi, 1978.

Dutt, K. N. — *Landmarks of the Freedom Struggle in Assam*, Calcutta, 1955.

Dutta, Anuradha — *Assam in the Freedom Movement,* Calcutta 1991.

" — 'Aspects of Growth and Development of Nationalism in Assam in the 19th century' in Bhuyan, Arun (Ed).

Dutta, Pramatha Nath — *Glimpses into the History of Assam*, Reprint, Guwahati 1994.

E

Edibe, Halide — *Inside India*, London, 1937.

Edwards, Michael — *The Last Years of British India*, London, 1963.

Engineer, Asghar Ali — *Indian Muslims.* *A Study of the Minonity Problems in India,* New Delhi, 1985.

F

Faruqui, Zia-Ul-Hassan — *The Deoband School and the Demand for Pakistan,* Bombay, 1963.

Fischer Luis — The Life of the Mahatma.

G

Gail, Minault — *The Khilafat Movement – Religious Symbolism and Political Mobilisation in India*, Oxford University Press, 1982.

Gait, E. A. — *A History of Assam*, Calcutta, 1926.

Gallagher Johnson and Seal — *Locality, Province and Nation*, Cambridge, 1973.

Gandhi M. K. — *Hind Swaraj or Indian Home Rule*, Ahmedabad, 1946.

" — *Indian Independence in Perspective*, *Young India*, dated 12th October, 1921 Published by Sasadhar Sinha, Delhi, 1964.

Gani, H. — *Muslim Political Issues and National Integration*, New Delhi, 1978.

Ghosh, P. C. — *Indian National Congress (1892 – 1909)*, Calcutta, 1967.

Ghosh, Shankar — *The Western Impact on India*, New Delhi, 1967.

" — *Indian National Congress, Its History and Heritage*, New Delhi, 1975.

Gokhale, G. K. — *The Making of the Indian Nation*, Delhi.

Gopal, Ram — *Indian Muslims, A Political History*, Calcutta, 1959.

Gopal, Sarvapalli — *British Policy in India (1885 – 1905)*, Cambridge University Press, 1965.

Gordon, Leonard — *Bengal, the Nationalist Movement (1876 –1940)*, Delhi, 1974.

Goswami, Priyam — *Assam in the Nineteenth Century Industrialisation and Colonial Penetration*, Gauhati, New Delhi, 1999.

Goswami, P. C. — *The Economic Development of Assam*, Bombay, 1963.

Graham, Major — *The Life and Work of Sir Syed Ahmed Khan.*

Griffiths, Sir Percival — *The British Impact on India*, London, 1952.

Guha, Amalendu — *Planter Raj to Swaraj*

Freedom Struggle and Electoral Politics in Assam, Delhi, 1977.

Guha, Arun Chandra — *First Spark of Revolution*, New Delhi, 1971.

Gunther, H. O. — *Muslim Sufferings under Congress Rule*, Calcutta, 1939.

Gupta, D. C. — *Indian National Movement and Constitutional Development*, Delhi, 1976.

Gwyer, Sir Maurice and A. Appadorai — *Speeches and Documents on the Indian Constitution*, Vols. I and II , London, 1957.

H

Hamid, Abdul — *Muslim Separatism in India, 1857 – 1947*, Karachi, 1967.

Haque, Mauzoomil — *Muslims in India*, Delhi, 1964.

Hardy, P. — *The Muslims of British India*, Cambridge University, 1972.

Harrison, Selig S — *India the Most Dangerous Decades*, Oxford University Press, 1960.

Hassan K. Sarwar — *The Genesis of Pakistan*, Karachi, 1950.

Hassan K. Sarwar (Ed) — *Documents on the Foreign Relations of Pakistan, The Transfer of Power*, Karachi, 1966.

Hasan, Mushirul (Ed) — *Communal and Pan-Islamic Trends in Colonial India*, New Delhi, 1981.

Hazma El — *Pakistan, a Nation*, Lahore, 1941.

Hunter, W. W. — *The Indian Mussalmans*, Reprint of 1871 Edition, Calcutta, 1945.

Hunter, W. W. — *A Statistical Account of Assam*, Vol. II, Reprint of 1879 Edition, Delhi, 1975.

Husain, Abid — The National Culture of India, New Delhi, 1956.

" — The Destiny of Indian Muslims, New Delhi, 1965.

I

Ikram, S. M. — *Modern Muslim India and Birth of Pakistan*, Lahore, 1950.

Ilbert, Sir C. — *A Brief Historical Survey of Parliamentary Legislation relating to India*, Oxford University Press, 1922.

Ispahani, M. A. H. — *Quaid-e-Azam, as I knew Him*, Karachi, 1967.

Iswari Prasad and S. K. Subedar — *Hindu-Muslim Problems*, Allahabad, 1974.

J

Jain, M. S. — *The Aligarh Movement, Its Origin and Development (1858 – 1906)*, Agra, 1965.

Jamil, S. M. — *The Muslim Year Book of India and Pakistan, Who is Who, Bombay*, 1948 – 1949.

Jinnah, M. Ali — Preface to *India's Problem of Future Constitution*, Bombay, 1940.

Jog, N. G. — *In Freedom's Quest (A Biography of Netaji)*, Orient Longman, 1969.

Jones, W. H. Morris — *Parliament in India*, London, 1957.

Joshi, Mahesh — *Assam, The Indian Conflict*, New Delhi, 1981.

K

Kabir, Humayun — *Muslims in India*, New Delhi, 1965.

" — *Muslim Politics (1906 – 1947)*, Calcutta, 1969.

Kakati Satish Chandra — *Discovery of Assam*, Second Edition, Calcutta, 1964.

Kapur, Anup Chand — *Constitutional History of India, (1765 – 1970)*. Revised Second Edition, New Delhi, 1970.

Kar, M. — 'Muslim Politics in Assam' in *'North Eastern Affairs'*, Shillong, July - December 1973.

" — 'Problems of Representation in Assam Legislature' in *'The Journal of the North East India Council for Social Science Research'*, Shillong, October, 1977.'

Kar, M. — 'Muslim Immigration to Assam' in *Social Scientist*, Trivandrum, April-May, 1980.

" — 'Khilafat and Non-Co-operation Movements in Assam' in Hasan, Mushirul (Ed). *Muslims in Assam Politics*, New Delhi, 1990.

" — *Muslims in Assam Politics 1946 – 1991*, New Delhi, 1997.

Karandikar, M.A. — *Islam in India's Transition to Modernity*, New Delhi, 1968.

Karim, Abdul — *Social History of the Muslims in Bengal*, Dacca, 1959.

Karunakaran, K.P. (Ed) *Modern Indian Political Tradition*, Calcutta, 1962.

Kaushik, P. D. *The Congress Ideology and Programme (1920 – 47)*, New Delhi, 1964.

Keath, A. B. *Speeches and Documents on Indian Policy, 1750 – 1921*, Oxford University Press, 1922.

" *Constitutional History of India*, London, 1936.

Keath, Callard *Pakistan, a Political History*, London, 1957.

Khaliquzzaman, Choudhury *Pathway to Pakistan*, Karachi, 1961.

Khan, Abdul Waheed *India Wins Freedom, The Other Side,* Karachi, 1961.

Khan, Aga *The Memoirs of Ahga Khan*, London, 1954.

Khan, Aga, H. H. *India in Transition*, London, 1918.

Khan, A. Ahmed *The Founder of Pakistan (Through Trial to Triumph)*, London, 1942.

Khan, Wali *Facts are Facts, The Untold Story of India's Partition*, New Delhi, 1987.

Khosla, Gopal Das *Stern Reckoning*, New Delhi, 1950.

Krishna, K. B. *The Problems of Minority*, London, 1937.

Kumar, R. (Ed) *Essays on Gandhian Politics*, Oxford, 1971.

L

Lahiri, R. M. *Annexation of Assam*, Calcutta, 1953.

Larry Collins and Dominique La Pierre *Freedom at Midnight*, New Delhi, 1976.

Latiff, Syed Abdul *The Muslim Problem in India,* Bombay, 1939.

Lovett, Sir V. *History of Indian Nationalist Movement,* London, 1921.

Lumby, E.W.R. *The Transfer of Power in India,* (1945 – 1947), London, 1954.

M

Mc' Cosh, John *Topography of Assam*, Reprint of 1875 Edition, Delhi, 1975.

Mahajan, Suchitra *Independence and Partition – The Erosion of Colonial Power in India*, Delhi, 2002.

Maitra, Jayanti *Muslim Politics in Bengal,* Calcutta, 1984.

Majumdar, A. K. *Advent of Independence*, Bombay, 1963.

Majumdar, Bimanbehari *Indian Political Associations and Reform of Legislature (1818 – 1917),* Calcutta, 1965.

" *Congress and Congressmen in Pre-Gandhi Era (1885 – 1917),* Calcutta, 1967.

Majumdar, J. K. (Ed) *Indian Speeches and Documents on British Rule, (1821 – 1918),* West Bengal State Archive, Calcutta.

Majumdar, K. N. *History of Mymensingh*, Calcutta, 1907.

Majumdar, R. C. History of the Freedom Movement in India, Vols. I and II, Calcutta, 1962, Vol. III, Reprint, Calcutta, 1996.

" *Three Phases of India's Struggle for Freedom,* Bombay, 1967.

Majumdar, R. C. (Gen. Ed) History and Culture of the Indian people.
1. Vol. IX, Part II, British Paramountcy and Indian Rennaissance.
2. Vol. X, Struggle for Freedom,
3. Vol. XI, Struggle for Freedom, Bombay, 1965, 1965 and 1968 respectively.

Majumdar, S. K. *Jinnah and Gandhi,* Calcutta, 1966.

Malla, N. (Ed) *Nationalism, Regionalism and Philosophy of National Integration,* New Delhi, 1998.

Mansergh, Nicholas (Ed) *The Transfer of Power, 1942 – 1947,* Vols. I and II, London, 1970 and 1972 respectively.

Mansur, F. *Process of Independence,* London, 1982.

Marbaniang, Iscot *Assam in a Nutshell,* Shillong, 1970.

Mary, Countess of Minto (Lady Minto) *India, Minto and Morley,* London, 1935.

Mathew, K. M. (Chief Ed.) *Monorama Year Book,* Kottayam, 1990 onward.

Medhi, Kunja *State Politics in India (A Study of Assam Legislative Assembly),* New Delhi, 1988.

Mehta, Ashok and Achyut Pattavardhan *The Communal Triangle in India,* Allahabad, 1942.

Menon, V.P. *The Transfer of Power in India,* New Jersy, 1957.

,, *An Outline of Indian Constitutional History,* Bombay, 1965.

Mills, A. J. Moffat *Report on the Province of Assam,* Calcutta, 1854.

Mitra, Bejan and Phani Chakravarty (Ed) *Rebel India,* Calcutta, 1946.

Mitra, H. N. *India in Parliament and Abroad,* Calcutta, 1919-1924.

Mitra, H. N. (Ed) *Indian Annual Register,* Calcutta, 1919-1930.

Mitra, Nripendra Nath (Ed) *Indian Annual Register,* Calcutta, 1931-1947.

Mitra, Sisir Kumar *Resurgent India,* Bombay, 1963.

Moon, Penderal *Divide and Quit,* London, 1961.

Moon, P. (Ed) *Wavell the Viceroy's Journal,* London, 1973.

Moore, R. J. *Liberalism in Indian Politics,* London, 1966.

,, *The Crisis of India's Unity,* 1917-1940, Oxford 1970.

Mosley, Leonard *Last Days of the British Raj,* London, 1962.

Mukherjee, Haridas and Uma *India's Fight for Freedom or the Swadeshi Movement,* Calcutta, 1958.

Mukherjee Hirendra Nath *India's Struggle for Freedom,* Calcutta, 1962.

Mukherjee, P. *All About Partition,* Calcutta, 1906.

,, *Indian Constitutional Documents (1773-1915),* Calcutta, 1915.

Munshi, K.M. *Indian Constitutional Documents,* Subtitled Pilgrimage to Freedom, Vols. I and II Bombay, 1967.

M.R.T. Preface to *Pakistan and Muslim India,* Bombay, 1945.

N

Nag, Sajal — *Roots of Ethnic Conflict-Nationality Question in North East India*, Delhi, 1990.

Nagarkar, V. V. — *Genesis of Pakistan*, New Delhi, 1975.

Nair, Jeevan and U. C. Jain — *Indian Parliament*, Privileges, Powers and Functions, Jaipur, 2000.

Narayan, Iqbal (Ed) — *State Polities in India*, Meerut, 1967.

Natesan, G. — *Swadeshi Movement*, Madras, 1906.

Navajivan Trust (Pub) — *The Selected Works of Mahatma Gandhi*, Vols. I-VI, Ahmedabad, 1993-1994.

Nehru, Jawaharlal — *The Discovery of India*, London, 1956.

,, — *Toward Freedom*, Boston, 1958.

,, — *A Bunch of Old Letters*, New Delhi, 1958.

Neog, Dimbeswar — *Introduction to Assam*, Bombay, 1947.

Nevinson, Henry, W. — *The New Spirit in India*, London, 1908.

Noman, Mohammad — *Muslim India (Rise and Growth of the All India Muslim League)*, Allahabad, 1942.

O

O' Dyer, Sir Michael — *India as I Knew It*, London, 1925.

P

Pal, Bipin Chandra — *Swadeshi and Swaraj*, Calcutta, 1954.

,, — *India's Struggle for Independence*, Delhi, 1992.

Pemberton, R. B. — *Report on the Eastern Frontier of British India*, Reprint, Gauhati, 1963.

Pirzada, Syeed Sharifuddin — *Leaders' Correspondence with Mr. Jinnah*, Bombay, 1944.

,, — *Foundations of Pakistan*, All India Muslim League Documents, Vol. II (1942-1947), London, 1970.

Pitt, I. J. — *A Short History of Hindu-Muslim Minds and their Reaction to Indian Politics*, London, 1944.

Poplai, S. L. (Ed) — *Select Documents on Assam Affairs (1947-1950)*, Volume One, Oxford University Press, 1959.

Pradhan, R.G. — *India's Struggle for Swaraj*, Madras, 1930.

Prasad, Bisheswar — *The Origins of Provincial Autonomy*, Allahabad, 1941.

Prasad, Dr. Amba — *The Indian Revolt of 1942*, Delhi, 1958.

Prasad Rajendra — *India Divided*, Bombay, 1946.

Prasad Rajendra — *Autobiography*, Bombay, 1957.

Punniah, K. K. — *The Constitutional History of India.*

Pylee, M.V. — *Constitutional Government in India.*

Q

Qureshi, I. N. — *History of the Muslim Community in India*, New York, 1961.

R

Raghu Vamsi, V.P.S. *Indian Nationalist Movement and Thought*, Agra, 1951.

Rahman, Mujibur *The Present Situation – Indian National Congress and Our Duty*, Calcutta, 1923.

Rai, B.C. *Constitutional History of India and National Movement.*

Rajkhowa, Benudhar *A Short Account of Assam,* Dibrugarh, 1915.

,,. *Historical Sketches of Assam,* Dibrugarh, 1917.

Rajkumar, N. V. *Indian Political Parties*, Delhi, 1948.

Rajput, A.B. *Muslim League*, Yesterday and Today, Lahore, 1948.

Rao, Shiva B. *Framing of Indian Constitution*, Vols. I and II, New Delhi, 1968.

Rao, V. Venkata *A Hundred Years of Local Self-Government in Assam*, Gauhati, 1963.

Rao, V. Venkata and Niru Hazarika *A Century of Government and Politics in North East India,* Vol. 1 (Assam) (1874-1980), Reprint, New Delhi, 1991.

Reid, Sir Robert *Years of Changes in Bengal and Assam*, London, 1946.

Reid, Sir Stanley *The India as I Knew* (1897-1947), London, 1952.

Reid, Sir Stanley and S. T. Shephard (Eds) *The Indian Year Book of 1927*, London, 1952.

Roberts, P. E. *History of British India*, London, 1952.

Rabinson, William *A Descriptive Account of Assam,* Reprint of 1841 Edition, Delhi, 1975.

Rosenthel, E.I.H. *Islam in Modern National State,* Cambridge, 1965.

Rudra, A. B *The Viceroy and Governor General of India,* London, 1940.

S

Saiyid, M. H. *Mohammad Ali Jinnah,* Lahore, 1945.

Saksena, R. R. *A Handbook of Indian Legislature*, Second Edition, 1937.

Sampurnanand *Memoirs and Reflections,* New Delhi, 1962.

Santhanam, K. *Transition in India*, New Delhi, 1964.

Sarkar, Sumit *The Swadeshi Movement in Bengal,* New Delhi, 1973.

Sarma, Siddhinath (pub) *A Note on Assam's Stand* (on Grouping), Gauhati, 1946.

Sastri, Biswanarayan and Promode Chandra Bhattacherjee This is Assam, Jorhat, 1958.

Sayeed, Khalid B. *Pakistan, the Formative Phase*, Karachi, 1960.

Seal, Anil *The Emergence of Indian Nationalism,* Cambridge, 1968.

Sen Gupta, Benoy Bhusan *Political Groupings in India,* Calcutta, 1940.

Sen, Sachin *The Birth of Pakistan,* Calcutta, 1955.

Sen, Shila *Muslim Politics in Bengal 1937-1947,* New Delhi, 1976.

Sen, S.P. (Ed) *Dictionary of National Biography,* Vols. 1 and II, Calcutta, 1972.

Sethi, J. D. *India in Crisis*, New Delhi, 1975.

Shakir, Moin *Khilafat to Partition*, Delhi, 1970.

,, *Secularisation of Muslim Behaviour*, Calcutta, 1973.

,, *Muslims and Indian National Congress,* Delhi, 1987.

Sharma, Jagadish *Indian National Congress. A Descriptive Bibliography of India's Struggle for Freedom*, Bombay, 1959.

Sharma J. S. *India's Struggle for Freedom, Selected Documents and Sources,* Delhi, 1962.

Sharma, Kushum *Ambedkar and the Indian Constitution*, New Delhi, 1992.

Sharma, S. R. *The Making of Modern India*, Orient Longman, 1951.

Sing, Hiralal *The Problems and Policies of the British in India*, 1885-1898, Oriental and African Studies, Asia Historical Series, London, New Delhi, 1963.

Singh, Bhavani *Politics of Alienation in Assam*, New Delhi, 1984.

Singh, G.N. *Landmarks in Indian Constitutional History and National Movement,* Vol. 1, 1600-1919, Delhi, 1950.

Sinha, M.P. and K. D. Gangrade *Inter-Governmental Conflicts in India,* Bombay.

Sinha, Pradip *Nineteenth Century Bengal,* Aspects of Social History, Calcutta, 1965.

Sinha Roy, B.P. *Parliamentary Government in India*, Calcutta, 1943.

Sitaramayya, Pattabhi, B. *History of the Indian National Congress,* 2 Vols., Reprint, Bombay, 1969.

Smith Vincent Travels in the Mughal Empire, A.D. 1656-1668 by Francois Bernier, (Revised version), New Delhi, 1982.

Smith, Wilford Cantwell Modern Islam in India, London, 1946.

,, The Muslim League, 1942-1945, Lahore, 1945.

Srinivasan, N. Democratic Government in India, Calcutta, 1954.

Suruchi Sahitya (Pub) What Ails India's North East, New Delhi.

Symonds, Richard A The Making of Pakistan, London, 1950

T

Tayabulla, M. *Between the Symbol and the Idol Atlast*, New Delhi, 1964.

Thomson, E and G. T. Garrat *British Rule in India,* Allahabad, 1962.

Thornton, Edward *A Gazetteer of the territories under the Government of the East India Company and of the Native States on the Continent of India.*

,, *History of the British Empire in India*, Vol. 1, London, 1854.

Tinker, Hugh *Foundations of Local Self-Government in India, Pakistan and Burma,* Bombay, 1957.

,, *India and Pakistan,* Second Edition, London, 1967.

Toye Hugh *Subhas Chandra Bose, The Springing Tiger*, Bombay, 1962.

Tripathy, Amalesh *The Extremist Challenge*, Calcutta, 1967.

Trivedi, V. R. (Mrs) — *Documents on Assam*, New Delhi, 1975.
Trumbell, Robert — *As I see India,* London, 1957.
Tucker, Sir Francis — *While memory serves: The Story of Last Two Years of British Rule in India*, London, 1950.

V

Venkatarangaiya, M and Pattabhiram (Eds) — *Local Government in India,* Calcutta, 1969.
Vithalbhai, K. Javeri and D. G. Tendulkar — *Life of Mohandas Karamchand Gandhi,* Vol. 2, Bombay, 1951.

W

Wade, John Peter — *Account of Assam*, Gauhati, 1972.
Wasti, Syed Razi — *Lord Minto and the Indian Nationalist Movement, 1905-1910,* London, 1954.
Weiner, Myron — *State Politics in India,* Princeton, 1968.
,, — *Sons of the Soil Migration and Ethnic Conflict in India,* Princeton University Press, India, 1988.

Z

Zakaria, Rafiq — *Rise of Muslims in Indian Politics*, Bombay, 1961.
,, — *Gandhi and the Break-up of India,* Mumbai, 1999.
Zacharias, H.C.F. — *Renascent India*, London, 1933.
Zaheer, Sajjad — A Case for Congress – League Unity, National Library, Calcutta, Accession No. E. 329.954/Sa 19.
Zinkin, Taya — Challenges in India, London, 1966.

Official Publications
Government of Assam, Shillong

1. Administrative Report – 1881-82, 1911-12, 1921-22, 1931-32, 1939-41.
2. Assam Gazette — (i) Proceedings of the Assam Legislative Council 1913-1936. (ii) Proceedings of the Assam Legislative Assembly– 1937-1950.
3. Eastern Bengal and Assam Gazette — 1907-12, Dacca.
4. Physical and Political Geography of Assam — Shillong, 1896.
5. Report on the Working of the Assam Legislative Assembly — 1946.

6. Resolutions of the Chief Commisioner on the Working of the Local Boards — 1887-1923.

Government of Bengal

1. Bengal District Records — Vols. I-V covering the period 1770-1791.
2. Gazette Notifications — 1874 – relating to the Reconstitution of Assam.
3. Gazetteer of Bengal and North East India — Reprint, 1979.
4. Papers relating to the formation of the Province of Eastern Bengal and Assam — 16 October 1905 – 31 March 1912

Government of India

1. Census Reports — 1871-1951.
2. Constituent Assembly Debates — 1946-1947.
3. Imperial Gazetteer of India – Provincial Series Eastern Bengal and Assam — Reprint 1999.
4. Muslims in India — 1952.
5. National Council of Educational Research and Training — India's Struggle for Freedom, Visuals and Documents, 1986.
6. Ninth Despatch — 1919.
7. Romain Rolland and Gandhi Correspondence — 1990.
8. Reports of/on the
   - (i) Franchise Committee (Southborough Committee) — 1918-1919.
   - (ii) Constitutional Reforms (Montague-Chelmsford) — 1918.
   - (iii) Reforms Enquiry Committee (Muddiman Commission) — 1925.
   - (iv) Indian Central Committee (Simon Commission) — 1930.

(v) Indian Statutory Commission (Simon Commission) — 1930.

9. The Collected Works of Mahatma Gandhi — Vols. LXXI to XC covering the Period from December 1, 1939 to January 30, 1948.

National Archives, New Delhi

1. Files of — Home Department, Political Deposit, Home Political and Home General Departments with particular references to Freedom Struggle in Assam (1906-1947) including the Viceroy's Report to the Secretary of State; also on the political situation and other related matters.

West Bengal State Archive, Calcutta

History Section

India's Parliament : Selections from the Proceedings of the First Session of the Legislative Assembly and the Council of State, Simla, 1921.

National Library, Calcutta

Accession No. :

1. GP. 352.05411 As 72/Vaa — Local Self-Government, Review of Working of Village Authority.
2. (i) GP. 352.05411 As 72/Sa — Annual Reports on the Working of the Local Boards 1883-1952-53.
   (ii) ,, — Municipal Institutions 1879-1953.
3. GP. 354.5411 AS 72 ac — An Account of the Province of Assam, Administrative Report 1901-2, found in Calcutta University Library.

Non-Official Publications, Indian National Congress

1. Report of the Congress Civil Disobedience Enquiry Committee, 1922.
2. Report of the Nehru Committee, 1928.
3. Report of the All Party Conference, Allahabad, 1929.
4. Report of the Sapru Committee – Constitutional Proposals, 1945.
5. Milestones of Liberty, Bombay, 1946.

Assam Pradesh Congress Committee Archive, Gauhati

Files and Manuscripts Packet Nos. 2(a), 4,6, 18, 22, 23, 26(A), 26(B), 30(A).

Report of the Khilafat Enquiry Committee 1922

Books in Assamese

Ali, Md. Nazar — Mor Jibonor Kichhu Katha (Autobiography), Mangaldai, 1969.

Assam Prakashan — Jiboni Sangraha (Biographies), Gauhati,

Parishad (Pub) 1962, 1969.
Bardalai, Gopinath Gandhiji, Gauhati, 1969.
Barkataki, Padmanath Swadhinata Ronor Sangsparsat (In the Vortex of Freedom Struggle), Dibrugarh, 1968.
Chaliha, Padmanath Jibon Binor Sur (Autobiography), Sibsagar, 1963.
Devi, Nalini Bala Smriti Tirtha (Biography of Nabin Chandra Bardoloi), Shillong, 1948.
Kakati, Satish Chandra Jiboni Mala (Biographies), Gauhati, 1940, 1947.
Sarma, Benudhar Congressor Kanchiali Rodot (Early History of Assam Congress), Gauhati.
Sarma, Sushil Asomiya (History), Gauhati, 1973.
Tayyabulla, M. Karagaror Chithi (letters from prison cell), Gauhati, 1962.

Books in Bengali

Ahmed, Abul Mansur Amar Dekha Rajneetir Panchas Bachhar (Witness to fifty years of Politics), Dacca, 1970.
Bagal, Jogesh Chandra Muktir Sandhane Bharat (India in quest of Freedom) Calcutta, 1367 B.S. (1961).
Bandapadhyay, Narayan Biplaber Sandhane (On way to Revolution), Calcutta, 1967.
Choudhury, Achyut Charan Srihatter Itibritta (History of Sylhet), Sylhet, 1903.
Das Gupta, Harendranath Bharatiya Jatiya Congress (Indian National Congress), 3 Vols., Calcutta, 1947.
Ghosh, Suresh Chandra 'Asomiya-Bangali Christir Sanghater Utsa Sandhane (In quest of the sources of Assamese-Bengali Cultural Conffícts) in 'Desh Patrika', Calcutta 23 December 1972.
Guha, Upendra Chandra Cacharer Itibritta, Reprint, Gauhati, 1971.
Gupta, Nirode Kumar Swadhinata Andolaner Smriti (Memories of the Freedom Movement), Silchar, 1974.
Kabiraj, Narahari Swadhinata Sangrame Bangla (Bengal in Freedom Struggle), Calcutta, 1957.
Mukhapadhyay Prabhat Kumar Bharate Jatiya Andolan (National Movement in India), Calcutta, 1960.

□□□

INDEX

Agha Khan, 51
Ahom Kings, 7
Ahoms, 6
AICC, 23, 217
see also Indian National Congress
Ali, Sadiq (Nawab), 63
All India Muslim League, 11, 70, 71, 110
All Party Convention, 223
Allahabad Pillar Inscription, 5
Almherst, Lord, 8
Ambedkar, B.R., 97, 99, 100, 103, 104, 105, 252
Ambedkar-Gandhi confrontation, 221
Anglo-Burmese War, 8, 10
Ansari, M.A., 88
Anti-Partition agitation, 16, 166
Anti-War Satyagraha, 22
Armed revolution, 16
Assam,
an anthropological museum, 2
and Simon Commission, 212
birth of Swarajya Party and politics in, 207
British intervention and annexation, 6
demographic and linguistic profile of, 12
early resistance to British rule, 9
first ever taste of legislature, 163
in nutshell, 1-26
in political mainstream, 203
local bodies and elective principles in, 131-162
elected local board system, 146
elected municipal system, 133
elected Panchayat system, 132
new political alignment in, 210
partition of Bengal, 14
period of parliamentary politics, 19
period of provincial autonomy, 22
physiography, ethnic and linguistic composition, 1
political awakening and freedom struggle, 15
political history, 3
reaction in, 206
reorganisation of Chief Commission, 11
representation in Central legislatures, 247
representation in Constituent Assembly, 253
Assam Association, 164
Assam Legislative Assembly,
list of members of, 356-
Assam Legislative Council, 19
background, 243
composition of, 244
depletion of under Chief Commissionarate, 256
presiding officers of, 246
upper house, 246
Assam Legislative Council (1912-1920),
local bodies constituency, 180
nominated members, 179
review of functions, 181
settled fact unsettled, 176
Assam Legislative Council (1921-1936),
list of Bill enacted by, 306-308
Swarajya Party members to, 309
Assam Local Self-Govt. Act (1915), 133
Assam Municipal Act (1923), 144
Assam Provincial Congress,
birth of, 203
Assam Swarajya Party, 207
Attlee, Clement, 24
Aurundel Committee, 55

Ayangar, Kasturiranga, 19

B

Bahadur Shah, 10
Bailey, 156
Baker, E.M., 53
Balfour, Arther, 65
Banerjee, Surendra Nath, 73
Bangladesh, 1
Bardalai, Nabin Chandra, 217
Barak Valley, 1
Baruah, Gohain, 151, 152
Baruah, Manik Chandra, 151, 165, 166
Battle of Plassey, 28
Beasant, Annie, 64
Ben, Wedgewood, 100
Bengal Municipal Act (1884), 138, 142, 143, 145
Bengali-Assamese Conflict, 165
Bengalis, 13
Bigge, J., 177
Bora, Phani, 4
Bordoloi, Gopinath, 19, 20, 24
Bose, Bhupendra Nath, 73
Bose, Subhas Chandra, 206
Botham, A.W., 217
Brahmaputra Valley, 2, 4, 12, 355
British Parliament, 28
Burgyone, 29

C

Cabinet Mission, 24
Cachar, 3
Cartier, 7
Central legislature, 68
Chaliha, Kuladhar, 205
Chanda, Kamini Kumar, 74, 76
Charter Act of 1793, 33
Charter Act of 1813, 34
Charter Act of 1833, 35, 37
  govt. of India, 38
  home government, 38
  significance of Act, 39
Chelmsford, 48
Choudhury Rohini Kumar, 217, 243
Choudhury, Ambikagiri Roy, 167
Chouri Choura, 18
  political development after, 205
Civil Disobedience Call, 18, 19, 20, 21
Civil Disobedience Enquiry Committee, 19
Civil Disobedience Movement, 22, 217
Clive, Robert, 6
Commerce and industry and planting seats, 337
Committee system, 146
Communal Award and Poona Pact,
  Assam's reaction to, 221
Communal Award, 101
Congress,
  towards Non-Cooperation of, 77
Congress Resolution, 64
Constitutional Reforms,
  continued struggle, 85
Cornwallis, (Lord), 7, 33, 34
Cotton, Henry (Sir), 149, 154, 164, 165
Council,
  character and functioning of, 175
Crewe, Lord, 176
Cunningham circular, 21
Curtis, Lionel, 72
Curzon (Lord), 14, 49, 165, 166

D

Das, Basanta Kumar, 195
Das, Kamala Kanta, 168
Das, Ram Prasad, 168
Das-Nehru group, 207
Datta, Promode Chandra, 223
Delhi Conference, 84
Depressed classes, 21, 97, 98, 101, 103, 104, 105, 106, 107, 222
Diengdoh, Berlina, 256
Disraeli, 40, 49
District Committees, 131
Dominion status, 220
Donoughmore, 73

Dowerah, Sadananda, 142
Duffrein, 47
Duke of Wellington, 37
Duke, William (Sir), 73
Dundas (Lord), 33
Dyarchy system, 75, 79
Dyarchy, works on, 202

E

Earle, Archdale (Sir), 132
East India Company, 3, 6, 7, 8, 9, 27, 28, 29, 31, 34, 36
  administration at home, 30
  govt. of Indian territories, 30
Edward, William E., 139
Electors,
  qualifications of, 299
Ellenborough (Lord), 36
Erle, Archdale, 155, 157
Excluded area, 232
Executive Councillors and Ministers (1921-1936), list of, 276-278
Executive Orders, 151

F

Faiznur Ali, 19
Fast Unto Death, 103
Federal Assembly, 124
Franchise, 144
Franchise and electorate, 75, 254
Frier, Bartle, 40
Fuller, Bamfylde, 14, 49, 50, 164, 166

G

Gandhi, 21, 80, 81, 92, 95, 96, 98, 100, 101, 103, 104, 105, 205, 209
Gandhi-Ambedkar Conflict, 97
  and scheduled caste problem, 97
Gandhi-Irwin Pact, 21, 93, 97
  reaction to and communal award, 220
Gauhati Congress, 83
Gaya Congress, 19
General Elections (1905), 49
Goalpara, 4, 7
Gokhale, 169
Gokhale, G.K., 49, 56, 59, 67
Gordon, PRT, 155, 167
Gour, Hari Sing, 196
Government of India Act (1854), 39
Governor General, 108
Govt. of India Act, 1858, 40
  govt. of India, 42
  home government, 41
  nature of parliamentary control, 42
  representation to Indians, 43
Govt. of India Act (1935), 107, 108, 243
  first schedule to, 122
  summary of provisions, 108
Govt. of India Act, 22
Grant, Charles, 35
Grow More Food Scheme, 22
Gunning, C.S., 222

H

Hamid, Abdul, 210
Hankey, M.P.A., 326
Hindu Mahasabha, 83, 99
Hindu-Scheduled Caste tangle, 106
Home Rule Movement, 71
Hopkinson, 136
Hore, Samuel, 86
House of Commons, 28, 29, 243
Hunter Commission Report, 77

I

Imperial Council, 59
Imperial Legislative Council (1909), regulations for election of member, 261-273
India,
  evolution of constitutional government in, 27-130
    age of parliamentary control, 28
    period of Charters, 27
Indian Constitutional Reforms (1918),
  illustrative List on provincial subjects, 121
  Report on, 115-
Indian Councils Act (1853), 163

Indian Councils Act (1861), 44
Indian Councils Act (1869), 46
Indian Councils Act (1870), 46
Indian Councils Act (1874), 46
Indian Councils Act (1882), 46
Indian Councils Act (1909), 59
provisions of, 59
Indian Criminal Law Amendment Act (1908), 18
Indian National Congress (AICC), 15, 18, 19, 46, 49, 71, 72, 77, 79, 83
Irwin (Lord), 96, 221
Iyengar, S. Srinivasa, 83

J

Jahangir, 27
Jallianwallabagh massacre, 77
Jenkins, John, 177
Jinnah, Muhammad Ali, 58, 76, 89, 90, 98
Joint Parliamentary Select Committee, 74
Jorhat Sarbajanik Sabha, 14

K

Kachari-Manipuri Conflicts, 3
Kalika Purana, 5
Kamala, 5
Keatinge, R.H., 11
Khaddar, 17
Khalji, Bakhtiyar, 5
Khan, Sir Syed Ahmed, 40
Khilafat Committee, 89
Khilafat and Non-cooperation Movement, 16
Khoja Muslims, 51
Khound, Parasuram, 141
King George V, 178
Kisan Sabhas, 15
Koch Kings, 6

L

Labour Party, 86
Lahore Congress programme,
and Assam's approach to legislature, 217
Lahore Resolution, 11
Lahore Session, 62
Lanedowne, 36
Legislative Councillors of Assam, 274
Legislatures and electoral politics,
evolution of, 163-260
Local Board,
constitutional structure of, 152
Lothian Committee Report, 107
Lt. Governors and Governors, 277
Lucknow Pact, 71
Luthian Committee, 107
Lytton, Lord, 190

M

Macaulay, 36
MacDonald, 99, 100, 104
Magna Carta, 72
Mahabharata, 5
Majumdar, R.C., 87, 95, 165
Malaviya, Madan Mohan, 62, 71, 82, 105
Medhi, Bishnu Ram, 20
Melitus, P.G., 156
Mill, A.J. Moffat, 10
Mill, James, 6
Minorities Pact, 99
Minto (Lady), 52, 64, 66
Minto (Lord), 50, 51, 52, 54, 55, 57, 59, 65, 66
Moniram, 10
Montagu Commission, 73
Montagu-Chelmsford Reforms, 15, 19, 74, 78, 88
composition of government, 196
implementation of, 187
reactions to, 195
Morley (Lord), 56, 57, 58, 150, 248
Morley-Minto Reforms, 13, 59, 69, 85
criticism of, 69
implementation of, 170
next phase of, 70
prelude to, 49
Mountbatten (Lord), 110
Mountbatten Plan, 24
Muddiman Commission, 78, 100
Central legislature on, 79

Munawar Ali, 20
Munawar Ali, 218
    constitution of for Assam L.C., 219
Municipal Board, tenure of, 145
Municipality,
    constitutional structure of, 142
Munro, Thomas, 35
Muslim Community, 171
Muslim League, 54, 63, 220

N

Naidu, Sarojini, 187
National schools, 17
Nehru Constitution,
    end of, 89
    failure of, 88
Nehru, J.L., 89, 90, 206, 226
Nehru's Resolution, 82
New Assam Legislatures, 227
Nichols Roy, J.J.M., 243
Non-Cooperation Movement, 15, 17
North (Lord), 29
Northbrook, Lord, 11

O

O'Connel, Dan, 56
Operation Partition, 165

P

Pal, Bepin Chandra, 167, 185
Pal, Bipin Chandra, 17
Panel system, 105
Party, 110
Patel, V.J., 207
Peasant uprising, 9
Phukan, Nilmoni, 201
Phukan, Tarun Kumar, 211
Phukan, Tarun Ram, 19
Pitt, William, 32
Pitt's India Act (1784), 32
    constitutional significance of, 32
Plaisted, Berthalomeo, 6
Poona Pact, 21, 105
    and Gandhi's Fast Unto Death, 103
    list of Scheduled Caste on basis of, 355
    summary of text, 106
Poona Pact, 21
Port of Chittagong, 173
Prabhakar, 43
Pragyajyotisha-Kamarupa, 5
Pratyanta Desha, 3
Press Act, 18
Provincial legislatures, 68

Q

Qasim, Mir, 28
Queen Elizabeth, 27
Quit India Movement, 22, 23

R

Raja, M.C., 105
Rajagopalachariar, Chakravarty, 19
Ramayana, 5
Ramsay MacDonald Communal Award (1932), 21
Rao, V. Venkata, 132
Reading (Lord), 81
Reforms and working,
    last phase of, 224
Regulating Act (1773), 29
    amending of 1781, 31
    constitutional significance of, 31
Reid, W.J., 155
Rennel, James (Major), 6
Revolt of 1857, 10
Ripon (Lord), 131
Ripon Reforms, 137, 140
Risley, H.H., 53, 57
Robertson, T.C., 8
Rose, J. Holland, 33
Round Table Conference (Second), 97, 103, 106, 107
Round Table Conference, 21
Rowlatt Committee, 76
Roy, J.J.M. Nichols, 200
Roy, Sitanath, 169
Royal Charters, 27, 28

Royal Commission on Decentralization, 132, 143, 150
Royal Proclamation, 166
Ryot Sabhas, 15

S

Saadula Govt., 22
Saadulla, Mohammad (Sir), 223
Samudra Gupta, 5
Sapru, Tez Bahadur, 105
Scheme of Communal Settlement, 96
Scott, David, 8
Seditious Meeting Act, 18
Select Committee Report, 201
Separate electorates,
  reaction to, 62
Shore, John (Sir), 7, 34
Simon Commission, 86, 107, 243
  Assam Muslim's case before, 214
Sinha, Lord, 64
Sirajudaulla, 28
Sitalbad, Chimanlal, 105
Sitaramayya, Pattabhi, 19
Society of Trade, 6
Solanki, P.G., 105
Stanley, Lord, 41
Statesman, 202
Struggle for Reforms, 184
Suhrawardi, H., 63
Sukapha, 6
Surendra Nath Banerjee's Resolution, 58
Surma Valley, 1, 11, 14, 20, 335
Swarajya Party,
  inside, 80
Sylhet, 3
Sylhet Referendum, 13

T

Tavernier, 6
Tayyabulla, 20
Tea industry, 172
Tea planters' franchise, 159
Treaty of Yandabo, 3, 8, 11
Triple Boycott Scheme, 17

V

Varmana dynasty, 5
Vasanji, Mathuradas, 106
Vasco de Gama, 27
Versailles Settlement, 77
Village Chowkidari Act (1870), 132
Vishnu Purana, 5

W

Ward, William E., 140, 148
Wellesely (Lord), 8
Welsh (Capt.), 7, 8
Willingdon, 107
Wilson, Woodrow, 72
Women voters, 353
Wood, Charles, 39, 43
Working Committee, 93, 94, 96
World War (Second), 23
World War I, 70

Y

Yervada Jail, 107
Yogini Tantra, 5
Young India, 205

❑❑❑